The Architecture
of the United States

An Illustrated Guide to Notable Buildings
A.D. 1115 to the Present
Open to the Public

The Architecture of the United States

Volume 2
THE SOUTH AND MIDWEST

G. E. Kidder Smith
Fellow, The American Institute of Architects

in association with

The Museum of Modern Art, New York

The South: Introduction by Frederick D. Nichols, FAIA
The Midwest: Introduction by Frederick Koeper

Anchor Books
Anchor Press/Doubleday   Garden City, New York
1981

The Architecture of the United States is published simultaneously in hardcover and paperback editions.
Anchor Books edition: 1981
Anchor Press edition: 1981

This book is the second of a three-volume series—*The Architecture of the United States*. The others are *New England and the Mid-Atlantic States*, and *The Plains States and Far West*.

PHOTO CREDITS

Jorgé Figueroa of *Modernage* made—beautifully—most of the prints in the book, with the rest made by the author. For "outside" photographs in this volume, the author is deeply indebted to the following:

Page   36   Courtesy of the architect
Page   43   Courtesy of the architect
Page   48   Courtesy of the Miami-Metro Department of Publicity and Tourism
Page 154   Courtesy of Hedrich-Blessing
Page 315   Courtesy of the Louisiana Tourist Development Commission
Page 479   Courtesy of the Ohio Historical Society, Inc.
Page 487   Courtesy of the Van Wert Court House
Page 675   Courtesy of the architect

Library of Congress Cataloging in Publication Data

Smith, George Everard Kidder, 1913–
    The architecture of the United States.

    Includes glossaries and indexes.
    CONTENTS: v. 1.   New England and the Mid-Atlantic states.—v. 2.   The South and Midwest.—v. 3.   The Plains states and Far West.
    1. Architecture—United States—Guidebooks.
I.   New York (City).   Museum of Modern Art.   II.   Title.
NA705.S578   917.3′04926
Hardcover edition ISBN: 0-385-14674-4
Paperback edition ISBN: 0-385-14675-2
Library of Congress Catalog Card Number 79–8035

To DFKS

Who enriched every page
—and every hour

FOREWORD

This guidebook was initiated (1967) and first sponsored by the Graham Foundation for Advanced Studies in the Fine Arts, Chicago, under its then-director (now emeritus) John Entenza. In 1978 the Foundation, under the directorship of Carter H. Manny, Jr., FAIA, gave me a supplemental stipend to complete and update my research. The National Endowment for the Arts, first under Roger L. Stevens and then under the ever-helpful Nancy Hanks, assisted by Bill N. Lacy, was co-sponsor with two substantial fellowships, while the Ford Foundation contributed two grants at critical moments, and the Museum of Modern Art a grant-in-aid. To the two Foundations, the Endowment, and the Museum, my lasting gratitude: this demanding project would not have been possible without their financial and moral support.

Objective of Book   The purpose of this guidebook is to help establish architecture more fully in the cultural life of the United States. For "architecture" is largely unknown to the public, all but ignored in general art courses at our universities, and—with the pioneering exception of New York's Museum of Modern Art—rarely shown in our museums. By pinpointing excellence and introducing the reader and traveler to distinguished building, it is hoped that the book will encourage interest in the heritage of this country's architecture. For unless we develop more discernment regarding urban and architectural quality, we will continue to commission and produce the mediocrity which characterizes most of our cities and buildings today.

This guide does not pretend to be a history of architecture in the U.S.A.—its author is an architect and critic, not a historian. The book is intended to serve as a commentary on a cross section of each state's architectural resources from earliest times to the present. It is by no means an inventory of memorable works—at only twenty buildings per state one arrives at a thousand entries—but it will critically examine structures considered representative of major periods of development. (There are, of course, many more than a thousand notable buildings in this country, but today's book economics severely limits the number which can be included.) Some states, particularly the older and the more populous, obviously have a greater range of distinguished work than the more recent or more sparsely settled.

Selection of Buildings   A compilation such as this must reflect the selective process of one individual. However, every building described has been personally examined and, with my wife's perceptive aid, an on-site, preliminary report written. The final choice represents a winnowing of over three thousand structures to half that number. With few exceptions each is at times open to the public.

The lengthy research connected with the preliminary selection of the historic buildings was greatly facilitated by the books and articles of architectural historians and other specialists in the field to whom I am deeply indebted. Though there is no up-to-date, overall history of architecture in this country at present (1980), several promising ones are now in production. There are, however, a number of useful volumes on various periods, regions, and architects, and these are mentioned in the text when quoted. For selecting contemporary examples I relied on my extensive architectural file which contains speedily retrievable articles on almost all buildings of merit published in the last forty years. Conversations with architects and historians kept matters topical. Because of limits of space, only those engineers, landscape architects, and related specialists who played a major design role are listed.

As regards choice of buildings, some readers may, of course, harbor favorites which have been irritatingly omitted, while other structures may be puzzlingly included. However, to bring *de gustibus* up to date, the late Mies van der Rohe and the late Walter Gropius—architects and educators of great significance in this country—each thought little of Le Corbusier's chapel at Ronchamp in eastern France, a building many hold to be one of the century's most important. Frank Lloyd Wright's disagreement with much of the architectural profession is well documented.

Omission of Some Building Types   No private houses have been included in this guide, though several harmonious streets of such houses are listed. A few private buildings are so stimulating on the exterior that they are mentioned with the cautionary note of sidewalk viewing only. Some contemporary suburban corporate headquarters and similar works of distinction were omitted at the request of their managements. All correctional institutions were bypassed and only a few mental institutions written up. The most sincerely regretted absence is that of a number of fine new buildings which had not been finished when we were last on the scene. More than twelve years were spent on this project and though three updating grants were made, inevitably in a country as large as this we missed some outstanding new work, plus some historic museum-houses which only recently have been opened. Sadly, some buildings discussed here undoubtedly will disappear in the next few years.

State and City Guidebooks Although this book of necessity omits many important buildings, old and new, this lacuna is partly eased by the realization that an encouraging number of comprehensive local architectural guidebooks is becoming available. One hopes every state and major city will eventually have a critical guide to its outstanding buildings. The local offices of the American Institute of Architects—listed in most telephone books—can often be of help, as can state tourist boards. Many cities and towns have an annual house tour, usually in the spring, when homes otherwise not open to the public can be visited.

For all architectural exploration, state and city maps are essential for time-saving travel.

As this book is primarily a field guide and reference source, the photographs are necessarily small. For a "visual data bank" of architecture in the United States see my two-volume *Pictorial History of Architecture in America* (American Heritage/W. W. Norton, 1976).

Caveats The structures described herein generally are open on the dates, days, and hours indicated, but it would be wise to check on these. Admission might range from 25 cents to a number of dollars, and, like hours, is subject to change. If no admission charge is indicated, the entrance is probably free although this, too, can vary.

There are times—a dreary winter day for instance—when even the Parthenon fails, when Pentelic marble cannot inspire. So it will happen that buildings extolled here can disappoint: moreover some might show their years before their due or have undergone serious alterations since last visited. In addition, this book is admittedly a cheerful report, probably at times too cheerful, but I am, for better or worse, an optimist in the first place and, secondly, if a structure was not considered outstanding it would not be included.

Prior to publication, the description of each building was sent to its architect or the appropriate historical body for correction of possible error. The responses were of the utmost help in corroborating and correcting data, and I am deeply grateful to those national and state agencies, dedicated historical societies and curators, fellow architects, and individuals who so generously and constructively helped check the text. I only wish that there were space to list them all individually.

It is well to keep in mind that in some cases even specialists will disagree, often in dating, occasionally even in the attribution of the architect of a historic building. The dates of the buildings given here begin with the generally accepted date for commencement of construction and the finish thereof. Major alterations, when known, are also listed. The facts given here represent the most recent research; in most cases data came from information at the source. The National Register of Historic Places (1976), U. S. Department of the Interior, was also of great help. If there are errors, however, the fault is, of course, mine.

In Summary The United States with its geographic range, size of population, ethnic richness, and financial means produces more architectural probing, offers more excitement, and achieves a greater volume of outstanding new work than any other single country. But lest this encomium seem comforting, it must be immediately added that for the most part, our town planning lags far behind that in Scandinavia, our land usage both in city and suburb is lamentable, and our low-cost housing generally inexcusable. Moreover I am uneasy about much work now being turned out. A few architects, properly publicized, seemingly are more concerned with conjuring novelty for novelty's sake, or with producing seductive exhibition drawings, than they are willing to be vexed by the tough, three-dimensional realities of a client's program, his money, or the annoying details of site and climate. Professional responsibility—let alone societal responsibility—appears to be of little moment. We are increasingly witnessing what Siegfried Giedion called "Playboy Architecture." Many of these idiosyncratic excursions will look trivial twenty-five years from now when, peradventure, the house or building will be paid for. Architecture should be concerned with creating significant space, not scene painting. Nonetheless we in the United States still have a workshop with a vitality unmatched elsewhere, and if we take a greater interest in what is being built (and torn down), we can create a finer tomorrow. This is what this book is about.
    Corrections and suggestions would be appreciated by the author.

G. E. Kidder Smith, FAIA
September 1980

163 East 81st Street
New York, NY 10028

ACKNOWLEDGMENTS

This book would not have been published had it not been for the constant help and encouragement of Martin Rapp, the Museum of Modern Art's spirited and talented Director of Publications. Stewart Richardson, former Associate Publisher at Doubleday—and a friend of long standing—was his stalwart cohort. Both have given me wonderful support. Editors Loretta Barrett, Elizabeth Frost Knappman, and Eve F. Roshevsky, and Harold Grabau, Adrienne Welles, and Patricia Connolly, copy editors, went over the manuscript with many suggestions for its betterment and shepherded a staggering mass of material through production. Thanks also to Marilyn Schulman, our designer.

I am particularly grateful to the four eminent architectural historians whose introductions give such illuminating perspective on the background and forces which helped shape the buildings in the three regional volumes. Dr. Albert Bush-Brown, chancellor of Long Island University and co-author with the late John Burchard of the encyclopedic *The Architecture of America,* contributed a superb introduction to the architecture of the Northeast—Volume 1—and also commented pertinently on the text for individual buildings. Professor Frederick D. Nichols of the School of Architecture of the University of Virginia and an author long known for his brilliant studies of Jefferson and the architecture of the South wrote the first introduction for Volume 2. Professor Frederick Koeper, a specialist on the buildings of the Midwest—his *Illinois Architecture* is one of the finest state guides—sets the stage for the second part of Volume 2. The indefatigable David Gebhard, whose guidebooks to the architecture in California and Minnesota are classics, gives great insight to the work of that vast sweep of states west of the Mississippi in Volume 3. To all four I am deeply indebted for their sterling contributions.

But the two individuals who dealt with every word of every sentence—always to their betterment—were my wife and Patricia Edwards Clyne. My wife advised on the field selections of buildings, wrote almost all of our on-the-spot reactions, navigated when not driving (we covered some 135,000 miles/217,000 kilometers), and shared twelve years of work, most of it under pressure conditions. (She also shared the delights of finding many extraordinary buildings in this extraordinary country.) The material simply could not have been gathered nor the book written without her constant help, judicious taste, and glorious companionship. When travel was over—once forty-seven different motels in fifty-six nights—and I had typed the text with semilegibility, Pat Clyne, the distinguished author and speleologist, took over. She tackled the oft-confused (and sometimes windy) language of 2,800 pages of manuscript, rationalized constructions, minimized malaprops, inserted the forgotten, removed the superfluous, all in a superb editing job. She then typed each page so beautifully that it could be framed. With these two lovely and talented daughters of Minerva the task became not only possible but pleasurable.

VOLUME 2 ACKNOWLEDMENTS

In addition to those who gave invaluable assistance in checking data on individual buildings, the following were of outstanding help:

Alabama Nelson Smith, FAIA, Birmingham; Jackson R. Stell, Alabama Historical Commission, Curator of Gaineswood; Joseph O. Vogel, Director of Museum of Natural History, University of Alabama.

Florida George F. Schesventer, Superintendent, Castillo de San Marcos National Monument; Mary Montgomery, The Tallahassee Junior Museum.

Georgia Professor Stanford Anderson, MIT; John A. Hayes III and Mills B. Lane IV, Historic Savannah Foundation; Elizabeth A. Lyon, Ph.D., and Kenneth H. Thomas, Jr., Georgia Department of Natural Resources; Lee Ann Caldwell Swann, The Augusta Heritage Trust; Minette Bickel, Georgia Trust for Historic Preservation.

Illinois William K. Alderfer, State Historian, Illinois State Historic Library; Ludwig Glaeser, Curator of the Mies van der Rohe Archive, Museum of Modern Art; Ken Hodorowski; Jethro M. Hurt III, Curator, Chicago Architecture Foundation; John G. Thorpe, FLW Home & Studio Foundation.

Indiana Richard H. Brennan, The Conrad Baker Foundation; Camille B. Fife, Historic New Harmony; Professor David R. Hermansen, Ball State University; Historic Madison Inc.; Craig Leonard; Connie Staton Smith, Tourism Development Division, State of Indiana.

Kentucky Grady Clay, Editor of *Landscape Architecture;* Marty Poynter Hedgepeth, Louisville Landmarks Commission; Bill Long, Kentucky Historical Society; Mrs. Eldred W. Melton, Executive Director, Kentucky Heritage Commission; Samuel W. Thomas, Director, Jefferson County Archives.

Louisiana J. Larry Crain, Ph.D., Department of Culture, Recreation and Tourism; Paul F. Stahls, Jr., Office of Tourism; Samuel Wilson, Jr., FAIA.

Michigan Marshall Historical Society.

Mississippi Mrs. Hector H. Howard, President, The Pilgrimage Garden Club, Natchez.

North Carolina Beaufort Historical Society; Raymond L. Beck, Historical Researcher, North Carolina State Capitol; Frances Griffin, Director of Information, Old Salem; Ava Humphrey, Historic Edenton; Archie C. Smith, Jr., Town Creek Indian Mound; Donald R. Taylor, Tryon Palace.

Ohio   Dorothy A. Babbs, Cincinnati Historical Society; Wilson G. Duprey, The Brumback Library; Ohio Historic Preservation Office; Gene Warman, Ohio Historical Society.

South Carolina   Mrs. J. Berry, Beaufort Museum; The Charleston Museum; Reverend Sam T. Cobb, St. Philip's Church; Mrs. S. Henry Edmunds, Director, Historic Charleston Foundation; Carl Feiss, FAIA, AIP; Canon Edward B. Guerry, Diocese of South Carolina; Historic Columbia Foundation; Shirley Ransom, Historic Camden; Gene Waddell, Director, South Carolina Historical Society; George W. Williams, Historiographer Emeritus, St. Michael's Parish.

Tennessee   Withers C. Adkins, Chief Architect, TVA; Ilene J. Cornwall and Carol Ann Wilson, Tennessee Historical Commission; John E. Hilboldt, Director, Belle Meade; James A. Hoobler, Tennessee Historical Society; Cathy Tudor, Tennessee Department of Conservation.

Virginia   C. Hill Carter, Shirley Plantation; Mrs. Leslie Cheek, Jr., and Judith S. Hynson, Stratford Hall; Chrysler Museum at Norfolk; Dexter P. Davis, Manager, Dulles Airport; Roy Eugene Graham, AIA, Colonial Williamsburg Foundation; James N. Haskett, Chief Park Historian, Yorktown; Tucker Hill, Virginia Historic Landmarks Commission; Mrs. Robert Sheeran, Foundation for Historic Christ Church.

West Virginia   Rodney S. Collins, Department of Culture and History, Charleston.

Wisconsin   Earl Gustafson and staff, State Division of Tourism; Kenneth Regez and Kenneth L. Ames, Rock County Historical Society.

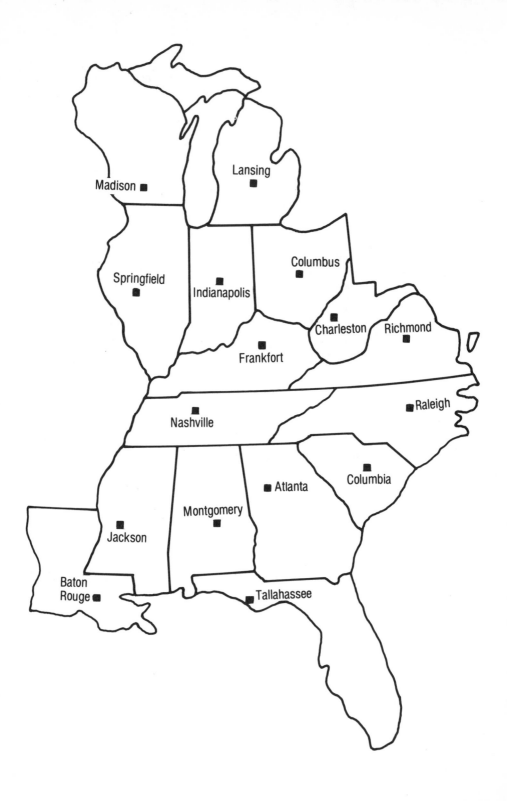

Contents

Introduction to The South

by Frederick D. Nichols, FAIA

In recent years, the hitherto largely ignored study of American architecture has suddenly found new admirers. A whole host of scholars are bent, at last, upon the task of writing on the building arts in the United States. The buildings in this guidebook, which surveys the development of eight hundred years in this country, illustrate the evolving traits of American design. In different parts of the New World, buildings took different forms—because of the severity of the climate in New England, the mildness of the climate in the South, and the arid heat of the Southwest. Moreover all influences from abroad suffered a sea change when Europeans began erecting structures on these shores. By the time the settlement of America had begun, wood in Europe had largely disappeared as a building material. Yet in the Colonies it is hardly an exaggeration to say that the first settlers practically had to cut trees down in order to land on the eastern seaboard, such was the abundance and density of the virgin forests. In addition, the clays of Virginia produced a brick so excellent it was being exported to Bermuda as early as 1622. It should be kept in mind that traditional English building technique was early modified by the cheapness of materials in the Colonies versus the expense of labor.

At this point it might be useful to provide a historic note on American architecture in order to give some sense of its chronological continuity. In the seventeenth century, the typical New England house was built around a single, central chimney with several fireplaces which kept the house warm and economized on fuel. In the South, chimneys were placed at the ends of the houses because of the mild winters and hot summers. Building throughout the century was basically of a primitive but often picturesque mold. Highlights are several churches (St. Luke's, Benns Church, Virginia, q.v.) and a few Jacobean houses such as Bacon's Castle, also in Virginia (q.v.). The Jacobean is a kind of medieval survival characterized by the use of Classical motifs grafted on medieval forms.

With increased wealth and population, the first phase of the Georgian period, 1700–35, became established in the New World. Particularly in the South, the large plantations and the similarity of the climate to the estates near Venice encouraged Palladianism—for similar circumstances tend to produce similar buildings. A Palladian symmetry was popular with outbuildings arranged in Palladio's method around courtyards or with isolated buildings. Sometimes the outbuildings were connected with quadrants, of which the most interesting example (later in the century) is Mount Vernon, Virginia (q.v.), with rusticated siding, all in wood.

Along the James River in Virginia many examples of plantation houses in this Georgian Style are preserved. Originally the exteriors of the Georgian houses emphasized the vertical with tall segmental windows and doors, and tall chimneys, like Westover, Virginia (q.v.). Plans were straightforward with pairs of rooms on either side of a central hall. With the High Georgian phase, 1735–65, some separation of function began to appear, and design became more sophisticated. Entries were used with stair halls separated from them with arches, and little lobbies were tucked between rooms to allow servants and family to enter without going through the main entrance. Roofs and openings were lowered and the horizontal was stressed as at Carter's Grove, Virginia (q.v.). Then just before the Revolution, during the Late Georgian period, 1765–76, houses were broken up into five- and seven-part compositions, such as Brandon (Virginia—q.v.), with wings, hyphens, and dependencies flanking the main block. With the coming of the Revolution, paneling began to disappear, and beautiful interiors with plaster walls, as at the Hammond-Harwood House (q.v.), Annapolis, by William Buckland, became the fashion.

After the Revolution a new style appeared, called the Federal. This is important because it represented for the first time the efforts of the people to create a truly American architecture. Due to the common language and to the close economic ties with England even after the Revolution, this movement was also influenced by the brothers Robert and James Adam in London, though a definite attempt was made to turn to France for esthetic inspiration. The brothers Adam were among the greatest architects and decorators of all English art. The delicate, elaborate Adam Style, which they developed, was transported to America via pattern books and magazines, and it quickly became the fashion in the New World. Interestingly enough, the small scale and the lightness of the plaster decoration were easily translated into wood, and the delicacy and lightness of the style were compatible with that material.

Plans began to open up into ovals, octagons, and circles. Domes became popular, especially flat domes, and also the simulation of a dome, which the Adam brothers had seen in Pompeii. There fluted fans were used in the corners of a square room to suggest a dome. Swags, garlands, and classical scenes became the fashion and are still to be found in American architecture. Porticos, particularly one-story porticos, flat planes, Palladian windows, and triple windows all were popular. Many beautiful examples are to be found on houses and plantations in South Carolina, particularly in Charleston. The most beautiful is probably the Russell House (q.v.) in that city.

The next important movement in the arts was the Roman Revival, initiated by Thomas Jefferson at about the same time that the Federal Style began in 1785. As usual Jefferson was very much ahead of the

times. In that year, 1785, Jefferson was asked by the building commissioners in Richmond to provide plans for the new state capitol, whose
foundation they had already completed. It is the first temple form
building revived after Roman times, if one does not count the small
garden temples which had been built in Europe several decades before.
It wasn't until twenty-two years later when Napoleon commissioned
the Church of the Madeleine in Paris that Europe had its first large
temple form building. However, Jefferson, with his original and inquir-
ing mind, was unwilling to use the temple form without making it practical; so he provided in the center of the building a circular rotunda-
shaped room, which allowed access to the Senate on one hand and to
the Representatives on the other. This was the first time in the Western
world that both houses of government in a democracy had been accommodated in the same building.

Jefferson's influence at first was primarily among his neighbors.
However, his influence extended finally across the entire country, and
during the rest of the century all the state capitols were domed buildings with porticos recalling Jefferson's Roman Rotunda at the University of Virginia (q.v.). It spread through the South after various
Southern planters had passed through Charlottesville on their way to
spend the summer holidays in the cool mountains among the spas of
Virginia. After they had seen the colonnades and the porticos at the
University they went home and added such to their own houses. Often
one thus finds a simple foursquare, eight-room center hall farmhouse in
the center of a splendid peristyle or behind a noble portico. Jefferson's
ideas prefigure forms which were to become characteristic of American
architecture during the creative energy which burst forth before and
after 1800—between the rigid European tradition and the mobile
American future; between contained, Classical geometry and the wish
to spread out horizontally over the vastness of a frontier, undeveloped
land.

About 1820, the Greek Revival was introduced. This was due in
part to a magnificent book published in London by James Stuart and
Nicholas Revett in 1762 called *The Antiquities of Athens*. It was also
due in large part to the Americans' enthusiasm for the Greek fight for
independence from the Turks. It is fascinating that the Greek Revival
Style was enthusiastically taken up by the countries which were in the
process of developing—for example, North America, Scotland, and
Russia were enthusiastic devotees of the Greek Revival Style. Europe,
however, generally took the style with a grain of salt and used it for inspiration. The Greek Revival in its domestic version in the Colonies
was characterized by the return to the old foursquare plan with a cen-

ter hall, a summer living room, square-rectangular high-ceilinged rooms, spacious staircases, and large porticos.

Until 1840, the Classical tradition of symmetry persisted. But when the Gothic Revival was introduced, with it came a new desire for the picturesque, for asymmetry, informal planning, and flowing spaces rather than rigidly contained rooms. This interest was partly stimulated by the popular novels of Sir Walter Scott and the teachings of John Ruskin.

Wars frequently change the direction of taste, and the American Civil War was no exception. While the Early Victorian styles and the influence of Napoleon III's rebuilding of medieval Paris had made tentative beginnings, it was not until after the Civil War that these various styles were developed in America. The Medieval Revival swept American church architecture, producing a few outstanding examples such as Grace Church, New York (q.v.), and Richardson's glorious Romanesque Trinity Church, Boston (q.v.). (Richardson's free handling of the medieval idiom here opened the way for the creative genius of the Chicago School.) Then the Italianate turned gradually into the Second Empire, and in the 1870s McKim, Mead and White made their famous trip through New England, and struck by the beauty of Early American building, they launched the "Colonial Revival," as it came to be called.

In architecture, the most brilliant creative effort of the nineteenth century was to be found in the work of the Chicago School after the Great Fire of 1871. There the skyscraper was born, and there—later— the Prairie House and the work of Frank Lloyd Wright achieved international distinction.

Inevitably, Kidder Smith's book will stimulate, and indeed for the first time will offer opportunities for study and evaluation of a large number of important American buildings. These are buildings that the people themselves think are important, for the people have seen to it that most of them are open to the public. The juxtaposition of photographs, alone, will act as a catalyst to a study of fresh currents of ideas that are endemic to American architecture. The typology of these structures and their regional characteristics are given fresh life in these stunning photographs by a man who is first of all an architect. Rarely have these two skills been brought together in a single person, so that the designer's taste and selection, which are emphasized in the photographs, are seen through the double lens of architectural training, as well as photographic dexterity. While Kidder Smith's earlier books concentrated on analyses of architecture in the 1950s and 1960s, this new volume surveys all of American architecture from the Taos Pueblo in New Mexico—an adobe Indian superblock—to Jefferson's Monticello—that most American of all houses—to the present. It will be indispensable to scholars, students, architects, and, indeed, anyone interested in the great story of American architecture. And, actually, who of our citizens can be ignorant of building? We spend most of our lives in buildings, and they contribute much to our health and happiness.

Introduction
to The Midwest

by Frederick Koeper

The buildings which record the comparatively brief history of the United States are spread over a vast continent. By contrast the small and ancient countries of Western Europe are dense with architectural monuments. (The combined area of only four Midwest states—Ohio, Michigan, Illinois, and Wisconsin—approximates the size of France.) As one travels across our spacious countryside, whether by automobile or vicariously at home turning the pages of this informative guide, one might ask: what are the peculiarly *American* qualities of American architecture? However risky it would be to answer definitively, one might plausibly look for them in that central part of the continental United States we refer to as the Midwest. Partially isolated from the cultural influences of Europe and unbeholden to those special conditions of climate and terrain of the Far West, the Midwest might be seen as the quintessential America. This is not to imply that Midwestern architecture is folksy or intellectually undistinguished. Indeed, America's greatest architect and the first American to achieve a truly international stature in the arts was, by his own definition, a proud product of this region which nourished his enormous talent; that architect was, of course, Frank Lloyd Wright.

Furthermore if one were asked to choose the most *American* city, not a romanticized ideal but a large city which best summarizes our aggressive pragmatism, one without benefit of special locale or historic gentility which accrue to Boston, New Orleans, or San Francisco, that choice—over Cleveland, St. Louis, or Kansas City—unquestionably would be Chicago. This choice would instantly be corroborated by Chicago's architectural preeminence, for it was here that the skyscraper was born as an ingenious architectural-engineering answer to the demand for commercial space in the crowded Loop district. The skyscraper is America's only truly creative contribution to the world history of architecture. Thus the Midwest as the heartland of America and Chicago as an innovative city have special standing for the historian and lover of architecture. In addition they symbolize those polarities of agrarian tradition and suburban preference versus industrialization and urban congestion which continue to enmesh our feelings and vex our decisions about the future.

In the middle of the last century the Midwest experienced, although tardily, those stylistic fashions of Classical and Gothic revivals which had already engaged the full attention of the Eastern seaboard. These styles were less intensely expressed beyond the Appalachians. The final wave of the Greek Revival, found in the simplified classicism of farmhouse, village church, and county courthouse, swept across Ohio, Indiana, and Illinois to leave its last wash on the upper banks of the Mississippi. The Taft House Museum in Cincinnati (q.v.) and the Smith Mansion in Nauvoo (q.v.) illustrate nicely the beginning and end of this flow. The succeeding wave of the Gothic Revival was less potent and survives, for example, in the occasional board-and-batten church, such as that in Delafield, Wisconsin (q.v.), reminding us of Grant Wood's *American Gothic*—which hangs in the Chicago Art Institute.

Individual "Gothic" elements are far more commonly found as an ingredient in the mixture of styles of the post-Civil War era which everyone loosely calls Victorian. The adjective embraces a wide spectrum of design but is unified by its disregard of stylistic purity, by restless ornament, and by love of color and picturesque irregularities. Eastlake and American Queen Anne are two of its several subdivisions but there is no need to be overly concerned with niceties of architectural distinction because historians themselves are still unraveling the complex strains woven into the building fabric of the 1860s and 1870s. Suffice it to say that no longer is "Victorian" a pejorative term—as modernists once would have it. Public appreciation for the late nineteenth century has come full circle. The historian makes only one request: that the real be distinguished from commercial imitations which have sprung up in this time of rediscovery of the Victorian era.

The amiable eclecticism of these years was diverted in the late 1870s by the appearance in the East of Henry Hobson Richardson's work. Two of his greatest buildings, however, together with those of Sullivan and Wright, are closely associated with the Midwest. Richardson reacted against the indiscriminate use of styles and, after making his initial and instant reputation with Trinity Church in Boston (q.v.), came to dominate the Romanesque Style he had adopted rather than allow the style to dominate him. Richardsonian Romanesque was immensely popular with Midwestern architects: John Wellborn Root, Henry Ives Cobb, and LeRoy Buffington to name a few. Harvey Ellis, sometimes Buffington's draftsman, was the designer of the Mabel Tainter Memorial Building in Menomonie, Wisconsin (q.v.), which imitates so well the rugged masonry and carved ornament characteristic of Richardsonian Romanesque.

But of greater portent were the late, drastically simple designs of Richardson that were a decisive influence on Sullivan and, through him, on Wright. This great triumvirate of architects constitutes a linked progression of architectural development unmatched in American history. In the mid-1880s in Chicago rose Richardson's Marshall Field Wholesale Store and the Glessner House (q.v.), both designs now regarded by historians as proto-modern. Then Louis Sullivan, that Chicago iconoclast, born in Boston, seized the essence of Richardson's drastically simple designs and created the beginnings of modern archi-

tecture itself. In particular it was the Marshall Field Store that guided
Sullivan's hand in the elevations for the Auditorium Building (q.v.).
Later Sullivan buildings, notably his skyscrapers, testify to Richardson's enduring spirit if not his individual manner. Sullivan, in turn,
influenced Wright in a profound way: he gave Wright (notwithstanding his sporadic attendance at the University of Wisconsin as a
special student in engineering) the only architectural education he ever
had during the six years Wright spent as draftsman in the Adler and
Sullivan firm, then located at the top of the Auditorium Building
tower.

The practicing architect, perhaps more than the historian, is aware of
the decisive role of economics and technology in shaping our buildings
and urban environment; to ignore them is to gain only a partial understanding of the history of architecture. The balloon frame is such an
example. It revolutionized wood building in the United States by utilizing machine-sawn lumber spiked together with the machine-made nail.
Balloon framing was introduced in the frontier city of Chicago in the
1830s and it immediately made obsolete hand-hewn timber construction held together with wooden pegs. Extremely strong and cheap
in cost, it was derisively called "balloon" on account of its light
weight. This new construction was responsible for the almost overnight
growth of new cities such as St. Paul and San Francisco as well as
Chicago. So historic is the balloon frame that a recently discovered
farmhouse in Peotone, Illinois, built in this manner in the early 1850s,
has been moved to the Smithsonian Institution's Museum of Technology in Washington to stand next to an example of the heavy timber
frame construction it "replaced," a house from Ipswich, Massachusetts.
  The Midwest development of the skyscraper was even more important. Here a steel skeleton superseded masonry bearing walls, allowing
for greater heights as well as far lighter construction throughout. The
earlier invention of the elevator and a systematic fireproofing of steel
members were combined with the steel frame for the first time by a
Chicago architect, William Le Baron Jenney, in the Home Insurance
Company Building (1883–85) in that city. This building's historical
authenticity as the first example of skyscraper construction was verified
by two separate professional groups during its demolition in 1931.
Today one can see a segment of the Home Insurance Company Building on display in Chicago's Museum of Science and Industry.
  Sullivan's part in the skyscraper story was an esthetic rather than a
technical one. He is remembered as having given valid artistic form to
the skyscraper at a time when architects were struggling, unsuccess-
fully, to design a building whose proportions had no precedent in ar-

chitectural history. Sullivan, always an opponent of historical eclecticism, asked simply that the skyscraper be "a proud and soaring
thing." His realization of this idea had its debut in St. Louis in his
Wainwright Building (q.v.), completed in 1891. But he applied the
Wainwright theme later to buildings in Chicago, Buffalo, and elsewhere.
Although remembered as the spiritual father of modern architecture,
the final outcome of Sullivan's career was a sad one: he lived to witness the return of eclecticism and the dissolution of his ideas—save
those which were carried on by his apprentice-pupil Frank Lloyd
Wright. But it must be remembered that Adler and Sullivan was not
the only firm contributing creative solutions to the skyscraper problem;
others were Jenney and Mundie, Burnham and Root, and Holabird
and Roche. These and others constitute what is known as the Chicago
School of Architecture.

The Midwest's rejection of Sullivan's creative approach was epitomized
by the Chicago World's Fair of 1893. Here huge crowds admired its
grandiloquent scenery of plaster facades, cast in a mélange of Classical
styles. It was a convincing display which set American taste firmly on
an academic course. Its effects on skyscraper design, for example, can
be seen in the Spanish Renaissance Style, derived from the cathedral of
Seville, which adorns the top of the Wrigley Building, and the late
French Gothic, derived from the cathedral of Rouen, at the top of the
Chicago Tribune tower.
   Despite Sullivan's negative verdict, much good came from the Fair.
It gave impetus to the City Beautiful movement which impressed upon
American cities harmonious arrangements of public buildings, tree-
lined boulevards, and other features derived from Haussmann's Paris.
The director of the Fair was Daniel Burnham, and his great success
projected his talents onto the national scene. He was a key member of
the McMillan Commission of 1902 which restored and enlarged L'Enfant's plan for Washington. He advised on plans for San Francisco,
Cleveland, and Manila before turning attention to his own city. Then
in 1909, in partnership with Edward H. Bennett, he unveiled his proposal for Chicago, impressive and comprehensive as no other city plan
had ever been. His academic tendencies, seen in the architectural
sketches, for example, were more than offset by such bold conceptions
as a continuous lakefront development and a connecting green parkway encircling the whole urban area.

The contrast between conservative and progressive architectural forces
at work in the Midwest could not be more sharply drawn than by com-
paring Daniel Burnham with Frank Lloyd Wright. Wright spurned (so

he related in *An Autobiography*) an offer from "Uncle Dan" for an all-expense education at the École des Beaux-Arts in Paris. But Wright, aware of Sullivan's own disillusion with this world-famous architectural school, curtly rejected Burnham's handsome offer. Instead Wright chose to set up an independent practice in Oak Park. (His home and studio there are now open to the public.) In 1900 Wright formulated the so-called Prairie House Style which he followed for a decade. The Robie House of 1909 in Chicago (q.v.) is an acknowledged masterpiece of these years. Another is Unity Temple in Oak Park (q.v.), the suburb which contains the greatest concentration of his buildings. The Prairie House expressed the flat landscape of the Midwest. Accordingly the plans were open and flowing, the silhouette low and horizontal. These felicitous designs of Wright's Prairie period were the subject of two German publications in 1910 and 1911, designs which gave encouragement to a rising young generation of European modernists, among them Dudok, Gropius, and Mies van der Rohe.

As fate would have it, another historic episode for Chicago began with the arrival of Ludwig Mies van der Rohe in 1938. Mies' practice in Chicago redirected skyscraper design back to the steel skeleton and curtain-wall principles which Jenney had introduced a half century earlier. Mies' rigorous designs, elementary yet eloquent, are regarded as the purest expression of skyscraper structural logic. His work and that of his many followers, Skidmore, Owings and Merrill among them, gave rise to the term Second Chicago School of Architecture. Indeed, throughout the country the Miesian idiom prevailed in the 1940s, '50s, and '60s. Acceptance of Mies, however, did not mean stagnation for Chicago; it was to lead again in the 1960s and '70s with the innovative tubular-framed skyscrapers, the John Hancock Center and the Sears Tower, the two tallest buildings in the world.

Another force, a most recent one which architects and historians failed to predict, is the rise of the historic preservation movement. Despite the losses of some important structures recently, historic preservation is nonetheless broadly favored by the public. Not only has it alerted our awareness of architectural heritage but it also, curiously, has had a marked effect on current architectural design, one too early to assess with accuracy. Yet it is quite clear that many architects are reacting against the self-imposed limitations set by the once-accepted European International Style and are exploring new—or more properly "old"—directions by reexamining the architecture of the past and its sense of place and meaning in our lives. All over the country there are success stories of projects which have benefited by heeding the existing fabric of the city and by intelligently adapting old buildings to new uses. The scorn which most architects once had for older buildings has disappeared, replaced by understanding and sympathy.

Kidder Smith himself is a precursor of this reawakened sensitivity to environment and the beauty of older buildings. His award-winning book of 1955, *Italy Builds,* reviewing the exciting work of that country's contemporary architects, gave equal praise to the tradition of the Italian vernacular and to townscape. In his description of American buildings, Kidder Smith likewise presents us with both sensitive and critical comment of broad range. He generously lends us his experienced eye. The sweep of his effort links the present with the past and stimulates us to make our own judgments and discoveries.

ORGANIZATION OF BOOK

The three volumes of this guidebook describe the architecture of three geographic regions with approximately the same number of buildings in each: Volume 1—New England and the Mid-Atlantic States; Volume 2—The South and Midwest; and Volume 3—The Plains States and Far West. The states in each volume are arranged in alphabetical order, and each state begins with a map showing by numbered dots the geographic location of cities containing buildings described in that state. The cities are also listed alphabetically and if there is more than one building in a city they appear in approximate chronology. As is explained, the structures which are in boldface in the state index are of general interest, whereas the others are more for architects, architectural historians, and other specialists. An index and glossary appear in each volume. Pertinent books and reference sources are listed in the text.

Alabama

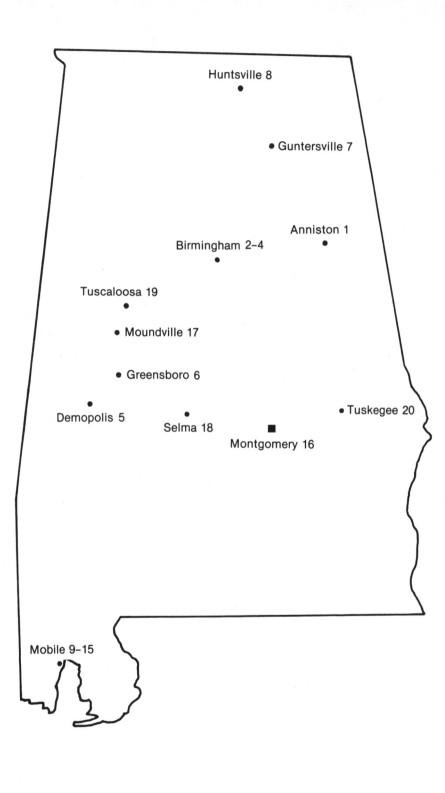

Huntsville 8

Guntersville 7

Anniston 1

Birmingham 2-4

Tuscaloosa 19

Moundville 17

Greensboro 6

Demopolis 5

Selma 18

Tuskegee 20

Montgomery 16

Mobile 9-15

ALABAMA

The buildings in boldface type are of general interest. The others are for the specialist.

Anniston	1	Anniston High School (1970–71)—Caudill, Rowlett & Scott
Birmingham	2	**The Theater of Birmingham-Southern College** (1967–68)—Warren, Knight & Davis
	3	Progressive Farmer Building (1972–73)—Jova/Daniels/Busby
	4	**Birmingham-Jefferson Civic Center** (1969–76)—Geddes Brecher Qualls Cunningham
Demopolis	5	**Gaineswood** (1842–60)
Greensboro	6	Magnolia Grove (1835–38)
Guntersville	7	**TVA Installations** Wheeler Dam (1933–36) and Guntersville Dam (1935–39)—The Tennessee Valley Authority
Huntsville	8	The First Alabama Bank of Huntsville (1835–36)—George W. Steele
Mobile	9	Fort Condé (1735, reconstructed 1976) and Fort Condé-Charlotte House (c. 1822–24)
	10	**Oakleigh** (1831–32)
	11	**Old City Hospital** (1833–36/1975–76)—William George
	12	Presbyterian Church (1836–37)—Gallier, Dakin & Dakin
	13	**Barton Academy** (1835–36)—Gallier, Dakin & Dakin
	14	**Richards/DAR House** (1860)
	15	**Bellingrath Gardens** (1927–32)
Montgomery	16	Teague House (Chamber of Commerce) (1848)
Moundville	17	**Mound State Monument** (c. A.D. 1200–1400)

1   Anniston High School (1970–71)
The Educational Park
Woodstock Avenue at 12th Street (3 blocks E of Quintard
   Avenue/US 431)
Anniston, Alabama

CAUDILL, ROWLETT & SCOTT, ARCHITECTS

As the first phase of the Anniston Educational Park—which comprises preschool through junior college—this high school building reflects the forward-looking, non-structured educational approach of the architects, the principal, and the teachers. Instead of a block of classroom "cells," there are, in effect, no classrooms at all, except specialized ones. To define a teaching area, freestanding chalkboards are set up around a group of movable desks. Flexibility is almost total. The obvious query —for all such schools—is whether there is any aural intrusion from the class on the other side of the chalkboard. Both teachers and students in Anniston feel that this does not constitute a serious problem, the "white noise" which flows through the building minimizing adjacent acoustic interference. There are, however, residual doubts on the part of some educators.

The two floors of the school focus on the double-height Material Resource Center (basically the library), which is the heart of both building and teaching process, and the home base of the student. Here is a bright educational agora, with one wall of glass facing the garden, while the activity on switchbacks of ramps and stairs at each end lends vitality between classes. Laboratories, language labs, and teachers' rooms, etc., are separately enclosed, with fully equipped auditorium and a gymnasium at far end, each with both inside and outside entries so that they can be used at night without entering the school proper. Construction is of white brick and white-painted concrete block. Poole, Pardue, Morrison & Dean were associate architects and also designed the adjacent Vocational-Technical Unit (1972). The aged (1914) but substantial house in the center belonged to former Governor Kilby and is now used for home economics instruction. It was designed by Warren, Knight & Davis.

Reception area open during school hours

2 The Theater of Birmingham-Southern College (1967–68)
8th Avenue (US 78) at 8th Street
Birmingham, Alabama

WARREN, KNIGHT & DAVIS, ARCHITECTS; DR. ARNOLD F. POWELL, THEATER CONSULTANT

One of the most exciting small (four hundred seats maximum) theaters in this country, this building was designed with close collaboration between John E. Davis, Jr., of the architectural firm and Dr. Arnold F. Powell of the College's Drama Department. It is intended as a teaching workshop as well as a community cultural asset. An intimate relationship between actors and audience, and maximum flexibility of facilities were prime concerns. The three main elements of the theater's adaptability can be seen in the treatment of ceiling, stage, and floor. The ceiling, instead of being a solid canopy over the audience with spotlights camouflaged, is crisscrossed by bands of white solids (radials and chords) which alternate with black voids. The space above provides the light loft, and the "voids," which are fully accessible by catwalks (on the solid bands), enable a variety of lighting or projection equipment to be easily installed, yet the geometry of the solid white bands gives definition to the room. The split-revolve-lift stage, 40 feet/12 meters in diameter and backed by a permanent cyclorama,

is divided into halves, the rear section of which can be lowered 25 feet/7.6 meters into the basement, rotated on a similar, lower round-table to expose a new set which is then speedily returned and, when appropriate, revolved into place, all in a matter of seconds. Three different sets are on immediate tap. The "used" set in the basement is removed and a new one, if needed, installed. There is, thus, no need for a fly loft, and a ceiling common to stage and auditorium further binds the two together. Folding side walls add to the adaptability of shape.

Inasmuch as the theater also has to double for ballet, cinema, television performances, and even chamber music, flexibility in seating was another essential ingredient. Thus all seats except the arc of four rows at back are removable and mounted on nine palletized "seat wagons," each holding from twenty-six to thirty-eight seats, which can be jacked up and pushed by hand (student power) across the flat floor. The first four rows of seats are on a lift for maximum options of arrangement. Almost any type of audience-to-stage relationship can be set up, from in-the-round, to proscenium, to thrust. When cleared of seats, the flat floor becomes a TV stage. Acoustics are tuned to fit this demanding range by electronic means.

A practice theater, classrooms, workshop, lower turntable, and storage fill the basement. The lobby is more than tight, primarily because of economics, and the front elevation is not masterfully coordinated, but the heart—the stage and auditorium—are superb. David A. Nibbelin, of Variable Acoustics Inc., was acoustic consultant.

Open during performances

3   **Progressive Farmer Building** (1972–73)
    820 Shades Creek Parkway
    Birmingham, Alabama

JOVA/DANIELS/BUSBY, ARCHITECTS

An ingenious publishing headquarters perched in the trees on a hillside at the southeast edge of the city. A thickly wooded, steeply sloping site posed more than ordinary difficulties, but the architects met these problems and in effect took advantage of them: the building (and the parking at the entrance) steps down the grade, airily upheld by exposed steel columns. Not a bush, let alone a tree, was removed that could be saved (at times to the consternation of the contractor).

The approach from parking deck leads via a flying walkway to the main entrance which is on the top floor. This reception lobby is both laterally spacious with its views outward and vertically spacious with the open double-height stairwell (with excellent photo-mural behind). The building is constructed largely of weathering steel and solar glass, each properly used (and with an influence of Saarinen's John Deere

Headquarters in Moline, Illinois—q.v.). The glass is shielded by a brise-soleil outrigging. The steel could be left exposed (i.e. not fireproofed), because each floor has direct exit to grade.

Grounds and lobby open during business hours

---

4 Birmingham-Jefferson Civic Center (1969–76)
9th–11th Avenues North between 19th and 21st Streets
Birmingham, Alabama

GEDDES BRECHER QUALLS CUNNINGHAM, ARCHITECTS

The somewhat fortified appearance of the exterior of this substantial Civic Center arose from conditions beyond the architects' control: it is bounded by Interstate 59 on one side and lies directly under the airplane approach to the nearby airport. To insulate the concert hall and theater from the noise outside, a heavily walled exterior of precast concrete panels plus a separate thick inner wall and ceiling (on steel frame) were mandatory, and successful. However, more suggestions of

festivity on the exterior would not be amiss. The flags of the fifty states?

The Center, occupying a four-block site on the edge of downtown, comprises four separate but attached units: an exhibition hall, concert hall, theater, and coliseum. Its design was premiated in a national competition which drew 276 entries. The exhibition hall provides a main-floor facility for trade shows and conventions, 100,000 square feet/9,290 square meters, with a large lounge and banquet room adjacent. It is an efficient, highly flexible space with columns on 90-foot/27-meter centers and a ceiling 25 feet/7.6 meters high. A 60 per cent expansion was completed in May 1980, permitting two major events to occur simultaneously.

The adjacent concert hall is introduced by a flowing lobby, while the hall itself, which seats 2,967, is one of the most impressive in the country. The treatment of the balcony (723 seats) and grand tier (908) is particularly dramatic, with sweeping angles and "trays" of well-scaled seats—as opposed to static layers. These are cantilevered in slightly asymmetric groups above and into the auditorium which has 1,336 seats. Maximum room width and minimum depth (125 feet/38 meters) were sought for greater intimacy between audience and performers. The proscenium measure 90 feet/27 meters wide by 28 feet/8.5 meters high. There are two lifts capable of accommodating 110 musicians or 150 extra seats when the orchestra is on stage. The ceiling of the auditorium is purposefully dark, rendering it almost invisible when contrasted with the bright red seats. It is made up of acoustic reverberation "doors" which can tune the hall precisely to accommodate a single voice or a full orchestra.

The theater, with a capacity of 1,071, is intimate with only 21 rows of seats. Red carpeting from the lobby sweeps in to complement the well-raked purple seats. The stage can be either thrust or proscenium, while the auditorium is used for cinema and speeches as well as theatrical productions. Overhead, as in the concert hall, a near-black ceiling conceals mechanics while giving flexibility. The theater lobby, however, is less satisfactory, being tight in circulation and exits, and on the antiseptic side visually; its tan tile motif (which occurs throughout the complex) is overly insistent. Rehearsal rooms and off-stage facilities are first-rate, as they are for all facilities.

The coliseum can be used for ice hockey, when it seats 16,756, plus virtually all other indoor sports and major entertainment. The courtyard on which the buildings focus forms a festive center with fountains, picnic areas, flowers, and trees. A 300-seat glass-walled restaurant will open in December 1980.

The Civic Center, which marks the centenary of the founding of Birmingham, is connected by landscaping to Wilson Park, the municipal core of the city. George W. Qualls was chief of design; Paul Weidlinger structural consultant; Bolt, Beranek & Newman, acoustical consultants; and Jean Rosenthal Associates, theater consultants.

Open for events

---

5   **Gaineswood** (1842–60)
    805 South Cedar Street (US 43)
    Demopolis, Alabama

Though Gaineswood is disjointed and of a scale which makes the house appear larger in photographs than in space, it carries itself with patrician grace. This highly unusual, basically Greek Revival mansion was designed by its owner, General Nathan B. Whitfield, an amateur architect and engineer who took a minute interest in every facet of the building, even to constructing personally some of the shop machinery for turning out parts. The plan of the house, which is of two stories

with only secondary bedrooms above, is unusual. The entry is not via the prominent portico across the front, but by the porte cochère at right. The balustraded parterre and the portico (the round Doric columns of wood, the inset square ones of masonry) are matched by a low portico at rear, also with balustraded parterre. In plan these are axially offset. A drawing room occupies the front of the house with master bedroom beyond and the "family" bedroom with half-round bay is appended to this. On the back side of the hall are the parlor and dining room, each dominated by a large and elaborately decorated domed ceiling of Italianate detail, with oculus for daylight in the center (the parlor being almost windowless).

The design of each room is sumptuous, the drawing room in particular containing some of the richest detailing to be seen in the waning days of the Greek Revival. Influenced, obviously, by various "handbooks" on the subject, the columns, capitals, cornices, and ceilings are wondrously intricate, pushed to the limit. The decoration of the domed ceiling in dining room and parlor are also of this ripe school.

Though heavily damaged by vandals, the house fortunately survived and is one of the most remarkable examples of its style in the country and unquestionably the finest house open to the public in Alabama. The dwelling was purchased by the state in 1971 and completely restored by the Alabama Historical Commission in 1975. Descendants of the builder have furnished the mansion with original family pieces.

Open Mon–Sat. 9–4, Sun. 1–4, except Jan. 1 and Dec. 25

---

6   Magnolia Grove (1835–38)
W end of Main Street at Hobson Street (ALA 14)
Greensboro, Alabama

The R. P. Hobson House, since 1947 a state shrine, will appeal for its luxuriant trees (primarily its giant magnolias [*Magnolia grandiflora*]) as much as for its chaste architecture. The house, with six slender Doric columns of brick plastered, tall windows, and balconied upper hall, sets an understated, somewhat "expected" but still attractive scene. Note the wrought-iron balustrade. The interior features the extraordinary exploits of Admiral Hobson.

Antebellum Greensboro (population about 3,500) is itself worth exploring, although its houses, with the exception of its finest (Magnolia Grove), are private. A descriptive map is available.

Open Thurs., Sat. 1–5, except holidays

7   TVA Installations

THE TENNESSEE VALLEY AUTHORITY, ARCHITECTS AND ENGINEERS

The TVA installations are among the most impressive architectural-engineering works in the United States. Although the Authority's seven nuclear plants are not open to the public, the water-powered and coal-fired installations can be visited (see Index) and almost all of them will reward the viewer. Among the finer in Alabama are **Wheeler Dam** (1933–36) on ALA 101, about 18 miles/29 kilometers east of Florence, and the picturesquely situated **Guntersville Dam** (1935–39), 3.7 miles/5.8 kilometers southwest of US 431 below New Hope. They have, of course, transformed the region.

Open daily

---

8   The First Alabama Bank of Huntsville (1835–36)
Civic Square and Fountain Row
Huntsville, Alabama

GEORGE W. STEELE, ARCHITECT

Designed by an architect who was obviously a Greek Revival cognoscento, with reputedly an outstanding library, this expertly pedimented bank is one of the finer—and one of the less known—buildings of its pe-

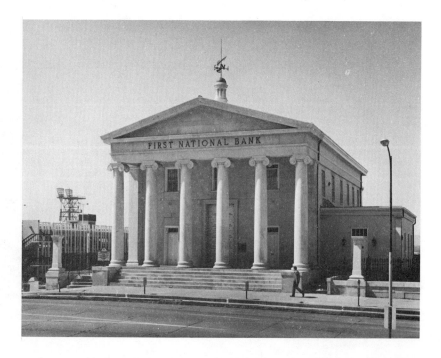

riod. Its six two-story Ionic columns were shipped to Huntsville by river barge from Baltimore; the limestone slabs comprising the front are thought to be local. All stonework is finished so smoothly that no mortar was used at the joints. The entire building was, indeed, so meticulously polished that the town's early settlers dubbed it The Marble Palace. Originally built as the Huntsville Branch of the State Bank of Alabama, it has been continuously used for banking purposes ever since, the present name dating from 1971. Since the 1950s the interior has been carefully adapted to modern conditions by a bank that obviously cares.

Open during business hours

---

9   Fort Condé (1735, reconstructed 1976) **and Fort Condé-Charlotte House** (c. 1822–24)
104 Theatre Street
Mobile, Alabama

Mobile in recent years has been making an effort to preserve and restore the slender remnant of its historic inheritance and part of this centers on Fort Condé Village. Included are a reconstructed section of

Fort Condé, the house next door (both discussed below), and a series
of restored and spruced-up dwellings from the middle of the nineteenth
century now devoted to shops.

The **Fort Condé de la Mobile** (originally just a palisade) was built by
the French (1724–35)—Mobile was the capital of French Louisiana
until 1719—then relinquished to the English after the Treaty of Paris
(1763), and captured by the Spanish in 1780. The Americans took
over in 1813 and its military days ceased, the fort itself being leveled
for its rubble. Using original French drawings, a section was reconstructed (1975–76) both for the Bicentennial and to give the city a
bulwark of its colorful past.

Part of the earliest **Fort Condé-Charlotte House** was first used as a
courthouse and jail, but in the 1820s it was remodeled into a good
Greek Revival residence. The double porch should be noted, particularly the second-floor Corinthian columns. At one time occupied by
the Department of Highways, in 1957 it was purchased by the National
Society of the Colonial Dames of America in the State of Alabama
and carefully restored, its furnishings representing the five periods
of its history.

*Fort open daily 9–5: admission; house open Tues.–Sat. 10–4,
except holidays: admission*

---

10   **Oakleigh** (1831–32)
     **350 Oakleigh Place at Savannah Street; S off Government Street, 4
        blocks on George or 3 on Roper**
     Mobile, Alabama

Oakleigh's masonry ground floor and its wood porticoed main floor
mark it a clear member of the French-influenced antebellum houses
that stretch along the Gulf of Mexico. Some historians feel that this
"raised cottage type"—often with Greek Revival details—originated
with the French in Alabama, then gravitated to Louisiana, where it
achieved its greatest popularity. Though not pretentious, Oakleigh is a
worthy companion to its sisters to the west. Its setting, a 33-acre/13-
hectare portion of an original Spanish land grant of some 400

acres/162 hectares, is surrounded by fine old live oaks (hence its name), azaleas, which were introduced by the French, and camellias (which are generally at peak blossom from mid-February through March). Though planned without benefit of architect—its original owner, James W. Roper from South Carolina, designed it—the house has a highly functional T-shape plan which permits cross ventilation (generally from three exposures) in the major rooms. It is elevated above ground because of dampness and insects, and is reached by an unusual curved outside stair set within the portico. The kitchen was placed in the rear as was the custom.

A number of changes were made in the house by its various occupants—it once even served as a youth center. Oakleigh was acquired by the city in 1955 and after full restoration and furnishing in the pre-1850 fashion, made into a museum-house plus headquarters for the Historic Mobile Preservation Society.

Open Mon.–Sat. 10–3:30, Sun. 2–4, except holidays and
Christmas week: admission

11   Old City Hospital (1833–36/1975–76) **now Mobile County
     Department of Pensions and Security
St. Anthony and Broad Streets
Mobile, Alabama**

WILLIAM GEORGE, ARCHITECT

Comprised of two stories on a raised basement, this rangy example of
the Greek Revival is one of the most original in the country—"naive
but impressive," wrote Hamlin (*Greek Revival Architecture in
America,* Oxford University Press, 1944). The naivety lies in some of
the proportions, particularly the low pediment with unusual Federal
window, the too-narrow entablature, and the stretched Tuscan columns. The east and west wings, incidentally, were added in 1907–8.
Designed, among other things, to keep off the heat of the Southern sun
—which it does well—the building served as a hospital until 1968
when the new Medical Center was opened. Following the termination
of its medical function, then desultory municipal use, the future of the
building—one of the most important examples of its kind in the South

—was long in doubt. Then in 1972 a civic-minded business executive, Mr. Joseph Linyer Bedsole, thoughtfully established a half-million-dollar trust for the building's restoration in memory of his sister, the late Lorraine Bedsole Tunstall, the first director of the Alabama Child Welfare Department. The building has been totally rehabilitated with matching city and county funds, and it is now used as offices for the Mobile County Department of Pensions and Security. Grider & Laraway were architects for the reconstruction, with George M. Leake consultant. This superb adaptive use gives Mobile not only a fine building but one of the most stalwart lineups of Tuscan columns—fourteen in all—in the United States.

Open Mon.–Fri. 8–5, except holidays

---

12 Government Street Presbyterian Church (1836–37)
300 Government Street at Jackson
Mobile, Alabama

GALLIER, DAKIN & DAKIN, ARCHITECTS

The Classic Revival devotee will want to include in his or her itinerary this sturdy church in downtown Mobile. The exterior falls into one of the standard patterns of its time with inset (in antis) porch, a form used here simply but boldly. The interior shows greater freedom with its diagonally coffered ceiling and confidently elaborate chancel wall with rich retable. Its tapered sides hint of the Hellenistic and even the Egyptian. The entire church was handsomely restored in 1975–76 for the Bicentennial. (Its original steeple—hit by lightning in 1852—was not replaced.) There has been dispute concerning the architects of the church—and of Barton Academy (q.v.)—with some historians crediting the design to Thomas F. James of Mobile who did a number of Greek Revival buildings in the city. However, James Gallier's own diary claims that he and the Dakin brothers were the architects of both church and Academy. Arthur Scully, Jr., in his *James Dakin, Architect* (Louisiana State University Press, 1973) dismisses Thomas James as "merely one of the contractors." Professor Scully also suggests that the chaste exterior of the church probably reflects the hand of James Gallier, while the sumptuously detailed interior is more likely the work of the Dakin brothers. It is pertinent to note that the Irish-born Gallier and the New York State-born James and Charles Dakin had all worked together in Town & Davis' office in New York before moving south where each remained, Charles unfortunately dying at the age of twenty-eight. Mobile, and the South, are richer for their efforts.

Open Mon.–Fri. 9–5, except holidays; Sun. service

13 Barton Academy (1835–36)
504 Government Street between Lawrence and Cedar
Mobile, Alabama

GALLIER, DAKIN & DAKIN, ARCHITECTS

Education in Alabama got off to an impressive start with this stately structure, the first public school in the state—although the building was also jointly used by private and parochial schools (and even clubs) to help with expenses. Designed by the same architects who produced the Presbyterian Church a few blocks east on Government Street, it constitutes one of the major Classic Revival buildings in the South. The facade comprises a raised and projected portico of six columns with minutely projecting pavilions at each end (all of brick

stuccoed). A sizable Ionic-bound drum on top with copper dome and a circular lantern add a jaunty touch. (Various additions at sides and rear were also made.) The building was preserved during the Civil War by being turned into a hospital, and wings were added in 1914. It was fully restored in 1969–70 to its considerable grandeur on the outside and remodeled within to house the administrative offices of the Mobile public school system. In the restoration—by architects D. T. March and N. H. Holmes, Jr.—the capitals of the portico were changed back to their original Ionic (to match those in the drum), while the contemporary metal windows were also replaced. Altogether an outstanding recycling job.

Open during business hours

---

14   Richards/DAR House (1860)
256 North Joachim Street
Mobile, Alabama

Mobile was on the verge of a cotton-booming economy after Alabama was admitted to the Union in 1819, but the town was devastated by fires in 1827 and 1839. The last conflagration occurred as the Classic Revival began to be challenged by new directions in architecture, and

among the best examples of this period is the ambitiously embellished
Richards House. (Charles Richards, its builder-owner, was a Maine-
born steamship master.) The house mass proper shows, with only
modest distinction, the bracketed Italianate then edging into mid-
nineteenth-century popularity. However the front portico and fence
are rich with a lacework of iron—cast iron with wrought iron used for
"framing"; it is among the finest to be seen. Such ornamental work had
been brought to the area toward the end of the eighteenth century,
some historians think by the French and possibly the Spanish—Spain
occupied Mobile from 1780 to 1813—and initially most of the ironwork in Mobile was of French manufacture. However, production soon
began in France's southern outpost. Note that the four seasons are
depicted in the lacelike iconography of the balustrade.

The house was bought and fully restored (1947) by the Ideal
Cement Corporation for its Mobile offices. When the company moved
to other quarters in 1973, it gave the house to the city of Mobile
in whose museum system it now belongs. That year the city leased
the property to the Mobile Daughters of the American Revolution for

twenty years on condition that the DAR furnish it appropriately—nothing more recent than 1870—and open it to the public. It is also available for party rentals and weddings. Thomas S. James, of Mobile, is thought to have been the architect. Incidentally, Mobile sustained no Civil War damage and many fine antebellum homes survive.

Open Tues.–Sat. 10–4, Sun. 1–4, except major holidays: admission

---

15   Bellingrath Gardens (1927–32)
**c. 19 miles/31 kilometers S of Mobile via US 90 or IS 10 (S of
   town of Theodore—well marked)**
near Mobile, Alabama

The almost 1,000 acres/405 hectares of Bellingrath contain one of the country's great gardens, and though there are seasonal heights— azaleas in February–March, roses in spring, and chrysanthemums in

October–November—there are pleasures at any month of the year. The variety is staggering (nine hundred varieties of autumnal camellias for instance) and so is the quality. If one tires of the 75 acres/30 hectares of plants and flowers, there are supposedly seventy kinds of trees and two hundred varieties of birds. The Bellingrath Home is also open to the public (daily 8 A.M.–dusk: separate admission).

Open daily 7–5: admission

16   Teague House (Chamber of Commerce) (1848)
468 South Perry Street
Montgomery, Alabama

The Teague House, its six Ionic columns upholding a rich but slightly heavy entablature, has come down to the present day remarkably untouched by the Civil War—when it was used as a Union headquarters —or by subsequent disasters. It has been doubly cared for since 1955 when it was acquired by the Alabama Chamber of Commerce. The house bears a relation to its flat-roofed, column-porched cousins in Athens, Georgia—which see—but it carries an air of its own. Though the second floor is occupied with business offices, the main-floor rooms have all been restored and refurnished (with strong early Victorian emphasis) and are open as house-museum to the public. Its walls are of solid brick both outside and in.

Open Mon.–Fri. 10–12, 2–3:30, except holidays

---

17   Mound State Monument (c. A.D. 1200–1400)
**1 mile/1.6 kilometers W of town on ALA 21, c. 17.5 miles/28
   kilometers S of Tuscaloosa via ALA 69**
Moundville, Alabama

The Mound State Monument consists of a series of twenty large earth platforms or mounds, mostly truncated pyramids but some ovoid, scattered over 315 acres/127 hectares of flat landscape edged by the Black

Warrior River. Designed as sites for temples and for residences of chiefs and priests (but not for burial) the knolls describe a very rough circle about the two largest outcroppings. The tallest, Mound B, at 58.5 feet/17.7 meters is now capped by a theoretical reproduction of a thatched-roof temple. (The only taller one in the country is the Cahokia Mound in East St. Louis, Illinois, which is roughly 100 feet/30 meters high.) The Indians who constructed these mounds were part of a sophisticated and complex culture known as Mississippian, a culture found throughout the Mississippi Valley and which developed among local agricultural groups. The most notable achievement of these peoples was the construction of monumental public works in the form of large mounds. The origins of this tradition are enigmatic, although some authors have suggested indirect Central American influence.

The nearby museum (1939) houses instructive material including a number of preserved *in situ* excavations, plus explanatory dioramas and displays. The first excavations at Moundville were made in 1905, and by 1933 the area was made Mound State Park, then a "monument" in 1938 when extensive excavations were begun. It was annexed to the University of Alabama in 1961. Altogether a revealing excursion.

Open daily 9–5, except Dec. 25: admission to museum

18   Sturdivant Hall (1853)
713 Mabry Street at McLeod Avenue
Selma, Alabama

THOMAS H. LEE, ARCHITECT

A stately house with several motifs from the mid-1850s peering around its earlier Classic Revival frame. Note, for instance, the touch of the Tuscan-Victorian in the square cupola atop the roof, and the regional, elaborate cast-iron balcony across the front (and also on the small porch to left as well as the portico at rear). The six two-story columns (30 feet/9.1 meters high) with cast-iron capitals give the facade an imposing order, which the rectangular shape of the building emphasizes. The interior has been well restored with sophisticated colors that echo the original ones. Note, too, the bold plaster cornices.

The dwelling was also known as the Watts-Parkman-Gillman House

after its trilogy of early owners, but was changed to the Sturdivant Mansion, or Sturdivant Hall, when the late Robert Daniel Sturdivant left an estate of fifty thousand dollars to the city to use the building as a house-museum. Behind are the kitchen, slave quarters, and carriage house. A fine addition to the town.

Open Tues.–Sat. 9–4, Sun. 2–4, except holidays: admission

19 Gorgas House (1828–29/1840/1890s)
University of Alabama
**N off University Boulevard (ALA 215) on Colonial Drive; Central
    Campus**
Tuscaloosa, Alabama

WILLIAM NICHOLS, ARCHITECT

An all-brick, Federally inclined house, combining the raised cottage style of the deep South with a Classic-inspired portico. The portico was possibly added later; it was certainly widened in the 1890s when it was expanded from one bay to three, its graceful curving twin stairs

simply being pushed farther apart. The brick was imported from England as ballast, with cotton filling the ship for the return trip home. Pegs instead of nails were used for most of its construction.

It was built as the university's first dining hall (and first permanent structure), and the dining area occupied the ground floor with quarters for the steward above. It was almost the only college building left after the Civil War had marched through Tuscaloosa. In 1840 it was remodeled as a private residence, later being used by the famous Gorgas family. (General Josiah Gorgas was once president of the university; his son, General William C. Gorgas [1854–1920], conquered yellow fever and controlled malaria in Panama, thus making the Canal possible). The Gorgas family occupied the house from 1879 to 1953, and the furnishings—more of comfort than distinction—date from their occupancy. One authority (J. Frazer Smith in his book *White Pillars,* Bramhall House, 1941) writes that the house was "Designed by Thomas Nichols, architect from Philadelphia," but most sources give the name William Nichols, and the university mentions his origin as Charleston. The dwelling, in addition to serving as mess hall, was also used as a hospital during the War Between the States, and later as a post office. It is now a house-museum, a key element of the Gorgas-Manly Historic District of the university, all of which is now in the National Register of Historic Places.

Open Mon.–Sat. 10–12, 2–5, Sun. 3–5

20 **The Tuskegee Chapel** (1968–69)
   Tuskegee Institute
   W of town on ALA 126
   Tuskegee, Alabama

**PAUL RUDOLPH, ARCHITECT; FRY & WELCH, ASSOCIATED
ARCHITECTS**

This exhilarating chapel bears little kinship to other churches, yet it is
one whose 1,100-seat nave states dramatically that the word of the
Lord is spoken here. The most striking feature of the inner design—
which looks almost exactly like Rudolph's original drawing published
in 1960—is the extraordinary flow, really ebb and flow, of spaces. This
is accentuated by the daylight which floods the side walls, the light
coming from glazed peripheral bands in the ceiling. The supporting
beams shield the direct light source so that glare does not result. The
enclosing walls are thus made "independent" visually, while the solid
central part of the ceiling, which carries the carefully balanced
artificial lights, "floats" as a canopy above the congregation. All sense

of confinement vanishes, while a seeming continuum of horizontal space "escapes" around the corner of the right-hand side.

The chancel is distinguished by its arrangement for the famous Tuskegee Institute choir—whose space is almost embraced by three sheer angled walls—and by the projected brick pulpit with its declaratory sounding board above. Though there is a passage to the left of the pulpit leading to the meditation chapel, this, surprisingly, does not distract or become a disturbing vacuum. Near the floor level along the sides note the incorporation of the ventilation units with the walls, their light-struck geometry stepping down the slightly canted floor. Overhead the carefully "pleated" ceiling fans in a broad curve then vanishes around the corner. The walls of the chapel, both inside and out, are of reddish-salmon brick—brick is used for the older buildings on the campus—laid with red mortar. (The first design for the church was in reinforced concrete: brick proved less expensive—and better.) There is an extravagance of planes, and even a disjointedness about the exterior, with its porch projecting in front, while windows push unnecessarily out the back, but the interior is spectacular, one of the most extraordinary religious rooms in the country. The lower level—there is a drop-off in grade—is used by the School of Music.

Open daily 9–4:30 during school year

Florida

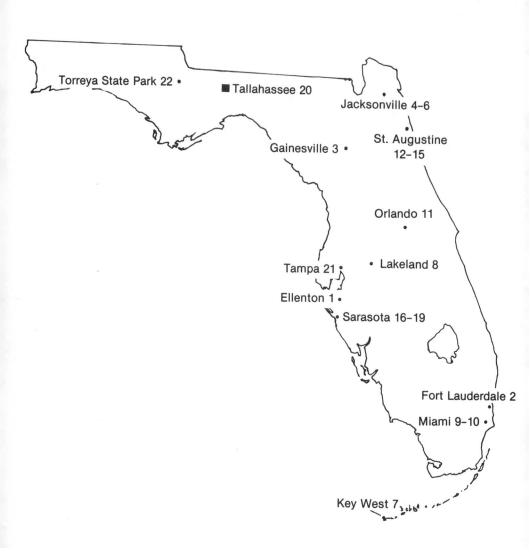

Torreya State Park 22 •

■ Tallahassee 20

Jacksonville 4–6

St. Augustine
12–15

Gainesville 3 •

Orlando 11

Tampa 21 •

• Lakeland 8

Ellenton 1 •

• Sarasota 16–19

Fort Lauderdale 2

Miami 9–10 •

Key West 7

FLORIDA

The buildings in boldface type are of general interest. The others are for the specialist.

Ellenton	1 **Gamble Plantation State Historic Site** (1845–65)
Fort Lauderdale	2 **United States Courthouse—Federal Office Building** (1975–79)—William Morgan
Gainesville	3 **Florida State Museum** (1971)—William Morgan
Jacksonville	4 **Gulf Life Center** (1966–67)—Welton Becket Associates
	5 **Police Memorial Building** (1974–77)—William Morgan
	6 **Florida Regional Service Center** (1977–78)—William Morgan
Key West	7 **Audubon House** (1830)
Lakeland	8 **The Frank Lloyd Wright Buildings, Florida Southern University** (1940–59)
	Spivey Fine Arts Center (1970)— Schweizer Associates
Miami	9 **Vizcaya** (1914–16)—Paul Chalfin and F. Burral Hoffman, Jr.
	10 Smathers Plaza Housing (1966–67)— Robert B. Browne
Orlando	11 Orlando Public Library (1965–66)— John M. Johansen & Associates
St. Augustine	12 **Castillo de San Marcos** (1672–95/ 1738–40/1752–56/1762)
	Fort Matanzas National Monument (1740–42)
	13 **Restoration Area** (1565–1821/1960– 1970s)
	14 The Oldest House (c. 1704–c. 1890)

	15 Flagler College (1886–88)—Carrère & Hastings
	Alcazar Hotel (1887–89)—Carrère & Hastings
Sarasota	16 St. Paul's Lutheran Church (1959/1968–69)—Victor A. Lundy
	17 **Plymouth Harbor** (1965–66)—Frank Folsom Smith
	18 East Campus, University of South Florida (1968)—I. M. Pei & Partners
	19 **Van Wezel Performing Arts Hall** (1968–69)—William Wesley Peters, of Taliesin Associated Architects
Tallahassee	20 **The Big Bend Pioneer Farm** (late 1800s)
Tampa	21 **Tampa International Airport** (1968–71)—Reynolds, Smith & Hill
Torreya State Park	22 **Gregory House** (1834)

1 Gamble Plantation State Historic Site (1845–65)
3708 Patten Avenue
2.3 miles/3.7 kilometers E of US 41, off US 301 at Central
Avenue
Ellenton, Florida

Primitively detailed without and haphazardly furnished within, the two-story Gamble Mansion, approximately 20 miles/32 kilometers north of Sarasota, is nonetheless a good example of "back-country classical." Eighteen capless columns, 25 feet/7.6 meters high, envelop three sides of the house, while an unusually buttressed back wing for kitchen and office (the first part built) stands at the rear, separated from the main house by a breezeway. A double veranda with both paired and single columns wraps about the dwelling on three sides. Almost all materials came from the 3,500-acre/1,416-hectare sugarcane plantation on which it stood. Red brick and "tabby" (oyster-shell lime, shells, and sand) were made by the plantation slaves, with much of the plaster having a binder of sugar. Wood came from the cypress and oak which abounded on the site. The house, which stood vacant and

dilapidated for many years, was privately purchased in 1925 and willed to the state, whose Board of Parks and Historic Memorials completely restored it in 1949. In addition to the regular furnishings of the period many Civil War memorabilia are also shown.

House open daily 9–4, except major holidays; tours on the hour: admission

2 United States Courthouse—Federal Office Building (1975–79)
299 East Broward Boulevard at Northeast 3rd Avenue
Fort Lauderdale, Florida

WILLIAM MORGAN, ARCHITECT; H. J. ROSS ASSOCIATES, ENGINEERS

An extraordinary government building which is best approached going northward on Broward Boulevard: one then appreciates its urban assurance, the parasol of its hovering roof, its cascades of water, and its tiers of planting. It is safe to say that few federal buildings and, in par-

ticular, fewer courthouses, are as ingratiating. Whether one's business is routine or a major courtroom ordeal, the architecture does its best to comfort the passage. Though there are architectural extravagances here, it is important to note that the project came in substantially under budget.

The complex contains four Federal courts, both civil and criminal, with full security and supportive functions; 150,000 square feet/13,936 square meters of office space for Federal agencies; and in-house parking for 230 automobiles. The structural system is based on reinforced concrete "trees" 30 feet/9.1 meters on center, cast-in-place concrete floor slabs, and concrete masonry infilling. In addition to the parasol roof which provides sun protection (and spatial venturesomeness), all windows are shielded by broad overhangs, while extensive shaded walkways are used where feasible in place of interior corridors. The watercourses amuse the eye, dampen street noises, and, with the ramps, provide agreeable linkage between the entry and the four-story-high atrium. Note the lateral offsets of the ramps. Extensive planting reflects the semitropical climate of Fort Lauderdale.

As the architect put it, "The underlying principle of design is that this facility must be an exceptionally delightful place for the citizen to visit at any time." H. J. Ross Associates worked in a joint venture with the architect; Stresau, Smith & Stresau were the landscape architects; Vida Stirby Brown the interior designer.

Open during office hours: atrium always open

---

3 Florida State Museum (1971)
University of Florida
Museum Road at Newell Drive
Gainesville, Florida

WILLIAM MORGAN, ARCHITECT

The architect faced difficult problems in the design of this combination museum and departmental offices because of its noisy site at the intersection of two roads and its steep fall-off in grade. He acquitted himself well on both counts. The approach side is bermed and grassed to echo quietly the park across the street, and to concentrate the emphasis of the complex on the terraced courtyard within, not the busy avenue. The court area has been creatively handled in its play of levels and

paths. It offers both circulation lanes and passive areas that are diverting to look down upon from the terraces which line the inner side of the museum and fun to use at ground level. The L-shaped building itself provides three well-canopied floors, with galleries and staff offices on main (i.e. upper) floor, natural sciences below, and the social sciences on the lowest level. The office space for the science disciplines opens onto the courtyard, with small inside laboratories across the hall and lab storage ranges (for research artifacts) cut into the slope. Having no above-grade contact, the storage area can maintain a natural, year-round temperature of 72° F/22° C. Construction is of waffle-slab reinforced concrete. The roof is extended by a series of precast, canted canopies that not only provide sun and rain protection but establish family unity.

The entry-level museum, providing 34,000 square feet/3,159 square meters of exhibition space, consists basically of one large L-shaped room divisible at will. Although its emphasis is on research connected with pre-Columbian Florida and the Caribbean, it harbors a wide variety of educational exhibits from natural history to the social sciences. Its walls on the terrace side have opaque and/or clear panels which can be interchanged for flexibility. Hopefully more of the collection will be placed outside on the broad bermed terraces and platforms, to join the reconstructed Temple House (second century B.C.–second century A.D.) from Vera Cruz that crowns the west mound.

The architect has been fascinated by "earth architecture" for years, and this is manifest in the courtyard landscaping. The bermed arena here is, indeed, so popular with students and townspeople alike that concerts and even weddings have taken place in it. The Sun Temple and complex at Teotihuacán (fl. A.D. 300–700) come to mind, but William Morgan has used Mesoamerica as lessons from the past, not models. As a consequence he has brought off an intriguing courtyard and building that edge the mannered but stay carefully within logic. Forrest M. Kelley was associate architect.

Open Mon.–Sat. 9:30–5, Sun. 1–5, except Dec. 25

---

4   Gulf Life Center (1966–67)
Gulf Life Drive—at Main Street Bridge (US 1 and 90)
Jacksonville, Florida

WELTON BECKET ASSOCIATES, ARCHITECTS; RICHARD R. BRADSHAW, INC., STRUCTURAL ENGINEERS

Gulf Life Tower brings a fresh look at skyscraper construction, with an exoskeletal, precast, post-tensioned concrete frame. The result not only produces an economical structure but a measure of sun control and effective modulation and play of light and shade. The twenty-seven-story building (plus concourse and mechanical floors) forms the pivotal unit of a complex which includes an adjacent hotel and shopping mall. The Center also helps spark Jacksonville's urban redevelopment, one which began with an older insurance building a few blocks away but which has been given positive testament with Gulf Life. The entire San Marco "peninsula," across the St. Johns River from the city's downtown core, had been a run-down area, crowded with depressed buildings. Gulf Life acquired a large section (12 acres/4.8 hectares) of this land, which is strategically adjacent to the Main Street Bridge and across the river from the new Civic Auditorium and other river-front improvements, and is rejuvenating much of the area. This handsome skyscraper and the adjacent Jacksonville Hilton are only the first units of this redevelopment. In 1978 construction began on an adjoining 16-acre/6.5-hectare site called St. Johns Place. This includes a 350-room hotel, shopping center, extensive boardwalk along the river, and a small office block (1981). Saxelbye, Powell,

Roberts & Ponder are the architects. Jacksonville is among the few river-front cities which has been farsighted enough to rediscover and utilize its lovely water location for other than industrial use. Most river cities in the United States either ignore the visual possibilities of their sites or erect a barrier reef of highways around their riparian periphery.

Gulf Life itself is a muscular building measuring 430 feet/131 meters high (above podium) and 144 feet/44 meters square. Its floors are supported by eight massive external concrete columns, two per side (near the third points), and the poured-in-place central service core. There are no interior columns. The prominent T-shaped beams are each made of fourteen prefabricated segments strung on 12.5-inch/32-centimeter high-strength cables or "tendons" and post-tensioned together in the method pioneered by the late Eugène Freyssinet. The beams taper horizontally to their ends and bulge outward from the building—reflecting their loads—and produce a mercurial sculptured effect as the sun moves about them. Strips of plate glass windows are set just behind the beams, their gray tint lending contrast to the white concrete frame. The tower rests on a podium and from this spring the eight supporting columns, here freestanding (49.5 feet/15 meters high to top of mezzanine) and making a dramatically scaled entry. Slung under the building and set back from the edge is the Sun Bank of Jacksonville reached by escalators from the glass-enclosed lobby. Underneath the terrace and facing the river is a six-hundred-seat cafeteria. The treatment of the top of the building is not altogether satisfactory as two floors masquerade as one, and the adjacent five-story garage is of indifferent design, but the basic building is a very superior joint product of architect and engineer. Kemp, Bunch & Jackson were associate architects.

The hotel part of Gulf Life Center—the Jacksonville Hilton—is intimately related to the tower and the plaza and shopping mall in front, having been designed by the same architects. Each of its 296 guest rooms has a sizable balcony, those on the riverside enjoying excellent views of the city across the water. Though the bar and dining rooms are inevitably prone to the architectural episodic, there is an atmosphere of restrained civility throughout.

Open during business hours

---

5   **Police Memorial Building** (1974–77)
    East Bay Street between Liberty and Catherine
    Jacksonville, Florida

    WILLIAM MORGAN, ARCHITECT

Terraces as a major architectural statement probably originated at Queen Hatshepsut's Temple at Dêr-el-Bahari (1550 B.C.). In our own time Le Corbusier at Marseilles demonstrated that a roof—as "terrace"—and its engagement of levels and forms can not only shield a building but constitute its chief delight, while utilizing 110 per cent of the site. William Morgan, always open to the lessons both of past and present, has not only made the roof of his Police Building an excursion in itself with its multiple terraces and surprises, he has added the kinetics of Rome's Piazza di Spagna, and embellished all with luxurious planting, a pool, and a fountain. Moreover the underlying philosophy of the building is perhaps of even greater significance than its physical rewards: the architect sought to transform a routine, often formidable if not hostile, municipal function into a public "park" which welcomes, day and night, the citizen, the visitor, and the lunchtime picnicker. The Police Building extends rapport and public accessibility to all in a "celebration" of the city and the people who make it up.

The design of this low-profiled neighborhood garden spot and official

headquarters—named for the Jacksonville police killed in line of duty
—was won in 1971 through a limited geographical competition. (The
building's program was subsequently changed when the state reorganized its judicial system and the design altered accordingly.) Its plan,
which fills a site measuring 700 feet/213 meters long, divides public
access on Bay Street from official use on the other side. Its two business floors are elevated above ground-level parking (for 244 cars and
some services), taking advantage of the 15-foot/4.6-meter fall-off in
grade.

The public is drawn to the building by a wide cascade of stairs,
flanked with planters, and it enters via an antimonumental door into a
towering central hall. Four freestanding columns uphold its roof while
a peripheral clerestory pours down a flood of indirect light. A comfortably scaled reception desk fills the far side, with ready access to the
Records Section adjacent. A generous, well-lit hall, lined with staff
offices, and highlighted by banners painted by local schoolchildren,
leads to a second skylit hall, primarily for official use, which is open
for the full height of the building and topped by a helipad. The building's concrete structure is dramatically stated here.

The expansive roof, as intimated, rejoices in an astounding parade of
levels, tiers of steps, and almost secret nooks, while a fountain gushes
water in front of the glass-walled cafeteria which welcomes the public.
The trees on several terraces will in time furnish generous shade: their
planting boxes—note stepped shape—are placed directly over structural columns. The chief cohesive element of the facades is the horizontal banding of smooth structural concrete which ties all together
and lends sophisticated scale to the vertically striated walls. Virtually

no windows were used because of security needs. Skylights provide most illumination.

In summary, the building flexibly integrates structural, mechanical, electrical, acoustical, illuminating, communicating, and partitioning systems through an economical, cast-in-place structural "tree" system designed with the help of William J. LeMessurier. William M. C. Lam was lighting consultant. Thomas A. McCrary was associate-in-charge. A nostalgic note can be seen in the late-nineteenth-century firehouse (on adjacent Catherine Street) which was carefully preserved and restored as a fire museum. Altogether a marvelous municipal concept.

Terraces always open, building open during office hours

---

6 Florida Regional Service Center (1977–78)
Coast Line Drive immediately E of US 1/17
Jacksonville, Florida

WILLIAM MORGAN, ARCHITECT

The Service Center stands only a few blocks west of the architect's Police Memorial Building and though only partly finished when last seen, it promises to be such an unusual structure that it is included here. As it is situated almost on the edge of the St. Johns River and

forms, moreover, a saddle between tall office blocks, Morgan sought a non-competitive building that would enhance the urban profile. And seizing on the fact that this is the narrowest span of the St. Johns, hence with the most concentrated activity (boat races, displays, etc.), the architect developed a design with a series of spectacular stepped terraces or esplanades facing the water and south sunshine. The building is divided in the middle by a spine of interior stairs which was enlarged and enhanced to encourage non-elevator intercommunication. This is precisely mirrored on the exterior to form a stairway-grandstand connecting the terraces.

The five-story structure serves as a combined state office building and downtown city parking facility whose air rights the state purchased. The federal government funded the bridge exit which cuts the northwest corner. The office areas have an extremely wide span (60 feet/18.3 meters) to provide maximum flexibility and "one room" layout. Prestressed beams were combined with poured-in-place concrete for the construction which uses a good deal of cantilevering. The building constitutes a searching attempt to tie the city to its sparkling waterside and to reawaken its citizens to "the quality of life downtown." Astonishingly, it came in $3 million under the budget of the Florida Department of General Services.

Open during office hours

---

7   Audubon House (1830)
205 Whitehead Street at Greene
Key West, Florida

A dwelling falling short of architectural distinction but revealing proper regional response to local building and subtropical climatic conditions. Note the upper and lower porches both front and rear, which provide shaded breezeways; the excellent planting, particularly the almond trees; and, lastly, the large roof to catch rainwater for household use. The house is almost enveloped by trees which not only shield it from the sun but allow a breeze, develop privacy, and produce visual/olfactory delights. The interior, which has been recently restored, boasts several good pieces of furniture plus a set of the original four volumes of Audubon's Elephant Folio.

Key West itself, though at one time (1830s) reputedly the richest town per capita in the United States, has little to show for its past,

while its present is being systematically encircled by high-speed high-ways that successfully amputate the town from the sea.

Open daily 9–12, 1–5, except Dec. 25: admission

---

8   **The Frank Lloyd Wright Buildings** (1940–59)
    Florida Southern University
    via South Florida Avenue, E on McDonald Street to Johnson
    **   Avenue**
    Lakeland, Florida

FRANK LLOYD WRIGHT, ARCHITECT

Time has not always dealt gently with the FLW buildings on the 1,800-student campus of Florida Southern, the first plans for which were drawn as early as 1936, while the last building dates from 1959 (the year of Wright's death). It is impossible (for this observer) to be enraptured by them. First, their broken, angled planes and surfaces do not take kindly to the insidiousness of their hot-humid climate which periodically drowns them with rain, occasionally lashes them with hurricanes, and in between bakes them with sun. Secondly, the

first structures (all but two of the original eight) were built largely by student labor with on-site, ill-controlled production of concrete blocks, so that the buildings' native naivety to environment has been compromised by material frailty. Their slightly moldy condition today was thus inevitable. (The college was built on a minimum budget.) Moreover, from the design standpoint there are questions too. The Ann Pfeiffer Chapel (1940), with prominent roof outrigging, though sensitively placed, disturbs some viewers, especially within, where its amorphous chancel, topped by a see-through grille, is uncomfortable visually. The adjoining Danforth Chapel (1955) is scarcely better, having an uneasily compacted shape, while behind the altar strips of orange and yellow glass alternate with clear panels to provide a view of the parking lot. (It is reported that Mr. Wright himself was unhappy with this glass.) The Ordway Arts Building (1955) on McDonald Street, and the Science Building (1952) are more satisfactory. The esplanades, or covered walkways, are highly useful in tying the buildings together and in providing weather protection but do so with absolutely minimum headroom.

However, in spite of this criticism, and with the cheerful note that they have recently (1980) been renovated, take a look, for they form the most extensive grouping—anywhere—of the maestro's work. And beyond the above negative remarks, the buildings do constitute a closely knit and harmonious grouping. Unfortunately, Wright's complete plan, with outdoor theater and contact with Lake Hollingsworth, all set in orange groves, did not materialize.

Some of the post-Wrightian buildings should be seen also, especially the fine **Spivey Fine Arts Center** off Johnson Avenue near the lake (1970—open during school year) by Schweizer Associates: Nils M. Schweizer was Wright's supervising architect at Lakeland for three years.

Campus open daily; map available at Administration Building

---

9   Vizcaya (1914–16)
3251 South Miami Avenue (immediately SW of Rickenbacker Causeway)
Miami, Florida

PAUL CHALFIN AND F. BURRAL HOFFMAN, JR., ARCHITECTS

One of the notable features of this seventy-room "Mediterranean" Xanadu is its direct embracing of the open bay and its capturing of the water via an impishly "tethered" stone barge. (The barge was designed by the architects and the sculptor A. Stirling Calder, Sandy Calder's father). This direct—and logical—relation of house and water was strangely rare in Florida at the time the mansion was built; but Vizcaya properly confronts and adapts to nature—here the sparkling Biscayne Bay. The house, whose architecture vaguely suggests a Brenta

Canal palazzo built by a Spaniard, stands weathered on the exterior but every surface of its pristine interior is alive with triumphant opulence. Though Italian Rococo predominates there is an array of rooms of almost every known fashion. The furnishings run from a second-century altar to 1915 gold plumbing fixtures.

The 10 acres/4 hectares of formal gardens, completed in 1920, are at times puzzlingly laid out but their parterred levels and their vistas are impressive. Many sections of the gardens have recently undergone extensive restoration and they should by all means be explored, especially along the water's edge. Diego Suârez was the landscape architect. This $25 million cold-weather retreat was acquired by Dade County in 1952, and now operates on a self-sustaining basis under its Park and Recreation Department. Don't miss and be sure to get a guide-folder to the different rooms almost all of which are now open to the public.

Open daily 9:30–5:30, except Dec. 25: admission

10   Smathers Plaza Housing (1966–67)
Southwest 29th Court at Southwest 10th Street
Miami, Florida

ROBERT B. BROWNE, ARCHITECT

Three strong, handsome buildings loosely related to each other form this center for the elderly. (Average age of the occupants is around seventy.) It is low-budget, high-imagination public housing built by the Miami Housing Authority; would that other cities' projects were as enlightened. The group is composed of a tower of thirteen floors with eight single rooms on all but the ground floor (ninety-six altogether), a six-story low-rise with fifty-one single apartments and thirty-five suites for couples, and a one-story community-recreation building or Senior Center with social hall, kitchen, meeting rooms, nurse, and offices. Each building was designed with assurance and sophistication. Exposed concrete, sealed and lightly stained, provides both structure and an "upkeep free" finish outside and in the corridors. The rooms are plastered to provide both a softer finish and furring space for wiring.

The heights and shapes of the two major buildings are broken into logical and expressive divisions to avoid a shoe-box insistence. Together with the low detached Center—also used by the neighborhood —they produce excellent scale. Moreover, in the long, six-story building there are three lateral offsets to break up the bulk, provide for entry, and to relieve what could have been a tedious corridor. Each room in the tower "projects" outward as a unit to get cross ventilation and a secondary source of light via windows in two walls (there being no air conditioning). These rooms are slightly splayed to make their minimum size seem larger. By using an identical room plan of bed-living room with bath and kitchenette, then angling and pinwheeling eight units around four identical light and air "slots," the architect has come up with a fresh and economical solution. Moreover these "broken" outside walls create strong visual variety and "forgive" errors in concrete workmanship. The injection of a reasonable number of slightly curved surfaces lends subtle vitality. The buildings, which occupy only 10 per cent of the lot, are angled relative to the site to prevent a static feeling and to allow several small areas for automobiles instead of one large one which would dominate the group. The parklike landscaping by Edward D. Stone, Jr., is good. As this is public housing, no furniture is provided except in common rooms. Altogether exceptional. Charles Harrison Pawley and Hernando Acosta were associate architects.

Grounds open daily

---

11   Orlando Public Library (1965–66)
10 North Rosalind Avenue at Central Boulevard
Orlando, Florida

JOHN M. JOHANSEN & ASSOCIATES, ARCHITECTS

There are not many raw concrete buildings that establish their corner with the civility and pride which this main library achieves. The exterior is not the bleak fortress which local citizens feared it would be, but a virile structure with welcoming authority. Its scale is largely developed by its orchestrated rhythm of three widths of windows. The play of these windows, some set flush and irregularly in panels of solid concrete, others ribbons 26 feet/8 meters high, lends interest to the facade, augmented by the several widths of the cornice "panels" at top.

The four-level, 200,000-volume interior is businesslike in the circu-

lation and reference sections and spatially airy at the several double-height reading areas (marked externally by the high windows). This vertical penetration of the main floor to that above—at four points including the two front corners—ties the two levels together and lends spaciousness to both. The second floor is largely devoted to open stacks, while the roof contains a large staff room (glazed on three sides), mechanical housing, and a terrace. The basement is devoted to work area, a two-hundred-seat auditorium (used by civic and cultural groups), and a children's room. Wood furniture (mostly walnut), rugs, Belgian linen curtains, warm colors, and planting relieve the hardness of the concrete. Expansion is anticipated. Take a look also at the bastioned back side. R. B. Murphy was associate architect.

Open Mon.–Fri. 9–9, Sat. 9–6, Sun. 1–5, except holidays

---

12   Castillo de San Marcos (1672–95/1738–40/1752–56/1762)
Castillo Drive (US 1 Business) and Matanzas River
St. Augustine, Florida

The Spanish, who were the first Europeans to settle permanently in what evolved to be the United States, made several determined but futile efforts to set up shop on the New World's mainland before finally

establishing a base at St. Augustine in 1565. (Spain was well organized in the West Indies by the early decades of the sixteenth century, having built a fort and town—Isabela, now in the Dominican Republic—following Columbus' second voyage in 1494.) Ponce de León, who had settled in Puerto Rico (1508), landed in Florida with colonists and cattle near present-day Charlotte Harbor (1521) but Indians soon drove them back. In 1526 Spain took five hundred men, women, children, slaves, and animals to Winyah Bay near Georgetown, South Carolina, but they, too, because of Indians, disease, and a bad winter, were forced to return to their West Indies base.

The Spanish, alarmed by the French Fort Caroline (1564) at the mouth of the St. Johns River (near today's Jacksonville), wanted a fortified settlement in Florida to prevent further European incursions. Though the struggle for bases in Florida was first between the Spanish and French, the English burned St. Augustine in 1586 and were moving southward down the coast. To counter the latter, the construction of an impregnable stone fort was finally ordered, previous ones of wood having been of short life and little value. Work began in 1672 and it lasted for many arduous years.

Massive, businesslike yet strangely elegant, the Castillo de San

Marcos (at one time called Fort Marion) stands as the finest and oldest example of military architecture in the United States. The star-shaped Castillo was designed by Ignacio Daza, who died shortly there-after. It was probably inspired by the principles for bastioned fortifica-tions worked out by Francesco de Marchi (1490–1574) and modified by Italo-Spanish and Dutch examples—with perhaps later influence from Vauban whose first *Mémoire* appeared in 1669. It was as success-ful as it is handsome, never having been taken in battle—though bit-terly besieged—and was used as recently as the Spanish-American War to house disciplinary cases. The fort, which is constructed of coquina, the local shell-based marine stone, was built on the edge of Matanzas Bay around a square courtyard with four-sided, spearlike bastions projecting diagonally at each corner. A 40-foot/12-meter-wide moat surrounds the whole. The thickness of the scarp or outer wall ranges from 13 feet/4 meters at base to nearly 5 feet/1.5 meters at the top of the parapet, which is approximately 30 feet/9.1 meters above the moat. (Until the 1738–40 strengthening, the walls were only 20 feet/6.1 meters high.) To provide sustenance against siege, wells were dug in the courtyard and several of the fort's twenty rooms were used for storing food. The garrison and the people of the village were to rely on these on several desperate occasions.

Modernization of the fort was carried out in three stages: 1738–40, when the previously wooden gundeck, or terreplein, on the east side was replaced by arched masonry walls that could withstand bombard-ment; 1752–56, when the other three sides were vaulted; and 1762, with the enlargement of the ravelin (a triangular outwork) in front of the gate. The fort was made a National Monument in 1924, and today, thanks to the U. S. National Park Service, is in grand shape. One of the world's great forts, it is among the chief secular inheritances of Spanish occupation in the United States. (Two other important ones are the Cabildo in New Orleans and the Palace of the Governors in Santa Fe—q.v.)

Open daily 8:30–5:30, except Dec. 25: admission

Fort Matanzas National Monument (1740–42—open 8:30–5:30 daily, except Dec. 25) lies 14 miles/22 kilometers south of St. Augustine off FLA A1A. Although it is nowhere near as impressive as the Castillo, the military buff will want to see it. Built to prevent a flank attack on St. Augustine, it is unusual structurally in that it is supported on wooden pilings driven into the marshland. Pedro Ruiz de Olano was the engi-neer. In ruins, the fort was made a National Monument in 1924, and restored by the National Park Service that year.

13   Restoration Area (1565–1821/1960–1970s)
N end of St. George Street
St. Augustine, Florida

St. Augustine is the oldest permanent town in what eventually became the United States. Its settlement, it must be kept in mind, was for almost two hundred years primarily a Spanish military outpost or, as it has been called, "a small poor garrison town." It never approached a fully rounded agricultural or trading colony such as the English established from Savannah, Georgia, to Machias, Maine. (Spain had to look after and support almost two hundred other bases or settlements in the New World in the sixteenth century. St. Augustine was their northernmost successful probing on the continent, the eleventh attempted in Florida, and the only one to survive through the years.) Built to discourage southward excursions by the French and English, as mentioned in the description of the Castillo, this Florida community was thus largely inhabited by poorly paid military and sometimes their families, not by plantation owners or city burghers. The resulting architectural peak was the superb Castillo, the adjacent village forming a picturesque if uneven background. Since it was a lonely outpost for so long, little *grandezza* was called for, while destruction by fires, both enemy and accidental (the last in 1914), have left but a slender residue of earlier days. There is no building, other than the fort, which survived Moore's burning of the town in 1702, virtually all construction until that time being of wood and thatch. After that date masonry was made mandatory with most structures of coquina or "tabby" concrete.

The early town naturally reflected the urban pattern and urban lifestyle of Spain, particularly those settlements along the Mediterranean and the West Indies. Streets were narrow to provide shade and create cool drafts. All dwellings lined the street; indeed their walls defined it. Most of them were built with fenced or walled, sometimes grassless patios where much living and work took place, and where the well, the precious vegetable garden, fruit trees, and chickens were safe. An open, south-oriented porch or loggia faced onto the patio, providing covered open-air work area and shielding the rooms from direct sun. The yard and porch also led to the entry to the house; almost no dwellings—as opposed to inns or shops—had a door onto the street. (Compare the somewhat similar Charleston "single house" with front door opening onto a veranda, thence a fenced garden. There is some thought that Britishers from Charleston, during their occupation, may

have influenced St. Augustine's development of second-floor running piazzas.) Few windows appeared in north walls and those facing west were small. Chimneys and fireplaces were infrequent, heat being supplied by charcoal braziers, and cooking via a hearth or in the oft-detached kitchen with only a roof smoke-hole. The modest (and most numerous) early houses were earth-floored, generally one-storied, and sometimes flat-roofed. Two-storied examples—not numerous in the First Spanish Period (1565–1763)—had covered balconies on the street-side and pitched roofs more often than not. During the British tenure of 1763–83, when the English took possession of Florida in exchange for British-captured Havana, many fireplaces and chimneys were added to existing houses, direct "front" doors cut, and glazed windows with outside shutters installed (previously shutters had been inside and little glass used). These innovations modified subsequent building, but relatively little permanent new construction was undertaken during those twenty years. The Second Spanish Period (1783–1821, when St. Augustine reverted to Spain)—a time of unrest for Spain in Europe (primarily due to Napoleon)—produced only a few new buildings, notably the church now known as the Cathedral of St. Augustine (1793–97) designed by the royal engineer but built largely by Irish monks. (It was fully restored for the town's 400th Anniversary.)

The citizens of St. Augustine as early as 1936 began to recognize the importance of this slightly unkempt treasure from its past, but it was not until 1959 that the Historic St. Augustine Preservation Board was set up and 1962 when non-profit St. Augustine Restoration, Inc. was established (though research and land acquisition had commenced earlier). With the nation's quickened interest in our extraordinary architectural inheritance, work has gathered speed. Now the highly appealing and revelatory St. George Street area, hard by the old City Gate and near the Castillo, is progressing handsomely. These few blocks re-create much of the atmosphere of the town's four major phases, though emphasis is on that of two hundred and more years ago. (The first three periods have been mentioned, the fourth began in 1821 with American occupation.)

Some thirty buildings have been restored or reconstructed with, it is hoped, more to come. Unfortunately the fire of 1702 which destroyed most of the town also incinerated many civic records which had been stored in the Cathedral, thus little cold documentation other than foundations and several informative maps exist to aid restoration. The work has been carried out, however, with as much authenticity as modern archeological research permits. The reconstructed dwellings range from the extremely simple **Gomez House** of wood, virtually a shack, the almost equally primitive **Gallegos House** of tabby, both typical of the First Spanish Period of 1565–1763, to the far more elegant eighteenth-century **Ribera House** directly across the street. This last is a two-story building of stuccoed coquina surrounded on two sides by an elaborate garden that bears witness to the wealth of its early owner. As one progresses from the Gate region southward along St. George Street, other buildings of interest (plus a bit of commercialism) reward the stroller, particularly the often-altered **Arrivas House** (eighteenth–nineteenth century). With more funding from the state, this area, which was laid out forty-two years before Jamestown and fifty-five before the landing at Plymouth Rock, could be one of our greatest historic streets: it almost is now.

Most buildings open 9–5:15 daily, except holidays: admission

NOTE: The Historic St. Augustine Preservation Board published (1971) a well-illustrated *Guidebook* to the area, while the St. Augustine Historical Society brought out (1962) an extremely thorough book by Albert Manucy entitled *The Houses of St. Augustine,* which the specialist will want to obtain.

A fascinating insight into the original (i.e. Amerindian) settlements in Florida and along the south Atlantic coast is given in *The New World:*

First Pictures of America, edited by Stefan Lorant (Duell, Sloan & Pearce, 1946). Jacques Le Moyne de Morgues sailed with René de Laudonnière in 1564 in an attempt to set up French Huguenot colonies in Florida with extensions to the north. Though Laudonnière was routed by the Spanish the following year (with help from a hurricane), Le Moyne, a skilled surveyor and artist, was able to make a number of excellent drawings showing the palisaded villages, granaries, and houses (generally circular and domical) which the French encountered among the native Indians. Some twenty years later John White, an English artist, made a series of illuminating watercolors of the Huguenot settlement (also short-lived—1585–90) in Virginia. The illustrations of both these men were vividly engraved by Théodore de Bry (1528–98), a talented Flemish artist, as shown in the abovementioned book. White subsequently (1577) went on to join Frobisher and to delineate "the first European pictures of the Eskimo"—Samuel Eliot Morison (*The Great Explorers,* Oxford University Press, 1978).

14 The Oldest House (c. 1704–c. 1890)
14 St. Francis Street
St. Augustine, Florida

Claims for The Oldest House stem from early propaganda days when the dwelling was privately owned and shown to visitors for profit. There is scarcely a stone in its present walls dating previous to the fire of 1702 when, as mentioned, British from the South Carolina Colony sacked the town. Moreover, the extremely thorough book titled *Evolution of the Oldest House,* Notes in Anthropology Volume 7 (Florida State University Press, 1962), says that "The site of the Oldest House was first occupied by the Spanish during the 1650–60 period." These dates would put it considerably later than the Thoroughgood House near Norfolk, Virginia (c. 1640—q.v.)—the oldest surviving dwelling of the English Colonies—plus several in New England. Whatever the claim, the Oldest House unfolds a useful and historical as well as picturesque architectural mélange of the domestic architecture of the city.

The coquina walls of the building now standing frame the rooms of the oldest section, the first of which was probably a single chamber. This was first expanded laterally, then, when the British took over, a wood-enclosed second floor was added (c. 1775). Through the years, subsequent additions and alterations were carried out, some as recently as late in the last century, with most changes haphazardly reflecting unsettled times. In 1918 the St. Augustine Historical Society purchased the house, but it was not until 1959–60 that a thorough archeological survey was made and the house carefully restored to its late-eighteenth-century appearance. The furnishings as restored reflect the Latin taste on the early first floor with an English flavor above. Admission to the house includes a visit to the patio and kitchen behind, as well as the historic museum and Tovar House.

Open daily 9–6: admission

---

15 Flagler College (1886–88)
King Street at Cordova
St. Augustine, Florida

CARRÈRE & HASTINGS, ARCHITECTS

The east coast of Florida as a winter refuge for ice-bound Northerners was developed by the perceptive Henry Morrison Flagler. As a background of this profitable acumen, Mr. Flagler, while clerking in Ohio, joined forces with a fellow upstate New Yorker named John D. Rockefeller, the two becoming the prime founders of the Standard Oil Com-

pany (1870). Later, seeking further fields and especially to demonstrate that a tropical sandbar could be transformed into a tropical Eden, Mr. Flagler established a hotel beachhead in the quaint village of St. Augustine. This salient—one incomprehensively removed from any beach, water, or view (except from upper floors)—was the Ponce de León Resort Hotel—named for the explorer who reputedly spent five days in the area in 1513. Realizing that a first-class railroad would be necessary to fetch his guests, the astute Mr. Flagler built the Florida East Coast Railroad (starting at Jacksonville) which he pushed down the peninsula as far as Palm Beach by 1894, Miami two years later, and finally Key West. For architects of his mid-city snuggery (his first of eleven in Florida), Flagler selected the untried but promising firm of John M. Carrère & Thomas Hastings, two young men, one twenty-six, the other twenty-eight years old. Both had been thoroughly trained in Paris' Beaux-Arts, and later had left McKim, Mead & White to start their own firm. (Their selection was not impeded by the fact that Hastings' well-known father was Flagler's Presbyterian minister.) The commission not only skyrocketed Carrère & Hastings, it locked the state of Florida in a neo-Iberian architectural embrace—perhaps logically for its day—which has lasted for almost a century. (Flagler had sent his young architects to Spain to study its outstanding buildings before designing his hostel.)

The result, though not without pastiche, is a functionally planned hotel constructed of solid reinforced concrete (six parts coquina to one of cement)—one of the first concrete buildings in the country—and trimmed with brick and terra-cotta. Moreover, the hotel, again ahead of the trade, generated its own electricity and boasted electric lights and steam heat, while its towers contained water tanks holding 8,000 gallons/36,370 liters for fire protection. The Ponce de León documents with éclat one facet of the eclecticism which characterized most American architecture for the last hundred and more years. Note, on entering, the dazzling 80-foot/24-meter-high rotunda and its murals those in the dining room by George W. Maynard, with many chandeliers by Louis C. Tiffany.

In 1968 its sturdy bulk was transformed into Flagler College, a 730-student, accredited liberal arts institution, its hotel rooms now serving as dormitories. Bernard Maybeck, also fresh from the Beaux-Arts, was an assistant designer of the hotel and supervised its construction before briefly moving to Kansas and then settling in California. (See Index.)

Only grounds and entry hall open to public: group tours can be arranged

Directly facing the college is the former three-hundred-room **Alcazar Hotel** (1887–89) also designed by Carrère & Hastings but in a simpler yet equally solid manner. The hotel closed in 1930, and now serves partly as the Lightner Museum (open daily 9–5, except Dec. 25: admission) with an exposition of toys, dolls, etc., while the remainder of the building houses the St. Augustine City Hall.

16   St. Paul's Lutheran Church (1959/1968–69)
2256 Bahia Vista Street
Sarasota, Florida

VICTOR A. LUNDY, ARCHITECT

The first unit of St. Paul's—now the Fellowship Hall—engages in a highly personal, almost Baroque expression of laminated wood beams. The boomerang curves of this "wood tent," moreover, extend beyond the building's sides, thus providing covered overflow space for the populous winter congregation while keeping a compact entity for the year-round residents during the other six months. Sliding glass doors alone separate inside from out. (The hall served as church for ten years until the present one was built.) The interlacing beams of laminated wood rest on steel columns encased with local coquina.

The "new" church is also tent-formed, its cable-suspended roof resting on eaveless concrete walls. The roof is supported by a triangular steel box beam, 3 feet/.9 meter deep, which runs the length of the building. From this are hung 2.5-inch/6.3-centimeter cables spaced every 18 feet/5.5 meters apart with 4 inches/10 centimeters of wood decking forming the roof-ceiling. The church itself measures 90 feet/ 27 meters wide by 139 feet/42 meters long. In addition to the nave and chancel, the bride's room, rest rooms, and office at entry are all contained under the "tent" of the roof. The statue of Christ is by Ejner Rasmussen, a member of the congregation. The architect's preference was for a simple, unadorned wall.

A Parish House (1962) is the third unit of the group.

Inquire at Parish House to visit

17 Plymouth Harbor (1965–66)
700 John Ringling Causeway
Sarasota, Florida

FRANK FOLSOM SMITH, ARCHITECT

An ingeniously planned structure which is in effect a twenty-six-story retirement "village." Superbly situated on Coon Key, between downtown Sarasota (two minutes away) and St. Armand's Key and the Gulf (even closer), with lagoons lapping two sides and the Yacht Club next door—its location could scarcely be improved upon. Occupying less than 10 per cent of the site, it is the tallest residential building in West Florida. Built by a non-profit church organization, and drawing its ecumenical occupants from all over the United States, it provides carefree living for its retired patrons. Instead of confining its dwellers to a lovely but lonely site away from the city, or instead of settling on an urban fringe on inexpensive but run-down land, the church trustees selected a glorious location, purchased sufficient land to give it elbow room, and topped it with a building of reasonable exterior and clever inner layout. Moreover, landscaping and furnishings were included in

the architect's contract, so the building has not been wrecked by plastic plants and department store *moderne* furniture.

Architecturally the most outstanding feature lies in its perceptive philosophy. This establishes a three-floor "colony system" of approximately forty apartment units per "neighborhood." The occupants of each bank of three floors are grouped both architecturally and socially into "clubs" for all sorts of activities. The center is the three-story elevator lobby (of slightly heavy detail) which connects these floors and forms an inner "clubroom" with, at one end, a large lounge with kitchenette and sizable open-air balcony opening onto the panoramic view. Thus the occupants of each apartment feel socially knit to only 39 others—not 349—while the short corridor lengths, which surround the "colony area," promote further intimacy and contact. All corner rooms have a balcony. Forty-two garden apartments fill the low left-hand wing while office, general dining, and common rooms occupy the main floor on the right, with twenty-eight apartments above. Covered open-air parking lies adjacent. There is a too slight expression of the triplex division on the exterior, and the symmetry is rigid (the architect's off-center proposal was rejected), but basic thinking and realization are enlightened. There is as a consequence a long waiting list to get an apartment in the building. Louis F. Schneider was associate architect; with considerable advice from Dr. John Whitney MacNeil, the founder.

Grounds open daily

---

18 East Campus (1968)
University of South Florida
NW edge of Sarasota on US 41 at General Spaatz Boulevard
     (adjacent to airport)
Sarasota, Florida

I. M. PEI & PARTNERS, ARCHITECTS

The east branch of the university's regional campus is composed of three two-story dormitory clusters—a combined common-room and dining-room building, and an L-shaped classroom group. It develops an intriguing mini-campus. The living quarters are treated like small-scale residential units, not regular straight-line college dormitories; and their grouping around labyrinthine courts and open passages produces not only around-the-corner but vertical stimuli. There is indeed almost

a casbah quality through these inner spaces. Formerly the private New College, this became a branch of the University of South Florida in 1975 when beset by financial problems: it is hoped that this East Campus will remain active.

Grounds open daily

---

19   Van Wezel Performing Arts Hall (1968–69)
1 block W of North Tamiami Trail (US 41) at 10th Street
Sarasota, Florida

WILLIAM WESLEY PETERS, ARCHITECT, OF TALIESIN ASSOCIATED ARCHITECTS

Perched on a point of land overlooking Sarasota Bay, its two-tone purple paint shining in the sun, the Lewis and Eugenia Van Wezel concert-hall/theater/auditorium suggests a geometric heliotrope. (Its

color scheme was selected by Mrs. Frank Lloyd Wright.) Van Wezel Hall is the key and thus far only unit in a new civic center which Taliesin Associated have planned for the city. Eventually this will include a community hall, an arena, and several miscellaneous smaller structures, all situated between 6th and 10th streets on Sarasota Bay. Van Wezel was designed primarily as a concert hall and auditorium, secondarily as a theater to be used mainly by traveling companies which truck in their own scenery. There are thus purposely few backstage facilities such as would be found in a repertory or experimental theater.

The auditorium's stepped rows of continental seating accommodate 1,778 (including space for four wheelchairs) in 28 double-angled rows. Three additional rows, holding 54 seats, can be placed on the forestage lift wagon. This number can be reduced to 1,200 or 900 by two drop curtains at rear which provide visual enclosure. Acoustic demands shaped the hall's plan and section, with "tuning" to fit most types of performances made possible by variable use of acoustic curtains invisibly hidden behind the range of grilles on each side. For each three rows of seats a side exit is provided, and these feed directly into the lounges overlooking the bay (or the front lobby). The Grand Foyer on the lower level opens onto the Garden Terrace with a panorama of Long Boat and St. Armand's Key across the bay. George C. Izenour was consultant for the theater; Vern O. Knudson guided the acoustics.

Open during performances as well as morning and afternoon tours, Mon.–Fri.

20   The Big Bend Pioneer Farm (late 1800s)
Tallahassee Junior Museum
3945 Museum Drive, c. 4 miles/6.4 kilometers SW of
Tallahassee, Florida

Folk architecture and rural buildings are, unfortunately, rarely accorded a proper place in the museum world. This instructive collection of farm buildings of the late nineteenth century sets out to correct such myopia. Comprising commissary, farmhouse (c. 1880), an almost elegant double-wing buggy house, and a host of ancillary units, the museum seeks to give an accurate depiction of a pioneer farmstead in northwest Florida's Big Bend country, a section of the state culturally far more Southern than the northern South. All structures were collected from within a 60-mile/97-kilometer area, the cypress commissary of 1898 coming from Georgia.

The farm succeeds admirably both in quality of building and in layout, being a model of its kind. Would that other states realized the importance of preserving and displaying the humble architectural inheritance which forms the backbone of the development of our "frontier" country. In a few streamlined years it will be too late.

Open Tues.–Sat. 9–5, Sun. 2–5, except holidays: admission

NOTE: Also located at the Tallahassee Junior Museum are the turn-of-the-century one-room Concord School House, Bethlehem Baptist Church, and Bellevue, an 1850s plantation home—and a good example of Southern cottage architecture. (It is open to the public on weekends, 9–5.)

---

21   Tampa International Airport (1968–71)
off IS 4/75 onto FLA 60 or Kennedy Boulevard
Tampa, Florida

REYNOLDS, SMITH & HILL, ARCHITECTS; J. E. GREINER & CO., ENGINEERS AND COORDINATORS; LEIGH FISHER ASSOCIATES, AIRPORT CONSULTANTS

The basic concept—and most of the reality—of the new Tampa Airport is brilliant. First of all it is based on a Landside/Airside plan (by the late Leigh Fisher) which divorces all ground-generated functions, that is passenger needs, from air-related ones, providing widely separated (c. 1,000 feet/305 meters) shelter for each. The Landside main building is connected with the four Airside units by high-speed, horizontal but elevated, automatic "shuttles." Secondly, its design is directly concerned with the automobile—that of the passenger driving his own car—instead of conjuring up a terminal as an end in itself and tolerating the private automobile as a nuisance. (An airport serves only as a ground-to-air transfer system: it is not a goal.) To this end the top half of the Landside building is a garage. Thirdly, Landside was developed as a "sandwich" of six floors, each classified for various passenger processing functions and services. The ground floor is devoted to deplaning passengers and baggage claim, and, there being no planes around, is surrounded by access roads; the second level—reached directly by car, taxi, or limousine via elevated ramps on each side—is given over to enplaning passenger and ticketing, while the third floor comprises the shuttle level and main concourse with concessions, restaurant, and cocktail lounge. On top of these three working floors are two floors and one open roof-deck for parking some 1,800 cars, with structural provisions built in for three additional levels of parking as needed. (Overflow parking is taken care of on surface lots.) The self-driven, ticketed passenger thus drives his car directly to a

parking spot atop Landside, drops down a floor or two by elevator to the concourse level, and is shuttled immediately to his Airside terminal and plane. If he needs a ticket, he proceeds, after parking, to the enplaning-ticketing floor and then by escalator to the third floor and by shuttle to the proper Airside satellite. Total maximum walking distance "from car seat to plane seat" was limited in the design process to 700 feet/213 meters, but generally it is a good deal less than half that.

The garden-surrounded exterior of the Landside building, which measures roughly 350 x 420 feet/107 x 128 meters, bristles with elevated straight ramps or helixes for automotive access both to the terminal and to the garaging above. The only "facade" it shows is that at the top, around the two semienclosed parking decks. All of this makes for a highly unusual and at times dramatic building, with cars dashing in and out or snaking up and down the concrete ramps. The open but undercover deplaning driveways at ground level are particularly impressive, with three-story high piers upholding the lateral overhang of the parking decks. Incidentally, both deplaning and enplaning passengers can—for a welcome change—proceed under cover to the rental-car annex directly adjacent. First-rate landscaping and fountains add to the spatial pleasures here. One million dollars was spent on the landscaping so that the passenger "would *know* he was in Florida the minute he arrived."

The second floor, which, as mentioned, is devoted to ticket offices and lounges, provides a spacious, quiet retreat, with good furniture, warm colors, and sculpture (by Roy Butler). The third, or transfer, floor, where one takes the shuttle or gets a bite to eat, is less satisfactory, its central area being so crowded with concessions, especially those in the center, that little spatial image comes forth. Moreover there is some confusion concerning orientation here.

But the four (eventually six) shuttle cars are admirable. Trimly designed by architect Eliot Noyes and built by Westinghouse, they are non-attended, automatic, horizontal people-movers accommodating approximately one hundred standees for a forty-second fun ride, and operating on a ninety-second or so headway. They are double-tracked to operate in both directions at once—on quiet rubber tires atop a concrete beam. (If only they went all the way to Tampa.)

The Airside terminals are leased to the airlines and were designed by them, hence vary in architectural quality. A three-hundred-room hotel was added in 1974. Joseph A. Maxwell & Associates did the terminal interiors, the graphics were by Architectural Graphics Associates, and the landscaping by Stresau, Smith & Steward. The Hillsborough County Aviation Authority played no small hand in the overall project, insisting from the beginning that the solution be passenger-oriented, not airline. It is the best airport in the United States.

22   Gregory House (1834)
c. 13 miles/21 kilometers N of Bristol via FLA 12
Torreya State Park, Florida

Bordering the once important Apalachicola River between Chattahoo-
chee and Bristol, the park takes its name from the rarely found but
here local evergreen *Torreya taxifolia*. (The tree was named for the
botanist John Torrey: because of its rarity it is now protected by law.)
The entire 1,063-acre/430-hectare park is being reorganized, and chief
among its features is this comfortable farmhouse recently moved from
its original site across the river. The dwelling provides a simple entry
porch on the approach side but a fine, pedimented two-story porch on
the west overlooking the river. An unusual—and airy—feature is the
semidetached office to the left. Furnishings, including some Gregory
family items, reflect the period. The building was in dilapidated shape
when the Florida Board of Parks acquired it in 1935. Completely
reconditioned and furnished, it was opened to the public in 1968. The
area was active in the Civil War, and at nearby Battery Point there are
still earthworks and gun emplacements to be seen. An unusual detour.

Open daily 9–11, 1–4, except major holidays: admission

Georgia

Toccoa 34 •

Athens 1–3
•

Marietta 23 •

Washington 35
•

■
Atlanta 4–14

Madison 22
•

Augusta 15–17 •

La Grange 19
•

Midway 24 •

• Milledgeville 25–26

• Macon 20–21

• Talbotton 33

• Columbus 18

Savannah 27–32 •

Waycross 36 •

GEORGIA

The buildings in boldface type are of general interest. The others are for the specialist.

Athens	1 Chapel, University of Georgia (1831–32)
	2 **Joseph Henry Lumpkin House** (c. 1843)
	3 **Taylor-Grady House** (c. 1845)
Atlanta	4 **The Ante-Bellum Plantation** (early 19th century)
	5 Flat Iron Building (1897/1976)—Bradford Gilbert
	6 **Swan House** (1928)—Philip T. Shutze—**and Tullie Smith House Restoration** (c. 1835–40)
	7 **Hyatt Regency Hotel** (1966–67/1969)— John Portman & Associates
	Peachtree Center—John Portman & Associates
	Trailways Bus Station (1967)—John Portman & Associates
	8 Sammye E. Coan School (1966–67/1970)— Morris Hall and Peter Norris
	9 American Security Insurance Building (1970–71)—Taylor & Collum
	10 **The Omni Coliseum** (1970–72), **Omni International** (1971–75), **and Georgia World Congress Center** (1974–76)—Thompson, Ventulett & Stainback
	11 **Colony Square** (1970–78)—Jova/Daniels/ Busby; Thompson, Ventulett, Stainback & Associates
	12 Gambrell Hall, School of Law (1971–72)— Stevens & Wilkinson
	13 Martin Luther King Jr. Middle School (1972–73)—Heery & Heery
	14 **Peachtree Plaza Hotel** (1974–76)—John Portman & Associates
Augusta	15 Harris-Pearson-Walker House (1797)
	16 **Old Government House** (1801),

River Esplanade (1975–78)—Gunn & Meyerhoff

Talbotton   33 Zion Episcopal Church (1848)

Toccoa   34 Traveler's Rest (c. 1815–20/1840)

                 35 **Robert Toombs Avenue** (late 18th/early 19th century)
Callaway Plantation (c. 1869)

Waycross   36 Baptist Village (1958–74)—Stevens & Wilkinson

1 Chapel, University of Georgia (1831–32)
off Broad Street, central campus
Athens, Georgia

Athens' classic inheritance traces back to this Greek "temple," which served as chapel and, for almost a hundred years, as assembly for the university. The picturesque exterior (of brick stuccoed) presents six sharply cut, unsubtle (no entasis, primitive capital) Doric columns upholding a simplified entablature. The interior is dominated by an enormous painting (23.5 feet/7.2 meters wide) of the interior of St. Peter's in Rome, the work of George Cook (1783–1857).

Open daily 9–5 during school year

2   Joseph Henry Lumpkin House (c. 1843)
     The Athens Woman's Club
     248 Prince Avenue
     Athens, Georgia

Athens, its name matching its architecture, developed in the early-middle nineteenth century a glowing and distinctive chapter in the history of Southern Greek Revival architecture. This finds echoes in nearby Washington and Madison and in slightly more distant Macon and Milledgeville (all represented in this guide), but the greatest of all was Athens. Its columned, flat-roofed houses are as functional, with their wide overhangs to keep off the weather, as they are beautiful. Their hide-and-seek, sun-and-shadow movements produce vitality even when it rains. Among the notable in this "Classic City" of 46,000 is the former Lumpkin House, home of Georgia's first Chief Justice and now owned by the Joseph Henry Lumpkin Foundation. When constructed, the house was surrounded by a large estate and was moved closer to the street in 1906 for greater convenience. Even with only a remnant of land left, the house—and some of its neighbors—are outstanding. Its most immediate feature is the colossal Doric portico that stretches across and "protects" the front. Then the unusual T-shape plan should be noted as it brings maximum cross-circulation of air to the rooms.

The house is handsomely furnished in period pieces and is undergoing restoration to serve the University of Georgia Law School and members of the state and local bar associations as a center for social and educational activities.

To visit contact Athens Welcome Center, 280 East Dougherty Street: they also issue a useful map

---

3   Taylor-Grady House (c. 1845)
634 Prince Avenue
Athens, Georgia

Although the interior of this outstanding Greek Revival house is not open to the public every day, a look at the exterior can be had at any time and at any time is worth it. The well-scaled porch wraps around the front and half of each side, upheld by thirteen Roman Doric columns, leading to the supposition that they represent the original states of which Georgia was the last proclaimed (1732)—and the largest. (The east side porch has four columns, that on the west five: note the

usual variation in intercolumniation across the front. The columns wrapped both front and sides of the original house; the rear section was added c. 1900.) Whatever the symbolism, the architectural effect is regal.

The house was purchased by the city (1966), then leased to the Athens Junior Assembly, which has recently restored and furnished it throughout with period pieces. Note the anthemion motif on the pilasters flanking the entry and the four curved "corners" within. The original smokehouse and pigeoncote-kitchen are on the grounds. The gardens are being renovated after years of neglect and in time will offer a solidly researched (but theoretic) landscape, complete with boxwood garden.

As the late Talbot Hamlin wrote, "nowhere did the Greek Revival produce a more perfect blending of the dignified and the gracious, the impressive and the domestic, than in the lovely houses of the thirties and forties in upstate Georgia and Alabama" (*Greek Revival Architecture in America,* Oxford University Press, 1944).

Open Mon., Wed., Fri. 10–2, Sun. 2–5

---

4   The Ante-Bellum Plantation (early 19th century)
Stone Mountain Park
via Stone Mountain Freeway (US 78), c. 16 miles/26 kilometers E of
Atlanta, Georgia

Stone Mountain Park—its "mountain" being at 825 feet/251 meters the largest outcropping of granite in the world—has in recent years drawn an extensive array of attractions. Among the historic pleasures is this collection of original buildings assembled here from various sections of the state but all dating from the early part of the nineteenth century and all basically typical of a well-established cotton plantation of the period. The anchor of the group is the Big House, built in the 1840s in the southwest corner of Georgia (Dickey) and moved to this site in 1961. Resting on a raised masonry basement, the one-story, clapboarded dwelling is reminiscent of the rural Greek Revival houses of this period which ranged from the Georgia coast to Louisiana. It is surprisingly poshly furnished inside. Surrounding the house are the formal gardens and the vegetable garden. The cook house, overseer's house, barn, store, and slaves' cabins fan out from the center.

There are nineteen buildings altogether, and collectively they give an illuminating picture of a Georgia cotton plantation 150 years ago, each unit being an authentic element. Be sure to take a look at the "doctor's office" diligently built of hand-hewn logs around 1826.

Open mid-June–Labor Day 10–9, rest of year 10–5:30, except Dec. 25–26: admission

---

5 Flat Iron Building (1897/1976)
Peachtree at Broad Street
Atlanta, Georgia

BRADFORD GILBERT, ARCHITECT

Five years before the more famous Flatiron Building which Daniel Burnham designed for New York City (q.v.), Atlanta's eleven-story Flat Iron was firmly holding down its difficult, triangular site. The multiple-bay windows, which stem from Chicago prototypes, undulate across the facade with a rich remembrance of things past. The city's

oldest high-rise, it has been completly renovated (1976) into competitive viability. It still forms a downtown focal point and has—because of its renovation—inspired renewed interest in and redevelopment of a number of neighboring structures. The building is now owned by Historic Urban Equities Ltd., a company specializing in the revitalization of heritage-type downtown (inner city) properties. The Flat Iron Building was listed in the National Register of Historic Places in 1976.

Open during office hours

---

6   Swan House (1928) **and Tullie Smith House Restoration**
  (c. 1835–40)
3099 Andrews Drive Northwest
Atlanta, Georgia

PHILIP T. SHUTZE, ARCHITECT OF SWAN HOUSE

The decade of the 1920s was perhaps the most indecisive in the development of American architecture. Freewheeling eclecticism had long been the only "acceptable" approach to building in this country, and it

was epitomized by the work following World War I. (This took place when much of Europe was eagerly exploring the future in an architectural development we now call the International Style. The phrase, incidentally, infuriates Europeans: their pioneering was not a style, it was a religion.)

With no design "restraints" and considerable fortunes (and little income tax), the sky was our architectural limit. Among the outstanding mansions of this period is the Swan House. Designed by local architect and Prix de Rome winner Philip T. Shutze it was built for Mr. and Mrs. Edward Hamilton Inman. The quiet exterior gives little hint of the richness that awaits within. There is, to be sure, a Doric porte cochere on the entry side and an elaborate door on the garden (i.e. approach) facade, but basically the exterior forms a simple, well-ordered mass. The interiors, however, are sumptuous and among the most beautifully detailed that one will see. Virtually all the rooms merit thorough study. With funds generously left it by the late Walter McElreath, the Atlanta Historical Society purchased the house (1966) for its headquarters, and opened it to the public, constructing a few years later a separate Historical Center (1972—Edward Shirley, architect) for a museum, auditorium, library, and offices.

In the woods a short distance behind the Swan House stands the **Tullie Smith House Restoration** (c. 1835–40), a grass-roots example of Plantation Plain Style moved (from nearby) to this site along with out-

buildings from other sections of the state. The group gives a bedrock impression of the less-than-regal life typical of Piedmont Georgia in the early-middle nineteenth century as opposed to the Greek Revival Mansion.

Open Mon.–Sat. 10:30–3:30, Sun. 1:30–3:30, except holidays: admission

---

7 Hyatt Regency Hotel (1966–67/1969)
265 Peachtree Street Northeast
Atlanta, Georgia

JOHN PORTMAN & ASSOCIATES, ARCHITECTS

This Peachtree Street gold mine, otherwise known as the Hyatt Regency, struck a rich vein via brilliant architectural imagination and know-how. Its twenty-one-story "lobby" restores the festive to that once-moribund species, the downtown hotel. Moreover, it has demonstrated—to the enormous satisfaction of its owners (who initially included its very astute architect)—that ideas still have a place in this world. One of the key notions here was three-dimensional exhilaration.

Down with tight lobbies, narrow, dingy corridors, and insipid rooms. Down with determining financial success by amount of rentable square footage instead of the quality of that footage. "The whole idea of Hyatt Regency is openness," said the architect, and the results are sensational. If the block which the hotel occupies was larger the management could probably run up two more additions instead of just one (200 rooms added to the original 826), so successful has it been.

The concept of a central open core for a skyscraper hotel with balconies from each floor opening onto it is not new. The Grand Court of the Palace Hotel in San Francisco (1875) had a marvelous top-lit six-story atrium; while the famous Brown Palace in Denver (q.v.), finished in 1892 (and still going very strong), boasts a tamer version. Then, too, Frank Lloyd Wright's Guggenheim Museum (q.v.)—which Portman admires—offers potent lessons wherein "negative" is positive. But John Portman has updated the three-dimensional vacuum, transforming nothingness into everything: turning elevators into mobile sculptures—they vanish through the roof to the revolving Polaris restaurant—placing a 40-foot/12-meter domed skylight on top of the "courtyard" to catch sunbeams, and rendering the scale agreeable by balconies and trellises dripping with vines. The bowered trellises prevent a "penitentiary" effect, serving in addition as contra-acrophobics. The guest or visitor also feels, thus, a spatially involved spectator-actor, comforted by the fact that he always knows where he is, and generally where he is going. This central area is exciting if restless, and at times details approach the overelaborate, but flair springs from this multi-tiered delight, and flair is no ordinary product in today's building world.

Open daily

The hotel is part of the overall **Peachtree Center,** also by John Portman & Associates, consisting of the twenty-three-story Merchandise Mart (1962)—whose somewhat routine exterior keyed the design of subsequent units—and several skyscrapers. The tightly packed mass tends to overwhelm, and there is an insufficient core (cf. Rockefeller Center), but numerous stimulating corners will be found. Among the finest units in Peachtree Center is the **Trailways Bus Station**

(1967—open daily). Though possibly confusable with garage above
(eight hundred cars), its interior is bright and colorful even to
graphics and growing plants. If any bus station will redeem the typically negative image of such transportation's staging points, this one
will. It should be added that almost all downtown Atlanta cries for
space, greenery, and better land control or it will strangle itself.

---

8 Sammye E. Coan School (1966–67/1970)
1550 Boulevard Drive Southeast (E via Memorial Drive)
Atlanta, Georgia

MORRIS HALL AND PETER NORRIS, ARCHITECTS

Requiring protection against vandalism—and with few views anyway
—the architects have designed a vigorous, windowless school for 1,500
students in the 7th–9th grades. Actually the school is busy from early
morning until late at night as it functions also as an adult education
and community center. The exterior problem was, of course, to get life
into a building without windows. This was accomplished by making the
piers narrow slabs of reinforced concrete (instead of square columns),

placing these at right angles to their respected facades, setting up thus a play of changing light, shade, and form.

The interior radiates from a two-story, commodious central "hall," off which open the glass-walled cafeteria and the class corridors. The hall doubles for informal assembly and to accommodate overflow from the auditorium placed a half floor lower. It is in addition a very popular "piazza" for students during the between-class periods. The flow of spaces here is stimulating, and is intensified at the upper level by the fact that the walls of rooms framing the court are glazed from top to bottom, allowing a spatial penetration at both levels. Even the corridor walls of most classrooms are of glass. There are no fixed seats.

Grounds and main hall open during school hours

---

9 American Security Insurance Building (1970–71)
**3290 Northside Parkway Northwest; off IS 75 at West Paces Ferry
   Road, 2 short rights to Howell Mill Road, NW edge of
Atlanta, Georgia**

TAYLOR & COLLUM, ARCHITECTS

The inherently handsome qualities of weathering steel have been often misunderstood. In a few notable buildings—of which this is one—this special steel has been used properly, as a structural "stick" or small-scale unit, not as a sheet where its weathering can be uneven. The

scale relation here of columns, beams, rails, banisters, and sun-panels shows keen feeling for the material's potential. This small, square, four-story office block has been carefully eased onto its wooded site, with every bit of natural cover retained where possible. The three top floors —upheld by twenty hollow weathering steel columns filled with 1,800 gallons/8,183 liters of water, antifreeze, and rust inhibitor—rest on a concrete platform, supported by concrete piers; these top floors visually float above the inset entry level. Lightness is further intensified by the thoughtful detailing mentioned, among them, the glass-walled elevators. The employment of water-filled columns for fire protection was developed with assistance from the U. S. Steel Corporation. It was the first use in this country though the system was patented, according to the architects, in England in the late nineteenth century. Altogether a topflight suburban office block.

Open during business hours

10   The Omni Coliseum (1970–72), **Omni International** (1971–75),
       and Georgia World Congress Center (1974–76)
       Atlanta, Georgia

THOMPSON, VENTULETT & STAINBACK, ARCHITECTS

The Omni, one of the most extraordinary sports, convention, office,
hotel, resort, entertainment, shopping, eating, and exhibition complexes in the United States, abuts the south edge of downtown Atlanta.
Together with The Decks, its 1,950-car parking structure, this 34-
acre/14-hectare coordinated group of mixed-use facilities has helped
make Atlanta one of the most popular convention cities in the country.
Almost all of it, it is pertinent to note, was built over railroad tracks
via air rights (23 feet/7 meters clearance), and all structures were designed by the same firm of architects. Located adjacent to downtown
and all mass transportation including MARTA, the now abuilding rapid
transit system (two sections of which opened in 1979), Omni forms an
important element in making the central business district alive for 200–
240 nights a year. The buildings, in order of completion, are:

The Omni Sports Coliseum, 100 Techwood Drive Viaduct. (Open
during events.) The gutsy, weathering-steel frame of Omni is matched
within by a mind-boggling, columnless space. It exudes power outside
by day as well as by night when pools of artificial light shine from its
glazed corners. The unusual structural expression of this 362-foot/
110-meter-square coliseum springs from four gigantic wall trusses
100 feet/30 meters high that rise from the centers of its four sides,
cantilever to the corners, and are joined and topped by a patented
"ortho-quad" roof truss. (One of the key reasons for this four-point
concentrated frame arose from the fact that the building is stilted over
railroad tracks, as mentioned.) A broad, landscaped concourse level—
useful at intermission in clement weather—surrounds most of the
building and provides entries at the midpoint of the seating ranks.
Inner peripheral circulation opens at the corners into lofty, bannered
lobbies (under the cantilevers) to form colorful interior gathering
spots. The arena within, which has a ceiling height of 130 feet/40 meters, is placed on the diagonal to obtain the maximum number of pre-
mium seats. It is roofed by sixteen 50-foot/15-meter-square pyramids
or pods which alternate in checkerboard fashion with flat ceiling panels
of the same dimension. The open, lightweight pods aid acoustics and

lend interest to the ceiling, while their pyramidal projection on the roof produces a distinctive exterior profile. The overall effect of the interior is strong but a few awkward corners appear when the area's angled placement meets the squared frame. Moreover the random intermixture of warm colors on the seats lacks zest plus the seat-finding ease of color coding. The lower service level is completely separate from that of the spectators. The outer concourse leads directly to a 1,950-car garage with over twice this automobile capacity at grade.

Omni's multivalent uses range widely, as its name implies, accommodating sports such as hockey and basketball, plus circuses, concerts, etc. Prybylowski & Gravino were the structural engineers. It is owned by the City of Atlanta and the Fulton County Recreation Authority.

Omni International, Marietta Street at Techwood Drive. (Always open.) The Omni International megastructure stands adjacent to the slightly earlier Sports Coliseum (though without covered connection), and provides a 470-room hotel—the Omni International—two eleven-story office blocks, three floors of shops, cafes, and restaurants. Though the exterior almost inevitably lacks coordination, these varied facilities are wrapped, with a purposefully irregular series of angles, around a sparkling, airy, twelve-story-high covered atrium—the Great

Space. (Though expensive to roof, substantial savings were effected on the non-weatherproof interior facings of all units.) An ice-skating rink forms the floor and focus of this arena, with two wide balconies along the sides and a skater-viewing and communications bridge across the center. The hotel, many rooms of which overlook these activities, is revetted in the same limestone employed for the other buildings, with white paint used extensively even to the Warren trusses of the roof. (One truss spans 180 feet/55 meters.) Two "cascades" of sculptured forms, ingeniously conjured from open-ended cubic boxes strung on the diagonal, give vertical accent to the ends of the court. A peripheral skylight surrounds the top level admitting slashes of sun, while glass encloses the west end. Seven hundred prisms were fixed on the skylights by Rockne Krebs to split and manipulate beams of colored light—"sun sculpture"—throughout. At night multicolored laser beams dart around the atrium. Sun and games, skaters and shoppers, visitors and office workers admix in a brilliant, non-rigid, three-dimensional pleasance. Prybylowski & Gravino were the structural engineers.

The George L. Smith II Georgia World Congress Center, 285 International Boulevard Northwest. (Open for events.) The Congress Center —adjacent to Omni—provides three mammoth interconnectable exhibit halls of 350,000 square feet/32,516 square meters of total space, a 1,952-seat auditorium, 32 meeting rooms, and all necessary backup facilities. With a ceiling height of 30 feet/9.1 meters it can accommodate an almost limitless range of exhibitions. The Center was not seen personally, so architectural assessment is withheld, but to judge from photographs—and the adjacent work of TVS—this should be very positive. There are plans for a substantial expansion. Byron Chapman was project architect; Armour & Cape Inc., the structural engineers.

---

11   **Colony Square** (1970–78)
Peachtree Street at 14th–15th
Atlanta, Georgia

JOVA/DANIELS/BUSBY, ORIGINAL ARCHITECTS, 1970–76;
THOMPSON, VENTULETT, STAINBACK & ASSOCIATES, ARCHITECTS,
1977–78

Colony Square is a 12-acre/4.9-hectare multi-use complex which could well be a prototype of the solution to our urban living-working-shopping-recreation problems. Located near the Atlanta Memorial Arts Center and convenient to the university and to the central business district, its intimately coordinated structures include a 24-story, square, and column-free office building (at 100 Colony Square), a larger 22-story office building (at 400 Colony Square), a 2-story, 18,000-square-foot/1,672-square-meter facility adaptable to either retail or office use, all facing Peachtree Street, and the 27-story, 500-room Colony Square Hotel (on 14th Street at Peachtree). All of the above are built around a central, enclosed, well-landscaped 2-level mall alive with restaurants, conference centers, and specialty shops. On the quiet east side of the complex, shielded by the tall buildings, rise three residential condominium towers containing a total of 264 units. Beneath the entire complex is a 3-level garage for 1,600 automobiles. The office buildings are of steel frame construction and white painted concrete except for the ground floor, which was left a natural tan finish. The color gives a useful accent that is picked up on the lower floor of the other buildings, and on walkways and exterior planters. Architecturally the complex holds together with efficiency, sophistication, and verve

with an appropriate touch of Le Corbusier influence in its design. Colony Square, though compacted, might be, as mentioned, a tuning fork for the resuscitation of the American city.

Grounds open daily

---

12 Gambrell Hall, School of Law (1971–72)
Emory University
North Decatur and Clifton Roads
Atlanta, Georgia

STEVENS & WILKINSON, ARCHITECTS

A handsome addition to the university campus (located in the northeast part of the city). To minimize size and maintain scale, the architects in effect made the building a "sandwich" of three main levels: a

substantial terraced base of light green color, an inset, fully glazed main floor, and a top floor projecting on all four sides. It is constructed of reinforced concrete. The stairs, the garden courts on the north side, and the terraces at the east and west (at the main floor level) add to the exterior pleasures. A two-story auditorium occupies the center of the two upper levels with the law library filling most of the three floors at the east end. Classrooms, faculty offices, and reading/study rooms are placed at the west. Graciously stated in the overall it is also well thought out in detail (note the inner circular stair).

Reception area open during school year

13 **Martin Luther King Jr. Middle School** (1972–73)
    **582 Connally Street Southeast (near Atlanta-Fulton County
        Stadium)**
    Atlanta, Georgia

HEERY & HEERY, ARCHITECTS

The King School is formidable on the exterior, being in effect a windowless box of raw concrete, but on entering one is greeted by a forum of animation. This is primarily created by the "auditorium" which steps down like an open amphitheater in the center of a common area with bright orange sounding boards hanging from the ceiling and dou-

bling as suspended sculpture. Activity continues in the cafeteria which opens on axis with the auditorium and in the glass-walled teaching units which frame the commons. In the current fashion, these seven educational clusters are open, self-contained, flexible, and loosely defined, reflecting an educational philosophy of team teaching. The library forms a study and reference retreat atop the cafeteria. Other facilities include a gymnasium, directly reachable from the outside, and a swimming pool.

Reception area open during school hours

---

14 Peachtree Plaza Hotel (1974–76)
Peachtree Street at International Boulevard
Atlanta, Georgia

JOHN PORTMAN & ASSOCIATES, ARCHITECTS

Having magnificently turned the design of hotels inside out with the breathtaking Hyatt Regency (q.v.), John Portman assayed another kind of spatial glamour in the nearby Peachtree Plaza. Abandoning the open atrium—the lot was too restricted—he placed public areas in a

rectangular podium consisting basically of five levels with more underground. He then injected sunlight into this core from a high peripheral glazed band, established as a focus a lagoon which covers a half acre (.2 hectare), and cantilevered miniature lounges over its placid waters. A floor of shops, a banquet level, a ballroom-conference level, with the whole topped by a swimming pool and deck, are the main elements in this base. Portman then surmounted this "public" area with a startling mirror-glass cylinder containing 1,100 bedrooms on its 56 floors, the usual revolving restaurant and bar crowning all. Ten substantial concrete columns carry the cylinder's weight to the foundations. The lower section is characterized more by intimacy than by the spatial euphoria experienced at the Hyatt, its nooks, its water, "islands," and bowered terraces probing three-dimensional directions. The unimposing Peachtree entry is lengthy and compressed and some lack of orientation can be felt within the cylindrical lobbies, but the overall atmosphere is intriguing. The architect himself, via Portman Properties, was the developer of the project, as he was of the whole Peachtree Center complex, of which this is, in effect, an extension.

Open daily

15 Harris-Pearson-Walker House (1797)
1822 Broad Street
Augusta, Georgia

Augusta, 127 miles/204 kilometers up the Savannah River from the city which names the stream, was one of the earliest towns founded in Georgia (1735). The main reason for its establishment was as a trading post with the Indians, a useful link with the interior. James Oglethorpe, who had laid out Savannah only two years earlier, also determined the plan of Augusta, but here a routine grid pattern was used.

This house on a hill at the west end of town—one of the oldest buildings in the region—was built as a residence for a prosperous tobacco merchant in what was then the village of Harrisburg. When the Augusta Canal was completed (1845), the area became industrialized and the neighborhood eventually declined. The house, once known as the Mackay House and the White House, after undergoing the usual trials and tribulations of unsympathetic additions through the years and even less sympathetic regard, was bought by the Richmond County Historical Commission (1947). It was then shorn of appendages and carefully restored by the Georgia Historical Commission, which opened it to the public in 1964. In 1975 the house's management was taken over by the Augusta-Richmond County Bicentennial Commission, Inc.

The visitor will be immediately struck by the strong but authentic colors of the exterior, and by the two-story veranda across the front which is framed under the gambrel roof. The prominent chimneys at each end add to its air of positiveness. The detailing reveals more talent than one would expect. Good late-eighteenth-century architecture in Georgia.

Open May–Oct., Tues.–Sat. 9:30–5; Nov.–Apr. 9–5, Sun. 2–5, except holidays

---

16   Old Government House (1801), **"Ware's Folly"** (1818), **Richmond Academy Building** (1802/1857), **and Old Medical College** (1835)
Telfair Street
Augusta, Georgia

These buildings along Telfair Street (with others closed to the public) provide an intriguing panorama of architectural fashions in late-eighteenth–early-nineteenth-century Augusta. The **Old Government House,** 432 Telfair (open 9–5 weekdays), served as the second Richmond County Court House from 1801 to 1821. Originally a Federal Style building, stucco wings and ironwork were added in the 1820s, giving it its present Regency appearance. At one time the residence of Dr. E. E. Murphey, the house at present belongs to the Historic Augusta Foundation, which has carefully restored and regardened it.

"Ware's Folly,"   *top photo facing page,* or the Ware-Sibley House, 506 Telfair, is now fortunately preserved as the Gertrude Herbert Memorial Art Institute. (Open Mon.–Fri. 10–12, 2–5, Sat.–Sun. 3–5, except holidays.) Its extraordinarily lavish exterior—the money involved here produced the nickname—is highly unusual with two semioctagonal bays squeezing a two-story rounded central porch, the whole elevated by a raised basement. Twin circular stairs lead up to the main floor. In plan a long central hall with oval stair splits the dwelling into halves with two rooms each. Frederick D. Nichols in his authoritative *The Early Architecture of Georgia* (University of North Carolina Press, 1957) writes that "This striking essay in the manner of the Early Republic is one of the finest houses of its type in the South." Thought by some to have been designed by Gabriel Manigault of Charleston, this attribution is not likely according to recent research.

Richmond Academy Building, 540 Telfair, is a castellated, symmetrical structure which now houses the Augusta-Richmond County Museum. (Open Tues.–Sat. 1–5, Sun. 2–5, except major holidays.) Built in 1802, it was completely remodeled in 1856–57 in the crenellated Gothic Style by W. H. Goodrich. It gives zest to the street.

The former **Old Medical College** of Georgia, 598 Telfair, presently headquarters for the Augusta Council of Garden Clubs (inquire to visit), is a hoary example of the Greek Revival but one with nostalgia. Its six precisely detailed Doric columns carry a plain but capable pediment. The building, designed by Charles B. Cluskey, is constructed of stuccoed brick.

To close this parade of Augustinian buildings, take a look at the **Sacred Heart Church** (1898–1900) at Greene Street (one block north of Telfair) at 13th, *bottom photo preceding page*. It is a fine example of late red brick Victoriana. There are reputedly fifteen brick patterns in its walls. Brother Cornelius Otten was its designer. Open daily.

Open as indicated

---

17   Georgia Railroad Bank & Trust Building (1967)
699 Broad Street
Augusta, Georgia

ROBERT McCREARY, WILLIAM HUGHES, ARCHITECTS

A smart locally designed bank and office building. The bank's contrast with its richly encrusted neo-Roman bank-ancestor on the corner illustrates much of the evolution of bank architecture since World War II. The relation of the new to the main street of the city is sympathetically worked out, with the wing along Broad Street containing the banking facilities kept low to maintain the scale of the avenue, while the seventeen-story tower rises from a setback position.

The bank's well-finished interiors include a civic function room on the second floor which seats as many as three hundred. It is loaned gratis to all civic organizations. A parking annex directly adjoins. More recognition of climate and sun control might have been in order, and the sign at the top is oversized, but otherwise the building is highly competent.

Open during business hours

---

18   Springer Opera House (1871)
1st Avenue at 10th Street
Columbus, Georgia

DANIEL MATTHEW FOLEY, ARCHITECT

Columbus, following its invasion by General Wilson's Union troops (a week after Lee's surrender), recovered more quickly than thought possible, and six years after Appomattox built an opera house. Restored in 1902, matters went handsomely for many years even through the Depression when movies took over; but by 1959 it closed down. Faced with destruction, the theater was saved (1964) by a stouthearted group of optimistic theater buffs and its Victorian gaiety has now been almost fully restored. The outside as well as most of the interior have been put back in fine condition and the theater is now in active use by the Springer Opera House Theatre Company, a Children's Theatre Company, and the Springer Ballet. It was designated the State Theatre of Georgia in 1971 and a National Historic Landmark in 1978.

Open for performances mid-Sept.–mid-May

19   Bellevue (1853–55)
204 Ben Hill Street
La Grange, Georgia

This late example of the Greek Revival, which crowns a hill on the western edge of town, is one of the most imposing in the state. It is, indeed, one of the great mansions; and when enveloped in the 12,000-acre/4,856-hectare plantation as claimed before the Civil War, the whole must have been magnificent. Its four sides are completely surrounded by a peristyle of two-story Ionic columns which functionally shade and esthetically gratify. The mass of the house is well attended to both in overall and in detail. Note the proper closer spacings of the columns nearer the corners, the strong entablature atop, and the richly balustraded balcony across the front. The now narrow grounds, with their magnolia and boxwood, should also be seen. The rooms within are spacious with high, decorated ceilings. The house recently has been thoroughly repaired, painted, and put in pristine condition by the La Grange Woman's Club which now owns it. Extremely handsome—and rightly a National Historic Landmark.

Open Tues.–Sun. 10–12, 2–5:30, except holidays: admission

---

20 Ocmulgee National Monument (c. A.D. 900)
off US 23, 80, and 129, c. 1.5 miles/2.4 kilometers E of
Macon, Georgia

It is thought that this central area of Georgia was settled by Indians at least ten thousand years ago, the earliest being nomadic hunters seeking the then existent mammoths, great bison, and other species of North American game which they—and possibly severe weather changes—eventually exterminated. The second lot of hunters and gatherers, having run out of large animals—as we in the last century almost ran out of buffalo—of necessity turned more to smaller game, fish, and to river mussels whose shells they made into sizable mounds. This group roamed central Georgia around 2000 B.C. The third or Woodland Period, which dates around 1000 B.C., saw the introduction of agriculture and a more settled life.

The Master Farmers of the fourth period, c. A.D. 900–1100, followed. They included Indian invaders and conquerors of the local tribes and probably came from the Tennessee or possibly the Mississippi area and established the settlement whose ruins and reconstruction we see today. These newcomers were largely sedentary, and, one would judge from their temple mounds, concerned with religion. Among their major constructions is this rectangular Great Temple

Mound. It has a height of 40 feet/12 meters, a base nearly 300 feet/91 meters, with two ramps angling up to the top. (It is possible that there was an influence from the Ohio Adena culture of mound builders in its concept.)

However, the most fascinating structure at Ocmulgee is the earthlodge, a circular council chamber or temple—compare the kiva of the Pueblos—which has been scientifically excavated, and then partially reconstructed, by the National Park Service. One enters via a "tunnel" to encounter a circular chamber, 42 feet/13 meters in diameter, upheld by four enormous oak "columns" which frame a central fire pit with, above, an open hole in the roof to permit smoke to escape and light to enter. The columns support a squared framework on which the inclined logs, which form the structural ceiling, rest with reed matting and 3 feet/.9 meter of red earth atop. Around the mysterious periphery of the chamber were forty-seven seats for the tribal elect. An arcane experience—and be certain to see the preparatory exhibit in the nearby visitor center. The Ocmulgee National Monument designation dates from 1936.

Open daily 9–5, except Jan. 1, Dec. 25

21   P. L. Hay House (1855–60)
934 Georgia Avenue at Spring Street
Macon, Georgia

T. THOMAS, ARCHITECT

An opulent, cubic, Italianate palazzo which adds a startling note to the architecture of the region. The mansion was originally built for a Mr. W. B. Johnston, a hugely successful merchant, who took his bride to Italy for their honeymoon, where the two decided on the "style" of their new home. (It is also known as the Johnston-Hay House.) Its red brick walls glow vividly against the green of the grounds and the white stone steps splaying from the front. The main floor finds shelter behind a porch which extends across the facade, breaking into a semicircle at the entry. The windows of the second floor bear heavy pediments (note the central one especially), while those on the third-floor "attic" frieze are round, somewhat like those in Palladio's Basilica at Vicenza. Statuesque chimneys, two per side, add a note to the roof which is climaxed by an outsize, octagonal cupola, banded by scrolled buttresses.

The interior, which is even more lavish than the outside, boasts two dozen rooms, most of them with a Carrara marble mantel. Mahogany and rosewood paneling, painted ceilings, sparkling chandeliers, opulent furnishings complete the scene. It is said that the architect brought over Italian workmen to construct this extraordinary house. It is doubtful whether local talent could match their craftsmanship. In 1977 the dwelling and its contents were acquired by the Georgia Trust for Historic Preservation, Inc., and are now managed by them.

Open Tues.–Sat. 10:30–5:30, Sun. 2–5, except holidays: admission

NOTE: The Greater Macon Chamber of Commerce, 640 1st Street, offers a free self-guiding map of the historic spots of the city. Though most are private they merit a look either from car or afoot.

---

22 Morgan County Court House (1905–6)
Town Square, Hancock and East Jefferson Streets
Madison, Georgia

J. W. GOLUCKE, ARCHITECT

Madison, laid out in 1809, is one of northeast Georgia's "presidential towns," and like Washington has a quiet community of comfortable houses (try Old Post Road) on tree-lined streets. Spared during Sherman's "March to the Sea," Madison, in addition to its dwellings, also trumpets this diverting pile where local law is meted out. Seemingly several structures atop one another, this small town *palais de justice* proclaims a startling civic grandeur with its two-story, red brick wings angled back from its diagonally placed Corinthian entry pediment. The building is topped by a gleaming white two-story squared "tower" crowned by a squared dome, clock, and belfry. The whole central section of town is listed in the National Register of Historic Places.

Open during office hours

---

23   John Knox Presbyterian Church (1965–66)
    1236 Powers Ferry Road, E via Roswell Road, c. 2 miles/3.2
        kilometers SE of intersection of US 41 and Roswell Road
    Marietta, Georgia

JOSEPH AMISANO, ARCHITECT

A wisely simple church of granite and white-painted wood. The exterior is distinguished by an extension of the side walls to enclose a square, open-air courtyard which acts as intermedium between the exterior world and the church, the secular and the religious. This walled parvis, moreover, creates an outdoor camaraderie which psychologically encourages the parishioners to tarry and talk with the pastor and each other; one does not erupt from the church after the service and head for the family car. The nave, which is square, provides a focused U-shaped grouping of pews (of white-painted wood) on three sides of the chancel seating a total of 460. This liturgical arrangement develops a close relation between congregation and minister and congregation with congregation. There is no central aisle to the altar, the approaches being on the diagonal. The sanctuary is "framed" by four square wood columns which rise to support the roof and the clerestory directly over the chancel. This clerestory provides the major source of daylight and is designed so that little glare results. A burnt-orange carpet gives visual warmth.

If closed, apply at adjacent parish house

---

24   Congregational Meeting House (1792) **and Museum** (1959)
US 17 at GA 38
Midway, Georgia

Midway (ex-Medway)—population c. 168—was settled in 1752, predominantly by Massachusetts Puritans who came via South Carolina as missionaries to the Indians. Their church, therefore, is a simple cypress version of a New England Colonial fane, primitively anachronistic amid live oaks and Spanish moss. The interior, remodeled (first in 1849), is disarmingly simple. The small museum which stands behind the church was designed by architect Thomas G. Little and is based on a raised-basement, verandaed eighteenth-century cottage typical of the coastal region. Take a look, too, at the tombs and trees of the cemetery across the street. Church, cemetery, and museum comprise most of the Midway Historic District which is now protected under the National Register of Historic Places.

Open Tues.–Sat. 10–4, Sun. 2–4, except holidays: apply for church key at museum

---

25   Stetson-Sanford House (c. 1820)
West Hancock and South Jackson Streets
Milledgeville, Georgia

Moved in 1966 to this site and partially restored (the dwelling had been an inn), the Stetson-Sanford House is a good example of a

Federal-inspired building modified by local mores. Its plan type, common to central Georgia, provides two large rooms in front with smallish entry hall giving onto a larger rear hall, generally, as here, graced with a circular stairway. Two modest rooms flank the rear hall and two larger the front, all four probably detailed by Daniel Pratt, a New England journeyman-cabinetmaker. The unusual feature of the Stetson-Sanford House (originally built for a G. T. Brown—it is also known as the Brown-Sanford House) is, however, not the plan but the two-story portico which dominates the front. Its pairs of semiclustered columns on each level with wide arced pediment make a monumental facade, probably influenced by Charleston examples. The master builder was John Marler. The house is operated by the Old Capitol Historical Society.

Open by appointment: see notice by entry

---

26 Old Governor's Mansion (1837–38)
120 South Clark Street
Milledgeville, Georgia

CHARLES B. CLUSKEY, ARCHITECT

Milledgeville, which was the capital of Georgia from 1807 to 1868—when the legislature was moved to Atlanta—possesses a number of distinguished houses. Most of these are Greek Revival-influenced, and the finest is the former Executive Mansion, since 1889 the President's House of Georgia College at Milledgeville. Built of brick covered with pinkish stucco, it is formalistic in its Palladianism, but note the bluish granite Ionic capitals on the two-story columns of the narrowly projected pavilion and the granite trim elsewhere. The plan is unusual in having down the center a rectangular entry, then a circular domed rotunda 25 feet/7.6 meters in diameter and 50 feet/15.2 meters high, with hexagonal library at rear. It is an imposing mansion outside and in, and has been impeccably preserved and was fully restored in 1965–67. Some historians feel that one Timothy Porter from Connecticut also had a hand in its design; he was certainly the builder. Cluskey is also spelled Clusky and McClusky, the first favored by recent research. A John Pell has also been mentioned as co-architect. The house is a National Historic Landmark.

Open Tues., Thurs., Fri., Sat. 10–12, 2–5, Sun. 2–5, except holidays: admission

27 The Squares of Savannah (1733–1855)
Savannah, Georgia

James Edward Oglethorpe (1696–1785) was a military man and a humanist, and it can be well argued that the plan he laid out for his new settlement in Georgia combined his career with his concern for mankind. His military experiences ranged from successfully fighting the Turks at Belgrade (1717) to chasing the Spanish from the seas around the Colonies (1742). His humanism, as expressed in his concern for prison reform and "the oppressed Protestant on the continent," was directly responsible for his asking George II if he could set up a colony for these lonely and troubled souls in the New World. This request was granted (primarily as a foil to the northward-looking Spaniards long established in Florida), and in February 1733 the last —and the largest—of the thirteen English colonies was established some 18 miles/29 kilometers up what came to be known as the Savannah River (named, rather misnamed, for the character of the countryside: a savannah is treeless).

The humanitarian castrum which Oglethorpe immediately began to

set up for some 114 colonists (including many debtors)—and which
he had determined in principle in England—was based on military
layout but military with a difference. Historians disagree as to the inspiration for Oglethorpe's plan—with theories ranging from the plan of
Peking, Palmanova (a marvelous star-shaped city of 1593 in Italy's
Veneto—which must have influenced Vauban), to London's squares,
and to an architect-friend's book, *The Villas of the Ancients Illustrated,*
which Oglethorpe possessed. In any case the plan that evolved for
Georgia was not the endlessly rigid gridiron, stereotyped by the Roman
city of Timgad, but a town plan based on a series of "wards," precisely
dimensioned, with each focused on its own open square. The wards
were composed of "Tythings" (lots) lined two rows across the north
side and two across the south, each row containing ten lots 60 x 90 feet/
18.3 x 27.4 meters—forty altogether. On these sat identical houses 16 x
22 feet/4.9 x 6.7 meters. Separating the north and south bands of dwellings in each ward was a broad space for community buildings with the
center, as mentioned, left open as a square. A net of streets, which
varied in width from 75 to 37.5 to 22.5 feet/23, 11.4, and 6.9 meters,
subdivided the whole. Such wards created a far more gracious layout
for living than an unrelieved grid, yet lacked nothing in military
ordination. The central open space of each ward also enabled
the outlying settlers and their animals to move into the palisaded town

and occupy the squares in case of danger. (Each family had, in addition to its town lot, a 5-acre/2-hectare garden plot in the outlying town common, with a 44-acre/18-hectare farm beyond.) Oglethorpe himself is said to have laid out the first four of his famous wards before returning to England (1743). His module, wondrously, was repeated as the town extended, until 1855, when available common land ran out. Savannah then boasted twenty-four squares, none, it should be added, identical. Mere open spaces—at times with a well and puzzingly few trees in the earliest days of the settlement—this network of *piazze* eventually flowered into a series of planted parks, establishing an organization unique to urbanism. Proper fencing and planting, it might be noted, did not appear until prosperity following the War of 1812.

Virtually all of the world's cities have squares but none uses them as patterned cadences that orchestrate the streets. Savannah, however, produced "a plan so exalted that it remains as one of the finest diagrams for city organization and growth in existence" (Edmund N. Bacon in his *Design of Cities,* Viking Press, 1967). The scale of these outdoor rooms is man's scale—the local automobile is tolerated, while through traffic is routed on wide avenues. Each square is different not only in planting but in statuary, the square's name and its sculpture recalling a long-deceased hero or statesman. Bull Street—William Bull was an Oglethorpe aide—is one of the most rewarding to stroll along, but meander about: would that later American cities had employed such pulsations of squares, street layout, and street variations. Instead we often entrust our urban patterns to our water commissioners. Savannah's great contribution, it should be emphasized, lies more in urban planning than in distinctive architecture. In this latter regard Savannah did not produce a domestic response equal to the felicity of the Charleston House (q.v.), though both deal with similar meteorological and ground conditions.

NOTE: For a thorough review of each square and the buildings on it see *Historic Savannah* (Historic Savannah Foundation, Inc., 1979).

Inquire at the Savannah Visitors Center, 227 West Broad Street at Louisville Street—open daily 9–5, except Dec. 25—for useful maps and data. It is housed in the 1860–76 Central of Georgia Railroad Station, accurately restored by Gunn and Meyerhoff in 1975: note the rich colors and the trusswork of the train shed—now the site of the annual Arts Festival. The Chamber of Commerce occupies the second floor

28   Davenport House (1815–20) and the Historic Savannah Foundation
324 East State Street, Columbia Square
Savannah, Georgia

ISAIAH DAVENPORT, MASTER BUILDER

The Davenport House stands as a monument to historic preservation and what such preservation can do for a house, a square, a section of town, indeed a city. The building was saved from imminent destruction —to become the inevitable parking lot—and purged from being a slum tenement (eight families were occupying it before its purchase in 1955 by the Historic Savannah Foundation). Sensitively rehabilitated on the exterior, and completely restored and refurnished within, it was the first—and key—purchase and restoration in the rescue operation to save Savannah's great, but dwindling, architectural heritage.

The dwelling, measuring 46.1 x 37 feet/14 x 11.3 meters, occupies a corner site facing Columbia Square, which had been laid out in 1799 and which recalls the domestic squares of London and New England in

its Georgian reticence. Davenport himself was born in Rhode Island and trained in Massachusetts and his building background favored exposed red brick and suppressed but elegant detail. Note the delicacy of the wrought-iron railing of the double stair that curves and rises to the equally fine front door. (Most Savannah houses rest on raised basements against dampness and street dirt.) The windows, with brownstone lintels, have exterior shutters, creating alternate bands of wood and glass across the facade. The interior, though maltreated through the years, was largely intact, even including the plaster cornices. Restoration, while extensive, was completely authentic. Davenport used an unusual proliferation of low arches in his house, starting with the fanlighted front door and continuing with the entrance hall where freestanding Ionic columns uphold a richly detailed arch that sets off the three-story elliptical stair hall at rear. Arches continue boldly in the drawing room, where each end is framed by an ellipse. The light color of the walls and the quality of the furniture make the interior uncommonly attractive. Very fine late Georgian, early Federal.

Open Mon.–Sat. 10–5, except holidays: admission

The success of the Historic Savannah Foundation with the Davenport House sparked a movement that no other city in the country can match. Charleston is beautifully preserving its patrician enclave and is beginning to broaden its activities elsewhere; New Orleans is conspicuously consuming its once unique inheritance; San Francisco fluctuates; but Savannah is reaching out to purchase, reconstruct, and resell (with controls) its hundreds of worthy, if badly undernourished, often vacant buildings. Almost all of these otherwise would have disappeared. The job which the Foundation has done is fantastic, and was, until recent federal help, all accomplished with private funds operating on a non-profit basis. Seven ladies—led by Miss Anna Hunter —saw the Davenport House in its slum condition, grabbed it before it was too late, then supervised its reconstruction, and went on to establish in 1955 the Historic Savannah Foundation, Inc. It is no overstatement to declare that they have transformed the city's present and future by its past. Leopold Adler II, the Foundation's onetime president, was an important spark plug. Over eight hundred houses of historic merit (plus a wedge of commercial structures) have been directly or indirectly resuscitated by the Foundation's efforts largely by non-profit "revolving funds." Thus, a house, having been bought by the Foundation, is sold under strict conditions of rehabilitation. The citizens of Savannah are turning back to the city instead of turning their backs on it. Along with most of the rest of the population the tax collector is beaming.

29   Owens-Thomas House (1816–19)
124 Abercorn Street, Oglethorpe Square
Savannah, Georgia

WILLIAM JAY, ARCHITECT

William Jay, a bright English architect, arrived in Savannah in 1817 at
the age of twenty-one to supervise the final design and the construction
of this spirited Regency house for Richard Richardson (the preliminary drawings for which Jay had finished in England). He is said to
have received the commission because Richardson's wife's brother
married Jay's sister. Jay went on to design several distinguished—but
hardly fully regional—buildings both in Savannah and Charleston before returning (1824) to his native England (and eventually to Mauri-
tius, where he died).

The exterior of the Owens-Thomas House reflects some of the flair
of Jays' natal Bath, where John Wood the Younger's Circus and Royal

Crescent (1764 and 1769) would have given any architecturally inclined young man memorable ideas. Nash's work in London, where Jay
studied, also stirred his ambitions. The basement walls of the Owens-
Thomas House are made of tabby (burnt oyster shells for lime,
crushed seashells for aggregate, water, and sand), further waterproofed
by stucco, and painted a light ocher. The distinguished features of the
facade are twofold. First is the graceful one-story portico which bows
subtly out in plan, with an entablature that carries around the house as
an outsize belt course. Secondly, the front entry is set in an arched
niche reached by twin curving stairs: good early Regency. Note that
the approach is within a low-walled garden, unusual for Savannah. The
busy sides are less well articulated, but examine the cast-iron balcony
(made in England) on the south facade.

One enters a ceremonial front hall with two gold-capped Corinthian
columns visually slowing the progression up the stairs. These stairs
split at the landing, double back on either side, and are bridged at top.
The salon is the most unusual room, being decorated with elaborate,
liberated-Greek plasterwork that fans out like palmettos onto the ceiling from the corners. The mantel, too, should be noted. Furnishings
throughout the house are superior. It might be said that in spots the interior shows more imagination than mastery of detail, but William Jay
in his seven years in Georgia and South Carolina left a definite imprint
on our architecture. Would that he had stayed. Many consider this to
be the finest Regency House in the country. This house was willed to
the Telfair Academy of Arts and Sciences in 1951 and opened to the
public three years later. The garden, too, is well worth inspection: most
of its plants are those available when the house was built. (The house
is now known by the names of its last two owners.)

*Open Tues.–Sat. 10–5, Sun.–Mon. 2–5; closed in Sept. and
holidays: admission*

Two other notable works in Savannah by William Jay are the Scarbrough House (1818–19) and Telfair House (1818–20), now Telfair
Academy. The two bear several key points of similarity.

The **William Scarbrough House,** 41 West Broad Street (open
Mon.–Wed., Fri.–Sat. 10–4, Sun. 2–4, except major holidays: admission), uses, typically for Jay, a one-story, four-column portico in front,
here strangely archaic with two piers and two early Doric columns. Its
entablature, as with all three Jay houses, carries as a belt course
around the front and sides, and is topped on the second floor of both
the Scarbrough and Telfair houses by a half-round lunette or fanlight.

This proved useful in ventilation as well as in looks. The effect is visually echoed by the roundheaded recessed windows aside the portico to set up a geometry which is partially obscured by the projection of the porch. Note the "gate" at the right. The plan of the Scarbrough House is unusual with a double-height atrium hall flanked by drawing rooms and with a ballroom across the back, a piazza at each end. The house was purchased by the Historic Savannah Foundation, Inc., in 1972, brilliantly restored (it had among other uses served as a school), and made into a museum in addition to serving as head-quarters of the Foundation.

The **Telfair Academy of Arts and Sciences,** 121 Barnard Street (open Tues.–Sat. 10–4:30, Sun. 2–5, except major holidays: admission), was built as a town house for Alexander Telfair with large central hall, the "wings" on either side having apsidal ends. The attic floor was added and the house converted into a museum in 1889 by Detlef Lienau, a prominent New York architect, hence the interior is not as Jay left it.

30   **Independent Presbyterian Church** (1817–19/1889–90)
     Oglethorpe Avenue at Bull Street
     Savannah, Georgia

JOHN HOLDEN GREENE, ARCHITECT

The church we see today is a copy of an earlier one which burned
completely in 1889. The commission for the first, which Greene won
by competition, shows the architect's Rhode Island background, including his own Providence Congregational Church, plus Wren and
Gibbs influences, all capably put together on the outside. The interior,
however, belongs to itself, and startles with its spatial grandeur, and its
enormous oval domed ceiling, one of the country's most monumental.

The copy is made in granite with cast iron for the steeple. W. G. Preston, architect of the Cotton Exchange (q.v.), supervised the rebuilding, utilizing drawings of the original which were found in the Boston Public Library.

Open 9–5 daily

---

31   Fort Pulaski (1829–47)
c. 15 miles/24 kilometers E of Savannah on US 80
near Savannah (Fort Pulaski), Georgia

Some 25 million bricks were reportedly used in the construction of this fort, plus eighteen years of labor. However, when it was bombarded by Union forces in the Civil War (April 1862) utilizing the latest rifled

cannon that knocked great chunks out of its walls (which are 7–11 feet/2.1–3.4 meters thick), coastal protection by forts, brick or stone, became obsolete. Pulaski had to capitulate in thirty hours.

The fort's construction—it was the third on the site—had been ordered by President Monroe after the War of 1812 revealed our coastal vulnerability. When a distinguished French military engineer and former aide-de-camp to Napoleon, General Simon Bernard—unemployed at home since Waterloo—sought to use his abilities in the United States, he was brevetted into our army, and among his first jobs was help with the design for Fort Pulaski. (General Bernard returned to France in 1830, eventually becoming French Minister of War.) Following the Civil War, some repairs were made (1869–72), but it lapsed into dormancy except for a brief period in the Spanish-American War. The fort was fully repaired and it and its 537 acres/217 hectares on Cockspur Island were made a National Monument in 1924. In World War II the fort was reactivated as "an active part of the defense system of the United States." It was named for Count Casimir Pulaski, the great Polish commander in the American Revolution who lost his life (1779) at the siege of Savannah. The site is administered by the National Park Service of the U. S. Department of the Interior.

Open June–Labor Day, Mon.–Sun. 8:30–6; rest of year daily 8:30–5:30, except Dec. 25: admission

---

32   Factors' Row (1840–86) **and Cotton Exchange** (1886–87)
Bay Street
Savannah, Georgia

In 1733 General Oglethorpe searched for a site for his new city upriver from the piratical perils of the Atlantic. He wisely chose a high bluff at the bend of the Savannah River, its height offering greater protection against both Indians and insects. At the foot of this bluff the town's port developed. With the boom in cotton shipping and naval stores, for which Savannah became famous in the early nineteenth century, the river's edge was stabilized; its 40-foot/12-meter cliff was faced with masonry (largely ships' ballast) in the 1840s. Charles B. Cluskey, who designed considerable local work of merit, injected ingenious arched "stores" in this embankment. A series of warehouses arose at this time and on these godowns and level with the top of the bluff were placed the two-story offices (mostly 1854–58) where the cotton merchants could not only transact business but reassure themselves as to operations and sailings simply by looking out the rear window. This became known as Factors' Row or Walk (Bull to Abercorn Streets) with the Cotton Exchange near the middle. Because Factors' Row rests atop the riverside warehouses, which, of necessity, are freestanding from the sloping bluff, a spider's web of cast-iron bridges connects them with Bay Street and its slender Emmet Park. With the bridges "flying" horizontally, and the stairs down to the lower levels adding detached angularity, the whole "pierced" by openings through which trees occasionally poke, an intriguing series of spaces develops. The place is indeed rich with atmosphere.

The **Cotton Exchange** (1886–87) was designed by W. G. Preston, a Boston architect (and contemporary of Richardson) who won its commission from ten other contestants. Built of elaborately molded red terra-cotta and red brick, it has been called "the most important sur-

viving building of the Romantic Revival, and one of the best examples of any period in Savannah" (*Historic Savannah*, 1979). It was also one of the first buildings in the country to be built on air rights (Drayton Street). Cast iron (locally produced), copper, and wood are its other materials. The Lion Fountain (1889) in front was also designed by Preston. Note, too, the gracefully arced *Stoddard's Range* (1859) directly adjacent. The warehouses below have taken on new life as nightclubs, restaurants, and shops.

The riverfront between Barnard and Lincoln streets—on which Factors' Row faces—has been stabilized via a bulkhead and embellished by an **Esplanade** by architects Gunn & Meyerhoff (1975–78) in an urban renewal project. The prime purpose of this was to prevent erosion by the tidal river with construction being built out 30–60 feet/9–18 meters to the harbor line. However, the project goes much further than bank stabilization and helps rejuvenate the entire midtown

waterfront via the esplanade mentioned, part of which is actually over the river. Approximately every 300 feet/91 meters of its half-mile/.8-kilometer length there is a small "park," while three semidepressed parking lots take care of the automobile. For strolling and ship-watching it makes an expansive riparian adjunct. The new concourse also gives a river's-edge pedestrian view of the northern facades of the Factors' Row warehouses. Hussey, Gay & Bell were the engineers; Lester Collins the landscape consultant.

Factors' Row open daily

---

33   Zion Episcopal Church (1848)
US 80, S of Town Square
Talbotton, Georgia

Miraculously preserved, we find in this small town east of Columbus a doughty, unrestored stained-wood example of village Gothic Revival. Reputedly even the nails were hand-forged. Peripheral but nostalgic. Several authorities feel that its design was influenced by Richard Up-

john's work. The church is listed in the National Register of Historic Places.

Generally open only on Sun.: key nearby

---

34 Traveler's Rest (Jarrett Manor—c. 1815–20/1840)
.2 mile/.3 kilometer N of US 123, 6 miles/9.6 kilometers E of Toccoa, Georgia

A rural outpost that once served as post office, stagecoach inn, and, in more settled times, a plantation. This rambling, unpainted, gabled group of buildings represents typical Georgia Plantation Plain Style with the two stories and shed porch across the front and shed addition at rear. Built on a random stone basement and against a large stone chimney, the house and its additions cover an extended building period. It measures almost a hundred feet (30 meters) long with full-length porch across the front, the porch and several of the expansions coming at the hand of Mr. Jarrett, who bought the place in 1838. Purchased by the state in 1955, the main house and outbuildings are now being completely restored.

Open May–Oct., Tues.–Sat. 9:30–5:30; Nov.–Apr., Tues.–Sat.
9–5, every Sun. 2–5, except holidays: admission

35   Robert Toombs Avenue (US 78—late 18th/early 19th century)
Washington (Wilkes County), Georgia

Washington, a small town (population c. 5,000) halfway between
Athens and Augusta, is one of those little-known architectural bypaths
which one occasionally encounters, always with pleasure. There are
several dozen Greek Revival houses in the unspoiled, very much lived-
in village, a handful of high quality. Though they are private, many
can be seen to advantage while strolling or driving. The town was laid
out in 1780, hence among the earliest of the thirty-one to be named
for the President, the first being in North Carolina according to the
George Washington Bicentennial Commission. The town has undertaken a commendable effort to make its attractions better-known and
publishes, as mentioned below, a map which visitors can use for a self-
escorted tour. Every "uneven" year in March or April there is also a
"House Week" when many dwellings are open. Most of the homes, as
the discerning will perceive, had their Greek Revival porches added
long after the original core. The finest are the Tupper-Barnett House,
corner of Allison Street, built about 1832, with eighteen-column Doric

portico around all four sides added in 1860; the Robert Toombs House (1797), east end of the avenue, with portico of around 1840; and, off Toombs Avenue, the Campbell-Jordan House, 208 East Liberty Street, house 1786, porch about 1825. The Washington-Wilkes Museum (c. 1835—open Tues.–Sat. 9–5, Sun. 2–5, except holidays), 308 East Toombs Avenue, has a regional collection as well as fine paneled interiors. All in all a surprisingly comely group of early-nineteenth-century houses for a small community.

Houses closed to public: inquire Chamber of Commerce, on Courthouse Square, for helpful map

Callaway Plantation (c. 1869), 5 miles/8 kilometers west of Washington on US 78 (open only Apr. 15–Oct. 15, Mon.–Sat. 10–5:30, Sun. 2–5:30), though not distinguished in detail, will interest the Greek Revival specialist. In addition to the house the outbuildings, including a 1775 log cabin, have been restored.

---

36 Baptist Village (1958–74)
Carswell Avenue (GA 122), c. 3 miles/5 kilometers W of Waycross, Georgia

STEVENS & WILKINSON, ARCHITECTS

Baptist Village's low-keyed architecture is concerned with the difficult problem of sympathetically housing both the ambulant aged and the infirm in a church-sponsored retirement center. Located in the southeast corner of the state on a 400-acre/162-hectare flat but well-treed site, it is composed of clusters of "cottage" groups, a dormitory, Intermediate Care Unit, and Nursing Unit, all of friendly scale. A high-rise solution was avoided because most of the people there are drawn from the countryside, hence like to feel in touch with the land. The architects have also created a small artificial lake to generate greater visual interest. All trees are meticulously preserved—one *Quercus virginiana* has a spread of over 150 feet/46 meters—and many new ones planted.

Each of the three clusters contains seven cottages deployed on both sides of a common dayroom-lounge-kitchen, the periphery of the complex being marked by covered walkways which afford open-air access to all units even in inclement weather. Two outer rows of cottages "frame" the third or inner row of one cottage and the nearby dayroom.

The cottages vary from living-bedroom units for single occupancy, to living room and separate bedroom for couples. All have bath and adequate storage facilities plus individual air conditioning. More extensive and more varied accommodations will be incorporated as the Village expands. Meals are served in the dayroom. In addition to the clusters which hold twenty-eight residents each, there is a main communal unit with administration, lounges, library, store, medical unit, chapel (and a proliferation of concrete "umbrellas" marking the entry). The architecture, especially of the clusters, is simple but it develops an inviting atmosphere. The first stage, which accommodated 100 people, proved so satisfactory, both sociologically as well as architecturally, that the Village was expanded through the years to take care of 350. It is owned and operated by the Georgia Baptist Convention.

Grounds open daily

Illinois

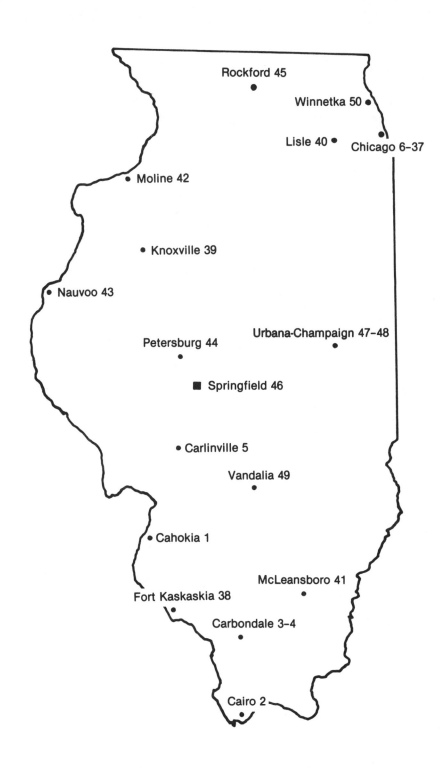

Rockford 45

Winnetka 50 •

Lisle 40 •

Chicago 6–37

• Moline 42

• Knoxville 39

• Nauvoo 43

Urbana-Champaign 47–48

Petersburg 44

■ Springfield 46

• Carlinville 5

Vandalia 49

• Cahokia 1

McLeansboro 41

Fort Kaskaskia 38

Carbondale 3–4

Cairo 2

ILLINOIS

The buildings in boldface type are of general interest. The others are for the specialist.

Cahokia   1 Old Church of the Holy Family
                                  (1786–99/1949)
                                  Cahokia Courthouse (1737)

Cairo   2 **Magnolia Manor** (1869–72)

Carbondale   3 **Polyspheroid Water Tank** (1965)—
                                  Chicago Bridge & Iron Company
                               4 Faner Hall (1975–76)—Geddes
                                  Brecher Qualls Cunningham

Carlinville   5 Macoupin County Court House
                                  (1867–70)—Elijah E. Myers

Chicago   6 **Old Water Tower** (1867–69)—
                                  William W. Boyington
                               7 **Glessner House** (1886–87)—
                                  H. H. Richardson
                               8 **The Chicago School of Architecture:
                                  The Evolution of the Skyscraper**
                               9 Rookery Building (1886–88/1905)—
                                  Burnham & Root, Frank Lloyd Wright
                              10 **The Auditorium Building** (1887–89/
                                  1967)—Adler & Sullivan
                              11 Monadnock Building (1889–91/
                                  1893)—Burnham & Root
                              12 **Museum of Science and Industry** (1893/
                                  1933–40)—D. H. Burnham & Co.
                              13 The Chicago Public Library Cultural
                                  Center (1893–97/1974–77)—Shepley,
                                  Rutan & Coolidge
                              14 **Reliance Building** (1890–91/
                                  1894–95)—Burnham & Root and D. H.
                                  Burnham & Co.
                              15 Frank Lloyd Wright Home and Studio
                                  (1889–95/1898)—Frank Lloyd
                                  Wright

16 **Carson, Pirie, Scott Store** (1899/
   1903–4)—Louis H. Sullivan
17 **Unity Temple—The Universalist
   Church** (1906–8)—Frank Lloyd
   Wright
18 **The Frederick C. Robie House**
   (1908–10)—Frank Lloyd Wright
19 Carl Schurz High School (1907–10)—
   Dwight H. Perkins
20 **The Wrigley Building and Neighbors—**
   Architects as noted
21 **The Tribune Tower** (1923–25)—John
   Mead Howells and Raymond Hood
22 Playboy Building (1928–29)—
   Holabird & Root
   333 North Michigan Building (1928)—
   Holabird & Roche
23 **Mies van der Rohe** (1886–1969)—
   His Chicago Contribution
24 **860 Lake Shore Drive Apartments**
   (1948–51)—Mies van der Rohe
25 **S. R. Crown Hall** (1955–56)—Mies
   van der Rohe
   IIT Campus (1939)—Mies van der
   Rohe
26 **Marina City** (1960–62)—Bertrand
   Goldberg Associates
   IBM Building (1971)—The Office of
   Mies van der Rohe
27 Central District Filtration Plant
   (1964–66)—C. F. Murphy &
   Associates
28 **Lake Point Tower** (1967–68)—
   G. D. Schipporeit and John C. Heinrich
29 **University of Illinois at Chicago Circle**
   (1965–79)—Skidmore, Owings &
   Merrill; other architects as noted
30 **Richard J. Daley Center** (1963–66)—
   C. F. Murphy Associates, Skidmore,
   Owings & Merrill, and Loebl
   Schlossman Bennett & Dart

31 **John Hancock Center** (1966–70)—
Skidmore, Owings & Merrill

32 **McCormick Place** (1968–71)—
C. F. Murphy Associates

33 Malcolm X Community College
(1971)—C. F. Murphy Associates

34 **First National Bank** (1968–71)—
C. F. Murphy Associates and The
Perkins & Will Partnership

35 **Federal Center** (1963–73)—Mies van
der Rohe, with Schmidt Garden &
Erikson, C. F. Murphy Associates,
A. Epstein & Son

36 **Sears Tower** (1971–74)—Skidmore,
Owings & Merrill

37 Illinois Regional Library for the Blind
(1978)—Stanley Tigerman

**Fort Kaskaskia State
Historic Site**

38 **Pierre Menard House** (1802)

Knoxville

39 Old Knox County Court House
(1837–39)—John Mandeville

Lisle

40 **St. Procopius Abbey Church and
Monastery** (1968–70)—Loebl
Schlossman Bennett & Dart

McLeansboro

41 People's National Bank (1881)—
Reid Brothers

Moline

42 **The Deere & Company Administrative
Center** (1962–64/1977–78)—Eero
Saarinen & Associates; Kevin Roche/
John Dinkeloo & Associates

Nauvoo

43 Joseph Smith Mansion (1844)

Petersburg

44 **New Salem Restoration** (1831–37/
1932–33)

Rockford

45 The Unitarian Church (1965–66)—
Pietro Belluschi and C. Edward Ware

Springfield

46 **Old State Capitol** (1837–40/1853/
1966–68)—John F. Rague

Urbana-Champaign   47 **Assembly Hall** (1959–63)—Max
                             Abramovitz of Harrison & Abramovitz;
                             Ammann & Whitney

                          48 **Krannert Center for the Performing
                             Arts** (1968–69)—Max Abramovitz of
                             Harrison & Abramovitz

Vandalia   49 Vandalia Statehouse State Historic Site
                             (1836–39/1857–59)—William Hodge
                             and John Taylor

Winnetka   50 Crow Island School (1939–40/
                             1954)—Saarinen & Saarinen, and
                             Perkins, Wheeler & Will

1 Old Church of the Holy Family (1786–99/1949)
at Intersection of ILL 3 and 157
Cahokia, East St. Louis, Illinois

As one of the few French-Canadian churches surviving from the eighteenth century, either in the United States or Canada, this medieval *poteaux-en-terre* structure takes on special importance. The church was constructed of hand-hewn walnut timbers set in the vertical fashion favored by the French. This is a curious construction technique, as the 6- to 8-inch-thick (15 to 20 centimeters) "studs," spaced 10 to 12 inches (25 to 30 centimeters) apart, have excess structural strength yet all the problems of caulking, plus the probability of rotting at the base. The in-filling or nogging at Cahokia is of rubble and lime.

The exterior, whose vertical "half-timbering" carries a distinctly medieval air, is largely unspoiled due in measure to the fact that the walls were at one time covered with clapboarding until the restoration of 1949. Note the angled end-bracing, and the slight inward cant of the sides. The interior walls are also of exposed construction but the inner atmosphere lacks the clear statement of the exterior.

Open June–Aug., daily 9–4, Sept.–Oct., Sat.–Sun. 9–4, services on certain feast days

Those interested in early French architecture in the Mississippi Valley—whose river served as the French highway between New Orleans and Canada—will also want to see the nearby **Cahokia Courthouse** (1737), also on 1st Street, but west of ILL 3. (Open daily 9–5, except major holidays.) Originally built as a private house around 1737, it was turned into a courthouse in 1793, making it the earliest surviving public building west of the Alleghenies. (Cahokia, the oldest town in Illinois—there was a French settlement here in 1699—was founded nineteen years before New Orleans.) Measuring only 35 x 43 feet/11 x 13 meters the Courthouse is of *poteaux-sur-sole* construction. The building, now a State Historic Site, has been moved and restored so often that little of the original remains; however the first foundations were found by archeological excavation in 1938, and the building reconstructed on its original site. (See, also, the completely rebuilt French church of 1715 at Fort Michilimackinac at Mackinaw City, Michigan.)

---

2 Magnolia Manor (1869–72)
2700 Washington Avenue
Cairo, Illinois

Cairo, at the confluence of the Mississippi and the Ohio rivers, never realized the importance which its desirable location might indicate. Events, including the Civil War and competition from railroads,

conspired against it. St. Louis to the north and Memphis to the south
—to mention only "neighbors," and less geographically endowed ones
at that—vastly surpassed it. Charles Dickens termed it "a dismal
swamp." There is, however, a nostalgic legacy—more Southern than
Northern—in Cairo (population c. 6,300), and chief, but not exclu-
sively, among its rewards in architecture is Magnolia Manor. It was, of
course, named for the trees found in its front yard as well as in
profusion throughout the town. Except for its superior window detailing, the exterior of the house represents a routine Tuscan-Victorian
bracketed style, but the interior, with many of its original century-old
furnishings intact, is excellent. The rich plaster cornices and ceiling
decorations, the paired columns upholding quarter-round arches, the
marble fireplaces, and the elaborate chandeliers set a splendid scene.
All of the rooms are completely furnished. A museum, largely of Civil
War mementoes, occupies the fourth floor, while the fully restored
kitchen in the basement is of interest. The house was acquired by the
Cairo Historical Association in 1952.

Open weekdays 9–5, Sun. 1–5, except Jan. 1, Dec. 25: admission

3   Polyspheroid Water Tank (1965)
West Chatauqua Street at South Taylor, SW edge of
Carbondale, Illinois

CHICAGO BRIDGE & IRON COMPANY, ENGINEERS AND
CONSTRUCTORS

The behemoth cylindrical water storage tank, stilted out of the ground, is giving way to more sophisticated, more comely versions. Much of this is due to an influence from advanced designs in Sweden and Finland. In these northern countries, the architects and engineers realized that one cannot prop such monsters up on the skyline, particularly in a flat residential area, and not pay an "ungainliness tax" on them. It is doubtful, however, whether in Scandinavia or the U.S.A., that one can match the sensuousness of these three conjoined spheroid

tanks (capacity 750,000 gallons/3,409,000 liters) of Southern Illinois University. Instead of being an object to tolerate, a water storage tank can be—as here—as much sculpture as vessel. (Unfortunately—but perhaps morphologically understandable—love messages have been scribbled on its legs.) A service ladder is provided inside one of the columns with access to a manhole at the top. Paul O. Hall & Associates were consulting engineers.

---

4 Faner Hall (1975–76)
Southern Illinois University
use Visitors Parking Lot by stadium
Carbondale, Illinois

GEDDES BRECHER QUALLS CUNNINGHAM, ARCHITECTS

The most obvious fact about Faner is that it is a long, long building—all 900 feet/274 meters of it. The most important fact about this Humanities and Social Sciences Center is that this stretched megastructure attains architectural distinction. Its length—a "linear grid"—was designed to stabilize the western edge of this part of the campus, separating active instructional, social, and athletic facilities from the quiet forested area, the Thompson Wood, which it abuts. To keep the great dimension of this three- and four-story, north-south-oriented building within acceptable visual bounds, the architects did the following: First of all they elevated the main bulk on stilts and inset the ground floor to make its campus (east) side a constant-height but variable-width galleria with functions freely arranged beneath. The facilities here range from the museum (at south end), to mechanical rooms, to lecture halls. The setback permits a lofty, arcaded communication link for most of the length of the building. The "pierced" quality of the ground level—the open spaces between enclosed functions—allows a sweep of space under the building which helps tie the campus to Thompson Wood.

To give cohesion to the building the architects lined the top floor of the east side with a continuous brise-soleil that protects the offices there from direct sun. (The west side is almost all shielded by louvers.) They then "broke" the length of the campus side by boldly projecting stairs and ramps at needed places.

The 132-foot/40-meter-wide building is divided on the upper levels into two parallel rows of offices, classrooms, and services, the rows

being sufficiently separated from each other to create three agreeable roof "courtyards" (on top of the lower floor). The scale, the quality of spaces, and the strong modular rhythm of the louvers produce a powerful building. Construction is of poured-in-place concrete. Robert L. Geddes was partner in charge of design. GBQC had been earlier (1967) retained by the university to prepare a master plan for the campus core.

Lobbies open during school year

---

5 **Macoupin County Court House** (1867–70)
   ILL 108—Main, East, South, and High Streets
   Carlinville, Illinois

ELIJAH E. MYERS, ARCHITECT

The worthy citizens of Macoupin County were paying for this elaborate hulk for over two generations after its completion (itself a tale of curious overruns and machinations). However, after more than a hundred years of use, most of them today would probably consider the money well spent. Almost the entire structure is of solid masonry except for the dome, stairs, and doors, which are of iron. The twin

Corinthian porticos, which climax the north and south ends, and the gold-painted dome are impressive, but be certain also to take a look at the lofty, rich courtroom on the top floor and the underside of the dome. Mr. Myers later went on to design the state capitols for Michigan (1871), Texas (1881—q.v.), and Colorado (1886).

Open during office hours

---

6   Old Water Tower (1867–69)
800 North Michigan Avenue at East Chicago Avenue
Chicago, Illinois

WILLIAM W. BOYINGTON, ARCHITECT

This castellated nugget arose through no Arthurian whimsicality, or because its designer simply liked towers; it was built to contain a standpipe 138 feet/42 meters high and 3 feet/.9 meter in diameter. This "cylinder" took up the pulsations and pressure variations in the old Corliss engines that once powered the pumps—now updated—which are still housed across the street. Water to supply Chicago's pumping stations, of which there are twelve, comes from the lake via

"cribs" placed several miles offshore, then piped underground. (See also the Central District Filtration Plant.) Though this tower is no longer needed (electric pumps have long ago replaced George Corliss' invention) its Gothic Revival fancifulness is still very much needed as an architectural celebration.

It is one of the few structures (the only public "building") that withstood the 1871 fire (which damaged the pump house). (It also survived 1918 street-widening plans.) The limestone tower and the pump house were both restored in 1913–16. One of the country's most wonderful relics, or as Carl Condit observed in his book *The Chicago School of Architecture* (University of Chicago Press, 1964), it is "as sacred as a religious symbol."

The Water Tower was renovated (1978) into a Visitor Information Center with an 1890s theme, complete with a new park. Loebl Schlossman & Hackl were the architects.

7   Glessner House (1886–87)
1800 South Prairie Avenue
Chicago, Illinois

H. H. RICHARDSON, ARCHITECT

Although he was born in Louisiana, H. H. Richardson's contribution to American architecture toward the end of the last century—either directly or by influence—can be seen over much of the northern half of the country. Seeking a virile robustness, as opposed to the effete pseudo-Classicism which was soon to mold the Chicago Fair of 1893, Richardson injected a forcefulness in domestic architecture, as in all his buildings, that is still revered in contemporary circles. The Glessner House, on the once "finest residential street" in Chicago (now The Prairie Avenue Historic District), well demonstrates this, its normal Richardsonian strength transformed almost into a granite arsenal (note stonework) as HHR skillfully turned the house inside out. He achieved this by putting the small-windowed halls and service quarters

on the 18th Street side, and opening the principal rooms onto a private garden court away from the north wind, noise, and dirt—one of the earliest examples of truly functional planning. Most of the house itself has been (and is being) well restored and refurnished with original pieces. The court has already been renovated.

Saved from impending destruction by the heroic efforts of the Chicago School of Architecture Foundation (now the Chicago Architecture Foundation), the dwelling—occupied by the family until Mr. Glessner's death in 1936—appropriately serves today as the headquarters of the Foundation. Richardson himself unfortunately died a month before the ground-breaking of his greatest house. His Chicago work left a lasting impression on John Root and Louis Sullivan (and Frank Lloyd Wright) of the famous "Chicago School" (q.v.) which did so much to launch what we call modern, as opposed to eclectic, or back-to-the-past architecture.

Open Tues., Thurs., Sat. 10–4, Sun. 11–5, except holidays: admission

---

8 The Chicago School of Architecture: The Evolution of the Skyscraper

Chicago has a vibrancy, and has exhibited a daring and vision, which no other city in the United States can match. As the town's incorporation dates only from 1837, brain and brawn have rarely been hampered by tradition. When its rail network of ten trunk lines was largely completed in the 1850s and 1860s to join its shipping potential (eventually becoming the world's largest inland port), Chicago easily outstripped the steamboat-oriented St. Louis as the transportation center of the U.S.A. Today its O'Hare Airport is also the world's busiest. Iron ore from Mesabi by inexpensive barge, coal by rail from not so distant Appalachia, and grain and edible animals from a crescent of nearby Plains States all converged on the city, drawing to it an extraordinary amalgam of the world's hopeful. The stifling heat of summer, the lake-borne chill of winter rarely deterred these migrants. With a population a bit over 100,000 in 1860, it boasted almost five times this number twenty years later and a million by 1890. And when that blessing in disguise, otherwise known as the Great Fire, broke out on the evening of October 8, 1871, and reputedly removed seventeen thousand mostly wooden and mostly nondescript buildings, leaving some one third of its inhabitants homeless, Chicago—to paraphrase Caesar Augustus—was found in wood and left in masonry, soon in masonry and steel. The detritus of the fire, incidentally, was shoved into the lake, its first landfill. It has been called the "city-as-process."

Before describing the so-called Chicago School and the development of the skyscraper,* it is important to mention an earlier stage of architectural contribution, indeed revolution, which occurred before Chicago attained the above-mentioned prominence. For it was in and around this city in the 1830s that the technique for constructing small wood buildings, particularly houses, was changed forever. Until then most structures had been put together with a heavy, mortised, and tenoned timber frame which was generally sheathed in clapboarding. This traditional "craft" approach required extensive forests and skilled carpenters, few of which were available in the waxing flat lands between the mountains to east and west. Then in the 1830s and '40s the machine production of nails cut their price to less than one tenth that of those previously made by hand, while the sawmills in turn became heavily mechanized. The notion thus evolved of using small-sized, closely spaced, one-man-handleable pieces of lumber often two stories high, creating frames of what we now call 2 x 4's (5 x 10 centimeters) spaced roughly 18 inches/46 centimeters apart. These studs are toenailed into a wood sill (which is bolted onto masonry foundations) and are topped by a plate, with a light wood roof truss spanning the whole—ergo the balloon frame. Such buildings could be put together with remarkable speed by only modestly trained labor—and at far less cost. They were even prefabricated in sections and shipped widely. They could be sheathed with wood or brick.

The "second" Chicago architectural revolution was even more momentous than the balloon frame for it turned the cities of the world into a bristle of upward-striving buildings instead of quiet profiles of four- and five-story walk-ups. It was made technically possible by the use of metal, particularly the Bessemer production of inexpensive rolled-steel members, and abetted by the invention of the elevator which in 1889 had become electrified (as opposed to clumsier earlier ones powered by steam or hydraulic power). The pragmatic architects and engineers of Chicago, working with admirable cooperation, devised this system of building, which for better or worse has changed much of the way urban mankind works, lives, and shops. (It became the greatest structural revolution since Gothic vaults and buttresses.) In this they were constantly prickled by forward-looking clients and

* Carl W. Condit's famous series of books are most useful on this. See in particular his *The Rise of the Skyscraper* (University of Chicago Press, 1952).

developers frantically trying to supply office and commercial square footage following the fire, a process intensified on recovery from the 1873 national financial panic.

Metal in the form of cast iron had, of course, been used for low-rise structures since the middle of the nineteenth century (earlier in English industrial buildings). It appeared first in facades where its slender dimensions could admit far more light than masonry. It was also used extensively for interior columns. But whereas cast iron has substantial compressive strength, it is weak in tension, thus in beams upholding floors. Steel, because it is highly resistant to compression, bending, and shear, thus rapidly replaced frangible iron and though like iron it demands a jacket of fireproofing, it remains to this day the basic American construction means for most commercial building. (It should be added that fireproofing by vitreous tile was pioneered in Chicago in the early 1870s.) With a single framing material, a cage of riveted (at times bolted) steel evolved, at first hesitantly and with a reliance on masonry. Shortly, however, it developed into a means of building whereby a skeleton with a regular grid of vertical columns and horizontal girders and beams takes all of the loads and stresses, leaving to the exterior walls only the function of enclosure. It should be noted that these outside walls are supported by brackets or spandrel beams at each floor level and not by the ground as may appear. With construction thus liberated, building height became nearly limitless. Whereas we have not attained Frank Lloyd Wright's 1956 proposal for a mile-high skyscraper (528 floors) we find (in Chicago of course) the two tallest in the world at a fifth of a mile—John Hancock and the Sears Tower, q.v. Parenthetically, the tallest masonry-walled building is Chicago's Monadnock (q.v.), its sixteen stories attaining an ultimate for a wall-bearing structure as it requires a ground-floor wall thickness of over 6 feet/1.8 meters.

Before discussing the development of the high-rise it should be mentioned that the first office block with an elevator (some historians even say the first "skyscraper" though it was only five stories high) is generally held to be New York's Equitable Life Assurance Company of 1868–70, designed by Gilman & Kendall with George B. Post. Five floors, of course, were formally considered to be a walk-up, and, as Mumford points out walk-up slums of mid-nineteenth-century Edinburgh sometimes had, unbelievably, "eight, ten or more" floors (*The City in History,* Harcourt, Brace & World, 1961). An earlier proto-skyscraper which also deserves mention is the Jayne Building, Philadelphia, 1849–51, eight stories plus tower, by William J. Johnston, which Ada Louise Huxtable was one of the first to mention (in an article in *Progressive Architecture* of November 1956). This startling cellular edifice, reputedly 130 feet/40 meters high (the same height, incidentally, as the mansarded Equitable) and with flanking six-story wings, was primarily a loft building for the storage of Dr. Jayne's patent medicines. Though it had freight hoists (two) there was no passenger elevator. (The first practical elevator dates from 1857, and was used in New York's five-story ex-department store, the Haughwout Building, q.v.). Mrs. Huxtable goes on to say of the granite-clad Jayne Building that "its direct link to the future was through the eyes of the young Louis Sullivan, who began his architectural career in an office [Frank Furness'] directly across the street." She also adds the surprising note that the building was "finished by Thomas U. Walter, later architect of the wings and the iron dome of the United States Capitol."

As to the skyscraper itself, it is essential to point out that there is basic disagreement among experts on what indeed constitutes a "skyscraper." Notable historians such as Montgomery Schuyler (1843–1914), Henry-Russell Hitchcock, and Winston Weisman claim that the nine-story Tribune Building of 1873–75 by Richard Morris Hunt and its contemporary the ten-story Western Union Building by George B. Post—both in New York, both fancifully turreted and both long destroyed—"may properly be considered the first skyscrapers." (Professor Weisman later favored the above-mentioned Equitable.) While both the Tribune and Western Union buildings had fireproofed metal frames and, of course, elevators, their outer walls were of load-bearing masonry. Thus Francisco Mujica, Siegfried Giedion, Carl W. Condit and Thomas E. Tallmadge feel (as does the author) that the above-mentioned New York structures were merely "elevator" or "high-rise" buildings with exterior bearing walls. They hold that a true skyscraper must have a metal cage, skeleton construction on which the exterior walls are hung independently as the building rises: in other words technical means, not feet in the air, are the definition determinants.

Initial efforts at metal-skeleton construction were both modest and evolutionary. William Le Baron Jenney (1832–1907) is generally considered the first to have designed a pure skeletal building, and is thus the genitor of the Chicago School. Jenney was both an engineer and an architect, educated at Harvard's Lawrence Scientific School and the Paris École Centrale (High Honors 1856), and was buttressed by considerable field experience in the Civil War. Moreover he knew Gustave Eiffel and the cast-iron work of Bogardus. Though his First Leiter Building of 1879 was of brick, timber beams, and cast iron, and only seven stories high, its design was almost dazzlingly anticipatory in its unadorned clarity and large windows. Hemmed in by elevated tracks, it still stands at 208 West Monroe Street. However Jenney's greatest contribution occurred a few years later when he produced the Home Insurance Building (1884–85/1891). "The first skyscraper actually erected upon modern principles of construction" (Giedion in his *Space, Time and Architecture,* Harvard University Press, 1941 et seq.). Even Russell Hitchcock writes that here "Jenney invented . . . what is specifically called 'skyscraper construction'" (*Architecture, Nineteenth and Twentieth Centuries,* Penguin, 1958). The exterior of Home Insurance, in spite of weighty appearances, was a mere curtain, supported at each floor level by the skeleton framing. Moreover it was the first to use steel beams, here for the upper floors when they came on the market (from Carnegie-Phipps in Pittsburgh) during construction. This somewhat encrusted, ten-story building (two floors were added later) has since been demolished. Though it was an esthetic retrogression from the First Leiter—let alone the Second Leiter of 1889–91 (now the Sears, Roebuck Store) and Jenney's masterpiece— the Home Insurance Building opened radically new possibilities for the skyscraper. High-rise building was subsequently taken to greater heights, literally and figuratively.

Jenney's pioneer was the opening wedge, with the climax of the Chicago School being, for many, the Reliance Building (q.v.). Amusingly, even among advocates of the metal-cage-curtain-wall in defining a skyscraper, there was once uncertainty as to whether Jenney's building was the first "true" example or whether it was Holabird and Roche's Tacoma Building, also in Chicago, of 1887. As both were taken down at the same time (1931), a panel of curious architects and engineers eagerly followed their dismantling. When they found that the Tacoma Building had "a solid masonry transverse supporting wall . . . extending its entire height" they had no hesitation in stating that "the Home Insurance Building was the first high building to utilize as the basic principle of design the method known as skeleton construction . . . We are also of the opinion that . . . the Home Insurance Building was . . . the true father of the skyscraper" (Tallmadge's *The Story of Architecture in America,* Norton, 1936). Jenney, we are told, got "his idea for skeleton construction from bamboo huts in the Philippines" (*Architectural Record,* August 1934). It is interesting to note that Graham, Anderson, Probst & White's handsome forty-three-story Field Building (1934), at LaSalle, Adams, and Clark streets, replaced the Home Insurance structure. When built it was the fourth highest in the world.

Chicago's World's Columbian Exposition of 1893 threw a classic-derived mantle on much subsequent building, but those ten to fifteen years of work of Jenney, Dankmar Adler, Daniel Burnham, William Holabird, Martin Roche, John Root, and Louis Sullivan—to name only the most prominent (none born in Illinois)—created a whole new dimension in the world of architecture. (H. H. Richardson's limited but notable work in Chicago was not concerned with the skyscraper, nor, excepting, of course, his much later mile-high proposal, was that of Frank Lloyd Wright, who had worked for several of the above architects.)

As Frederick Koeper writes in the preface of his valuable book *Illinois Architecture, A Selective Guide* (University of Chicago Press, 1968): "There is no state in the union whose history of architecture can match in total importance that of Illinois." He might well be right.

---

9   Rookery Building (1886–88/1905)
209 South LaSalle Street at Adams
Chicago, Illinois

**BURNHAM & ROOT, FRANK LLOYD WRIGHT (LOBBY),
ARCHITECTS**

The exterior of this squarish, doughty, eleven-story building (179 x 167 feet/55 x 51 meters) is nobbly and dark, but its capacious domed, skylit lobby is full of light. Measuring 71 x 62 feet/22 x 19 meters, the first renovation of this "graceful, semi-private square" (to quote the Landmarks Commission) was done by Frank Lloyd Wright in 1905, at which time were added the balcony enclosure and the touches of marble and gold leaf that make the place refulgent under his geometric lamps. The elaborate structure of the perforated I-beam trussing, indeed the whole lacy atmosphere, should not be missed. Recently it has been completely refurbished. In *The Meanings of Architecture, Buildings and Writings by John Wellborn Root,* collected by Donald Hoffman (Horizon Press, 1967), the central court is termed "An example of interior spatial organization without parallel in the architecture of the Chicago School." The building's foundations, incidentally, represent one of the first uses of crossed railroad rails embedded in concrete to form a steel grillage.

Open during office hours

---

10   The Auditorium Building (1887–89/1967)
430 South Michigan Avenue at Congress Parkway
Chicago, Illinois

ADLER & SULLIVAN, ARCHITECTS; HARRY WEESE, RESTORATION ARCHITECT

Behind this unlikely facade hides one of the finest auditoriums in the United States; Frank Lloyd Wright termed it the finest "in the world— bar none." Yet the exterior of the building is a model of homeliness and confusing scale. One expects more from Louis Sullivan, even if his client's program did call for a building to house office space, a hotel, and a theater, the first two intended to pay for most of the overhead. The load-bearing exterior, as is obvious, denies the building's largest space (the commercial rooms wrap around the auditorium), which is unfortunate but perhaps inevitable. Moreover the top six floors are almost a blatant copy of H. H. Richardson's Marshall Field Wholesale Store, built in 1885–87 and demolished in 1930. (This, seemingly without question, can be ascribed to the Auditorium's directors' admiration of the Richardson building.)

However, inside lies one of the country's most dazzling interiors.

There is a golden glow to this auditorium which visually captures festivity; aurally it rewards with acoustics which are nothing short of sensational. As Giedion wrote, it is "the finest assembly hall of its period." The design of the room, which seats as many as 4,237, was almost all Sullivan's; the ingenious engineering, flexibility (rear sections can be closed off), and acoustics were by Dankmar Adler— whose reputation for acoustics got the firm the job. The detail flanking the proscenium employs "arches" set in panels (foreshadowing Sullivan's Transportation Building of 1893) to fill the spaces between the ends of the projecting boxes and the stage and this is distracting. And it can be argued that the precise rectangle of the proscenium itself stands uncomfortable under the soft arch which embraces it, but these obliquities vanish in the overall triumph. Young Frank Lloyd Wright reputedly detailed the ornament sketched by Sullivan. In 1967 Harry Weese and his associates restored it with keen sensitivity, even down to getting matching carbon-filament bulbs. Crombie Taylor and George Izenour were key consultants. The heavy money needed for the restoration was raised by the energetic Auditorium Theater Council: Harry Weese graciously contributed his services. The offices and hotel since 1946 have been occupied by Roosevelt University.

Open during performances

11   Monadnock Building (1889–91/1893)
53 West Jackson Boulevard at Dearborn Street
Chicago, Illinois

BURNHAM & ROOT, ARCHITECTS

The Monadnock is a dinosaur among skyscrapers. It is the last of a species in that its floors are upheld not by iron or steel—as were its cohorts then rising in Chicago, including others by Burnham & Root—but by wall-bearing masonry. (The floors themselves, however, carry steel beams.) Its client, apparently, distrusted the longevity potential of steel columns, though this is what the architects originally proposed. It might be pertinent to quote here *The New Columbia Encyclopedia* (Columbia University Press, 1975) and its definition of Monadnock, which is a mountain in New Hampshire: "The peak lends its name to the geomorphic term *monadnock,* an isolated mountain remnant standing above the general level of the land because of its greater resistance to erosion." Thus the Monadnock's sixteen-story-high outer walls are

enormously thick at street level (6.3 feet/1.9 meters) to support a
load which could easily have been carried on fireproofed metal columns of considerably less square footage. Burnham & Root did their
best to lighten this bulk visually by creating a lively oscillation of windows and bays, and by keeping to a pared simplicity (also the client's
wish); in this they succeeded with aplomb. It is one of the first major
buildings in this country to eschew all ornamentation: its smooth
flanks are totally free of embellishment. The elegance and finesse of its
brickwork—many special molds were employed—and its flared base
find imitators even today. Note the champfered corners and details of
the projecting bay windows. When completed it was the tallest office
building in Chicago and the largest office block in the world. The south
half of the building was added (using steel) in 1893 by Holabird &
Roche. Its interior was remodeled in 1938 by Skidmore, Owings &
Merrill.

Lobby open during business hours

---

12   Museum of Science and Industry (1893/1933–40)
57th Street and South Lake Shore Drive
Chicago, Illinois

D. H. BURNHAM & CO., ARCHITECTS

Chicago's famous World's Columbian Exposition of 1893 was the most
momentous Fair ever held in the Americas. Not only was that gleaming
White City of overwhelming beauty to most of its viewers (but not all
of its critics) by day, it was magically illuminated at night—the first
time buildings of such scale had been floodlit. Moreover the Fair's
mostly "Roman" stage-set gave an imprimatur to neo-Classical architecture which thereafter was a decisive factor in shaping a large share
of the "official" buildings (and banks) throughout the United States.
A Classical influence continued for more than the fifty years which
Louis Sullivan mournfully predicted. Though the Fair's other buildings
and most of its lagoon by Frederick L. Olmsted are long gone, the Palace of Fine Arts, designed by Charles B. Atwood in Burnham's firm, is
still with us. It is important, and surprising, to note that the Fine Arts
building "was not constructed as a temporary structure; the main walls
are of solid brick and perfectly sound, and the foundations of brick
and concrete and the entire structural features are [today] in good
condition" (*Architectural Forum,* July 1921).

Chicago's former Palace was initially used after the Fair as a natural history museum with much of its collection coming from the Fair itself. It was first known as the Field Columbian Museum, then the Field Museum of Natural History. However when the present Field Museum in Grant Park was completed in 1920, Graham, Anderson, Probst & White, architects, the old Palace was deserted. In 1921 Julius Rosenwald, who earlier had been deeply impressed by Munich's Deutsches Museum—the greatest technical museum in the world—offered to contribute $1 million if the city would establish a similar institution. Though this was not acted upon, it seemingly planted a seed, for on June 9, 1922, the American Institute of Architects staged a banquet in the great 1893 Rotunda to focus public attention on saving the building. In 1925 a substantial bond issue was passed to rehabilitate (with a museum in mind) Chicago's only relic of its famous Fair, and the next year the ever-generous Mr. Rosenwald offered $3 million if the city would make it a museum of science and industry. (He later doubled his gift.)

This largesse was, of course, welcomed and the long-term process of reconditioning and planning begun, the museum opening in the spring of 1933 for Chicago's Century of Progress Exposition. It was not until 1940, however, that all of the interior and its installations were completed. Today probably the Museum's only rival in fascination of ex-

hibits is its famous inspiration in Germany. The architects for rehabilitating the exterior of this Athenian-inspired Classic Revival example
were Graham, Anderson, Probst & White, with Shaw, Naess & Murphy
responsible for the interior. Whether, as claimed of the original, the
building constituted "a result unequalled since the days of Pericles"
seems moot, but at least we have one of America's most fascinating
museums and a souvenir of the country's most famous Fair.

Open Memorial Day–Labor Day, daily 9:30–5:30; rest of year,
Mon.–Fri. 9:30–4, Sat.–Sun. and holidays 9:30–5:30

---

13   The Chicago Public Library Cultural Center (1893–97/1974–77)
Michigan Avenue between Washington and Randolph Streets
Chicago, Illinois

SHEPLEY, RUTAN & COOLIDGE, ARCHITECTS

The five-story exterior of the former Central Library, now library and
cultural center, fits into a reasonable if unexciting Beaux Arts mold.

The current brochure, in quoting the 1892 *Instructions to Architects* (five firms were interviewed), says that "A classical order of architecture without dome and tower is to be employed, and it is to be executed in granite or Bedford bluestone." (It should be kept in mind that Shepley, Rutan & Coolidge's Art Institute was being finished [1892] just down the street, and that Chicago's famous neo-Classic world's fair was to open the following year.) But if the Cultural Center's exterior is pedestrian, the main entrance off Washington Street is one of the city's highlights. The curves of its Carrara marble main stair take one to the scintillating Preston Bradley Hall on the third floor, a room whose mosaics are probably not equaled this side of Isphahan. Originally designed by Robert Spencer of the architectural firm, the mosaics were executed by Louis Comfort Tiffany, who was also responsible for the fine dome. Bradley Hall, which formerly housed the Humanities Department, is today actively used for concerts and civic functions. With the help of City Architect Jerome R. Butler, Jr., and historian Ira J. Bach, the building was fully restored and updated mechanically by Holabird & Root (1974–77), with C. H. Carlson restoration designer. It was then rededicated as the Public Library Cultural Center. The building rests, incidentally, on 2,375 piles driven into Chicago's unstable soil.

Open Mon.–Thurs. 10–8, Fri. 10–6, Sat. 10–5, Sun. 1–5: tours Thurs. 11 A.M. *and 1* P.M., *Sun. 1* P.M., *except holidays*

---

14   Reliance Building (1890–91/1894–95)
32 North State Street at Washington
Chicago, Illinois

BURNHAM & ROOT AND D. H. BURNHAM & CO., ARCHITECTS

The cluster of new skyscrapers on nearby Dearborn Street, several of which can be seen behind the Reliance Building, are lineal descendants of this fourteen-story, last-century masterpiece. The Reliance, many feel, is the most advanced skyscraper of The Chicago School. In it we find skeletal steel construction with internal wind bracing, prodigious panes of glass, curtain walling (here a narrow band of glazed terra-cotta, reputedly its first high-rise use)—all prototypes of the new technology. The Reliance epitomizes steel-skeleton, glass-skin more than any of its contemporaries. In addition, it refined the bay window

treatment of earlier high-rises, all seeking light on narrow streets. Glass here forms a wall, not a hole in a wall, and as a consequence it rises with a refined lightness which its more masonry-freighted friends could not match. As Giedion points out in his *Space, Time and Architecture* (Harvard University Press, 1967 edition), the Reliance Building was a direct precursor of Mies van der Rohe's 1920–21 project for an all-glass-sheathed, thirty-story skyscraper.

The building had a curious construction history which is told by Donald Hoffman in his informative book *The Architecture of John Wellborn Root* (Johns Hopkins University Press, 1973). The site of the Reliance Building (including a previous structure) had been purchased in 1882 by a developer who wished to put up a high-rise (fifteen to sixteen stories) office block, but the lease of the ground floor and basement did not run out until May 1890, while that of the upper three (originally four) continued until 1894. Burnham & Root waited until 1890 and then cranked up the top three floors, laid a new spread foundation, constructed upon it a glass-lined shop and mezzanine—taken by Carson, Pirie & Scott—and established a full-service basement. In January 1891 young John Root died—he was forty-one. Moreover his design for the remainder of the building has never been discovered. The distressed Burnham, after consulting friends, took on the Massachusetts-born, Harvard-educated Charles B. Atwood. Early in 1894 Atwood—soon to become the design partner of the firm—produced the drawings for the thirteen floors to go atop the new base, and when the lease of the old floors was up that May they were removed and the tower we now see was erected. The steel was topped out on August 1, 1894, at exactly 200 feet/61 meters, having taken only eighteen days to complete. (Atwood made substantial contributions to the 1893 World's Columbian Exposition of which Burnham was Director of Works. This brilliant, too-little-known architect also died young—at forty-seven.)

The structural plan of the Reliance is unusual in that its supporting column grid is not uniformly aligned to form square bays, and though columns frame each of the three projecting or oriel bays per floor (that in front slightly wider than the two on the side), this is not indicated on the exterior. The lower floor has since been remodeled, and in 1963 the cornice was removed for safety reasons. The Reliance's white terracotta is perhaps fussily detailed, its windows are sullied today by glaring signs, and fire escapes obscure its prismatic clarity, but this ninety-year-old veteran is still one of our very greatest pioneers.

Lobby open during business hours

---

15   Frank Lloyd Wright Home and Studio (1889–95/1898)
951 Chicago Avenue at Forest Avenue
(Take IS 290 from downtown, Harlem Avenue exit N)
Chicago (Oak Park), Illinois

FRANK LLOYD WRIGHT, ARCHITECT

Mr. Wright was twenty-two years old when he designed his own first house, and, somewhat like Jefferson at Monticello, he evolved an oft-changed "laboratory" domicile. The result of expansion and experimentation—the expansion occasioned by the need to accommodate a family which eventually included six children, and then the need for a studio—ended with a house of little purity of design but one with instructive evolution. (Compare Wright's beautifully composed Winslow House of 1893.) Architecturally, the studio, which was added several years after the dwelling was started, is the more interesting and certainly the more prophetic part. The house was designed while Wright

was working with Adler and Sullivan, and shows, as might be expected, some cautiously historic influences from them. (Note the prominently triangular Queen Anne gable.) Changes were made through the decades (some by Wright as late as 1956), and in 1974 acquisition of the property was jointly funded by the National Trust for Historic Preservation, which holds title, and the Frank Lloyd Wright Home and Studio Foundation, which leases, operates, and is restoring the property. Intriguing for the specialist.

Open Tues., Thurs. 1–2:30, Sat.–Sun. 1–4, except holidays: admission

The Oak Park Tour Center, 158 North Forest Avenue (between Lake Street and Ontario), conducts guided tours of the **Frank Lloyd Wright National Historic District.** The Center is open Mar.–Nov., daily 10–5: admission for tours. Telephone: (312) 848-1978. Recommended.

16 Carson, Pirie, Scott Store (1899/1903–4)
State Street at Madison
Chicago, Illinois

LOUIS H. SULLIVAN, ARCHITECT

In addition to the balloon frame, the skyscraper, and Wright's open-plan "Prairie Houses," Chicago gave the world a special kind of window, "the Chicago window." This consists of an enormous fixed crystal pane in the center and smaller, double-hung sash for ventilation on one or both sides (note the bowed ones in the Reliance Building, q.v.). No enterprise could employ these windows to greater advantage at the time of their development than a department store, and the great Sullivan here used glass to maximum advantage. Today's fluorescent lighting and year-round air conditioning have transformed mercantile emporia into windowless boxes, except for the ground-floor showcases, but at the turn of the last century Carson's achieved a fenestrational grandeur (while directly reflecting the structural frame) which has never been equaled. State Street carries one of architecture's most important walls.

To give relief to the building's basic plainness, and to entice customers into the corner front door, Sullivan traced out, and George G. Elmslie detailed, a filigree of incredible cast-iron ornament—"coiling thickets of iron ribbons" (Scully)—which traces along the lower two floors and blossoms at the entry. Take a long look at this entrance ornament: the world is not apt to see such inventiveness and such craftsmanship again. The rounded corner of the store (insisted upon by the owners) ill-adjusts in the upper levels, and the building's profile is not the most svelte, but in taking the window wall to exquisite proportions and in developing an ornament of legendary skill, Sullivan rose to scintillating heights.

The building, which was originally the Schlesinger and Mayer Department Store, started (1899) under Sullivan as the three-bay, nine-story unit to the east (nearest the lake) on Madison Street; then in 1903–4 Sullivan designed the twelve-story addition attached to this, adding three more bays along Madison, the rounded corner, and seven bays on State, while D. H. Burnham & Company added a matching extension on State Street in 1906. There were later additions and alterations, but the great contribution lies in the Sullivan facade and the entry at northwest corner.

In late 1979 the City completed the State Street Mall in front of Carson's and other important stores. This nine-block landscaped

"Great Street" is limited to buses and emergency vehicles and includes ample bus shelters and subway access. It is hoped that it will also spark redevelopment of the side streets as well.

Open during business hours

---

17 Unity Temple—The Universalist Church (1906–8)
875 Lake Street at Kenilworth Avenue (Take IS 290 from
   downtown, Harlem Avenue exit N to Mall Parking)
Chicago (Oak Park), Illinois

FRANK LLOYD WRIGHT, ARCHITECT

Throughout the nineteenth century in both the United States and Europe, Christian religious architecture in the main was strangely content to dust off past historical styles (as, of course, were most building

types). The greatest periods of church building—Early Christian, Byzantine, Romanesque, Gothic, Renaissance, and our own Colonial, to name only the most obvious—had always looked forward. The Gothic age especially exhibited a fierce ambition to build higher and more boldly with each new cathedral. (It was, of course, named for wild men, the Goths.) Against the eclectic stagnation of the nineteenth and early twentieth centuries a monumental shock arose when Wright, near the beginning of this century, evolved this Unitarian-Universalist Church with almost no historical reference—and very little money ($45,000!). To the specialist there is a hint of the Mayan, or even Egyptian—which is fascinatingly reflected around the entry of Walter Gropius' 1914 "Werkbund" Exhibition Building in Cologne—but Unity Temple itself shows little stylistic reminiscing. The walls of solid concrete—"the first concrete monolith in the world" (FLW)—and the high, smallish windows materialized from Wright's desire to screen out disturbances from the church's busy corner with its streetcars. The economy of concrete—until then almost never so frankly used in a "dignified" building—was also a factor. (See Flagler College, 1888, in St. Augustine, Florida.)

The church is divided into two conjoined units, the 64-foot/20-meter-square worship room (most prominent from Lake Street), and a rectangular parish house, both being entered via a low nexus off Kenilworth. As one approaches the entry there develops that spatial involvement generally found in penetrating Wright's buildings, here with both ambiguities (as to which section is which), and excitements (at the multilevel interaction). Once hesitancy has been resolved and one turns left to the church proper, another cunning manipulation of spaces begins, for one enters behind the chancel at a half-level below the nave floor via a "cloister," or ambulatory, which allows glimpses of the auditorium, while permitting latecomers to enter without disturbing others. The church room itself, though intimate in feeling (it seats four hundred), attains, however, a strangely monumental quality with pews in the central and squared floor area framed on three sides by two levels of alcoves. This produces both liturgical closeness and a stage-like emphasis on the sanctuary, a theatrical effect intensified by the fact that most of the daylight floods down from amber-colored roof skylights (with the artificial lights placed behind them). The resulting room is probably the first in centuries to establish a totally fresh church interior. Whether it conjures a religious ambience depends upon what one brings to it, remembering that the church is a Unitarian house of worship. Architecturally the auditorium reveals, and revels in, a sequential family of squares from its overall plan, down to its light-ing fixtures, and to its surprisingly Mondrianesque treatment of the glass in the roof monitors. Some find too much visual restlessness in this treatment and the restored (1961) colors too strong; others might object to the fact that a large proportion of the congregation is relegated to balcony seats. Still Unity Temple represents a monumental step in architecture in the United States and in religious architecture of the twentieth century. Money, however, is sorely needed for its upkeep, indeed its preservation.

Note: The Frank Lloyd Wright Home and Studio (q.v.) is not far distant.

Open Tues., Thurs., Fri. noon–3; advisable to telephone (312) 848-7123: donation. Services Sun. morning. A taped tour is available

---

18   The Frederick C. Robie House (1908–10)
The University of Chicago
5757 South Woodlawn Avenue at 58th Street
Chicago, Illinois

FRANK LLOYD WRIGHT, ARCHITECT

In the history of twentieth-century domestic architecture there are two houses which are of transcending importance: the Robie House in Chicago and the Villa Savoye (1927–31), some 17 miles/27 kilome-ters west of Paris, by Le Corbusier, the Swiss-French architect. Both

have been snatched from imminent destruction and both pioneered directions in domestic shelter which subsequently changed the shape of many of the world's dwellings. The Robie House's immortality—a word not casually used—lies in the fact that it, and the others by Wright that led up to this climax, transformed the typical house plan comprising a cluster of boxlike rooms into a free-flowing series of interrelated spaces. The major rooms have their identity, but it is a shared identity which extends a hand to the next room: space becomes a continuum, not a closet. This "liberation" of the plan, this demolition of the box cincture, the "cellular sequestration" as Wright called it, is today a constituent concept in the planning of even our "tract" houses, but in the early part of this century, house-planning was an uptight affair, and it was every room for itself.

Mr. Wright also epitomized in the exterior of the Robie House a concept which he had been nurturing for years but had hitherto been unable to express so fully. He tied the house to the land so that it rises as an extension of the plain, a house in strict league with its setting. (His first client house, the Winslow of 1893, hints of this.) This partnership of man and land was always with Wright: its most spectacular manifestation leapt a waterfall—see Fallingwater, Ohiopyle, Pennsylvania. The "binding to the soil" process of the Robie House was accomplished by boldly cantilevered roof lines of sharp eaves (whose steel-braced extensions were calculated to admit low winter sun, but not the high and hot sun of summer), and by unbroken horizontal bands of brick alternating with continuous strips of windows. (The "window wall" across the front of the living room and dining room is 56 feet/17 meters long!) Note the finesse with which these broadly etched bands and walls of brick "slow down" and develop their ends with a series of stabilizing shapes—reminding one of the velocity diminution of the figures of the Parthenon frieze as they approach the corners. The low outer wall marking, indeed nudging, the property line, and the shadow-casting balcony over the billiard room and children's playroom on the lower level accent this horizontality. The stretched hipped roof planes cap all, and with their cross-axis establish subtle tensions.

The entrance to the house, like so many of Wright's, is convoluted: one does not know the first time whether one will end up above or below.

Once inside, however, the sequence of spaces commences. They are liberated outward via the window wall (whose sash head is near ceiling height), and they jog upward in the angled ceiling planes. The focus of the living room—a half-flight above ground (cf. the Villa Savoye)—is the large fireplace that acts as semidivider between it and the dining room, making the seating arena around the fire a semicirculation area —hence somewhat restless—but creating a masterful flow laterally. (Note that one can "see through" the top of the fireplace into the dining room.) The bedrooms on the upper floor are routine, but there is nothing routine on the two lower floors.

Wright stunned the world with the Robie House: domestic architecture was never again the same. *Chicago's Famous Buildings,* edited by Arthur Siegel (University of Chicago Press, 1969), says of it that it is "one of the most brilliant designs in the history of architecture." The building has been sympathetically remodeled (1968) for university purposes by J. Lee Jones and Skidmore, Owings & Merrill.

Closed to public except via arrangements of Office of Special
Events: telephone (312) 753-4429. Much can be seen from street

19   Carl Schurz High School (1907–10)
3601 North Milwaukee Avenue at West Addison Street
Chicago, Illinois

DWIGHT H. PERKINS, ARCHITECT

Assured and dignified and with a fine assortment of angles and planes, the Carl Schurz School possesses a character which time has not eroded. A slight influence from Berlage and the Dutch brick tradition (even Lutyens) can be felt, but the Tennessee-born, MIT-educated Mr. Perkins states his solution of massing and of imaginative detail with confidence and skill. Most of the architect's professional life was concerned with school design with a strong input of the philosophy of John Dewey and "education as a tool." Although formalism can be seen here, particularly in plan, those interested in early-twentieth-century architectural developments will certainly want to see this Carl Schurz School. Originally designed as a technical high school, the building underwent several changes and additions through the years.

Lobby open during school hours

20   The Wrigley Building and Neighbors
all visible from Michigan Avenue Bridge
Chicago, Illinois

ARCHITECTS AS NOTED

The Michigan Avenue Bridge affords a vantage point in a meeting of
sky, water, and building that encompasses much of the excitement of
downtown Chicago. Louis Jolliet and Père Marquette, the first Europeans to explore the region, landed at the nearby mouth of the
Chicago River in September 1673, as the bridge plaque proclaims.
Fort Dearborn was erected on this spot in 1803 and its outlines are

thoughtfully traced in today's concrete and asphalt. Similarly, in the surrounding skyscrapers one can discern much of the evolution of the building form which Chicago gave the world.

From the engineering standpoint—always advanced in this city—it is pertinent to point out that the very direction of the river under the bascule-type bridge was reversed in flow by constructing (1892–1900) a 28-mile/45-kilometer-long Drainage Canal that carries river and its pollution away from the lake, not into it. Moreover beneath bridge and buildings near the river there extends an entirely different stratum of service streets and rail spurs—proposed for much of the city (mostly for freight) in the famous Burnham Plan of 1909. This should be seen for the lesson it gives in traffic classification. Would that all cities (including the rest of downtown Chicago) had such separation. Burnham's suggestion was no doubt inspired by the fact that in 1855–60 most of the downtown area was raised 7–12 feet/2.1–3.6 meters to lift it higher above the lake level—an act of extraordinary municipal boldness.

The buildings observed from the bridge begin, reading from left to right, with the thirty-four-story **Wrigley,** 400 North Michigan (1921, addition 1924), by Graham, Anderson, Probst & White. It is among the elite of the terra-cotta school which mantled much building, especially skyscrapers, in the earlier part of the century and was the first tall building to be floodlit at night. An influence of New York's Woolworth Building (q.v.) can be seen in its design. The **Tribune Tower's** (q.v.) Gothic aspiration, 435 North Michigan (1925), by John Mead Howells and Raymond Hood, stands across the avenue. Shining in the background to right rises Harry Weese's bright **Time-Life Building** (1970), East Ohio and Grand Avenue, while nearer at hand the **Equitable Building,** 401 North Michigan (1965), Skidmore, Owings & Merrill and Alfred Shaw & Associates, architects, offers high-level design while its plaza, Pioneer Court, unfolds a refreshing open space leading down to the river. On the south side of the bridge, diagonally across from the Wrigley, stands **#1 Illinois Center** (1971), one of the last works of Mies van der Rohe, its minutely detailed brown steel and dark glass presenting a contrast of classic sobriety to its neighbors. Altogether an instructive mixture of building types, unexpected spaces, constant but amiable activity of vehicles and pedestrians, plus the sparkling waters of the river and its sometime traffic.

Open during business hours

21   The Tribune Tower (1923–25)
435 North Michigan Avenue
Chicago, Illinois

JOHN MEAD HOWELLS AND RAYMOND HOOD, ARCHITECTS

For "the most beautiful office building in the world," the Chicago *Tribune* staged the most famous international architectural competition (1922) ever held in the United States. Not only were there 223 entries from 23 countries, but in many respects it marked a turning point in America's architectural outlook. As the *Tribune* itself proclaimed in assessing the entries, the designs submitted "may be considered an encyclopedia of the architecture of the skyscraper."

Howells and Hood's prize-winning eclecticism occasioned doubts when contrasted with many of the more advanced entries from Europe, especially the design of Eliel Saarinen from Finland which won second prize. There were many who thought that his project should have placed first, and Saarinen's "non-historic" design versus the "Gothic-

inspired" winner had a strong influence on many younger architects, including, it might be fairly hypothesized, Ray Hood, the co-winner. Louis Sullivan, with his well-known foresight, wrote in reviewing the competition winners that "The Finnish master-edifice is not a lonely cry in the wilderness, it is a voice, resonant and rich, ringing amidst the wealth and joy of life. In utterance sublime and melodious, it prophesies a time to come, and not so far away, when the wretched and the yearning, the sordid and the fierce, shall escape the bondage and mania of fixed ideas" (*Architectural Record,* February 1923). Perhaps equally important for the development of architecture in this country, the competition brought Eliel Saarinen (1873–1950) and his son Eero (1911–61) to the United States, where the latter's short-lived genius bequeathed us many of our most stimulating structures. (See Index.)

None of the above background seeks to deny virtue in the Howells-Hood design, for it is a very clever building even if the rationale of using a steel frame in a medieval stonemason's garb seems oblique. Its strength lies not in its Tour de Beurre (A.D. 1485) remembrances of profile nor in the "Gothic" drapery (cf. the Woolworth Building) of top and base. Much of its neglected contribution can be seen in the wraparound "oneness" of its main shaft (not the adjuncts), a three-dimensional design concern which is finding imitators today. Important, too, are the rhythmic pier-and-mullion variations which lend a briskness to its limestone and glass exterior which most contemporary skyscraper fenestration simply does not possess. It is not irrelevant to note that Raymond Hood was subsequently one of the chief designers of the RCA Building in New York's Rockefeller Center (q.v.), whose fenestration and pier pattern were possibly foreshadowed here.

Lobby open during office hours

---

22 Playboy Building (1928–29)
919 North Michigan Avenue at Walton Street
Chicago, Illinois

HOLABIRD & ROOT, ARCHITECTS

In the late 1920s and early 1930s, Holabird & Roche (Holabird & Root after 1927) with Graham, Anderson, Probst & White were pioneers in developing what might be termed the proto-modern skyscraper. Their symmetrically stepped, high-rise buildings, generally

clad in Indiana limestone and basically bereft of historical detail, were, and are, outstanding contributions of their time. (Their "stepped profile" reflected zoning then in effect. Elements of Art Deco can be seen in their modest decoration.) Possibly Holabird & Root's finest example is the thirty-seven-story Playboy (ex-Palmolive) Building, whose carefully built up setbacks and bay expressions help punctuate the north end of Michigan Avenue. As the *Architectural Forum* wrote, "The main structure, buttressed in a manner suggestive of pyramidical completeness, attains great individual distinction in the soaring verticals of the central mass" (May 1930).

Farther south along Michigan Avenue, just across the Chicago River, stands the **333 North Michigan Building,** by Holabird & Roche (1928). Of the same genre as the Playboy Building, its thirty-five floors are more commandingly sited and more fully visible since the Playboy has been hemmed in by recent construction. Measuring 62 x 200 feet/19 x 61 meters, 333 splendidly dominates its Michigan Avenue axial site. It is revetted with shot-sawn limestone.

Lobby open during business hours

23   Mies van der Rohe (1886–1969)—His Chicago Contribution

As has been remarked earlier, the late maestro from Aachen—who dropped formal schooling when fifteen—probably influenced the development of more of the world's architecture than any man since Andrea Palladio (1508–80). This influence was especially strong in Chicago where Mies lived, taught, and practiced for the last thirty years of his life. If the Swiss-French Le Corbusier was this century's poet-architect, Mies—Corbusier's virtually precise contemporary (he was born a year later)—was the Cartesian rationalist. For him the building was an end in itself, a precious, almost religious object of fantastic precision with an identity only a little troubled by climate or, occasionally, even occupants. It was an approach to architecture of consummate, even ruthless dedication, a purification rite which twentieth-century *Baukunst,* the art of building, much needed following World War I. It was, as Mies put it, "architecture for a technological society." In stressing the science of the art-science syndrome which makes up architecture, such driving consistency can generate problems, and not all of Mies' work will offer refreshment. But when, as often, conditions and construction are propitious the results can be almost spiritual. (Mies' lack of what might be termed "social concern" is in pointed contrast to that other great pioneer of the Modern Movement, the late Alvar Aalto.) Parodied endlessly by lesser practitioners, Mies perhaps even boxed himself in as his buildings got taller and wider and grouped together. Because of an evolutionary approach to "universalize" design (Jordy), particularly high-rise, it might be said that his work gains immeasurably when set next to buildings by others, but tends to some desiccation when self-multiplied. To paraphrase, more (clusters of his buildings) can possibly become less.

Mies van der Rohe's first great building (following several prophetic projects) was the German Pavilion at the 1929 Barcelona Fair. This was a low structure of such flow of space and such elegance that it alone was the exhibition "material," and to have designed only this would rank him among the greatest. This glorious work—glorious to judge from photographs and its plan, for it was taken down when the exhibition closed—opened the eyes of the world of architecture by the quiet dynamism of its interwoven, counterpointed spaces (cf. Frank Lloyd Wright's Robie House) and by its freestanding walls—now mere area definers. There was a total separation of support, that is structure, from enclosure. (Moreover it was for the Barcelona Pavilion that Mies designed his still-famous and still-produced Barcelona Chair. Though this is the most elegant chair of our time it should be mentioned that it is a structural tour de force, its bending moment being taken by the vertical juncture of two Vs, one of the legs, the other of back and seat.)

On settling in the United States in 1938 at the age of fifty-two Mies puzzlingly abandoned his exploratory probing and yearning for an indoor-outdoor continuum of space as seen in his country-house projects of the early 1920s and in the Barcelona Pavilion. Instead he concentrated on form, in effect a "box," and the "box" characterizes virtually all of his later work. Instead of projecting outward to tie the interior to infinity, Mies wrapped up and packaged space, and the exquisite tidiness of this packaging and its "fanaticism for pure form" (Giedion) brought him, again, everlasting fame. Moreover being a prophet of technology, he concentrated on steel and glass—the materials that epitomize our time—and with only a few exceptions the post-World War II buildings by Mies have been of steel, dark steel (or bronze), and since the Seagram Building in New York (q.v.), with dark glass between. The result is characterized by a somberness, but an undying, if at times repetitive, classic somberness, always rectangular, always symmetrical, always of dignity, unsurpassed *clarity* and impeccable detail. L. Hilberseimer, a sometimes Mies associate, goes so far as to write, "Mies van der Rohe thinks the structure of a building more important than its use. Use may change, he argues, but the structure remains" (*Contemporary Architecture,* Paul Theobald, 1964). Or as Professor James Ackerman put it, in describing Palladio, "The essential factor is a sense of order" (*Palladio,* Penguin, 1966).

To keep his masses from being too ponderous, Mies almost always elevated them on stilts or inset the entry level, "detaching" the building, so to speak, so that it could more graciously meet the ground. When he did not do this (Memorial Hall in Des Moines for example), the effect is almost a dark, uninviting wall. Moreover since Crown Hall (q.v.) of 1956—an electrifying design which revels in exposing four enormous roof trusses—Mies showed little interest in expressing structure other than the exposed columns of the inset ground floor. Construction was his obsession but revelation of structure is rarely seen. (It is pertinent to observe that in his famous all-glass-wrapped skyscraper projects of 1921 and 1922 the plans contain no hint of supporting columns.) Even in the enormous bulk of the Federal Center (q.v.) there is in the facade no expression (except at ground level) of columns, hence bay size. In this regard it is instructive to contrast the Mies-inspired Daley Center (q.v.) down Dearborn Street where Jacques Brownson, the Center's chief designer (and a former student of Mies), made a tremendously effective exterior expression of structural organization and support.

Only a cross section of Mies van der Rohe's Chicago buildings can be shown here (several admirable local architectural guidebooks are available). Still they are enough to demonstrate vividly that this city, whose vitality and daring in effect created "modern" architecture almost a hundred years ago—its architects in close association with its engineers—has been enormously enriched by the genius from Germany. He rationalized architecture, he epitomized steel in construction, and in many of his works he rose to heights unmatched in our time. Praise be that the United States recognized his talents and gave him ample opportunities. What he gave in return is part of our imperishable legacy. As Arthur Drexler succinctly wrote, "With Mies architecture leaves childhood behind" (*Ludwig Mies van der Rohe,* George Braziller, 1960).

24   **860 Lake Shore Drive Apartments** (1948–51)
860–880 Lake Shore Drive between Chestnut Street and Delaware Place
Chicago, Illinois

MIES VAN DER ROHE, ARCHITECT

Mies' first buildings to excite the American scene—which had been alerted by the earlier units of the IIT campus (q.v.) and the concrete Promontory Apartments (1946–49)—was this conjoined group of two twenty-six-story apartment buildings overlooking Lake Michigan. Identical in form (though the south building contains only six-room apartments and the north three and a half) these two three-by-five bay apartments stand at right angles to each other, carefully offset by one bay, with a flat column-free canopy connecting them. In plan they measure 64.9 x 106.9 feet/19.7 x 32.5 meters: Lake Shore Drive angles in front. The framing is of steel, with poured concrete floors and concrete used for fireproofing the skeleton, while steel cover plates encase the concrete and were used for part of its formwork. Steel "wall-frames" of combined mullions and spandrels were prefabricated and lowered into place, while the light-colored aluminum window frames were installed from within.

The buildings have been criticized in that the mullions (the vertical steel window dividers) also appear on the columns, where, of course, they are not structural. Mies explained these "rhetorical I-beams" (Venturi) as necessary to maintain "the rhythm which the mullions set up," and also to stiffen the steel plates covering the other face of con-

crete fireproofing. Rationalized or not, the result is a stunning pair of buildings. (Note that in order to maintain the constant 5.25 feet/1.6 meters on center of mullion spacing, the two end windows of each bay are slightly narrower than the two center ones.)

The twin blocks' exterior airiness comes from their being elevated above largely open ground floors through which the sun streams and confinement evaporates. Their dark, impeccably understated elegance —"monastic severity"—carries on above. (The penthouse treatment for the water tanks is, however, not satisfactory.)

From within, the lobbies are classic entries, while the apartments themselves, with windows from ceiling to within a few inches of the floor, form heady accommodations. The exterior curtains are all the same beige color to maintain harmony from without, but the tenants, who own their apartments, can hang inner curtains if desired. (Since the building became a condominium upkeep has lapsed.) Air conditioning should have been installed initially—the recent individual units are not coordinated—and there might have been another elevator per building. But so sought after have the apartments become, that anyone fortunate enough to have had one when the buildings were first opened could now sell it at considerable profit. PACE Associates, and Holsman, Klekamp & Taylor were associate architects.

It is illuminating to compare 860–880 Lake Shore Drive with the adjacent Esplanade Apartments at 900, also by Mies, but completed five years later (1956). The newer buildings are even more refined in detail (note window treatment), have central air conditioning and more facilities, but the use of dark plate glass (for sun control) and the dark window framing tend to sap the vitality of their facades.

Lobbies only open to public

---

25   S. R. Crown Hall (1955–56)
Illinois Institute of Technology
South State Street at 34th
Chicago, Illinois

MIES VAN DER ROHE, ARCHITECT

Crown Hall represents an ultimate in steel construction, the most keenly honed ferric exercise that will be seen today, or even tomorrow. It is, thus, a procreant building in the development of contempoary architecture, a building with an exhilaration of its large-scale inner space that is matched by the small-scale meticulousness of its detailing. When Mies said that "God is in the Details," and "Simplicity is not Simple," he must have had Crown Hall foremost in mind. (The statement "Less is More" is attributed to Peter Behrens.) The building, the design of which began in 1950, comprises only one vast, transparent, upper enclosure which rests 6 feet/1.8 meters above grade on a semiraised basement containing classrooms, workshops, and services. The major room is completely wrapped in glass, clear in the top part, translucent below. Note that the framed height of the translucent section when added to that of the lower window (in basement) exactly equals the dimension of the clear glass above. The steel-framed concrete roof of this great rectangular structure, which measures 120 x 220 feet/37 x 67 meters, is hung externally from four mammoth plate-girder trusses 120 feet/37 meters long, 6.3 feet/1.9 meters deep, and 60 feet/18 meters on center, with a 20-foot/6.1-meter cantilever at each end. This completely eliminates the need for interior columns—and thus achieves Mies' total universal space. Peripheral I-beam mullions and the supports for the trusses occur every 10 feet/3 meters. It is a totally explicit assertion of structure. As the building has only one main floor

above ground, there was no need for fireproofing the steel (as at 860 Lake Shore Drive, etc.); it is thus the material's ultimate expression.

The interior, being liberated of supports (there are two utility ducts), is unobtrusively subdivided into exhibition space (at main entrance), drafting rooms (on either side), and administration (behind central area), with 8-foot/2.4-meter-high movable oak partitions creating an undulation of space beneath the 18-foot/5.5-meter-high ceiling. This space mates with the lateral limitlessness of the glass exterior walls. The sweep which results is visually incomparable—and pedagogically stimulates interchange between the older and younger architectural students. On the debit side, noise transmission can be a nuisance at times; when the rear door in the administration area is opened the sweep of winter's drafts is uncontrolled in the Windy City, and the acoustic ceiling, venting, and lighting are not distinguished (largely because of economics). But walk up those twelve exquisitely tensioned travertine steps (whose tread separations lend weightlessness to the whole), pause to take in the detail of steel on steel (note ventilators), and steel meeting glass, then step into this chamber of transparency and you will have encountered one of our greatest buildings. PACE Associates were associate architects.

Two years after his first arrival in the States, Mies was also asked to plan the complete **IIT Campus** (in 1939—31st–35th streets, along State Street. Ludwig Hilberseimer, a Bauhaus associate of Mies, helped with this). In addition to Crown Hall Mies was responsible for many of the other buildings, the early ones generally with steel frame and yellow brick walls. Incidentally, the first sketches for Crown were in this same mold: an on-the-ground, internally columned affair with little of the exaltation of the present building. The campus itself is too rigid, too hierarchically static for many observers (it cries for a vertical accent, a rallying point) and architecturally too much of a oneness (a 24-foot/7.3-meter module runs throughout except for the 10-foot/3-meter one used at Crown). This is, however, one of the most coordinated groups of buildings in the country—and there are certainly spots of interbuilding brilliance. As for Crown Hall itself, "Not since the Gothic has there been such clarity of expression"—Philip Johnson (*Architectural Record,* July 1956).

Tour of campus Sept.–May, Sat. at 10 A.M.: *exhibition area of Crown Hall open during school hours*

---

26   Marina City (1960–62)
300 North State Street at Chicago River
Chicago, Illinois

BERTRAND GOLDBERG ASSOCIATES, ARCHITECTS

The observer of these two fantastic towers will certainly be impressed by their appearance. But even more important is the architect's acute analysis of the specific problem—and even the future of the metropolis. Bertrand Goldberg writes, "We cannot burden business buildings used 35 hours a week or apartment buildings used at night and over weekends with our total tax loads. We can no longer subsidize the single shift use of our expensive city utilities. In our cities within cities we shall turn our streets up into the air, and stack the daytime and nighttime uses of our land. We shall plan for two shifts within cities, where the fixed costs of operating a city can be shared by commerce, recreation and education at the lower levels . . . and by housing above. As we spread taxes and other expenses over shared uses, we help diminish the traffic problem caused by the trip to work. Our specialists living and working in the same building complex need only vertical trans-

portation" (*Architectural Record,* September 1963). Thus the concept and design of Marina City began with the time clock ticking off occupancy hours and the tax burden applied to multiple use, aspects which too few architects and developers consider.

Goldberg has, of course, arrived at a microcosm of the city wherein one lives and works, finds recreation and exercise, shops and dines, and parks one's car and boat, all without leaving the premises, or even going outdoors. Whereas a few of the architectural details might be questioned, the concept is brilliant. (One wonders whether this multiple-use notion was not subliminally sparked by the Auditorium Building of Adler & Sullivan, q.v., who in 1889 combined office building with hotel and theater.)

Placed on the edge of the Chicago River and within a few hundred yards of Lake Michigan, near the spot where the city was founded as a trading post, Marina City obviously occupies a strategic and expensive piece of real estate. Most of the important functions of the city, whether business or pleasure, are within a few minutes' walk. When one adds to this convenience the project's own attractions, the imagination of both architect and client becomes clear. (The client is the Building Maintenance Employees International Union, which conceived the idea of downtown housing and which helped finance it.)

The specific site—once covered with railroad tracks—was adjacent to land spotted by the architect five years earlier.

The twin towers rise 60 stories and number among the highest concrete buildings in the world. The lower 19 floors are devoted to open spiral ramps on which attendants park the automobiles belonging to the 896 apartments which sprout 40 floors above. Laundry and storage facilities are placed in the area between cars and flats. At water level there is a 500-boat marina. (The office and commercial spaces utilize river water as a source of cooling energy.) A 16-story office block occupies the north side of the site, while a television station, theater, exhibition hall, an extensive series of shops, service facilities, ice-skating rink, and restaurant occupy the base.

The construction of the circular towers was based on a central core of reinforced concrete, about which the apartments, like petals on a daisy, fan out—"kinetic space" as the architect calls it. Each of these great utility-transportation cylinders, which are 35 feet/10.7 meters in diameter, were erected first and the ramps for cars and floors for the apartments poured later, the overall diameter being 105 feet/32 meters. The circular construction reduced wind loads, shortened utility runs, and produced an excellent ratio of floor space to exterior wall.

The building's round plan readily enables it to be divided into apartments from one-bay, or one "petal" efficiencies (256 units), to one-and-one-half-bay, one-bedroom apartments (576 units), to two-and-one-half-bay, two-bedroom apartments (64 units), the latter occupying the 52nd to 60th floors. The slight pie-shape plan of each apartment provides a maximum of glass and light and a minimum of back wall. The semicircular balconies form small open-air rooms, being approximately 20 feet/6.1 meters wide (except for half-bays) and 10 feet/3 meters deep. Besides providing a private aerie they are useful for shielding the glass from the high sun, for window washing, exterior painting, and maintenance for the unit air conditioners above each door. (Unit air conditioners are more economical for the mixed uses of the building.) The innermost space of the apartment is occupied by the kitchen and bath. Electric heat is used throughout, the heat from lighting fixtures providing a major source. The project was planned to attract single tenants and small families.

From the critical point of view, the towers are perhaps a bit close together for as much privacy as one might like, but at 70-foot/21-meter separation—the width of many streets—one could scarce ask for more space for in-town living. In addition the office building, whose verticality stems from the fact that its mullions double as columns, sits uneasily with the near-horizontal curves of the parking ramps. A quiet, neutral statement might have been better here. The whale-backed, lead-sheathed auditorium elbows its way into the plaza too forcefully, cramping an already crowded area. (Its size, however, was occasioned when the original plan for a 1,200-seat theater was greatly enlarged to accommodate a television studio tenant.) But if its expression is slightly uneven in spots, basically Marina City stands as a brilliant, pioneering prototype for today's midcity living. Moreover it is an urban solution, not an urban problem-maker—as most gigantic buildings are. Because its lowest apartment is twenty floors above the street, there is far less dirt and noise than in typical apartment blocks, while conversely there are spectacular views of Lake Michigan and half the city at one's feet. Commuting time is infinitesimal for those working in the adjacent office building, and only a short walk for most others. One's car and boat are just downstairs, while amusement, culture, shopping, and exercise facilities are a mere elevator ride away. What more can the central city provide?

Adjacent, rather uncomfortably adjacent, rises the fifty-two-story **IBM Building,** 1971, by The Office of Mies van der Rohe (now Fujikawa, Conterato, Lohan & Associates) with the C. F. Murphy firm associated.

Lower concourse always open

---

27   Central District Filtration Plant (1964–66)
E end of Ohio Street on Lake Michigan
Chicago, Illinois

C. F. MURPHY & ASSOCIATES, ARCHITECTS

Those with a civil engineering bent will want to see Chicago's famous water-filtration plant—one of the outstanding examples of contemporary architectural engineering—projecting into Lake Michigan adjacent and parallel to Navy Pier. The plant, the world's largest at 1,700 million gallons/7,728 million liters a day, draws water from one of four intake cribs located several miles offshore, then treats this chemically with chlorine, aluminum sulfate, iron sulphate, lime, anhydrous ammonia, carbon, and fluorides. After passing through settling basins the treated water is filtered and distributed to pumping stations, thence, via over 4,000 miles/6,437 kilometers of mains, to users. The architecture which houses this 51-acre/21-hectare complex is a model of decorum, with its good, though slightly boxy, proportions, its extensive landscaping, and its five electronically programmed fountains (illuminated at night) which erupt on this strategic point of man-made land. The panorama it offers of the city is unequaled. S. Z. Gladych of Murphy Associates was chief of design.

Open for public tours Tues., Thurs., Sat., Sun. 1–4, except holidays

---

28   Lake Point Tower (1967–68)
505 North Lake Shore Drive, off Grand Avenue
Chicago, Illinois

G. D. SCHIPPOREIT AND JOHN C. HEINRICH, ARCHITECTS

Dominating the Navy Pier promontory of Chicago in isolated splendor, this "visual instrument responding to the sky and light" (AIA Honor Award description) enjoys one of the most enviable sites in the country. Lake Michigan laps its edge, while a dazzling panorama of the city unfolds on the other side. Though admittedly influenced by Mies van der Rohe—its architects worked for some years in Mies' office—this seventy-story building housing nine hundred luxury apartments possesses a boldness and imagination all its own. Man is free here: no one breathes down one's neck, no neighboring window pokes its friendly face at one (which a cross plan would allow). The trefoil tower rests on a rectangular base containing a four-level garage for seven hundred cars, two floors of commercial and retail facilities, and a restaurant, the base topped by a 2½-acre/1-hectare "park," complete with pond, swimming pool, and putting green. Atop the building,

the Lake Point Club is housed in a rotunda penthouse. Some of Chicago's finest shopping is only a few blocks away.

An equilateral triangle forms the structural core of the building, housing elevators, stairs, and utilities in its spine and framing its circulation lobby. Three short arms from this central hall give access to the apartments, which range from efficiencies to three-bedroom, all bedrooms having their own bath. Interapartment partitions are arranged so that there is some freedom in altering available sizes. Living rooms with dining alcove and shielded kitchen occupy the end of each rounded arm, the "soft" form of this totally glazed shape being surprisingly agreeable. Ingenious, low components containing individual air conditioners and direct fresh-air vents line the peripheral walls.

Lake Point Tower is obviously a retreat, a very private roost unimpinged upon by others, but there is room, and need, in this world for such a building. The concrete frame—when built it was the highest concrete structure in the world—is sheathed in bronze-toned aluminum of excellent detail (note ventilators), with tinted glass providing most of the skin: very fresh, very handsome. Graham, Anderson, Probst & White were associate architects.

Lobby and grounds only open to public

29   University of Illinois at Chicago Circle (1965–79)
West Harrison Street at South Halsted
Chicago, Illinois

SKIDMORE, OWINGS & MERRILL, CHIEF ARCHITECTS AND
PLANNERS; OTHER ARCHITECTS AS NOTED

This unusual commuter campus comprises one of the nation's few coherent groups of university buildings. Bold and provocative in concept,
it is at times perplexing in detail. Occupying (after early neighborhood
resistance) 118 depressed acres/48 hectares near the southwest edge of
downtown, it lies only 1.5 miles/2.4 kilometers from the Loop with its
job opportunities and cultural and recreational facilities. The university is available to both rapid transit and surface lines and to the free-
ways which border its north and east sides. Private cars are allowed
only in designated areas and in peripheral parking lots and/or structures.

The campus was planned for 8,000 students in Phase I, 14,000 in
Phase II, and an "ultimate" expansion for 20,000. The central core of
communal buildings was calculated and built with this figure as its
limit. Later the University of Illinois Board of Trustees projected an
enrollment to an eventual 34,000 (by 1980), but in September 1977
this was revised to maintain a total of approximately 20,000, and with
an added emphasis on graduate work and adult education. Present enrollment (Fall 1980) is 21,001 including 3,462 graduate students.

A meticulous analysis of urban education for commuting students,
and its proper architectural expression, preceded any actual building
concept. Basic to these conclusions was the decision to group facilities
by function rather than by discipline: that is, one cluster of rooms for
lectures (no matter what the subject), all laboratories together (whatever the science), and separate office building for professors (as opposed to departmental buildings). The main advantages of this organization lie in the considerable savings effected in both building and
staff, for it produces a far higher occupancy rate for lecture halls and
greater internal flexibility. Moreover it concentrates the learning kernel
of the entire campus—lecture halls, classrooms, library—in one compact core, demanding the least between-class movement for students
(but more for professors). On the debit side, it leads to some "social"
anonymity and a rootlessness as the student has no "home base" except his locker. There is also a minor linear inconvenience to the faculty and, unquestionably, a separate-pathness between instructor and

student, as they have no common departmental ex-cathedra meeting ground. Moreover the university now has ten times as many graduate students as initially anticipated—students who need more "clustered" facilities than undergraduates—and this has inconvenienced the scene (though this is obviously not the fault of the architect).

The epicenter of the Chicago Circle campus is the rooftop agora over the cluster of lecture halls, which are grouped together to form an enormous rectangle (300 x 450 feet/91 x 137 meters). Here at the confluence of the elevated granite walks, which knit much of the campus into "a unified totality," and placed strategically between library and student union, lies a roof piazza of pure inspiration. Near the sky-borne corners, where they mirror the shapes of the lecture rooms below, stand four anti-agora, inward-oriented "exedras," while in the center, twin flights of opposing steps march down to the lecture-room level in the form of a "split" curved amphitheater, each side of which can hold 500 students. This elevated core is one of the great spaces in college planning (at least in reasonable weather). Beneath are grouped one 500-student lecture hall, two of 250, twelve of 125, and six of 75: maximum concentration of education on bottom, maximum relaxation and interaction on top.

The elevated granite pedestrian "expressways" are to some observers of dubious merit because in dirty weather most people naturally prefer to walk underneath, but their weight is such that a veritable hypostyle of columns is needed for support: this renders the covered walks not only crowded but gloomy, at night even dangerous—until recent outside lighting. (Granite was used instead of concrete because it is unaffected by the salt needed in snow removal.) Small classroom buildings—three stories, thirty students per room—are grouped to form courts on the north and south sides of the lecture block, playing a stepping-down-in-scale role. As mentioned, the "plaza's" aerial felicity is framed by the library on one side (by Skidmore, Owings & Merrill—undistinguished) and by the Chicago Circle Center, the student union, on the other (by C. F. Murphy Associates). The union promises much on the exterior, for it is a broadly assertive block; however, within there is too little of the welcoming large area hinted at without. As this is a commuter college of "locker-livers," the need is acute for more spacious lounge-centers, as many students will have several hours between classes and no dormitory to repair to. (This lack is now being partially corrected.)

On the third side of the campus core rises the Science and Engineering Laboratories (by SOM), which both abuts and respects the Chicago Circle Center. The science unit—the boldest-scaled and for many the most resolute building on campus—is compartmented into three lower floors of laboratories, all windowless for greater utilization of wall area, while the top floor is open and column-free to be totally flexible for future developments. The building was designed so that it could be expanded, as has been done (but not as originally foreseen). Near the west end of the Science and Engineering Laboratories and convenient to the library, rises the thirteen-story Science Office Building. The higher buildings, incidentally, occur near the edges of the campus, with the lower ones near the center: "activity decreases and specialization increases with outward movement."

The tallest unit on campus is University Hall, the striking twenty-eight-story building near the rapid transit entrance of the campus. This gets wider as it rises instead of vice versa, its shape evolving from the engineering postulate that a partial cantilever delivers the greatest efficiency of material. Obviously in a skyscraper there are limits to this concept because the demands of vertical circulation decrease with height, while wind loads increase, but Walter Netsch of Skidmore—and the chief of design for the entire University of Illinois at Chicago Circle campus—has brought forth an eyebrow-raising university trademark and a useful vertical accent. Note that the height is divided into three horizontal groups (atop a two-story, largely open base and under a double-height top floor): the grouping comprises twelve, eight, and five floors—the division arrived at via the Golden Section (which has characterized many other buildings). Note too that the increased loads on the lower part of the concrete structure are expressed by doubling the number of columns in each of these three groups, instead of increasing column sizes. The unusual—and dubious—windows throughout University Hall and much of the campus are set in precast concrete frames, with a tall, narrow central glass section and small trapezoidal panes at top and bottom—"a capricious and thoroughly unconvincing fenestration" it has been termed (*P/A Observer,* October 1965). In the classroom area, however, the ground floors are largely all-glass to emit a comfortable "night light" onto the adjacent walks.

Opposite University Hall (across a previously existing transformer station which could not be moved) stands the red brick Art and Architecture Building (SOM), where Walter Netsch purposefully eschewed the rectangular shape which jackets the other and earlier buildings. Its plan grew from Netsch's "Field Theory," which is based on a complex geometry which occasionally takes off into a realm of pattern-making that can compromise needs. It reflects "sociocultural, biomechanical, and motivational forces . . . It is iconic, volumetric, and spatial" (*P/A Observer,* March 1969). In brief, the plan of the Art and Architecture Building is based on 10- and 85-foot (3- and 26-meter) squares, rotated 45° to produce multifaceted facades on the exterior, and modules of work space within. In addition to this resulting intricacy, each floor or studio area is a quarter floor higher than the previous, an intentional vertical change designed to "expand perception of space." The result makes for a confusing but exciting building—a laboratory of three-dimensional interactions—one with a dynamic series of ramps, corridors, unexpected pulsations. On the exterior, a lively profile and geometric interplay result.

Netsch's ultimate in "Field Theory" design (at least here) are the Phase II Behavioral Sciences Building (1970), on the opposite side of University Hall from the Art and Architecture Building, and the Science and Engineering South Building (1971), behind the first science block. The plan intricacy in both of these is unbelievably labyrinthine, but out of them has percolated a new direction in today's architecture, one requiring diligent discipline to avoid disaster. The well-appointed Physical Education Building (1971) was designed by Harry Weese & Associates.

As mentioned, there are faults at the campus, but many of these can be ascribed to the harsh demands of a midcity commuter institution now aggravated by broad changes in pedagogical attitudes (and even in students). When all is added up, the University of Illinois at Chicago Circle makes firm contributions.

Campus open daily

---

30 Richard J. Daley Center (1963–66)
Dearborn, Washington, Clark, and Randolph Streets
Chicago, Illinois

C. F. MURPHY ASSOCIATES, SKIDMORE, OWINGS & MERRILL, AND LOEBL SCHLOSSMAN BENNETT & DART, ASSOCIATE ARCHITECTS

A startling scale and a businesslike certitude characterize Chicago's Richard J. Daley Center (formerly the Civic Center). The "center" comprises one new courthouse—the skyscraper to be discussed—one elderly Cook County (ex-City Hall) Building by Holabird & Roche (1907–11), and a polished plaza 345 x 220 feet/105 x 67 meters. The design of the thirty-one-story Center posed a number of unusual problems in that the bay size (i.e. the free floor area establishd by four columns) had to be unusually large to accommodate the numerous, intermixed courtrooms, which make up much of the building. Moreover the ceiling height had to rise correspondingly, some courtrooms actu-

ally piercing through two floors. The resulting bay of 48.3 x 87 feet/14.7 x 26.5 meters is the largest yet achieved in any office building. The columns needed to frame these bays and support the building—twelve on the periphery, four within—are authoritatively expressed on the exterior, the key factors in generating the astounding scale, the well-tempered backbone of the Center. Built up in cruciform plan, the columns measure 5 feet/1.5 meters across at the base (note detail of juncture of vertical and horizontal), and step back (i.e. reduce in size) thrice to 2 feet/.6 meter across at the top, lending a subtly tapered profile to the building.

The Center—which reflects the design influence of Mies van der Rohe—is clad with Cor-Ten steel, its rich, almost velvety finish complemented by bronze-colored, heat-absorbing plate glass, the near monochrome of steel and glass combining to produce majestic solemnity. However, any tendency toward visual heaviness is ameliorated by the nobly proportioned, glass-encased ground floor which is inset from the edge of the building and by the plaza which flows under the building and into the sunshine on its south side. Continuity is emphasized by using the same granite paving throughout.

The planning of the Center's floors could not proceed as with a routine skyscraper, each floor subdivided at will into peripheral offices. In this case, the building not only had an extremely complicated elevator system to contend with (separate cabs for judges, public, prisoners, freight), it had to accommodate a vast and varied collection of courtrooms (121 in seven different sizes, some small, some two-story and holding 150 people), and to provide public circulation plus office space, in addition to its own corridors, for judges, clerks, and related personnel. To meet these needs the architects devised first the large bay size mentioned, then grouped all the courtrooms on the interior of the building, the courts not needing windows but definitely requiring sound insulation. Along the outer walls (on the court floors) are the corridors—turning the building inside out, so to speak—where they provide excellent access to the elevators, the various courts and offices (and offer wide-ranging views of the city). Across the east and west ends on most floors are placed the offices for the judges and secretaries. Inner circulation enables the justices to move in privacy to any courtroom. In addition to having an intermixture of large-sized courtrooms as a structural determinant—producing the gigantic bay—the architects had to contend with another factor which exerted an impact on structure: ventilation in the courtrooms. This required duct sizes up to 4.5 feet/1.4 meters in diameter, hence determined a truss pattern through which the ducts could be "woven." The corresponding depth of these trusses, plus the high ceilings needed, make a floor-to-floor height of 18 feet/5.5 meters or 50 per cent greater than a routine building. Except for the equivocal treatment of the ninth and tenth floors, which accommodate mechanical equipment, the building is magnificent, the Center and its plaza and sculpture standing without question as one of our great achievements in high-rise urban architecture and land usage. Jacques C. Brownson was in overall charge of design.

In the plaza itself, sun and light changes play tag with Picasso's sculpture, the low jets of the fountain sparkle, and the leaves of well-placed trees rustle. Picasso's *Woman,* all of 50 feet/15 meters high and weighing in at 324,000 pounds/147,000 kilograms, was installed in 1967, and masterfully accents the square. It is constructed of the same Cor-Ten as the building, but as Sir Roland Penrose, Picasso's biographer, writes, "The materials of which it is made are primarily air and light, held together decisively by the rigid metal." And if the sculpture seems less "Woman" than, say, "Pegasus," we must recall the artist's famous words that it is no more important to understand art than "to try to understand the song of a bird." Picasso himself, in an act of wonderful generosity, donated his design and its model "to the people of Chicago." Its construction was made possible by private donations and foundations.

Facing the plaza on the south rises the **Brunswick Building** (1964) by Skidmore, Owings & Merrill, its light color (of painted concrete) lending freshness, while just visible on the diagonal corner stands the dark, granite-clad **Connecticut General Building** (1966), also by SOM. The west side of the Civic Plaza is framed by the old City-County Building and though the old is heroically Roman, it has been said that the new is "more purely classical" (*Architectural Review,* October 1977). On the east and north there is a mishmash of unfortunate buildings whose days, one hopes, are numbered. Underground pedestrian circulation and shopping allées provide a network connecting Daley Center with the old Court House and the new buildings mentioned, plus the subway system. Daley Center itself has two underground floors, including a garage.

Lobby floor open during business hours

31   **John Hancock Center** (1966–70)
      **875 North Michigan Avenue between East Delaware Place and
        East Chestnut Street**
      Chicago, Illinois

SKIDMORE, OWINGS & MERRILL, ARCHITECTS AND ENGINEERS

The John Hancock Center is Chicago's bold and gutsy—and inescapable—landmark. Exoskeletal skyscrapers have been tried before and tapered buildings constructed, but none has sprung from the structural demands or delivers the startling visual impact of John Hancock—Big John. It dominates much of the city, and whereas no one can avoid seeing it—and there must be only a few who would so want—do not miss the observation floor and/or cocktail lounge at dusk if the weather cooperates. (It might well be cloudy down below but sunny above.)

Bruce Graham, the architect who was in charge of the building's design, is technical-minded, "interested in that part of architecture that is related to structural engineering," and this sometimes ignored approach is evident here. Graham likes to explore the many possibilities, the new options of working with today's tools including the computers extensively employed on this job. Compare, for instance, this excursion with the even taller Sears Roebuck Tower (q.v.) which he also designed. For the Hancock tower, Graham and his cohorts, principally Dr. Fazlur Khan as chief structural engineer, arrived at the straight tapered form as a strictly structural, basically wall-bearing, trussed-box response to heavy winds and great height. (The building takes almost the full blast from nearby Lake Michigan, as opposed to the mutually sheltered Loop group.) Structurally, the floors of Hancock contribute only a minor stiffening element to the frame. The prominent exterior diagonals form the least expensive way of bracing (in transferring lateral wind forces to the entire structure) because they use less steel. Moreover they are also effective in establishing scale, thus the exoskeleton.

John Hancock is not just a building, it is indeed a "Center," with shops, offices, and apartments stacked like a vertical town (and probably inspired in this regard by the pioneering, not distant, Marina City). A specialty store and shops occupy the first 5 floors, parking for 1,200 cars (reached by strident exterior ramp) on floors 6–12; offices and mechanical services occupy 13–17; commercial office space 18–41; mechanical 42–43; with the "sky lobby" the 44th–45th, where all

apartment dwellers and visitors change elevators—and, on these floors, swim in their own pool, shop in their own shops, or dine in their own restaurant. Above this, 705 condominium apartments (efficiencies to four-bedroom) occupy the 46th–92nd floors, with observation lounge (94), restaurant (95–96)—by IDS Inc.—and television and mechanical (100) above. The total height, without masts, is 1,107 feet/ 337 meters. Amusingly the apartments with diagonals crossing their windows were the first rented: the occupants wanted to identify with the structure!

An assessment of a building of such Brobdingnagian size and so many occupants obviously should take into account the milieu in which it rises, and it is here that criticism has been leveled. But as Bruce Graham put it, "People say that it is on the wrong site, but of all areas in Chicago that are changing, it is this portion of town—and not because of John Hancock." (The building, incidentally, occupies a bit less than half of its ground.) Moreover if this were solely an office building disgorging almost a hundred floors of workers every afternoon at 5:03, the building in this largely upper-bracket apartment and shopping section of the city would be intolerable. But, as indicated, there are only 27 floors of offices and 46 of apartments—certainly not menacing numbers. Each group follows its staggered hours and keeps the area alive throughout the day and much of the night. A number of occupants themselves work in the building.

The exterior finish is dark aluminum and bronze-tinted glass except for the light travertine on the ground floor. (The meeting of tower with base is ill-resolved.) The sharp eye will note from the street that the office floors have higher ceilings than the apartments above, and it will also readily pick out the garage decks, sky lobby, and restaurant, but there are no other—there really could be no other—expressions of occupational function. John Hancock is brutal, dominating—but breathtaking.

Observation floor and 95-to-96th-floor restaurant and cocktail lounge open daily 9 A.M.–midnight: admission

---

32 McCormick Place (1968–71)
Lake Shore Drive at 23rd Street
Chicago, Illinois

C. F. MURPHY ASSOCIATES, ARCHITECTS AND ENGINEERS

Since the publication of the famous Burnham Plan of 1909, Chicago has been the most progressive city in the country in reclaiming and extending a lakeside site. It has built up a near continuous strip of waterside parks by landfill—almost 17 miles/27 kilometers of them—useful and vital for both recreation and unimpeded motor traffic. Carl Condit has called this "the greatest civic project ever undertaken by an American city" (*American Building Art, 20th Century,* Oxford University Press, 1960). Moreover there are plans to double its scope. It should be added also that the "inland" landscaping of Frederick Law Olmsted and Jens Jensen was another and equally important facet of the city's realization of the need for comprehensive, far-seeing planning and planting. And even today Chicago's architecture is, as it almost always has been, the most exploratory in the United States. (The skyscraper, after all, was invented here and taken to many of its greatest heights.)

This new exhibition hall and theater, perched on filled land—and extending new architectural horizons—fits boldly into the city's historic contributions. Even at a distance the enormous overhangs of its cantilevered roof give one pause, while close up its black triangulations visually enmesh the observer in the structural geometrics of its 15-foot/4.6-meter-deep, two-way trusses. The approach itself is dramatic on the upper level as one drives right through the building via a wide mall (the end of 23rd Street—spacious enough for buses to turn), a concourse which separates the gigantic exhibition area on the left from the theater group at right. At the end of this sheltered esplanade one emerges onto a terrace, with Lake Michigan, enlivened by sailboats, and Meigs Field, busy with its planes and helicopters, forming the backdrop. Traffic specifically for McCormick Place approaches via a tunnel on the lower level, parallel to the long side. Both outdoor and covered parking are adjacent. A fire (1967) destroyed most of the upper section of an earlier structure, but the architects were able to utilize much of the two lower floors. The building, as mentioned, is divided into two separate sections on its glass-wrapped main floor. A highly flexible exhibition area of 302,000 square feet/28,000 square meters occupies the left (north) part, its roof upheld by reinforced concrete columns 150 feet/46 meters on center (!) and 50 feet/15 meters high; a 4,451-seat theater (filling two levels, and entered from the lower) takes up the right-hand (south) section, along with two 1,200-seat auditoriums, various meeting rooms, a restaurant for 2,000,

and service facilities on its two floors. There is also a large exhibition area on this second level. Below are mostly services, including the kitchen. The great projection of the roof overhang (75 feet/23 meters) was calculated so that trucks could load and unload exhibition material (which has a rapid turnover) under cover on both east (lake) and west sides, and at upper and secondary levels.

The interior of the cavernous exhibition arena can be exciting or confusing, depending completely on what is going on inside. Lined with precise rows of chairs (or when empty), it delivers structural punch; cluttered with exhibition stands, each outshouting the other, one is not tempted to tarry. The theater, on the other hand, is a good-looking conventional auditorium useful for conventions.

By quietly hugging its hillock, and being sandwiched tightly between lake and expressway, the building makes a minimum instrusion on the landscape, and a maximum expression of controlled architectural strength. A tremendous job. Gene Summers was chief of design with Sherwin Asrow structural engineer.

Open for events

---

33   Malcolm X Community College (1971)
1900 West Van Buren Street at Ogden Avenue (parallel to Eisenhower Expressway)
Chicago, Illinois

C. F. MURPHY ASSOCIATES, ARCHITECTS

A long, low (three-story) precise rectangle housing a dynamic, two-year community college dedicated to Black Excellence. Its architecture, obviously Miesian inspired, reflects this philosophy—being both black and excellent—and while demanding in its severity, it is rewarding in its positiveness and its precision. Concentrating all facilities in one building, which operates all day and much of the night, the college serves as many as 10,000 students, plus the surrounding community. A 450-seat theater, a gym, and two large top-floor lounges supplement approximately 100 classrooms. A tough, disciplined job. Gene Summers was in charge of design.

Public areas open during school hours

---

34   First National Bank (1968–71)
Dearborn, Monroe, Clark, and Madison Streets
Chicago, Illinois

C. F. MURPHY ASSOCIATES AND THE PERKINS & WILL
PARTNERSHIP, ARCHITECTS

At one stage architects hestitated to use a tapered curve form for skyscrapers, not only because of technical difficulties, but even more because such a form might seem arbitrary (as it usually is). But with the First National Bank the bell-bottom was completely logical. The bank wanted to stay adjacent to its former strategic, mid-Loop location, but the gross buildable area of the site covered only 60,000 square feet/5,570 square meters, and they needed 40,000 square feet/3,716 square meters for the Savings Department alone on the ground floor, plus services and elevators. (Illinois does not permit branch banks, hence the extreme importance of this space availability.) The Chicago building code demands, as do others, either a reduction in size as a tall building rises or a "contribution" of unbuilt-on ground space. Hence, as this is the tallest building in the Loop at sixty stories, the architects, after trying various setback schemes, most of which had been done to death, evolved this tapered form (which is of uniform width above the forty-third floor). This shape produced a ground-floor area almost twice that of the upper stories. They then created an adjacent plaza. First National is, it should be added, the first slope-sided major building in the country—if one excepts the thirty-two-story Foshay Tower (1929—q.v.) in Minneapolis, built as an office building imitation of the Washington Monument. The resulting bank tower (850 feet/259 meters high) turned out to be both imaginative and compelling, its eight enormous piers per side (of steel covered with granite fireproofing) setting a unique profile, its facades accented by its forthrightly expressed utility floors and by its glass-lined 56-foot/17-meter-high main floor.

The chief problem inside, with the enormous open banking space taking up most of the area, was where to put the elevators. Some of these (for security reasons) could only serve the twenty-one floors belonging to the bank, some the "lower" tenant floors, others the topmost, while freight elevators must be available to all. This was finally solved by a split system, with groups of elevators at each end of the building, their masses projecting slightly from the flat sides. The main banking floor itself is handsome throughout, with stimulating three-dimensionality, keyed by a "floating" balcony, and numerous works of art.

For their outdoor space "contribution" the bank created a marvelous breathing spot in the crowded downtown area that also serves as a discreet attention-getter. This skillfully stepped-down forum forms the Loop's most refreshing and gregarious meeting-watching and fair-

weather-picnicking spot, complete with fountain (not inspired) and excellent planting. Concerts and exhibitions are regularly scheduled in summer. Several restaurants and shops look out on this tiered space with a two-story banking pavilion on west edge. A freestanding Chagall mosaic mural embellishes the terrace. Altogether a skillful, very professional job. Carter H. Manny Jr. was principal-in-charge for Murphy Associates, Albin B. Kisielius for Perkins & Will. Novak & Carlson were the landscape architects; IDS Inc. were associated with the architects for the interiors of the lower floors, with Ford & Earl Design Associates responsible for the fourth to twenty-first floors.

Open during business hours

---

35 Federal Center (1963–73)
South Dearborn, Adams, Clark Streets and Jackson Boulevard
Chicago, Illinois

LUDWIG MIES VAN DER ROHE, WITH SCHMIDT GARDEN & ERIKSON, C. F. MURPHY ASSOCIATES, A. EPSTEIN & SON, ARCHITECTS

The Center comprises three units: the forty-two-story John C. Kluc-zynski Federal Building, the thirty-story Everett McK. Dirksen Federal Building at right angles, which because of its block-long length is the dominant structure, and a one-story post office. The architects' concern for urban values in a congested area prompted the inclusion of one major plaza (on Dearborn Street) plus one smaller (at Clark and Jackson). The mutual disposition of the three buildings was, of course, meticulously evolved, with the Jackson Boulevard side of the forty-two-story skyscraper flush with its thirty-story neighbor to form a broken "L," and the front (plaza side) of the post office aligned with the midpoint of the taller structure. The varying heights and bulks of the three, plus the plaza in front, modify the architectural sameness which might otherwise have resulted, while the 53-foot/16-meter-high, exuberant red *Flamingo* stabile by Alexander Calder excites the plaza. The ground floors of both office blocks are well inset, glazed on all sides, and are devoted to lobbies. The well-scaled post office—probably the most distinguished that one will see—is glass on three sides.

The Dirksen Building, housing the U. S. Courthouse and Federal offices, was the first unit finished (1964) and presents an almost re-

lentlessly massive facade 368 feet/112 meters high, one broken only by the tall inset ground floor and the grilled utility level at top. Its main internal feature—besides a cheery entry—are the double-height courtrooms on the top ten stories, the lower part of the building being devoted to more routine federal office needs. Above there are fifteen identically sized, purposefully internal courtrooms, four per floor. Measuring 42 x 56 feet/12.8 x 17 meters by 18 feet/5.5 meters high each, they are surrounded by a belt of corridors and offices. The corridors narrow on the "official" side (judges, clerks, juries) and widen on the west side where there is public access to courtrooms, lounges, and miscellaneous offices. Bruno Conterato was partner-in-charge for Dirksen as well as Kluczynski and the post office. He is from The Office of Mies van der Rohe, (since 1975 Fujikawa, Conterato, Lohan & Associates). The forty-two-story Kluczynski Building, like the Dirksen Building, is a fireproofed steel structure based on a 28-foot/8.5-meter-square bay and 4.7-foot/1.4-meter module with a steel skin painted matte black. The column grid for both lies completely within the outer walls.

The post office uses the same 4.7-foot/1.4-meter module but a structural bay of 65.3 feet/19.9 meters to produce a 197-foot/60-meter-square building with an interior height of 27 feet/8.2 meters. It provides a lofty room which with its clear glass walls on three sides expands to the plaza with its sculpture in front. Because it is only one floor high its steel structure did not have to be fireproofed. The super-sized Calder outside, installed in 1974, was made possible by a commendable decision of the General Services Administration (which controls federal buildings) to provide up to 0.5 per cent of building costs for fine arts. Altogether our finest government-commissioned group.

Open during office hours

---

36 Sears Tower (1971–74)
South Franklin, Adams, Wacker, and Jackson
Chicago, Illinois

SKIDMORE, OWINGS & MERRILL, ARCHITECTS AND ENGINEERS

The Sears Tower, at 110 floors (1,454 feet/443 meters) the tallest building in the world, is technically extraordinarily ingenious. Its designers have likened it to a clutch of squared cigarettes of varying

lengths mutually bundled together, and this structural simplification is translated into nine statically independent units, each 75 feet/23 meters on a side, all nine strapped together, so to speak, as one. Five 15-foot/4.6-meter bays comprise a unit's side. At the fiftieth, sixty-sixth, and ninetieth floors two of these square "tubes"—on opposite corners— terminate, producing the notched profile on the exterior and marking skylobbies for elevator changes within. The remaining two, structurally bound like the others by belt trusses and internal diaphragms, rise the full height of 1,454 feet/443 meters, a limit set by the Federal Aviation Administration. The steel frame is clad with black aluminum and 16,000 bronze-tinted windows. But the building's relation to the horizontal, where it meets the street, is not amiable—"an un-Chicagoan brutishness" (*Architectural Review,* May 1977)—particularly on the Adams and Jackson sides. Moreover the most used entry (on Franklin) lacks the bravura one might expect. In addition, the building raises urbanistic questions of whether some 16,500 office workers should be housed in any single high building, pouring in and out, more or less en masse, and with limited transportation options. (The not-distant John Hancock Building, q.v., by the same architects, though rivaling Sears in height at one hundred floors, is approximately half devoted to more casual-hour apartment occupancy.) Though a technical triumph—and obviously an impressive sight—the Sears Tower raises questions for future building limits in all major cities. Bruce Graham of the Chicago office of SOM was partner in charge of design, Fazlur Khan chief structural engineer. The lobby and bank interiors were by SOM, the Sears interiors by Saphier, Lerner, Schindler Inc.

103rd-floor Skydeck open daily 9 A.M.*–midnight: admission*

---

37 Illinois Regional Library for the Blind (1978)
West Roosevelt Road at Blue Island Avenue (S of Circle Campus)
Chicago, Illinois

STANLEY TIGERMAN, ARCHITECT

Spritely, at times even playful, this small triangular library does much to spruce up its neighborhood. Designed primarily for the blind and the physically handicapped, but with small community facilities, even the passing motorists will be cheered by its oft vibrant colors. Red baked enamel panels enclose most of the two-story structure offset by

yellow at entry. The 165-foot/50-meter-long wall on the avenue side by contrast is of gray-painted concrete, perked by a narrow wavelike window which runs along much of its length. Seemingly—and perhaps actually—capricious (but very refreshing), the curves of this window "reflect" the curves of the top of the service counter within. The dips in the counter help the blind locate by touch various sections of the library such as braille and talking books, as well as aiding wheelchair users. Braille stacks lie beyond. The layout, being designed for touch circulation, has narrow "mnemonic" passageways. Some shapes appear arbitrary but all in all a lively voice is heard. Tigerman's work is both provocative and zestful; when it has satisfied basic requirements, it is almost always "architecture that is fun" (*P/A* 4:78). Jerome R. Butler of the Bureau of Architecture, City of Chicago, was associate architect of this Regional Library.

Open Mon.–Fri. 9–5:30, Sat. 9–5

---

38 Pierre Menard House (1802)
1.8 miles/3 kilometers SW of ILL 3 on Kaskaskia Road
Fort Kaskaskia State Historic Site, Illinois

A simple, functional French Mississippi River home on the south-western edge of the state (9 miles/14 kilometers northwest of Chester), Pierre Menard reflects, like its sisters in Louisiana, both cli-

mate and building conditions. The lower floor is of masonry to shield
against dampness and flooding by the river; a porch protects the front
and two sides from excess sun, while providing room access and open-
air living; the kitchen is detached at rear to lessen the danger of fire.
The exterior of the house above the basement is of oak and walnut
vertical logs covered with poplar wood siding. The interior is of pine
with ashwood floor. Elaborately carved mantels form the chief decorative feature. A number of the furnishings are original; all are of the period. Be certain to visit the kitchen and smokehouse.

Though France lost all North American territory (including Canada) to England following the Treaty of Paris (1763), French cultural
influence continued for many years. This simple but appealingly direct
house is an informative expression of those days. Purchased by the
state in 1927, the house has been repaired and is today well maintained. Kaskaskia itself (of which little today remains but this house,
the river having taken its toll) was the first capital of the state.

Open daily 9–5, except major holidays

39 Old Knox County Court House (1837–39)
Main Street (US 150), just SE of Galesburg
Knoxville, Illinois

JOHN MANDEVILLE, ARCHITECT

A trim Greek Revival courthouse by an architect whose only other known work is the nearby library (old Hall of Records). Set off by the village green, the courthouse is a first-rate example of the style popular in the 1830s and 1840s in the South (compare Mills's little church in Camden, South Carolina), but little seen in Illinois. The brick Doric columns and the detailing of the whole portico are superior. A cast-iron stair was added in the 1870s, the better to serve the upper-floor courtroom, which now houses the Knox County Museum. A cupola once adorned the roof but was taken down years ago. Of the relatively few Greek Revival public buildings in Illinois, this small courthouse ranks among the finest—along with the State Capitol at Springfield (q.v.).

Open Mon.–Fri. 8:30–4:30, except holidays

40   St. Procopius Abbey Church and Monastery (1968–70)
off Maple Avenue and College Road, SW of town
(take Lisle exit off ILL Tollway)
Lisle, Illinois

LOEBL SCHLOSSMAN BENNETT & DART, ARCHITECTS

The impact of this Benedictine complex (about 28 miles/45 kilometers west of Chicago) lies in its brilliantly calculated interior progression to the church proper, in the natural lighting of its nave, and in its use of simple materials to produce an austere but superb room. The worshiper advances via a "hall" that wraps around a third of the church, and this blank-walled, angled path builds up a theatrical sense of anticipation. One then turns as nave and simple chancel slowly "open" spatially to extend their welcome. All walls, including those of the hall, are of brick rising unbroken to the ceiling. An enormous, and largely invisible, clerestory window (90 x 13 feet/27 x 4 meters in size) pours a flood of light over the nave and in the process accentuates the geom-

etry of the wooden trusswork and the wood (Douglas fir) ceiling versus the angled planes of the brick envelope. (A 120-foot/37-meter-long steel truss 20 feet/6.1 meters deep fills and supports the window structure.) Total simplicity characterizes the atmosphere of the worship room: the chancel is defined by a single step, the altar is a quiet oak table. The pews, which seat seven hundred, are divided into two groups, one for the general congregation, the smaller at right for the resident monks. The tiny Blessed Sacrament Chapel opens behind the right-hand wall with entry near the chancel. This is one of the finest religious interiors in the country and quite probably the best of the Roman Catholic faith.

The monastery, which is attached to the church, angles in two levels about a cloister garden but with generous rooms for each of the sixty-five monks (eventually one hundred) facing outward. A two-story refectory stands opposite the entrance to the complex with a small Blessed Virgin Chapel opening off the hall which gives access (slightly ambivalent) to both church and monastery. Architecturally the latter is good, while the church—primarily the design of the late Edward D. Dart—is brilliant. Frank Kacmarcik and Lyle Yerges were consultants. The firm is now known as Loebl Schlossman & Hackl.

Visitors welcome during daylight hours

---

41 People's National Bank (1881)
Washington Street opposite Courthouse
McLeansboro, Illinois

REID BROTHERS, ARCHITECTS

Half the architectural motifs known to man in the latter part of the nineteenth century (plus the striped awnings of the twentieth) were gathered together for this marvelous bank. Among the more prominent elements of its design cornucopia are: "blocked" or banded columns, segmental central pediment, roundheaded windows, red brick and white stone facade and sides, a richly decorated frieze, several cornices, outward-splaying chimneys, a Mansard roof enthusiastically punctured by dormers, all topped by a clocked, squared dome surmounted by filigreed ironwork. There is a compactness of elements here which even hints of the work of Frank Furness (see Index). As one of the most ebullient statements of late-nineteenth-century "cul-

tural aspirations" in the United States, its photograph rightfully graces the cover of *Illinois Architecture* by Frederick Koeper (University of Chicago Press, 1968).

Open during business hours

---

42 The Deere & Company Administrative Center
(1962–64/1977–78)
**John Deere Road, c. 3.9 miles/6.3 kilometers E of IS 74 on ILL 5,
c. 7 miles/11 kilometers SE of
Moline, Illinois**

**EERO SAARINEN & ASSOCIATES, ARCHITECTS OF HEADQUARTERS;
KEVIN ROCHE/JOHN DINKELOO & ASSOCIATES, ARCHITECTS OF
DEERE WEST**

The Deere Headquarters forms one of the very greatest of America's new buildings: many feel that it is Saarinen's most brilliant achievement. With a superb site (1,060 acres/429 hectares of wooded, rolling countryside), an enthusiastic, knowledgeable client (William A. Hewitt, chairman and chief executive officer of Deere), and a (then) pioneering material (Cor-Ten, the weathering, self-preserving steel), the late Eero Saarinen (1910–61) wrought one of his seminal buildings. Lamentably he died four days after the final building contract had

been signed and before ground had been broken. Saarinen always sought to express the psychology of use in his architecture (such as "the excitement of air travel" at the TWA Terminal in New York, q.v.), plus the "personality" of his client's product—and this, of course, is the chief reason why his buildings vary so widely. (Compare Mies van der Rohe's antipodal philosophy: his buildings are distinctly all of a family.) For the administrative headquarters of the vast John Deere organization, one concerned basically with the rough, tough world of farm machinery and related products, Saarinen chose a rough, tough material. Though inaugurating Cor-Ten's architectural usage, as mentioned, Saarinen fully understood the material's limits, both upper and lower, and concentrated on its "stick" form optimum. Dutiful imitators think that any manipulation of weathering steel will fit any need, and slap up large sheets of the material, many of which are inappropriate.

The Deere headquarters is divided into three units: an exhibition hall for Deere products with adjacent auditorium, a detached administrative block, and (in 1978) the West Office Building by Roche/Dinkeloo. (The auditorium is a 378-seat theater for special presentation of products and a variety of other Deere programs and is also available to local community organizations.) The 210-foot/64-meter-long exhibition hall forms a rectangle 36 feet/11 meters high abutting the hill on entry (east) side and fully glazed along the west (toward offices). Entrance, because of grade drop-off, is at midheight with an elevated passerelle bisecting the hall to form the main entry (at the fourth floor) to the main building. (The bridge also offers a survey of Deere products below.) The movement of personnel across this bridge injects elevated motion into the showroom while its exhibits constantly remind staff of the company's range of products. The highlight of the hall is an ingenious, 174-foot/53-meter-long, three-dimensional "mural" of some two thousand items relating to John Deere and early farming memorabilia, brilliantly assembled and composed by Alexander Girard.

The seven-story (plus basement) main building stretches 330 feet/101 meters (eleven bays of 30 feet/9.1 meters) across a benign valley, and faces the smoothly landscaped approach to the complex. The approach includes two artificial lakes (one of which cools the water for the air-conditioning system), and Henry Moore's *Hill Arches* on an island in the upper pool. The main building contains all amenities for a town-detached headquarters, with its own dining facilities for its approximately one thousand employees. Its architecture—"an iron building" requested the client—represents a consummate expression of the headquarters of a farm machinery manufacturer, the antithesis of a frangible glass box. An outrigging of weathering steel louvers surrounds and projects from the building, with four slightly haunched and suspended "vanes" shielding the offices from the sun without interfering with the view. (They provide redundant "sun protection" on the north side.) Open grille decking, also of weathering steel, projects out to provide balconies for window washing. The placement of beam on beam, and of beam fastened to column as expressed on these balconies suggests the simplicity of the finest in Japanese wood temple joinery, but here logically expressed in welded steel. (Exposed, that is, non-fireproofed steel could be used because the structure stood outside urban zoning limitations.) The upper five floors of the building are given to general office space, with a maximum of employees near the windows, while directly beneath is the executive floor, with private offices lining the periphery, and largely open secretarial spaces down the middle. The ground floor is devoted to building services and an executive dining room, lounge, and gallery projecting almost into the lake. The cafeteria and executive floors are inset from the outer walls. All are sheathed with solar-reflecting bronze plate glass. Ammann & Whitney were the structural engineers; Sasaki, Dawson, Demay Associates (now Sasaki Associates) designed the landscaping. A stupendous building with an integrity not likely to be seen again soon.

In 1978 the **West Office Building** was opened on a site which had been selected for possible expansion by Saarinen himself. Only three stories in height—so as not to impinge on the headquarters—the new structure is set back on the hillside and connected to the older by a glazed bridge 194 feet/59 meters long. The exterior uses the same weathering steel that was pioneered in the Saarinen building. The most spectacular aspect of Deere West is its interior garden "court." This rises 54 feet/16 meters to a glazed roof composed of two main "vaults" and several minor ones, the court acting as separator of the two identical but slightly offset office rectangles. The "open" offices are in visual touch with the garden: a 315-seat cafeteria includes a number of seats in the garden area. Numerous works of art are found throughout. To judge from photographs (the building was not finished when last visited by the author), the Roche/Dinkeloo addition is a sympathetic partner to the headquarters. It contains 200,000 square feet/18,580 square meters. As might be recalled, Kevin Roche and John Dinkeloo were formerly members of and successors to the original Saarinen firm.

Museum-display building open daily, including holidays, 9–5: tours of Administrative Center Mon.–Fri. 10:30 and 1:30

---

43 Joseph Smith Mansion (1844)
Main Street at Water
Nauvoo, Illinois

Nauvoo, on the Mississippi River a bit upstream from Keokuk, Iowa, was one of the key points in the historic development of the Mormon faith. It was here that Prophet Joseph Smith—founder of the Church of Jesus Christ of Latter-day Saints—hoped to settle, only later to be killed by a mob along with his brother Hyrum (1844). The Mormons' subsequent banishment from Illinois took place at Nauvoo in 1846, and under Brigham Young most of them left, eventually to settle in Salt Lake City. The Mormon Church of Utah is now busily engaged in restoring, via Nauvoo Restoration Inc., as much of the early town as possible, turning it, it is hoped, into "a Williamsburg of the West" (although Mormons occupied it only for seven years). In addition to this comprehensive effort by Utah Mormons, which will include the reconstruction of the Nauvoo Temple (dedicated in 1846, incinerated in 1848), the Reorganized Church of Jesus Christ of Latter-day Saints—a group at some odds with their Salt Lake City cousins (and most of whom remained in Nauvoo)—has restored the Joseph Smith Mansion shown here. Formal, even formalistic, it is a suprisingly accomplished dwelling for its time and place, and has been properly restored and furnished with period pieces. The whole town is of interest; a useful guide leaflet is available.

Open Memorial Day–Labor Day, daily 8–8, rest of year 8:30–5, except major holidays

---

44   New Salem Restoration (1831–37/1932–33)
off ILL 97, c. 2 miles/3.2 kilometers S of
Petersburg, Illinois

Almost all of this tiny village, where Abraham Lincoln lived for six years (1831–37) as a young man, has been restored, much of it hypothetically but with meticulous research and care. (Lincoln was born in 1809 in Hardin County, Kentucky, and did not reach Illinois until he was twenty-one years old.) The restoration gives as reasonable a picture as feasible of this 1830 hamlet in the central part of the state. Many buildings are reconstructed on their original foundations, establishing a country village atmosphere as opposed to a random collection. William Randolph Hearst was the first (1906) to stir public interest in the restoration of New Salem which in the 1830s was the size of Chicago—twelve families. Mr. Hearst bought the land and subsequently donated it (1918) to the state. Actual reconstruction, how-

ever, did not begin until 1932. Since then a dozen houses, a number of stores, a school, and a tavern have been rebuilt, while the only surviving original structure, the Onstot Cooper Shop (1835), has been put back in its early condition (after having traveled to nearby Petersburg and being brought back to New Salem in 1922). By coincidence, shortly after Lincoln was appointed to the state legislature and moved to Springfield, some 18 miles/29 kilometers to the southeast, New Salem withered, and eventually was abandoned. The restoration and its furnishings give good insight into backwoods life and shelter in Illinois in the 1830s.

Open daily, summer 9–5, winter 8–4: tours daily except major holidays

45 The Unitarian Church (1965–66)
Dawn Avenue and Turner Street, N off East State Street
Rockford, Illinois

PIETRO BELLUSCHI AND C. EDWARD WARE, ARCHITECTS

The Unitarian Church and fellowship hall create a compact grouping as they survey a 10.5-acre/4.2-hectare site from the crest of a hill on the southeast edge of town. The concrete-framed, flat-roofed buildings

set an unusual religious stage: as one approaches, the pleasures unfold. A small but delightful garden atrium welcomes the visitor who then enters the relaxed narthex, and proceeds to the nave, where a reserved but friendly atmosphere envelops one. This church room is first-rate: no maudlin historicism, no structural acrobatics, simply a well-designed rectangular chamber of quiet dignity. Its precast "split" concrete columns (with narrow panels of stained glass between their halves) form, with the ceiling beams, structural "U" sections on which are laid the precast concrete ceiling planks. Natural stain board-and-batten redwood forms the side walls between the exposed structural members—as they do on the exterior—and carry across two thirds of the chancel to "establish" the pulpit and table. The right third of the sanctuary wall, slightly inset with a thin strip of window marking its separation, is of white concrete covered with growing vines which rise from a tiny "garden." The natural light is comfortably handled, flowing from high clerestories between the beams on each side, and augmented at chancel by a redwood-and-glass grille which gives a proper illumination accent to the sanctuary (and sun on the small garden). The fellowship hall, or multipurpose room, flexibly adjoins the narthex at left on entering; furnished with its own kitchen, it can be turned to a number of group activities. On the lower level, taking advantage of the change in grade, are a series of classrooms for religious instruction, a small chapel, a youth lounge, and utilities.

Visitors welcome Mon.–Fri. 9–5, Sun. service

46   Old State Capitol (1837–40/1853/1966–68)
Adams, 5th, Washington, and 6th Streets
Springfield, Illinois

JOHN F. RAGUE, ARCHITECT

A tawny, weather-beaten temple of considerable architectural appeal.
Doric porticos adorn the north and south sides, while the eternal
dome, here jacked high into the air and painted maroon, states its
function from afar. Rague was following much of the "formula" used
by Town & Davis for state capitols but early references to Town &
Davis as architects of the Springfield state house are incorrect. Although parts of the building were in use in 1840, it was not completed
until 1853. With the rapid growth of the state, the capitol was soon
outgrown and a new building erected, the old becoming (1876) the
Sangamon County Courthouse. When space here became cramped, instead of building a new courthouse, the old one was jacked up 11
feet/3.3 meters and a complete new floor slipped underneath (1898).
In the 1960s, however, a new courthouse being called for, the state
General Assembly decided to turn the ex-capitol, ex-courthouse into a
Lincoln "site," reconstructing the building to the original condition

which Lincoln, himself, knew so well—and in which he lay in state before burial.

To effect this properly, the entire building was taken down stone by numbered stone, and put back together (1966–68) to give us the building we now have, one which in almost all particulars resembles Rague's original. The rebuilding has been beautifully carried out, and the result is not content to be a lifeless restoration, but provides an active forum for the city. A State Historical Library has been incorporated beneath the Old State Capitol, while a 465-car garage has been injected under the grounds to provide parking for visitors and to lure shoppers back to midtown. Ferry & Henderson were the restoration architects.

Open daily 8:30–5, except major holidays

---

47   Assembly Hall (1959–63)
University of Illinois
Florida Avenue between 1st and 4th Streets
Urbana-Champaign, Illinois

**MAX ABRAMOVITZ OF HARRISON & ABRAMOVITZ, ARCHITECT;
AMMANN & WHITNEY, ENGINEERS**

A powerful, ingenious, multipurpose assembly hall whose structure is superbly expressed outside and in. The concrete ribs of its carapace revel in the movement of the sun across its folded plates. In simplistic terms, the hall is composed of two bowls, a roof bowl over a seat bowl, each 400 feet/122 meters in diameter, the inverted, domical upper one resting on the upturned and straight-angled lower, creating an interior completely free of columns. (The lower bowl is partially set into the ground to provide midpoint access to the seats.) This audacious space supersedes in span the somewhat similar dome of Pier Luigi Nervi's famous Palazzo dello Sport for the 1960 Olympics in Rome which has a diameter of 328 feet/100 meters. The Assembly dome is, indeed, the mightiest in the world. Incidentally Nervi's elegant roof was built of prefabricated small elements, the Assembly Hall was poured in place.

The upper dome, of folded plate construction, as mentioned, sends out "fingers" of branching folds toward the perimeter compression ring, post-tensioned by 2,467 lappings of high-tensile wire to contain its thrust. The roof load is then transferred via forty-eight radial

buttresses to the ring footing of the foundations. The folds of the roof
not only provide greater strength (like folding a sheet of paper), they
add greatly to the appearance, outside as well as within, where they
also aid in the acoustics. The thickness of the concrete in the dome is
only 3.5 inches/89 millimeters with a further 2 inches/51 millimeters
added for acoustic material. Inasmuch as the upper half is supported
by the inward-canted buttresses of the lower, and not by external vertical columns, the whole hall rests lightly on the horizon like some gigantic spaceship. The shell represents magnificent coordination between architect and engineer: nothing should be added, nothing could
be taken away—it is theory defined. A glass-enclosed concourse,
reached by six external ramps, provides access to the hall, the width of
this annular concourse being sufficient to double as exhibition area. All
services are below.

The interior forms a dazzling, unencumbered space, 128 feet/39 meters high and, as mentioned, 400 feet/122 meters in diameter. Note the
excellent scale of the ribbing of the folded roof. The Hall accommodates ice shows, basketball, and convocations—"any type of event that
might appear on a stage." Capacity varies from 3,500 to 15,823 on
permanent seats with 1,000 extra on portable chairs. Since the building
of the Krannert Center (q.v.), the Assembly Hall is used primarily for
large-scale events. The mechanics of the light ring and "grid" are complex, but overall this intriguing campus magnet is superb. Abe Feder
was lighting consultant; Bolt, Beranek & Newman, acoustic consultants.

Open during events

48   **Krannert Center for the Performing Arts** (1968–69)
       University of Illinois
       Goodwin Avenue between West Illinois and Oregon Streets
       Urbana-Champaign, Illinois

MAX ABRAMOVITZ OF HARRISON & ABRAMOVITZ, ARCHITECT

This gigantic five-theater complex for the performing arts, ranges in
capacity from the 200-seat Studio Theater to the impressive 2,100-seat
Great Hall. No multiple use was considered: each unit was designed to
house best its speciality. Besides an open-air amphitheater, there is a

small experimental theater, a drama theater, a music theater, and an orchestral hall. Constructed to serve the conjoined cities of Urbana and Champaign as well as being a teaching adjunct for the University of Illinois (with some 35,000 students), its facilities have vastly increased the cultural possibilities of the region. Being compressed on two city blocks, it was necessary to raise the lobby terrace almost a full floor above the street to accommodate services and adjacent garage. With three major theaters (of red brick) rising above this terrace, an effect of almost Pergamean monumentality results. The lobby terrace connects with the plaza terrace above it by utilizing the steps of the 560-seat, semicircular amphitheater to provide ingenious access. A vast, low-ceilinged lobby, or public level, connects all four theaters.

In fair weather the plaza terrace can be used for promenading and "observing" during intermissions. Rehearsal rooms, studios, and shops fill the lowest level. Each theater has its own inner lobby and public facilities.

The small Studio Theater presents a totally flexible box for experimental work; even the seats are movable. The Playhouse (at left)—the drama theater—provides 678 seats in a particularly handsome, steeply raked room with Venetian-red seats and deep-blue, almost black, walls and ceiling, their dark color making the auditorium "enclosure" almost disappear when the house lights go off. The Festival Theater (at right), seating 965 and designed for musicals, opera, and the dance, sets a more effusive note with the same red seats as in the Playhouse but with white walls and ceiling. The effect, however, is not as successful, being choppy with "paneling," especially about the stage. The Great Hall (on axis at center) was designed for orchestras—it seats up to 120 musicians on its stage—and for choral programs, and is, in contrast with the two other major theaters, a "self-contained" auditorium with no proscenium and no curtain. It functions solely as a 2,100-seat concert hall—and it functions with excellent acoustics. Lined with butternut paneling and with a faceted, light-colored plaster ceiling suspended free of the side walls, and with even the seats in the same muted color, the interior is impressive: understated, uncluttered, elegant. Jo Mielziner and George C. Izenour were theatrical consultants; Dr. Cyril M. Harris, acoustical engineer. The Center was made possible by a munificent gift by Mr. and Mrs. Herman Krannert.

Daily tours 2–5, except holidays; also open for
performances

49   **Vandalia Statehouse State Historic Site** (1836–39/1857–59)
Gallatin Street at Kennedy Boulevard
Vandalia, Illinois

WILLIAM HODGE AND JOHN TAYLOR, ARCHITECTS

The exterior proportions of the statehouse are naive—it was constructed in less than four months—especially the mammoth square
brick piers of the portico which date from the 1857–59 remodeling.
However, the setting is dulcet, the lawn on four sides well tended, and
the interior competent. Nothing monumental, but a reasonable example of federal architecture with classical portico enhancing its mass.
Vandalia served (1820–39) as the state's second capital (with this the
fourth Capitol building). The capital was then moved to the more centrally located Springfield. Remodeled, as indicated, during later years,
the building was completely restored in 1933–39. It stands along the
famous Cumberland Trail, the country's first great national road which
began in Cumberland, Maryland, in 1811.

Open daily 9–5, except major holidays

50 **Crow Island School** (1939–40/1954)
**Willow Road at Glendale Avenue, c. 2 miles/3.2 kilometers E of
IS 94**
Winnetka, Illinois

**SAARINEN & SAARINEN, AND PERKINS, WHEELER & WILL,
ARCHITECTS**

The Crow Island School, which helped revolutionize the architecture of elementary education, is still in fine shape, forty years later. Its evolution, which started with the design of an ideal classroom—as opposed to the monumental self-important building then popular—still carries lessons. Note its child scale, its L-shaped rooms with ample window seats, and its close association with nature. (Much of this innovative designing was inspired by the school's superintendent Carleton Washburne.) Pedagogical shelter has changed abruptly in the past few decades—the classroom unit itself has largely given way to an undefined flexible teaching space—but Crow Island lies behind much of the evolution. It was added to in 1954 by Perkins, Wheeler & Will. One of the great pioneers.

Open during school hours

Indiana

Crown Point 13

Fort Wayne 15–16

Bluffton 2

Lafayette 22

Indianapolis 17–21

Columbus 3–11

Aurora 1

Mitchell 24

Madison 23

New Albany 25

Corydon 12

New Harmony 26–27

Evansville 14

INDIANA

The buildings in boldface type are of general interest. The others are for the specialist.

Aurora	1	**Hillforest** (1852–56)
Bluffton	2	Wells County Court House (1889–91)— George W. Bunting & Son
Columbus	3	**Columbus and Its Building Program** (1940–)—Architects as noted
	4	**First Christian Church** (1940–42)— Eliel Saarinen
	5	**North Christian Church** (1963–64)— Eero Saarinen & Associates
	6	**Cummins Engine Company Technical Center** (1966–68)—Harry Weese & Associates
	7	Fire Station #4 (1967)—Venturi & Rauch
	8	**Cleo Rogers Memorial County Library** (1966–69)—I. M. Pei & Partners
	9	**L. Frances Smith Elementary School** (1968–69)—John M. Johansen
	10	Columbus East High School (1970–72)— Mitchell/Giurgola
	11	**Fodrea Community School** (1972–73)— Caudill, Rowlett & Scott
Corydon	12	Corydon Capitol State Memorial (1814–16)
Crown Point	13	Old Lake County Court House (1878–79)— John C. Cochrane
Evansville	14	**Old Vanderburgh Court House Center** (1888–91)—Henry Wolters
Fort Wayne	15	**Allen County Court House** (1897–1900)— Brentwood S. Tolan
	16	**Concordia Theological Seminary** (1955– 58)—Eero Saarinen & Associates
Indianapolis	17	Indianapolis-Marion County Public Library (1916–17)—Paul Philippe Cret

18 **Clowes Memorial Hall** (1962–63)—John M. Johansen and Evans Woollen

19 **John J. Barton Apartments for the Elderly** (1966–67)—Evans Woollen

20 **Christian Theological Seminary** (1965–66)— Edward Larrabee Barnes

21 **College Life Insurance Company of America** (1971–72)—Kevin Roche/John Dinkeloo

Lafayette

22 Tippecanoe Court House (1881–84)— Elias Max

Madison

23 **The Sullivan, Lanier, and Shrewsbury Houses**—(1818–55)

Mitchell

24 **Spring Mill Village Reconstruction** (1817–1850s)

New Albany

25 Culbertson Mansion State Memorial (1867–69)

New Harmony

26 **Historic New Harmony** (1814–24)

27 **Roofless Church** (1959–60)—Philip Johnson Paul Johannes Tillich Memorial Park (1966)—Zion & Breen

1 Hillforest (1852–56)
Main Street at 5th
Aurora, Indiana

A buoyant semi-Italianate villa built for Thomas Gaff, a nineteenth-century Ohio River shipper and industrialist. Resplendent in yellow, white, and dark green, it is perched on the hillside at the end of Main Street, its elevation allowing a panorama of town and the nearby Ohio River. (Cincinnati lies about 25 miles/40 kilometers up the river.) The Italian villa fashion was just beginning in this country in the 1850s, and this example with semicircular main bay, cylindrical "cupola" (probably influenced by riverboat pilothouses), and simple side wings stands as a chaste example. Shortly thereafter the brackets proliferated.

The mass of the dwelling, whose rear section is not as satisfactory as the front, is painted a clean yellow, while the white and dark green mentioned are found in the trim and shutters. The interior represents early Victorianism in its furnishings, all of which have been carefully maintained. Cornices, chandeliers, and fireplaces are the most notable features. The house, in addition to being open to the public for much of the year, also serves as a cultural center for the town.

Open Apr.–Dec., Tues.–Sun. 10–5: admission

---

2   Wells County Court House (1889–91)
South Main Street at West Market (IND 1)
Bluffton, Indiana

GEORGE W. BUNTING & SON, ARCHITECTS

The courthouses of Indiana, especially those of the 1880s and '90s, unfurl the most splendiferous cavalcade of municipal building in the United States. No state in this world can equal their determined ostentation. Individually they are generally awe-inspiring, collectively overwhelming. They range from the Greek Revival to Second Empire, Baroque to Richardsonian—to name only the most prominent. Professor David R. Hermansen, at Ball State University in Muncie, has been one of the deepest delvers into this "Hoosier Hysteria" as he calls it, and has written that "During the 19th century all 92 Indiana counties built at least two and several as many as five courthouses in a span of less than 90 years" (*Historic Preservation,* May–June 1971). Professor Hermansen has also prepared a comprehensive traveling exhibit on the subject. His help with research for this book is much appreciated. Only a brief cross section of Indiana's vast panoply can be included here, but many others are worth investigating. Among them (alphabetically by city) are: Decatur (1872), Frankfort (1882), Greensburg (1860), Lagrange (1879), Plymouth (1870), Richmond (1892), Rising Sun (1845), South Bend (1854), Wabash (1892), and Warsaw (1882).

The Bluffton Court House—with obvious influence from H. H. Richardson—stands as one of the more adventuresome "Romanesque" examples. The square corner tower with cantilevered round turret is outstanding, as is the stonework. (Note the stringcourses with delicate

friezes.) The courtroom itself is also well handled. Its ceiling was dropped c. 1925, but the original ceiling with its stencils was left in place and will be restored. The entire building, having received National Register certification (1979), is now being rehabilitated. Its architect, George W. Bunting (1829–1901), "was without question the most prolific designer of county courthouses to reside in Indiana" (*Indiana County Courthouses of the Nineteenth Century,* David R. Hermansen, 1968, Ball State University Press). Around 1886 he was joined by his son.

Open during office hours

3   Columbus and Its Building Program (1940–   )
Columbus, Indiana

ARCHITECTS AS NOTED

The First Christian Church (q.v.) was the initiating unit of the most extraordinary architectural design and building program in any city in the United States. Through the enlightened generosity of J. Irwin Miller and the Cummins Engine Foundation many of the outstanding architects in the United States have been commissioned to design local buildings, the Foundation picking up the tab for their services. (The Columbus-born Mr. Miller is the Chairman, Executive and Finance Committee, of Cummins, the largest manufacturer of diesel engines in the world.) The architects themselves are chosen by the citizens from a panel recommended by outside experts. Mr. Miller often only meets the designer for the first time at the dedication of his building. The result has been an astounding parade of good, often great, buildings, only a few of which, because of space limitations, can be described here—a comprehensive guidebook to all is available. Even the largely Victorian main thoroughfare (Washington Street) has undergone a partial rehabilitation of colors and signs under the skilled eyes of Alexander Girard. As a result of this stimulating rejuvenation, plus a startling number of new buildings and facilities—including two outstanding factories—Columbus has been able to make the attractions and the life of a semiremote small city (population around 32,000), lying 42 miles/68 kilometers southeast of Indianapolis, outpull much larger centers in the competition for bright young engineering and managerial talent. An indexed map and, as mentioned, an excellent, inexpensive guidebook to some forty new structures of merit are available at the Visitors Center (1864/1973). Exhibits and rest rooms are available with free parking nearby.

Obviously with a program that began in the early 1940s—and which of financial necessity had to proceed via scattered buildings to meet diverse needs through the decades—little urban coherence could be established. However, new comprehensive planning will in part ameliorate this condition—as per Washington Street—and knit the city together more fully and also to its setting. In the meantime let us bless what has been done—and done under private initiative.

The 1874 Bartholomew County Court House, Washington Street at 3rd, Isaac Hodgson, architect, should also be seen.

Guide booklet available at Visitors Center, 506 Fifth Street; open
from Apr.–Oct., Mon.–Sat. 9–5, and also on Sun. 12–4, except
major holidays. Bus tours available

---

4   First Christian Church (1940–42)
531 5th Street
Columbus, Indiana

ELIEL SAARINEN, ARCHITECT

Frank Lloyd Wright's 1908 Unity Temple in Oak Park (near Chicago
—q.v.) was the first church in the United States to break out of the
stultifying rehash of past styles which then (and even now) mocked
the once-progressive spirit of Christianity. The First Christian Church
in Columbus gives us another step forward in the evolution of American religious building. Unity Temple, unfortunately, exerted little architectural influence on the country; we were not then ready for such
boldness. But the First Christian Church can claim to be a progenitor

of revitalized church building in the United States. Its "paneled" exterior, elevated chancel, and its stretched austerity date it, but it is still a handsome, strong proclamation of Faith. Note the tensions between the lofty bell tower (166 feet/51 meters high) and the broad horizontals. The church itself is part of a religious grouping which is angled around a sunken garden (originally a pool). A large auditorium lies beneath the nave, while the elevated wing at right contains the Bible School, and the west wing houses the primary department. The nave is "as simple and fundamental architecturally as the gospel it proclaims" to quote the church pamphlet. The chapel, located behind the main chancel, and provided with a separate entrance, should also be seen. Eero Saarinen was his father's associate.

Open daily 8–4

---

5   **North Christian Church** (1963–64)
    850 Tipton Lane, E off Washington Street
    Columbus, Indiana

EERO SAARINEN & ASSOCIATES, ARCHITECTS

Conceived in symbolism and nurtured by perceptive talent, of all his work this church was among the architect's favorite designs. It was completed by his associates after his death in 1961. Symbolism generated its plan, which is an oblate hexagon somewhat reminiscent of the Star of David, hence the Judeo-Christian tradition. Symbolism also raised the spire 192 feet/59 meters toward heaven and topped it with a cross of gold leaf on steel. The continuation upward of the six steel roof ribs, which double-bend to form the spire, provides one of the smoothest facets of the church's design; spire and church are organically fused. The dominating roof extends like a conical hat of steel and slate over the elongated hexagon of the concrete base. The slightly elevated nave rests in the center of this hexagon, surrounded on both narthex and lower levels by classrooms, meeting rooms, and offices. The brim of the "hat" projects as a shield over the peripheral windows —as it also emphasizes the dominance of the primacy of worship over the ancillary of services. This envelopment by the roof is intensified by a berm which surrounds the building and largely conceals the fenestration of the narthex level, while completely hiding the windows of the moated basement.

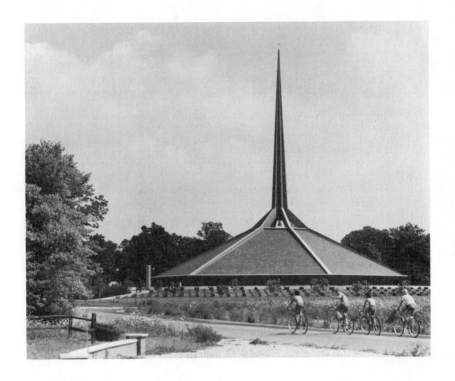

When one first enters, the nave seems small though it seats 465 in a stepped dish in the center of the church, while 150 more can be accommodated in the upper ranks. This smallness, this withinwardness, is intensified by the fact that the six ceiling planes that enclose the upper part of the worship room slant up toward a central oculus or skylight. Daylight enters from this round skylight plus a peripheral, invisible glazed band of borrowed light (somewhat insufficiently borrowed) which entirely surrounds the nave and separates it from its sloping hexagonal ceiling. (Compare Saarinen's earlier chapel with similar lighting at MIT, Cambridge, Massachusetts.) In the North Christian nave, one is celestially isolated; however, the nave is wonderfully altar-centered—the long altar rests in the middle of the hexagon—and develops an admirable liturgical intimacy. The communion dais and tables are removable, creating a versatile worship space that can also be used for dramatic and musical presentations. A stepped chancel and boldly silhouetted organ pipes form the only accents. A youth activities center, kitchen, auditorium, and services are found on the lower level.

Open Mon.–Fri. 9–5, Sat. 9–2, Sun. service 10 A.M.

6 Cummins Engine Company Technical Center (1966–68)
1900 McKinley Avenue
Columbus, Indiana

HARRY WEESE & ASSOCIATES, ARCHITECTS

An engine-block precision and robustness characterize this office building and conjoined technical unit, well reflecting the company's products. The square, six-story administrative and "think-tank" unit stands
separate from and at a 45° angle to the two-story research and testing
building. A slender, glass-enclosed bridge plus an underground passage
connect them. The administrative unit is angled to "loosen" the space
between the two. Both buildings are made of reinforced concrete, but
the largely glass administrative wing (of poured concrete frame)—its
plate glass a deep tan in color—dominates the almost windowless technical adjunct. The windows of the office block are given some sun protection and interesting scale by bifurcated concrete hoods—like
squared sunglasses—bolted atop and projecting from each window.

The walls of the research-testing building, which measures 386 x 450
feet/118 x 137 meters, are of prefabricated concrete panels, ribbed to
give a scale relationship to the administrative building. Its lower floor
is devoted to service and supplies, with an enormous and totally

flexible work area above. This lofty space can be subdivided at will, with machine shops alternating with enclosed evaluating offices directly alongside. The noise and venting problems involved in scrutinizing huge diesel engines run at full throttle have been thoroughly engineered. Expansion is possible. A very competent technical facility.

Contact administration for visiting information

---

7   **Fire Station ✳4** (1967)
    4950 25th Street (IND 46—NE edge of town)
    Columbus, Indiana

    VENTURI & RAUCH, ARCHITECTS

This puzzling building represents an architectural direction—the anti-heroic—of curious fascination. It very consciously makes architecture a stage set, in effect a paint job which is spatially disorienting—and to some professionals annoying—in its desire to shake us, to challenge us,

as observers. Its goal is to turn the ordinary, the superordinary, supereconomical—here on a superdull road—into an object which we cannot ignore. In this non-escapability, "this masonry garage," it achieves its goal, its teleology. The trapezoidal plan—angled across the back to express space requirements and two sizes of fire engines—places dormitory at left rear, lounge (too small, say the firemen) on front left corner, 36-foot/11-meter-high hose-drying tower as fulcrum near center, and engine room at right. The parapet of the latter is purposefully "false" as it extends over the lower left section. The white brick filling most of the facade stops short of the corners so that the red brick of the sides could wrap around and bedevil the scale, making a small building appear larger, and, as Venturi puts it, "more pert." Take a look.

Open daily 8–5

8　Cleo Rogers Memorial County Library (1966–69)
5th Street at Lafayette Avenue
Columbus, Indiana

I. M. PEI & PARTNERS, ARCHITECTS

The Rogers Library and the space around it were not designed *in vacuo,* but as urban components of the elderly Irwin Home adjacent and the First Christian Church directly across the way. The architects have fashioned thereby a composed downtown piazzetta that is active and attractive both day and night. The pavement of this plaza is red brick, and red brick steps upward to make a low podium for the library, then rises vertically to form its walls. Angled sharply, these walls are smart exercises with that most ancient of man-made building materials. Contrasting with these ruddy walls are the concrete for spandrel beams and concrete waffle ceilings. Setting off the plaza in front stands a walk-through *Large Arch* (1971) by Henry Moore— one of the country's finest pieces of urban sculpture, and a gift of Mr. and Mrs. J. Irwin Miller.

The library interior at the entry lacks eloquence, primarily because the tall stacks bully the space, but the mezzanine, devoted to the fine arts (plus the director's office), provides a private retreat centered about a skylit garden. The entry floor at rear expands outward onto a garden terrace. The lower level, largely underground, is filled with the adult section, 150-seat auditorium, workrooms, and, best of all, the

children's library opening onto a partially sunken court that also connects with the upper terrace. The total book capacity is 175,000 volumes.

Distinguished as a library, the achievement is also significant as an urban partnership of three strikingly disparate buildings. These were pulled together by first blocking Lafayette Avenue (at the architect's request), then designing the library to pick up the scale of the 1911 house (note that the library's right window head lines with house eave), and transferring with harmony the facade of the library to coordinate with that of the 1942 church, with Mr. Moore's great Arch the catalyst. Outdoor art shows and concerts also take place on the plaza. Kenneth D. B. Carruthers was partner-in-charge.

Open Mon.–Thurs. 8:30 A.M.*–9* P.M.*, Fri.–Sat. 8:30–6*

---

9   L. Frances Smith Elementary School (1968–69)
4505 Waycross Drive, E on 25th Street (IND 46), S on
**   Timbercrest Drive, 1st right**
Columbus, Indiana

JOHN M. JOHANSEN, ARCHITECT

An assemblage of "exploded" parts, tied and interlaced by multicolored ramp-tubes—almost a non-building—make this one of the country's intriguing schools. In spite of apparent and actual complex-

ity, the concept is relatively simple: three classroom wings of varying length and height fan out from an elevated administration unit and library at center, the whole being interconnected by ramp-tubes and, from the second floor, by open exit ramps. The classroom wings vary in length and formation to fit their size requirements. Each accommodates six rooms with approximately thirty students each. They are built of demountable steel, and can be changed, while administration and library, and the ground-level units for kitchen-dining, multipurpose room, mechanical services, and kindergarten are of concrete.

One enters a small courtyard under the elevated administration block to find an immensely dynamic, but slightly confusing, game of brightly colored ramp-tubes seemingly taking off in every direction. Colors, forms, and angles here generate a three-dimensional experience approaching kinetic sculpture. At the head of each class wing there is a nodule which commands that wing, and which also serves for special projects. Use was made of the upper-level open ramps to provide direct access to the playground and to serve as emergency exits. They also visually bind the school to the flat land about it, in curious fashion energizing both. Highly arbitrary at times, with, occasionally, faulty finish and questionable details, the school is enormously provocative. When seen under construction, it appeared to offer architectural anarchy; when experienced after completion, enthusiasm sang out (notwithstanding the faults mentioned). Children and staff love it.

Open during school hours

10   Columbus East High School (1970–72)
230 South Marr Road (SE on State Road 7, left on Marr)
Columbus, Indiana

MITCHELL/GIURGOLA, ARCHITECTS

An advanced high school for 2,100 students, businesslike on the exterior, keen in concept and organization. Its instructional block in center is flanked at left by the freestanding Physical Education Building (primarily a gymnasium with 4,200 seats), with separate pool having retractable roof directly behind. Both units are available to the community. An "unnecessary" but effective brick "arch" heralds them. At extreme right rises the auditorium (892 seats), also with direct access for the public. The hub of the building—its educational workshop—comprises a three-level main block with a two-level industrial arts and service wing angling at 45° at rear. Across the front half of the slightly elevated ground floor of the academic section extends a "gallery level" containing a planetarium, a series of varyingly sized lecture or seminar rooms, and audiovisual facilities, these specialized rooms being bunched in three two-bay groups with entry/exit stairs between. Ad-

ministrative services fill part of the largely glazed rear of this floor of the building, along with lofty student "commons" and the adjoining cafeteria, both opening onto an outdoor terrace. Food preparation is adjacent in the first half of the angled wing.

These multiple levels and spaces and their dramatic continuum and lighting make this gallery level exciting. There is a spontaneous "forum" quality of social interacting here which gives the school much life. The prime instructional floor (i.e. the second) is based on three Y-shapes. The resource center, teachers' station, and individual student carrels form the base of each Y with arms containing classes branching from this. A bank of seminar rooms and enclosed labs line the entire front, illuminated (at times insufficiently) by the angled continuous skylight seen in elevation plus small horizontal windows in every third exterior panel. On the far side (i.e. the rear) of the second floor are more study carrels and two instructional material centers along with three open deck areas. The third floor, less than half the width of the two below, contains thirty-three enclosed seminar rooms, all the same size (sixteen seats), and all stepped to face onto open decks. As is apparent, the three levels proceed from the general to the specialized.

Built on a steel bay module of 44 x 32 feet/13 x 9.7 meters, the school is enclosed by red, bricklike tile on the ground floor and a white aluminum sandwich panel above when not of glass. Behind all planning was the goal to spur the "development of self-direction, initiative and deciding one's own destiny."

Public area open during school hours

---

11   Fodrea Community School (1972–73)
2775 Illinois Street at Hughes
Columbus, Indiana

CAUDILL, ROWLETT & SCOTT, ARCHITECTS

Fodrea's white metal exterior, being largely windowless, gives few hints of the spatial largesse that greets one within its open-to-sky inner court. This forum, elevated a half-flight above ground, is framed by two L-shaped arms. The larger of these is the two-story instructional building with Materials Resource Center across its inner angle, the whole fully glazed onto the planted, sunny court. (The street-side walls are solid except for a clerestory running their length.) The east arm of the other side contains the two-story multipurpose gymnasium

with stage and music arena at far end, and at right angles to this dining-kitchen wing which closes the court. Three corner stairways give access. Both gym and cafeteria can be used by the community when the instructional wing is closed. In addition to the careful landscaping in the raised concourse, another prominent "court" feature can be seen in the freestanding columns of the space-frame roofing of the main building.

The interior of this teaching block is completely open, class groups forming as needed. At the angle of the instructional "L," a Pueblo "kiva" steps down in circles to form an intimate teaching or studying spot. Accommodating a maximum of 640 students from kindergarten to eleven years old, the school's design evolved through lengthy consultation on the part of the architects with children, their parents and teachers, and the school board. There are opportunities for adult instruction—and, of course, activities—as well as for the young. The school was named for the three now-retired Fodrea sisters, all teachers. Paul Kennon and Truitt Garrison of CRS were in charge, with A. Dean Taylor of Columbus, associate architect.

Building open during school hours, court always open

12   Corydon Capitol State Memorial (1814–16)
North Capitol Avenue at Beaver Street
Corydon, Indiana

A sturdy limestone municipal building, built as the Harrison County Court House, but on completion (1816) made the first capitol of the state. (In 1825 the capital was moved to Indianapolis.) The 40-foot-square (12-meter-square) building, topped with a cupola, stands in a shaded plaza in a still little-spoiled village. Its exterior walls are unusual in that they are made of inner and outer facings of local blue limestone with sand between for a total thickness of 30 inches/76 centimeters. Unfortunately, only a small amount of the original woodwork remains. The ground floor, formerly used by the House of Representatives, forms one entirely open room, with dais for the speaker of the House across the back. On the second floor are located the Senate Chamber and the Supreme Court. Though not of stylistic significance, it gives a solid glimpse of early Indiana building, when the territory, on mustering a population of 60,000, could qualify as a state. The building was completely restored and refurnished in 1929–30, and is now under the supervision of the Department of Natural Resources—

Division of Historic Preservation. The surrounding Historic District should also be seen.

Open Mon.–Sat. 9–12, 1–5, Sun. 1–5, except holidays: admission

---

13   **Old Lake County Court House** (1878–79)
      Courthouse Square
      Crown Point, Indiana

      JOHN C. COCHRANE, ARCHITECT

An architecturally transitional courthouse that combines geometry with color and dash. Red bricks, white quoins, and white stringcourses —the latter roller-coasting over roundheaded windows—are topped by three determined pediments, heavily modillioned. A clock tower rises behind in the center with a smaller turret on each side. Note that though the five bays of the facade are of three different widths, each carries the constant module of a single-width window, the center window alone being unique. An addition was made in 1907–9 by Beers & Beers, with another in 1928 by Albert Turner, architect, but the Main Street facade, fortunately, has not been touched.

The building's legal functions were moved to new quarters in 1974

and the Old Court House was acquired the next year by the nonprofit Lake Court House Foundation Inc. Under the direction of architect David J. Katz a complete restoration was then commenced under the Foundation's aegis. Adaptive uses are now being sought: a number of shops have been opened on the lower level and it is hoped that a museum will occupy part of the upper floor. The building is in the National Register of Historic Places.

Open during business hours

14 **Old Vanderburgh Court House Center** (1888–91)
The Conrad Baker Center
Court Street between 4th and 5th
Evansville, Indiana

HENRY WOLTERS, ARCHITECT

In most of the larger (and many minor) cities of Indiana, the court-houses were conceived with Medician grandeur, and the Vanderburgh County building—now the Conrad Baker Center—is no exception. Its limestone pile set stiff competition for its neighbors for trade and prestige. (The smaller towns splurged on their courthouses for the chance to be named the county seat.) The Center was designed by a German-born architect educated at the Paris Beaux-Arts. The profligacy of architectural motifs at Evansville bears testament to a civic pride and a civic willingness to part with cash which seems totally lacking in our present program of watered-down, minimal civic struc-tures. The 216-foot/66-meter-high cupola and central bay alone must be seen to be believed. When to these are added the domed, half-round bays, their circular windows at top suitably wreathed, the building overflows with varietal Second Empire fashions. Its exuberant sculp-ture by Franz Englesmann is worthy of binocular scrutiny.

Though the interior is cut up in places, the Blue Room (ex-Law Library) is not only good but available for public and private functions. Municipal usage being considered inefficient, the courthouse's future remained unclear until the non-profit Conrad Baker Foundation ac-quired the building in 1969 on a ninety-nine-year lease, and is using the restored building for a cultural center housing exhibitions, a hundred-seat repertory theater, a number of shops, and other functions pro bono publico. One wishes the Foundation and the citizens of Evans-ville the greatest of success: this is one of the most distinguished build-ings in the state.

Open Tues.–Sat. 9–5, Sun. 12–5, except holidays: donation

---

15   Allen County Court House (1897–1900)
South Calhoun Street between Berry and Main
Fort Wayne, Indiana

BRENTWOOD S. TOLAN, ARCHITECT

The Allen County Court House carries "a combination of the Renais-sance, Roman and Grecian, in architecture" as the illustrated guide (available within) attests, and though it certainly does not flag in its external aspirations, its greatest ambitions lie inside. The view from the rotunda looking upward reveals a whirling kaleidoscope of dome,

pendentives, and arched supports, all ablaze with colored glass or bright murals, each facet loaded with allegory and/or historical depiction of the episodes of the area. The entry floor houses various county offices and a law library, the second floor is largely devoted to records, while the third is filled with richly finished courtrooms. Constructed of the famous Indiana limestone, the building was designed by Brentwood Tolan whose father, Thomas J., had previously built a number of courthouses throughout the state (and in Ohio). As the aforementioned guide alleges, "It can also be claimed as the largest, most beautiful, costly, safe, and the most splendid structure designed for County uses, of any in Indiana, or indeed, the entire West."

Open during office hours

16   Concordia Theological Seminary (1955–58)
6660 North Clinton Street (1.6 miles/2.5 kilometers N of US 30)
Fort Wayne, Indiana

EERO SAARINEN & ASSOCIATES, ARCHITECTS

North European vernacular, particularly Scandinavian, produces an unexpectedly romantic academic "village" from the Saarinen office. The college is grouped about an artificial 9-acre/3.6-hectare lake and develops a homogeneity of small, simple units dominated by its chapel. It was largely designed and built at one time. Approximately 450 students attend the seminary, almost all of whom will enter the Lutheran ministry (Missouri Synod). Its 198-acre/80-hectare site, northeast of Fort Wayne, was formerly farmland.

The 575-seat Kramer Chapel, triangular in section, rests on a terraced podium at the head of the lake, where its geometry and location make it the visual dominant and circulation crossroads of the campus. The chapel interior is effectively illuminated by a skylight which runs the length of the ridge, plus a panel of glass from ridge to floor on the

right side of the chancel, with peripheral indirect bands of light (in the Saarinen fashion) along the base of each side. As a result, light flows in, enlivening the somewhat austere architectural treatment of the interior. The church's sharp roof angle measures 23.5° from the vertical, those of the secular buildings 23.5° from the horizontal, all thus are geometrically locked together, and all are covered with dark gray tiles The slender, triangular bell tower, 103.5 feet/31.5 meters high, adds the proper vertical accent. A variety of art (mosaics, wall carvings, bronzes, terra-cottas, and wood carving) is found throughout.

Campus and chapel open daily

---

17 Indianapolis-Marion County Public Library (1916–17)
40 East St. Clair Street
Indianapolis, Indiana

PAUL PHILIPPE CRET, ARCHITECT

A limestone, Doric-inspired library which is generally considered the French-born Cret's finest work. Bound strictly to Hellenism, here with freshness, it stands high in the period of the eclectic development of U.S. architecture. It has, indeed, been called "the best classic building in America." The main reading room approaches the grandiose. Zantzinger, Borie & Medary were associate architects.

Open Mon.–Fri. 9–9, Sat. 9–5, Sun. 1–5, except major holidays

---

18 Clowes Memorial Hall (1962–63)
West 46th Street at Sunset Avenue
Indianapolis, Indiana

JOHN M. JOHANSEN AND EVANS WOOLLEN, ASSOCIATED ARCHITECTS

Clowes Hall was placed at the entrance to the campus of Butler University so that it could conveniently serve both college and city. This combined concert hall and theater is given architectural prominence by its clustering of tall, boxlike forms, the varying heights and projections of which develop a massive rhythm and shadow play. However, in spite of the inviting color of the limestone facing and an engaging roof line, some formidableness is evident, resulting from the "palisade" of the many box-forms that frame and enclose the building. An "invitation" to enter is missing.

The main lobby itself is four stories high and laterally constricted as it continues the rigorousness seen without. The auditorium, on the other hand, with watermelon-red curtain, red seats, and gold acoustic wire-hung "clouds," is an exciting space. This heart, this rationale, of the building is inviting while its acoustics are excellent. The 2,200 seats of Clowes are arranged in gentle curves in the Continental (aisleless) manner. As this seating arrangement demands exits no more than 15 feet/4.6 meters apart (fire code), the architects took this mandatory module and enclosed the sides with a series of the aforementioned staggered boxlike "wall elements" which reflect the shape of the hall. Interior safety demands of the building code thus became a design key. The generous lateral lobbies pulsate between the uneven (but carefully calculated) spaces formed between auditorium and outer walls (of concrete), and are arranged so that they provide alcoves for conversation, some with seats, away from the circulation flow. The large stage

can accommodate a variety of performances ranging from a symphony orchestra to Broadway shows to films. It is topped by a high stage loft. The two pits in front can be raised to orchestra level or stage height. Clowes Memorial was financed in the main by a generous grant from the Clowes Foundation. Fink, Roberts & Petrie were the structural engineers; Jean Rosenthal, state consultant; Bolt, Beranek & Newman, acousticians.

Open during performances

---

19   John J. Barton Apartments for the Elderly (1966–67)
555 North Massachusetts Avenue at Michigan Street
Indianapolis, Indiana

EVANS WOOLLEN, ARCHITECT

Any architect who can survive the bureaucracy of the public housing gauntlet in the U.S.A. deserves to be congratulated, especially if he arrives at a solution as capable as this. Designed on a rock-bottom budget, the tower contains 248 apartments for those over sixty-five. The majority (170) of these are for single occupancy, but 78 are doubles requiring bedrooms of sufficient size to hold two beds, and correspondingly larger living rooms. These latter units are logically expressed in the faired-out upper section—reminiscent of BBPR's Torre

Velasca in Milan. The same plumbing and utility chases run throughout. Sandwiched between the upper six floors and the lower fourteen are the main lounge and community room, with a generous balcony along each side. This floor is airy and pleasant and offers extensive views over the city. All furnishings in the apartments are by the occupants so that nostalgic possessions will lend identity to a new setting. Construction throughout is of reinforced concrete poured in place with excellent form-marks. The hollow, angled spandrel sections were precast: they contain heating coils and also shield the windows. Subsequent low-rise expansion—good but not great—was added (1971) by bridging the street.

Lobby open to public

---

20 Christian Theological Seminary (1965–66)
1000 West 42nd Street at Haughey Avenue
Indianapolis, Indiana

EDWARD LARRABEE BARNES, ARCHITECT

A well-laid-out, beautifully detailed building, the first stage of a fuller development. The seminary provides instruction for approximately three hundred (eventually four hundred) graduate students from a number of Protestant churches, plus Roman Catholic and Jewish

representation—some twenty-five denominations each year. Living quarters at present are provided off campus, some under the aegis of the religious organizations with which the students work part-time. Dormitories will be built later. Seminary construction is of prefabricated, pebble-faced, sand-colored concrete panels, precisely detailed and manufactured. Panels of the same material also pave the back terrace. Variety is given the low wings by the projection of the student lounge (in front), the high mass of the auditorium (rear), and by the changing monitors of the roof lines. Contact with the unspoiled 36-acre/15-hectare setting on a bluff overlooking the White River (beyond the northwest edge of town) is intimate, even when viewing nature from within, while several landscaped, open-air gathering spots are also provided. Internal passages are frequently lit by skylights that liberate the corridors. The steeply raked auditorium, which seats 411 (somewhat rigidly) is finished entirely in wood; the other rooms, all of which are bright and airy, are plastered. The scale and atmosphere of the building are excellent. The numerous works of art were largely the gift of Mr. and Mrs. J. Irwin Miller (of Columbus, Indiana).

Open Mon.–Fri. 8–5, except holidays

21 College Life Insurance Company of America (1971–72)
3500 DePauw Boulevard, just SE of intersection of IS 465 and US 421 (c. 10 miles/16 kilometers NNW of downtown via Northwestern Avenue and US 421)
Indianapolis, Indiana

KEVIN ROCHE/JOHN DINKELOO, ARCHITECTS

Architecture as a prismatic sculptural expression was first, and most substantially, made evident by that vibrating collection of pyramids at Gizeh, where the interaction of profiled angle on profiled angle practically shakes the Sahara. Today, the back-to-the-pyramids, mathematical approach toward the sculptured aspect of architecture has probably reached a climax in this group of three startling forms northwest of Indianapolis. They represent a far-out but by no means frivolous approach in sheltering a keenly competitive business whose architectural image is certain to influence sales impact. One may or may not be sympathetic to these truncated, strangely scaled, quarter-pyramidal forms,

with vertical (but splayed) walls of solid concrete forming two sides, and sloping, right-angled walls of mirror glass forming the other two. However, one will certainly not forget their oscillation on the plains of Indiana, or the reflections of their mirrors inching across those mighty walls of concrete. The interiors, all interconnected by bridging, provide highly satisfactory work spaces, with bands of windows overlooking the countryside and the group's own pool and landscaping.

Reception area and grounds open during business hours

22   Tippecanoe Court House (1881–84)
Main, 3rd, 4th, and Columbia Streets
Lafayette, Indiana

ELIAS MAX, ARCHITECT

The battle between General Harrison's troops and Tecumseh's Shaw-nees (November 7, 1811) made Tippecanoe famous, but this court-

house gives its county distinction. It possesses a lateral ferment—recessions, progressions, angles, returns, porches, and pilasters—which make this one of the most three-dimensional building blocks in the country. And like Palladio's famous Villa Rotunda, all four facades are basically alike. No sleek envelope for the *citoyens de Lafayette* (the town was named for the general), but a gutsy limestone monument to their taste and their pocketbooks. The interiors do not live up to the outside. Although Max is credited with the design (as per cornerstone), local opinion holds that his superintendent, James F. Alexander, was responsible.

Open during office hours

---

23   The Sullivan, Lanier, and Shrewsbury Houses (1818–55)
Madison, Indiana

Madison, comfortably hugging a curve in the Ohio River about 50 miles/80 kilometers from Louisville and 75 miles/121 kilometers from Cincinnati, was for five years (1850–55) the largest town in Indiana (population c. 5,000). However, rail was soon to supersede river for communications, and the Indiana towns, such as Indianapolis which developed trunk connections with the Eastern markets (as also did Cincinnati and Louisville) soon surpassed the water-oriented Madison. Now a pleasant town of some 13,000—with the unspoiled riverbank of Kentucky across the Ohio as a backdrop—Madison has architectural richness for its legacy and our enjoyment. The three most interesting houses which are open to the public are (chronologically) the Sullivan House (1818), the Lanier Mansion (1840–44), and the Shrewsbury House (1846–49). The Greek Revival Auditorium, 101 East 3rd Street, designed by E. J. Peck and built in 1835, also merits a look. It is frequently open for exhibitions and meetings.

The **Jeremiah Sullivan House** (1818), 304 West 2nd Street (open May–Oct., Tues.–Sat. 10–4:30, Sun.–Mon. 1–4:30: admission), is a representative Federal Style dwelling of reddish brick, white woodwork, and black shutters with fan-lighted entrance reached by a five-step small porch with good wrought-iron balustrade. (The ironwork of Madison became so well known that it even supplied New Orleans.) The Sullivan kitchen in the basement should also be seen.

The **J. F. D. Lanier Mansion** (1840–44), 1st Street between Elm and Vine (open daily summer 9–5, winter 9–4: admission), is a nonconformist Greek Revival house set in grounds (once elaborate gardens) that roll down to the river's edge. It was designed by Francis Costigan (1810–1865), who did a number of houses in town, and who is generally recognized as the state's leading architect of his period. Its two-story porch with 30-foot/9.1-meter columns (topped by amateurish capitals) forms the highlight of the exterior, but notice, too, the wrought-iron railings, and the octagonal cupola-observatory on the roof. The interior boasts an ambitious circular stair. Acquired as a State Memorial in 1925, the house has been fully restored and furnished.

The **Shrewsbury House** (1846–49), 301 West 1st Street at Poplar (open Mar.–Dec., daily 9–5: admission), was also designed by Francis Costigan. Quietly restrained on the exterior, with touches of the Greek Revival (note corner pilasters) it now serves as an antique shop. The restored interior is notable for an ingenious freestanding circular stair which leaps three flights from the middle of the entry hall. Detailing in the drawing room, with coupled columns providing semidividers

of space, is good. Madison's Historic District is listed in the National Register of Historic Places.

Open as indicated

---

24 **Spring Mill Village Reconstruction** (1817–1850s)
Spring Mill State Park
just N of IND 60 and c. 3 miles/4.8 kilometers E of
Mitchell, Indiana

A well-reconstructed "village" of the early 1800s, dominated by the three-story stone gristmill (1817) with its 24-foot/7.3-meter (in diameter) waterwheel and its aerial flume which supplies the overshot wheel. The mill machinery has been restored to top condition, its wooden gears grinding corn for visitors. A museum occupies the top two floors, outlining the early history of the region and of Indiana— which was admitted to the Union as a state in 1816 when this mill was being constructed. The other buildings which make up the village include, besides residences, a tavern, distillery (conveniently next to the

former), mill office, hat shop, loom house, apothecary, etc. Many of
the houses even when of wood themselves, are surrounded by low
stone walls enclosing lawn and garden. (These also kept out roaming
hogs being raised for the village pork market.) The establishment of
the railroad a bit to the north eventually siphoned off all residents, and
by the early 1890s the village had become a ghost town. It was
acquired by the state in 1927 and fully restored to give a good insight
into early Indiana building practices. It rests in a 1,319-acre/534-
hectare park complete with stands of virgin timber plus a good lake
for boating and fishing. There are also campgrounds.

Grounds open all year, Mill open Apr.–Oct., daily 9–6: admission

25   Culbertson Mansion State Memorial (1867–69)
914 East Main Street
New Albany, Indiana

A Second Empire-inspired Victorian dwelling on Mansion Row, overlooking the Ohio River (and Louisville, Kentucky). Its exterior combines light yellow walls, a dark Mansard shingled roof, topped by an
unusual balustrade, and a spry variety of arched windows and doors.
Although the interior furnishings are not original with the house—
which in the past had accommodated numerous occupants including
the American Legion—they have been carefully collected. Note especially the drawing room and its painted ceiling (restored). The house
is a distinguished example of its time. In 1976, Historic New Albany
Inc. donated the mansion to the State of Indiana to be operated as a
State Memorial.

Open daily 9–12 and 1–5, except major holidays: admission

26   Historic New Harmony (1814–24)
Main Street
New Harmony, Indiana

The German refugee Harmonists (via Pennsylvania)—dissident Lu-
therans from Württemberg—were the first of two unusual experimental
groups to settle in New Harmony in the early decades of the nineteenth century. The community begun by Robert Owen was their
successor. The first (1814–24) was made up of some eight hundred
souls who believed in communal property, celibacy, and the almost immediate Second Coming of Christ (as, of course, did the Shakers), and
who worked diligently to prepare themselves for it. The group, with its
organizational ability and native industry, soon prospered. Their town
plan was specific, their buildings standardized. Unfortunately, material
"enchantment" and dissension, aggravated by distance from ready
markets, began in the early 1820s. Father George Rapp sold their land
—30,000 acres/12,141 hectares—and possessions (1825) to Robert
Owen and William Maclure. With his followers Rapp returned to
Pennsylvania to set up a new base at Economy (q.v.).

Robert Owen (1771–1858) was an extraordinary, if at times im-
practical, idealist. Among his disciples was his son, Robert Dale Owen
(1801–77), one of the first publicly to advocate birth control in the
United States. (He was also Chairman of the Building Committee for
Washington's Smithsonian Institution.) The entire Owenite community
was highly talented and sought "Universal Happiness through Universal Education." They introduced one of this country's first kinder-
gartens, first free public schools, first trade schools, etc. In theory
Owen and Maclure hoped to set up similar communities across the
country. (Though these two were born in Scotland, the balance of this
gifted group were Americans and Europeans from many countries.)
Unfortunately, bickering as to means, plus lack of organizational and
agricultural expertise, soon caused the "commune" itself to dissolve.
Robert Owen himself returned to England (1827) though five of his
children stayed on. However, a number of the brilliant men and
women whom Owen and Maclure had attracted to New Harmony
remained to make New Harmony a renowned scientific outpost for more
than thirty years. By the time of the Civil War the town had changed
character, many of the early scientists and idealists having died or left.
In the twentieth century descendants encouraged the creation of a state
memorial commission (1937) which at least saved several key historic
sites.

In the early 1940s Jane Blaffer Owen and her husband, Kenneth, a great-great-great-grandson of Robert Owen, came to New Harmony and were largely instrumental in reactivating this interest. Mrs. Owen's enthusiasm and the efforts of local residents inspired others so that now New Harmony is one of the significant restorations in the United States.

The architectural heritage of both Harmonists and Owenites left the village (population c. 950) with a varied collection of buildings, primarily brick or frame structures, the early ones of logs. Reputedly some 30 of 160 Harmonist structures remain as well as a number of Owen buildings. So that restoration would not proceed on a casual basis, a comprehensive long-term coordinated approach was drawn up in 1973 by Ralph G. Schwarz, an urban planner. Then a second state commission was created which formed Historic New Harmony Inc., under Mr. Schwarz's guidance. Mr. Schwarz and his staff acquired in the public interest many key properties, and have received considerable financial backing from various private foundations, including the Lilly Endowment of Indianapolis. New Harmony has also benefited from the investments of Mr. and Mrs. Owen and the major contributions of The Robert Lee Blaffer Trust. Mr. Owen's early purchase of some 6,000 acres/2,428 hectares of his ancestors' land, and his preservation of several key historic buildings, set the present stage.

The oldest building is a 1770s double-log house located in the northwest part of town near an assemblage of log cabins (1814–19) re-erected on West Street, with the David Lenz House (c. 1822) facing them across North Street. The most accomplished early instructional structure is Dormitory #2 (1822), Main Street at Granary, a brick edifice which once served to house single men (and later became school, tavern, post office and fraternal lodge). It is now owned and maintained by the State of Indiana. There are also several, near-identical two-story wooden or brick houses with standardized beams and an ingenious form of wall and ceiling insulation, locally called "Dutch biscuits," formed from short boards daubed with clay and wrapped in straw. A series of subsequent buildings, including the mandatory "opera house," filled the nineteenth century. (The opera house was originally a Harmonist dormitory for women, converted to a theater in 1856 and restyled in 1888. It is now owned and maintained by the state.)

In our time four noteworthy structures have been built: the Roofless Church (1960) by Philip Johnson (q.v.); the forty-five-room New Harmony Inn, North at Brewery, by Evans Woollen (1974); the Sarah Campbell Blaffer Studio for Pottery (1978), by Richard A. Meier & Associates; and the Atheneum (1979) with two-hundred-seat auditorium, by Richard A. Meier & Associates. (It was not finished when last seen.) The seventeen-minute orientation film in the Atheneum gives a review of New Harmony's 165-year history beginning in 1814, through the phalanstery of the Owen-Maclure period, and ends with today. The building seeks to "mirror the evolution of society toward an ideal harmony." Historic New Harmony Inc. also sponsors a year-round series of films, plays, lectures, concerts, seminars, and exhibits. New Harmony conjures much thought concerning our early-nineteenth-century philosophical pioneers—and their shelter achievements. The whole village has been a National Historic Landmark since 1965.

For tour of sites and buildings apply at Atheneum, North Street near Arthur, open daily 9–5, except Jan. 1, Dec. 25: admission

27   Roofless Church (1959–60)
North Main Street at West Worth
New Harmony, Indiana

PHILIP JOHNSON, ARCHITECT

Weather can be a problem, and services difficult, however there is little question but that one can commune more intimately with heaven in a roofless church than in one hammered over by man. The silent, crumbling walls of Tewksbury, and the half-blitzed old St. Michael's leading to the new Coventry Cathedral, both provide spiritual experiences of the highest order—and do not, likewise, the awesome pylons of Stonehenge? So it is here in New Harmony. Philip Johnson has created his open "church" wrapped within a 12-foot/3.6-meter-high brick wall, 231.9 feet/71 meters long x 127.5 feet/39 meters wide, and then punctuated it with a softly undulating yet mathematical sanctuary of impeccable inspiration. 50 feet/15 meters high and covered with cedar shingles over laminated wood arch frame, the shrine's profile is based vertically on a parabola, while its lateral undulations stem

directly from a plan of six circles interlocked with a central seventh, all identical in diameter. At the intersection points of the peripheral circles are placed the six ovoid limestone "piers," 4 feet/1.2 meters high, on which the arches of the sanctuary rest. The convoluted geometry— vaguely suggestive of a Buddhist stupa—hovers compassionately over the late Jacques Lipchitz's bronze *Virgin* in the center, a Virgin faceless for self-effacement. Lipchitz also created the strikingly handsome, gilded ceremonial gate (1962) at the east end, with five sculptured wreaths, the topmost of which, with the Lamb of God inside, is supported by angels. (The day-to-day entrance is via a gate in the south wall.) Just inside the processional gate lies the "narthex," framed by trees. A giant golden rain tree dominates one side of the nave. The balcony on the north wall, its opening "remembering" the world outside, is overly framed in semiclassic fashion, but this small detail is soon forgotten in the aura of the most profound religious shelter in the United States today. There are plans to add (adjacent to the south wall) a small roofed chapel for year-round services and personal devotions. The shrine was made possible by a grant from the Robert Lee Blaffer Trust.

Just opposite the processional gate stands the **Paul Johannes Tillich Memorial Park** (1966), designed by Zion & Breen as landscape architects with James Rosati, sculptor. It should also be seen.

Open daily sunrise–sunset

Kentucky

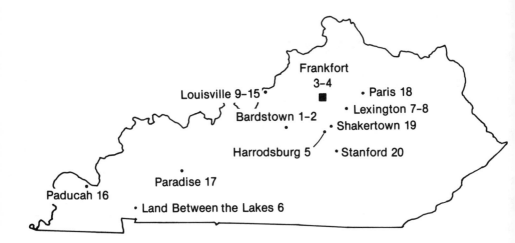

Louisville 9–15

Frankfort
3–4

• Paris 18

Bardstown 1–2

• Lexington 7–8

• Shakertown 19

Harrodsburg 5

• Stanford 20

•
Paradise 17

Paducah 16

• Land Between the Lakes 6

KENTUCKY

The buildings in boldface type are of general interest. The others are for the specialist.

Bardstown	1 **Federal Hill** (1795–1812)
	2 Wickland (1813–17)—John Marshall Brown and John Rogers
Frankfort	3 **Liberty Hall** (1796–1800)
	Orlando Brown House (1835)—Gideon Shryock
	4 **Old State House** (1827–30)—Gideon Shryock
Harrodsburg	5 **Old Fort Harrod State Park** (1775–76/ 1926)
Land Between the Lakes	6 **Land Between the Lakes Recreation Area** (1966–70)—Tennessee Valley Authority
	Kentucky Dam (1938–44)—Tennessee Valley Authority
Lexington	7 "Old Morrison" (1831–34)—Gideon Shryock
	8 **The Horse Farms** (mid-20th century)
Louisville	9 **Locust Grove** (1790–91)
	10 Farmington (1808–10)
	11 Jefferson County Court House (1835–60)—Gideon Shryock
	City Hall (1870–73)—John Andrewartha
	12 **The Actors Theatre/Old Bank of Louisville** (1835–37)—James H. Dakin
	13 **Water Company Pumping Station** (1858–60)—Theodore R. Scowden
	14 **Old Main Street Rehabilitation** (19th century/1970s)
	Louisville Museum of Natural History and Science (1977–78)—Louis & Henry
	American Saddle Horse Museum (1977)—Lawrence P. Melillo

Riverfront Plaza and Belvedere (1973–74)—Doxiades Associates with Lawrence P. Melillo and Jasper Ward

American Life and Accident Insurance Company Building (1971–72)—The Office of Mies van der Rohe

First National Bank of Louisville (1970–72)—Harrison & Abramovitz

15 Lincoln Income Life Insurance Building (1965)—Taliesin Associated Architects

Paducah

16 New City Hall (1967)—Edward Durell Stone & Associates

Paradise

17 **Paradise Steam Plant** (1959–70)—Tennessee Valley Authority

Paris

18 Duncan Tavern (1786–88)

Shakertown

19 **Pleasant Hill** (1805–59)

Stanford

20 William Whitley House (1785–92)

1   Federal Hill (1795–1812)
My Old Kentucky Home State Park
.8 mile/1.3 kilometers E of downtown on US 150
Bardstown, Kentucky

The carefully symmetrical facade of Federal Hill with faded red bricks, dark-green shutters, and white trim adds quiet colorfulness to its State Park setting. Behind, in the standard manner, projects the service wing containing kitchen and smokehouse which were completed in 1795. The body of the house dates from 1812. The main rooms—three on the ground floor and three above—are all approximately 22 feet/6.7 meters square and 15 feet/4.6 meters high and are lit by unusually large windows. A substantial entry and stair hall divides the house down the middle. Detailing—from the front door to the mantels, and especially in the parlor—is first-rate. The house and 234 acres/95 hectares are now part of My Old Kentucky Home State Park, named, of course, for a visit (by some disputed) of Stephen C. Foster, who was so moved that he composed the famous song as a result (copyrighted in 1853). Whether or not the unfortunate Mr. Foster (who died in great poverty at the age of thirty-eight) did visit the house, it is worth a visit on its own. Built for Judge John Rowan, a noted jurist, Repre-

sentative, and U.S. senator from Kentucky, it was occupied by the judge's descendants until 1922 when it was acquired by the state. Its architect is unknown.

Open mid-June–Aug., daily 9–7:30, rest of year 9–5, closed Mon. from Dec.–Feb. and Jan. 1, Dec. 25: admission

---

2   Wickland (1813–17)
on US 62, c. 1 mile/1.6 kilometers NE of
Bardstown, Kentucky

JOHN MARSHALL BROWN AND JOHN ROGERS, ARCHITECTS

A red-brick, white-shuttered Georgian house, distinguished on the exterior by its two roundheaded doors (on adjacent sides), simple dormerless gabled roof, and almost windowless north facade. The plan is locally typical, with rectangular two-and-a-half-story main mass (64 x 42 feet/19.5 x 12.8 meters) and lower service wing as an "L" behind. The interior is notable for its several Adam mantels, a set of four gold-framed mirrors, and its 12-foot/3.7-meter-high doors. Restrained elegance throughout.

Open Mon.–Sat. 9–sundown, Sun. 12–sundown: admission

3   Liberty Hall (1796–1800)
218 Wilkinson Street at Main
Frankfort, Kentucky

A dignified Georgian-Federal mansion—possibly the oldest brick
house now standing in Frankfort. Its red-brick exterior with central
pedimented bay (of minuscule projection), Palladian window (with
strangely "dropped" side lights), and its minutely detailed cornice are
well conceived, while the white-painted, solid shutters (restored) on
ground floor and the dark, slotted ones on bedroom level add a cheerful, functional note. There is an influence from Virginia and, perhaps,
Delaware in its features, but the notion that Thomas Jefferson designed
it does not hold up. Jefferson was a friend of John Brown, the owner,
and made suggestions concerning the house, but none of them seemingly were carried out.

The interior lives up to the outside promise. Besides being well designed, it is well preserved, having been lived in and cared for continuously until 1937, and possessing almost two thirds of its early furnishings. The plan is standard, with a wide central hall dividing both
floors, the stair hall separated from the front hall by an arched portal.

The trees on all sides and the garden, which at rear borders the Kentucky River, embellish the setting.

Restoration of the house, the kitchen in the "L" at rear, and the garden has been properly carried out, and the furnishings augmented to produce a fully rounded example of its time. It is now operated by the National Society of the Colonial Dames of America in the State of Kentucky.

Open Tues.–Sat. 10–5, Sun. 2–5, except holidays: admission

The **Orlando Brown House** (1835—open Tues.–Sat. 10–5, Sun. 2–5, except holidays: admission), 202 Wilkinson Street, was built for John Brown's second son and designed by Gideon Shryock, Kentucky's famous native-born architect who designed the Old State House (q.v.). With its pedimented front and Greek Revival porch, the house is well worth a look. It, too, is operated by the Colonial Dames.

---

4 Old State House (1827–30)
St. Clair Street at Broadway
Frankfort, Kentucky

GIDEON SHRYOCK, ARCHITECT

Gideon Shryock, 1802–80, was the outstanding Kentucky-born architect of the nineteenth century just as Paul Rudolph is of the twentieth. However, the exterior of Mr. Shryock's former State Capitol, restored (1973–75) and preserved by the Kentucky Historical Society, will probably not garner first prize among Greek Revivalists. In spite of the fact that the hexastyle portico of Mr. Jefferson's Capitol in Richmond (q.v.) was of influence, Frankfort's State House is too antiseptic and its detailing not sufficiently refined. Nonetheless the impact of the building was widespread, for it carried the new word of the Classic Revival into this section of the country. Shryock won the competition for the capitol's design (1827)—the third on the site, the two previous having burned—when only twenty-five years old. He had studied diligently with William Strickland in Philadelphia for a year, after which he returned home and was soon master of the Greek Revival in areas that were remote from Eastern seaboard culture. His influence extended as far as Little Rock, where he designed Arkansas' distinguished State House (q.v.). It should be added, as regards the Frankfort capitol, that not one of the five plans submitted in the com-

petition met the "entire approbation . . . of the commissioners."
Shryock, however, was chosen to amalgamate the best features of each;
we thus do not know precisely which was his own contribution.

The interior of the State House is highlighted by the marble stairway
in the rotunda near the center of the structure. This starts with a
straight flight of nine risers then branches to right and left in sweeping
curves to the second floor. The steps are not cantilevered but are self-
supporting, built like a horizontal arch with the upper floor the key-
stone. Supposedly Shryock remarked that if they had been a sixteenth
of an inch (1.6 millimeters) out of line they would have fallen! A
dome on pendentives with rich reliefs and lined with rosetted panels
arches above. Clay Lancaster points out that Shryock was probably
influenced by McComb's New York City Hall (q.v.) in the design of
these stairs (*Journal of the Society of Architectural Historians,*
III/70). Though the building is no longer used as a museum, two former courtrooms are employed as galleries. More restoration is in progress. *Antiques,* July 1978, regards the Frankfort building as "the first
Greek revival state capitol in the United States."

*Open Mon.–Sat. 9–4, Sun. 1–5, except Dec. 25; open other
holidays 1–5*

5 Old Fort Harrod State Park (1775–76/1926)
US 68 and US 127 (South College Street at West Lexington)
Harrodsburg, Kentucky

Old Fort Harrod is a restoration of a fort built for the first permanent
English-speaking settlement west of the Alleghenies. The restoration is
perhaps questionable in part but it is as accurate as 1926 research
could muster. (The Castillo de San Marcos in St. Augustine, Florida,
q.v., built by the Spaniards, dates from 1672–95; Fort Michilimackinac at Mackinaw City, Michigan, q.v., was constructed by the French
in 1714.) Located on the Wilderness Road to the West, Fort Harrod's
stockade was 12 feet/3.7 meters high, 200 feet/61 meters square (the
original measured 264 feet/80 meters on a side), forming a key refuge
against Indian attack, and providing safety for families in the area, including their livestock. Several families lived in the fort permanently.
Even a one-room schoolhouse—Building #8—was provided. Most of
the population came from Virginia, for the region at that time was part
of this state, Kentucky not gaining independence until 1792. Three

blockhouses command corners of the fort, while grouped along one side are six cabins. Everything was built of logs, limiting construction dimensions to pieces readily handled by a few men, generally 12–15 feet/3.7–4.6 meters. The logs were then chinked against the weather.

Each cabin, all of one room initially, rests on a stone base with a fireplace-stove on one side. Note that the upper exterior sections of the chimneys were sturdily framed by notched logs set with thick mortar—known as "cats and clay"—and lined with lime mortar within to make them more or less fireproof. A pole stood adjacent to push over the chimney in case it caught fire! Windows were made of oiled paper, sometimes greased with bear fat, or of skins, with heavy shutters put in place at night. The early floors were generally packed earth. The reconstruction of Fort Harrod gives revealing insight into the earliest buildings of trans-Appalachia.

Open Apr.–Oct., daily 9–5, Nov.–Mar., Tues.–Sun. 9–5:
admission

---

6   Land Between the Lakes Recreation Area (1966–70)
S of US 62 on KEN 453 (20 miles/32 kilometers E of Paducah)
Land Between the Lakes, Kentucky

TENNESSEE VALLEY AUTHORITY, PLANNERS AND ARCHITECTS

The 170,000 acres/68,797 hectares of Land Between the Lakes have been developed for outdoor recreation and environmental education. Made almost an island by Kentucky Lake and Lake Barkley and their respective dams (1944 and 1965), the area stretches some 40 miles/ 64 kilometers, to beyond the Tennessee border. Though there are campgrounds, most visitors come for a day's outing of boating, fishing, picnicking, and nature observing. The camps are divided to appeal to specific groups such as families, organizations (scouts, etc.), and trailer users.

Part of the land had been government property (game, fish, and wildlife); TVA owned part, some belonged to industry. Congress asked the Tennessee Valley Authority to develop the overall region—now bounded by two of the country's largest man-made lakes—giving the Authority power of eminent domain to acquire approximately 100,000 acres/40,469 hectares in addition to those which TVA and the government already owned. A few people were dispossessed but in general

the area was not developed—the land is marginal—its early ironworks having lost out to richer veins long ago. Policy has been to keep the land semiprimitive, even wilderness in part. It does not seek to be in competition with the private motels and facilities on the far shores of the two lakes. With one exception, the few shelters thus far erected are for toilets, wash- and shower-rooms, and related conveniences. They have all been designed with a simple but imaginative touch: an abandoned concrete silo has, for instance, been turned into a tree-top observation post by means of an airy ramp. The only major building is the Youth Activities Station with six dormitories, classroom and cafeteria; schoolchildren are brought here for a week's "education in conservation."

Open all year, some campsites only spring–fall

The **Kentucky Dam** (1938–44) at the head of Kentucky Lake (just east of Gilbertsville) is the only TVA dam in the state—but see also the TVA Steam Plant at Paradise. The dam follows the commendable pattern of direct, well-tailored simplicity which has characterized TVA's architecture and engineering since it began its momentous work in the early 1930s. With a length of 8,422 feet/2,567 meters and total height of 206 feet/63 meters, it is majestic outside, while the powerhouse interior with five turbines (open to the public daily 9–5) should not be missed.

7 **"Old Morrison"** (1831–34)
Transylvania University
**Gratz Park, West 3rd Street between Mill and Market (1 block E of
   North Broadway)**
Lexington, Kentucky

GIDEON SHRYOCK, ARCHITECT

Mr. Shryock stuck with the Greek Revival throughout most of his career. Here for what was earlier known as Morrison College, but which was absorbed by the older, adjacent Transylvania—the first (1780) institution of higher learning west of the Alleghenies—Shryock achieved his most monumental facade. (Compare his Old State House in Frankfort, q.v.) Poised on a high platform, with six widely spaced Doric columns across its front, topped by a simple entablature and unadorned pediment, the building asserts majesty though of a pared variety. Badly damaged by fire in 1969, it has been fully restored through the gener-

osity of many friends, being rededicated in 1971. The interiors include a chapel, early medical museum, and administrative offices of the University. A number of paintings by Matthew Jouett (1787–1827) and other artists are on display.

Open Mon.–Fri. 8:30–4:30, except holidays

---

8 The Horse Farms (mid-20th century)
US 27, US 60, and area around
Lexington, Kentucky

The thoroughbred horse and cattle farms, which virtually encircle the northern arc of Lexington, rank high in man's interweaving of enclosure with surroundings. The choreography of the white-painted fences extends across the undulating countryside to create a soul-satisfying geometry of white and green. The famous Blue Grass countryside—its "blue" best observed in Spring, especially May—might well be the most sympathetically "fashioned" landscape in the United States. This glorious regional expression of man and land in harmony can be seen from both main and minor roads, while the Lexington Chamber of

Commerce, at 421 North Broadway, has lists of those few horse farms the general public can visit, at least at certain times of the year. In addition there are commercial bus tours which operate from this same building from April to October. The Keeneland Race Course, some 6 miles/10 kilometers west of the city off US 60, is generally alive with training activities (6–10 A.M.) in addition to its scheduled race periods several times a year (primarily April and October). But even if one does not enter a farm, a drive through the region, especially off the major roads, can be a happy revelation of a well-loved bit of earth.

There is, however, an ugly note on the horizon: because of the industrial and commercial development of the Lexington area, much of this incomparable countryside—one limited in extent because of its unique limestone-phosphorus undercroppings—is being plowed into tract suburbs or sprawling, albeit generally clean, industry. Grady Clay, the eminent Louisville editor of *Landscape Architecture Quarterly,* calls this hideous gobbling the "Bluegrass Blues," adding that "Lexington must realize that the horse farms are a civic asset which are wholly irreplaceable." Let us hope that the troika of long-range planning, Kentucky's preferential property tax for farms, and a strong Bluegrass Land and Nature Trust will insure the salvation of one of this country's greatest landscapes.

A few open to the public: see above

9   Locust Grove (1790–91)
561 Blankenbaker Lane, NE edge of
Louisville, Kentucky

A well-restored group which gives an excellent idea of a Kentucky plantation at the time when the area was changing from pioneer days to more settled conditions. (Kentucky joined the Union as the fifteenth state in June 1792.) The main house, modest in its frontier simplicity, naturally forms the architectural focus, but the numerous outbuildings, including a reconstructed log cabin, also merit inspection. In use as a working farm when purchased by the state and county (1961), the dwelling though structurally intact required several years of restoration by the Historic Homes Foundation to return it to its original condition. (A front porch, an ungainly wing, and Victorian brackets all had to be removed.) The interiors are particularly handsome with their walnut paneling and fully restored second-floor ballroom. The grounds, too, are well tended.

Open Mon.–Sat. 10–4:30, Sun. 1:30–4:30, except holidays: admission

10 Farmington (1808–10)
3033 Bardstown Road (US 31E) at IS 264, c. 6 miles/10 kilometers S of
Louisville, Kentucky

Farmington is a one-story, Federal- and Jefferson-influenced dwelling atop a semiraised basement. Strict symmetry characterizes its plan from entry to rear porch. Not overly impressive from the outside (it takes a quiet, boxy turn), the interior opens into a fine series of high-ceilinged rooms (14 feet/4.3 meters), of which the most gracious are the elongated octagons which form the music room on one side and the dining room across the generous hall. (It is pertinent to recall Jefferson's use of octagons in the Farmington Country Club in Charlottesville, Virginia, and in his Monticello—q.v.) Neglected for decades, the house was purchased in 1958 by the Historic Homes Foundation. That same year, an 1840 inventory was discovered so that proper refurnishing with precise period pieces could be carried out. In addition to the house and grounds, the outbuildings should also be seen.

Though almost copied from Thomas Jefferson's *unexecuted* plan for

Poplar Forest, a modest summer home he designed for himself in Virginia, there is, to date, no documented evidence that Jefferson was actually responsible for this house in Louisville—as sometimes claimed. (Poplar Forest, 1806, was eventually built as an octagon.) The strong similarity in the two house plans lies in the fact that both have twin octagonal main rooms axially projecting from a squarish structure. However, Plan Number 191 in the Massachusetts Historical Society—mentioned by Jeffersonian proponents—shows porticos fronting the semiprojection of each octagon, while Farmington has porticos on the *flat* sides. But as John Speed, for whom Farmington was built, reputedly knew Jefferson well, it is quite possible that the unused plan of Poplar Forest was borrowed and slightly changed en route over the mountains. Desmond Guiness and Julius Trousdale Sadler, Jr., in their book *Mr. Jefferson, Architect* (Viking Press, 1973) claim that Jefferson was the architect of Farmington. It is listed on the National Register of Historic Places.

Open Mon.–Sat. 10–4:30, Sun. 1:30–4:30, except major holidays: admission

---

11   Jefferson County Court House (1835–60)
Jefferson Street between 5th and 6th
Louisville, Kentucky

GIDEON SHRYOCK, ORIGINAL ARCHITECT

Shryock's Court House stands strong in three-dimensional statement, albeit weak in some details (for many of which Shryock was not responsible). Recent research reveals that his attribution is limited to the 1835–42 period. (He resigned, or was forced out, in 1842.) Note, for instance, the ramrod Doric columns (no entasis or subtle curvature of profile) and their understated capitals. Moreover the cornice was drastically simplified in 1932 because of crumbling stone. It is the building's blunt positiveness of form and its setback from the sidewalks that lends force to the street and to the city.

Construction took an abnormally long time because of difficulties with funding. Engineer-architect Albert Fink (1821–97) is credited with altering, expanding, and completing the building (1858–60)—and with adding the tetrastyle porticos, constructing the unusually handsome rotunda and dome, and finishing the upper floor. He also

changed the planned hexastyle front portico to tetrastyle and omitted completely (possibly wisely) the towering cupola which Shryock had designed. Following a fire in 1905, Brinton B. Davis redid (1912) much of Fink's interior except the rotunda gallery, thus most of the detailing is ascribable to him. A complete renovation and mechanical updating was undertaken (1978–79) by architects Bickel-Gibson Associates.

From its earliest days, the building has not been without criticism. The *Daily Courier* (September 1, 1858) termed it an "elephantine monstrosity of architecture" and less than a year later the *Daily Louisville Democrat* said "It stood like a gigantic stone scare-crow on the most beautiful square in the city" (July 1, 1859). The *Herald-Post* predicted (January 31, 1926) "that antiquated pile on Jefferson street, known as the courthouse . . . is going to be razed. That is the pile's destiny as surely as the sun shines on a cloudless day." In addition to verbal abuse, the building, like many of its peers across the country, was threatened with physical demolition as facilities became inadequate and/or civic aspirations demanded the latest in architectural fashions. Fortunately "pragmatic rehabilitation" won the day and Louisville thus is a more abundant city.

Facing the Court House across 6th Street stands the **City Hall** (1870–73), designed by John Andrewartha. Because only the east wing was built, it appears an uncommonly mixed-up structure. Note the sculpted locomotive yclept *Progress* in its tympanum.

Open during office hours

---

12   The Actors Theatre/Old Bank of Louisville (1835–37)
320 West Main Street
Louisville, Kentucky

JAMES H. DAKIN, ARCHITECT

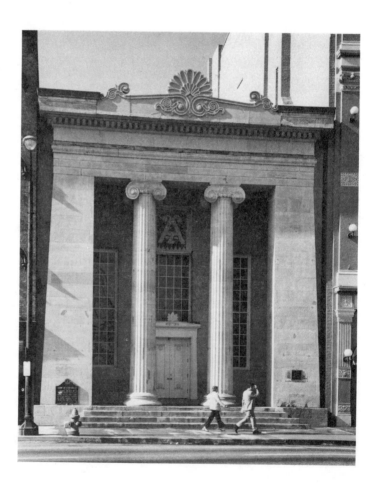

Though a mere 38 feet/11.6 meters wide (and the same dimension to the cornice), surprising monumentality is proclaimed by Mr. Dakin's Greek Revival bank. At one time used by the Louisville Credit Men's Association, since October 1972 it has been the Actors Theatre of Louisville. Its august facade quality is achieved by the two towering *in antis* Ionic columns (columns set within enclosing side walls), by the "unequal" space divisions in this porch, and by the strategic inward angling of the outer edges of the "pylon" of the facade, all measures producing a visual impression of greater height and scale. This dexterity is topped by an acroterion (of cast iron) which sets an opulent note that is repeated at small scale on the front door.

The interior, beautifully restored by Harry Weese & Associates, is bathed with daylight from an oval oculus above the old banking floor, and forms a splendid lobby to the theater. The original offices and vault behind the banking room (of no architectural interest) were removed and a 641-seat theater, almost a semicircle in plan, put in by expanding into the late-nineteenth-century warehouse adjacent, a building now housing a second theater and offices. Until recently it was thought that Gideon Shryock was the designer of the bank, but with the discovery of some 180 original drawings by James Dakin, it is clear that the latter was the architect with Shryock carrying out the supervision. In any case we have not only a jewel of the Greek Revival (with tinge of the Egyptian) but a highly viable use of a great building plus its hearty neighbor. (See Arthur Scully, Jr.'s book *James Dakin, Architect,* Louisiana University Press, 1973.)

Open for performances

---

13   Water Company Pumping Station (1858–60)
River Road at Zorn Avenue (NE on IS 71, off at Zorn Avenue
    exit)
Louisville, Kentucky

THEODORE R. SCOWDEN, CHIEF ENGINEER

One of the esthetic glories of mid-nineteenth-century engineering, the engine house and standpipe tower of the Louisville Water Company Pumping Station ⌗1 is also a marvelously inventive example of the Classic Revival. The brick engine house—its central section more than similar in form to the Temple of Fortuna Virilis of 100 B.C.—might

suffer a bit in its details, its Corinthian columns and terra-cotta capitals being a mite heavy. But the building could rest on the banks of the Tiber instead of the Ohio River, so splendid is its Roman concept and mass. Its Cornish pumps, which pushed water 6 miles/9.7 kilometers to Louisville, yielded long ago to electricity and are now dismantled, their rooms turned to shops and a garage. (Maintenance of the building has been excellent.)

The triumphal standpipe tower, which absorbed jolts in the mains (primarily from the nearby Veterans' Hospital) and equalized water pressure, rests on foundations 13 feet/4 meters deep. A *tempietto,* 38.4 feet/11.7 meters in diameter and almost exactly as high, encircles its base, the top of its coping decorated by nine Classic statues and one American Indian with his dog. Above this well-populated coping rises a 134-foot/41-meter-high, Tuscan-inspired column containing a 4-foot/1.2-meter-diameter standpipe and four overflow pipes, the whole topped by a lantern and small dome for a total height of 169 feet/52 meters. A tornado toppled the shaft in 1890, seriously injuring it, but it was immediately rebuilt with steel plates imitating its original wood construction, and since then has been kept in fine condition though no longer in active use.

Incidentally, the anachronistic statue of the Indian dates from the reconstruction of the standpipe housing. It replaces the only piece of sculpture destroyed by the tornado. The pumping station, now under lease from the Louisville Water Company to the Art Center Association, is being adapted for offices, exhibit spaces, and work areas for artists, with the exteriors restored to their original pristine condition. The structures were made a National Historic Landmark in 1972.

Grounds open daily

---

14   Old Main Street Rehabilitation (19th century/1970s)
Main Street W from 2nd
Louisville, Kentucky

In addition to its bourbon whiskey, of which it distills roughly half of the world's supply, Louisville has long prided itself for its strategic location at a cascade of the Ohio River. Moreover the city has a collection of nineteenth-century commercial buildings—many with handsome cast-iron fronts—which is one of the richest in the country. However, through the years the river was not only ignored, it was amputated by Interstate 64, while its historic buildings were bypassed for more up-to-date facilities. Fortunately the city has now recognized the urban contribution of its venerable structures on Old Main Street (a block or two south of the river), and with the close cooperation of the Louisville Landmarks Commission has begun their systematic recycling. The results will fascinate all interested in urban business blocks and warehouses of a century ago. Too many structures have been destroyed in headstrong "rehabilitation," but much still remains, and the present upgrading of this riparian edge where the town was founded is producing both isolated gems (see the Actors Theatre/Old Bank of Louisville at 320 West Main), and several marvelously continuous blocks of architectural bouillabaisse.

The finest of these is probably that between 7th and 8th streets, highlighted by the old Carter Dry Goods Building at 731, built in 1878 to the design of C. J. Clarke, an architect born in nearby Frankfort. Its street floor facade is of cast iron (Snead & Bibb Ironworks) and its upper three of light masonry. The Carter Building and the two side

structures were totally transformed (1977–78) into the **Louisville Museum of Natural History and Science.** Several bays of the front (behind the facade) were cut back to make a dramatically inviting three-story open entry, while part of the center of the middle building was gutted to create a five-story skylit atrium. Much of the old structure, however, was saved, including the cast-iron Corinthian columns. The result is admirable. Louis & Henry were the architects with R. Jeffrey Points principal-in-charge. The elaborate Hart Block building opposite at 730 West Main Street, built in 1884 with Charles D. Meyer architect and the local Merz Iron Works, has also been rehabilitated (1977), Lawrence P. Melillo architect, and now houses the **American Saddle Horse Museum** (open Mon.–Sat. 10–4, Sun. 1–5, except major holidays: admission). Its five-storied cast-iron front is one of the richest to be seen.

Up and down the street, activity is taking place with sturdy old structures being carefully modernized to refresh the present—financially, historically, and urbanistically. The buildings on the 600–700

and 800 blocks are listed in the National Register. At Main Street and 5th, the **Riverfront Plaza and Belvedere** (1973–74) demonstrates current recognition of some of the key new elements needed in the city's central business district. With plans originally proposed by Doxiades Associates in the 1950s, coordinated with overall city development by Gruen Associates (1968–69) the Riverfront Plaza opens, rather re-opens, the city to the Ohio River by providing a two-block-long elevated park and viewing platform with a 1,600-car garage underneath. A series of pergolas on stepped terraces gives geometric organization to the whole, and this is further enlivened by cascades of pools (with amusing multidiametered concrete "lily-pads"), and good planting. As almost half of the Belvedere is built over the Interstate mentioned, one can enjoy a grand sweep of the river, the only wheel visible being that on the stern of the *Belle of Louisville*. (There are riverboat excursions Memorial Day–Labor Day.) The Riverfront Plaza and Belvedere was designed in joint venture by Doxiades Associates with Lawrence P. Melillo and Jasper Ward. Simonds & Simonds were the original landscape architects.

Further architectural faith in Louisville's new as well as old downtown development is manifest in a number of recent structures of which the strongest architecturally are the **American Life and Accident**

Insurance Company Building (1971–72) on the edge of the Plaza, The Office of Mies van der Rohe, architect (Bruno P. Canterato in charge), and the **First National Bank of Louisville** (1970–72), across the street at 101 South 5th, by Harrison & Abramovitz (reception area of each open during business hours). The insurance building rises five floors above the plaza (with three below), utilizing wide-span (42 feet/12.8 meters) structural bays typically inset at base, weathering steel, and dark glass. The handsome forty-story bank is of the "dark tower" idiom (of bronzed aluminum over steel frame), its 517 feet/157 meters height (it is the tallest in the state) rewarding most of its tenants with a variety of panoramas. A little park gives pleasure to the Market Street side, but the four-story garage is of lesser caliber. The bank's windows and spandrels are nearly flush so that the entire structure can be washed along with the glass. The First National, it should be added, has committed a substantial sum at low interest for rehabilitating Old Main Street.

There is, thus, considerable vitality along Louisville's Main Street. If its nineteenth-century inheritance is properly preserved and rehabilitated, the entire central business district, and the city, will be enormously enriched as the old will, of course, lend visual counterpart to the new. But the new must not be allowed to become so jam-packed that there is no breathing space. Moreover, it should never be forgotten that the city's "very roots cling to the riverbank" (*Louisville, July 1974*).

---

15   Lincoln Income Life Insurance Building (1965)
6100 Dutchman's Lane, NW off US 60/264 at Breckinridge Lane
**   Intersection**
Louisville, Kentucky

TALIESIN ASSOCIATED ARCHITECTS

An extraordinary office building on the east edge of the city, with an eye-popping exterior of filigreed salmon-and-white concrete panels. The unusual facades are wrapped around a highly ingenious structural frame. Eleven of the building's fifteen floors are suspended from the top on steel tension members sized 6 x 1.25 inches/15 x 3.2 centimeters. This supporting floor, which measures 80.9 feet/24.5 meters on a side, is comprised of double-cantilevered steel trusses, 12 feet/3.7 me-

ters deep, atop a 24 x 60-foot (7.3 x 18.3-meter) concrete utility core. The exterior might not be everyone's cup of tea, but the structure is brilliant, its high-tension suspension eliminating all columns. A dining room and observation lounge occupy the top floor. William Wesley Peters was chief architect. Wilson, Andros, Roberts & Noll were the structural engineers.

Visitors welcome during business hours

---

16 New City Hall (1967)
South 5th Street between Clark and Washington Streets
Paducah, Kentucky

EDWARD DURELL STONE & ASSOCIATES, ARCHITECTS

This quietly formal city hall is a welcome addition to Kentucky's western gateway. It rests calm and shaded under its generously overhanging roof, a roof upheld by columns used functionally but also with a hint of the antebellum—and the late Mr. Stone's Embassy in

New Delhi. Surrounded by a shining moat, the building, 216 feet/66 meters square in plan, consists of two upper stories and full basement. The peristyle surrounds the two main floors on all sides, with entry leading to a central two-story "atrium" with small fountain in center and a court brightly illumined by the architect's characteristic skylight. Various civic offices and functions, plus the offices and facilities for mayor, occupy the surrounding floors, while the largely windowless basement is mostly taken up with police facilities, a jail, and the maintenance department, with a drive-through passage in the middle. An extensive park is planned for the area in front. Civic comeliness without civic bombast. Lee Potter Smith was associate architect.

Open during office hours

---

17   Paradise Steam Plant (1959–70)
**7 miles/11 kilometers SE of Central City on US 431 to
    Drakesboro, then c. 7 miles/11 kilometers NE to
Paradise, Kentucky**

TENNESSEE VALLEY AUTHORITY, ARCHITECTS AND ENGINEERS

"Constructivist" sculpture is now working with forms so large that much of it has to be shown out-of-doors. It is doubtful, however, that the work of any artist in this field can approach the esthetic impact of

the Paradise Steam Plant. Three enormous hyperbolic cooling towers stand 437 feet/133 meters high with base diameter of 320 feet/98 meters and strictly mathematical profiles—their curves being straight-line generated. Together, they produce a mighty geometric interplay with three venting chimneys (the tallest being 800 feet/244 meters in height) whose tops are painted in alternate bands of red and white for airplane visibility. Against these major elements, a secondary, eerily horizontal composition of brown-painted, elevated conveyors—which feed coal to the boilers—adds an almost surrealist touch. The first two generating units were constructed 1959–63; unit 3 construction began in 1965 and when completed in 1970, Paradise became the largest steam-generating plant in the world with a total capacity of 2,558,000 kilowatts. It is also one of the country's great architectural-engineering achievements, sculpture on perhaps an ultimate scale.

The plant was purposely located atop extensive coal beds, the coal obtained by the much-maligned stripping process. Though early activities of the Peabody Coal Company—which has a seventeen-year contract with TVA to supply this fuel—were perhaps deleterious, a concentrated land restoration process is now taking place. The stripping shovels are, according to the brochure, "the largest self-propelled land vehicles in history, and can scoop up, swing and dump a third of a million pounds [c. 151,000 metric tons] of earth at a time"!

Some facilities open to public during business hours

18 Duncan Tavern (1786–88)
323 High Street on Court House Square
Paris, Kentucky

Considering that Kentucky was not even a state when this inn was
erected—thus building conditions primitive—the substantial, even
handsome result is a tribute to its builder. Constructed of local limestone, fitted with a proper (but smallish) Palladian window, and
trimmed with green shutters, it holds its own even today. The **Ann
Duncan House** (1800—same admission) adjoins, built as a residence
by the widow of the innkeeper. Both have been well restored and
furnished.

Open Tues.–Sat. 10–12, 1–5, Sun. 2–5, except holidays:
admission

19 Pleasant Hill (1805–59)
on US 68 at KEN 33 (c. 22 miles/35 kilometers SW of Lexington, 7 miles/11 kilometers NE of Harrodsburg
Shakertown, Kentucky

An extensive and informative restoration of a village of twenty-seven buildings, the westernmost outpost of the United Society of Believers in Christ's Second Appearing, otherwise known as the Shakers. The community numbered as many as five hundred in the early nineteenth century (generally less), and these worshipful, industrious, and celibate Kentuckians—converted by missionaries from Shaker settlements in New York and New England—constituted a phalanx in developing scientific agriculture (especially seeds), handicrafts, and cattle breeding. All property was communal, and growth of the sect was maintained, for a while, by conversion of adults and adoption of orphans. The group disbanded in 1910 but many buildings remained in use though most slipped into quiet neglect. To stop this erosion and save the buildings, a public-spirited non-profit group was incorporated in 1961, the entire settlement purchased, and restoration begun (1963).

All of the buildings have now been restored for a variety of adaptive uses, and their collective impression strung along a cobbled lane is one of harmony and brotherhood. Local wood, local stone, and brick were used for construction, and the proverbial Shaker simplicity and thoroughness are manifest throughout. The Meeting House (1820), a building used only for the four services formerly held each Sunday, is perhaps the most intriguing: its entire second floor is suspended from roof trusses so that the meeting room below, which measures a surprisingly large 44 x 60 feet/13.4 x 18.3 meters, would constitute one open space for the Believers' famous dancing. This represents an architectural-engineering achievement of a high order. The twin circular stairs in the Trustees' Office (by Micajah Burnett, 1839) rank with the finest in the country. The largest structure (and the one shown in the photograph) is the three-story, T-shaped Center Family House (1824–34) whose front section measures 55 x 60 feet/16.7 x 18.3 meters, with kitchen-dining wing extending 85 feet/26 meters behind. Burnett was also responsible for the layout of the village and the design of most of its buildings.

The competition of mass-produced factory items after the Civil War, the drastic decline of Southern markets then, and the lure of the city initiated Pleasant Hill's decline. Hastened, too, by celibacy and dissen-

sion, it finally closed down, as mentioned, at the beginning of this century. (The last Sister died in 1923).

Other Shaker settlements of architectural interest and open to the
public are the Hancock Shaker Village just west of Pittsfield, Massachusetts (q.v.), and the Shaker Village near Canterbury, New Hampshire (q.v.). Both, because of a more demanding climate, are even
more spartan than the basic but appealing buildings and furnishings
seen in Shakertown. All combine simplicity of conception, refinement
of detail, with probity of construction. A unique attraction of Pleasant
Hill is that lodging for the public (in sixty-three air-conditioned
rooms) is available in twelve of its restored buildings, while excellent
meals from Shaker recipes can be had in the Trustees' House. It is,
thus, very much alive, and very worth a visit. The restorations, which
opened in 1968, were under the direction of James Lowry Cogar, with
Washington Reed, Jr., chief architect.

Open daily 9–5, except Dec. 24 and 25: admission

20 William Whitley House (1785–92)
W off US 150, 2.5 miles/4 kilometers NW of Crab Orchard and c.
9 miles/14.5 kilometers SE of
Stanford, Kentucky

This combination dwelling and "fort" is reputedly "the first brick house west of the Allegheny Mountains." Architecturally it reflects the Virginia background of its owner-builder and militarily its location on the Wilderness Road west. Of simple Georgian style, the house was constructed with walls of handmade brick garnished by prideful initials in front and diamond pattern at sides. The walls were made extra thick against possible Indian attack, and the windows raised high and kept small for this same reason. The floor joists are so substantial that the partitions are not structural. The interior has been well restored (1939)—note, especially, the paneled parlor—and the house is now operated by the Department of Parks.

Open June–Aug., daily 9–5, Sept.–May, Tues.–Sun. 9–5: admission

Louisiana

Natchitoches 10

St. Francisville 23–24 • Clinton 7

New Roads 20•

Darrow 8

Baton Rouge 1–5 ■

• Ponchatoula 21

St. Martinville 25

Burnside 6

New Iberia 11 •

New Orleans
12–19

Napoleonville 9

Vacherie 26

Reserve
22

LOUISIANA

The buildings in boldface type are of general interest. The others are for the specialist.

Baton Rouge

1 Pentagon Barracks (1819–23/ 1966–67)

2 **Old State Capitol** (1847–49/rebuilt 1880–82)—James H. Dakin

3 Union Tank Car Repair Facility (1958)—Battey & Childs; Synergetics Inc.

4 LSU Rural Life Museum (19th century)

5 The LSU Union (1960–61)— Desmond-Miremont & Associates

Burnside

6 Houmas House (1840)

Clinton

7 **Court House and Lawyers' Row** (1840) —J. S. Savage

near Darrow

8 **Ashland-Belle Hélène** (1841)—James Gallier, Sr.

Napoleonville

9 **Madewood Plantation House** (1846–48) —Henry Howard

near Natchitoches

10 **Melrose Plantation** (late 18th/early 19th century)

New Iberia

11 **Shadows-on-the-Teche** (1831–34)

New Orleans

12 **The Vieux Carré** (1721–1856)

13 **Madame John's Legacy** (1726–28/ 1788)

14 Pitot House (1799–1800)

15 **The Louisiana Cemeteries—St. Louis ⚜1** (1789) **and ⚜2** (1823)

16 Gallier Hall (1853)—James Gallier, Sr.

17 **Gallier House** (1857–60)—James Gallier, Jr.

18 615 Howard Avenue Building (1888–
    89)—H. H. Richardson
    Confederate Memorial Hall (1889–
    90)—Thomas Sully
19 John Hancock Building (1960–62)—
    Skidmore, Owings & Merrill

New Roads   20 **Parlange** (c. 1750)

Ponchatoula   21 D. C. Reeves Elementary School
                            (1969)—Desmond-Miremont-Burks

Reserve   22 **San Francisco Plantation** (1853–56)

St. Francisville   23 Oakley (c. 1799)
                        24 **Rosedown Plantation and Gardens**
                            (1834–35/wings 1844)

St. Martinville   25 **Acadian House Museum** (1765)

Vacherie   26 **Oak Alley** (1837–39)—Gilbert Joseph
                            Pilié

1 Pentagon Barracks (1819–23/1966–67)
Riverside Mall
Baton Rouge, Louisiana

The Pentagon Barracks provide us with a surprisingly competent, Classic-inspired example of early American military architecture. After the Civil War the barracks were used by Louisiana State University until acquired by the state in 1950. They were then fully restored and remodeled on the interior in 1966–67, with one building converted to apartments for state employees, while the other three contain offices for state agencies. It is informative to note that the prominent red color was selected from nineteenth-century United States Army Archives, the sample chosen being called Baltimore brick red. A fifth side once existed but apparently it was pulled down shortly after completion—wisely opening the group to views of the Mississippi. Captain James Gadsen, of the Corps of Engineers, was the barracks' designer.

Grounds always open

2   Old State Capitol (1847–49/rebuilt 1880–82)
North Boulevard at St. Philip Street
Baton Rouge, Louisiana

JAMES H. DAKIN, ARCHITECT

There are few entrance halls of any architectural period that can match
the sheer inebriation of this one in the Old Capitol. It develops a lusty,
joyful space with a circular stair coiled at the entry waiting to propel
one to the main floor above where an umbrella of multicolored panes,
spewing glass fireworks from the top of the central column, provides
the ceiling. Exposed structure (cast iron) and decoration (intricately
colored and fabricated glass) are masterfully fused. Gothic Revival
arches and arcades mark each level of the hall, and from it open the
major rooms. These have been respectfully adapted (1968–69) from
political chambers to create an art gallery (the former Senate), lecture
hall, and administrative offices, under the careful direction of George
M. Leake.

The Old Capitol—the design for which was won by competition—
was gutted by fire during the Civil War (1862), but was restored
twenty years later, serving in its original capacity until 1932 when the
new Capitol was built. The restoration of 1880–82 was under the direction of William A. Freret, who made some changes, including the
dome and the addition of the fourth floor. Concerning the original
design—which possibly also had a dome—it is worth noting that
James Dakin had for several years been a member of the New York
firm of Town & Davis (see Index for their buildings), famous for their
Greek Revival structures. Here, however, Dakin opted boldly for the
"newer," more up-to-date Gothic Revival because the former "appeared in every city and town of our country." He practiced the rest of
his life in Louisiana except for brief excursions to Mobile, Alabama.

The exterior of the Old Capitol is tame, forming a stiffly symmetrical
block, with two towers standing beside both river and land entrances.
The water approach is perhaps the better from an architectural point
of view, with a long straight flight leading to the arched door hemmed
by octagonal turrets. The street turrets are square (and vaguely Assyrian), a machicolated "cornice" running around all. Though the outside is thus reasonably quiet, the exuberant central hall is the finest
Gothic Revival civic interior in the United States.

Open Mon.–Fri. 9:30–5, Sat. 10–5, Sun. 1–5, except holidays

3   Union Tank Car Repair Facility (1958)
off US 61 near Alsen, c. 12 miles/19 kilometers N of city
near Baton Rouge, Louisiana

BATTEY & CHILDS, ENGINEERS AND ARCHITECTS; SYNERGETICS INC., DOME ENGINEERS

"Visitors and Salesmen by Appointment Only" proclaims the sign, but the admirers of Buckminster Fuller (who founded Synergetics Inc.) can see enough from the gate to make the drive up from Baton Rouge worthwhile. For this is the largest geodesic dome yet built (but not the largest steel-ribbed—which is at Pittsburgh at 415 feet/126 meters). Its unobstructed interior diameter measures 375 feet/114 meters and its height, 116 feet/35 meters. (The spheroid U. S. Pavilion at Montreal's Expo '67, which Bucky Fuller also designed, was 250 feet/76 meters in diameter.) The Union Tank Car Repair Facility is also the country's first all-welded steel dome. Its ingenious shell is made up of 321 yellow-painted, identical, hexagonal, diamond-shaped units forming the skin, supported by an exoskeleton geodesic "spider web" of blue pipe framing. The whole was put together by an inside crane,

rather than scaffolding. The 11-gauge steel plate is that also used in
the tank cars. All the elements employed in the dome's construction—
pipes, plates, nuts, bolts, and washers—were distilled into a total of
seven standardized parts! The tank cars to be serviced or rebuilt move
in onto a circular, off-center transfer table and are rotated to the
proper repair slot, of which there are thirty. An inner "control tower,"
80 feet/24 meters high, coordinates movement. The long low structure
seen at left from the gate is the paint tunnel. A brilliant building and
one so successful that Union Tank has constructed two others.

Visible only from gate

---

4   LSU Rural Life Museum (19th century)
Burden Research Plantation
SW corner of IS 10 and Essen Lane, SE edge of
Baton Rouge, Louisiana

The rural vernacularist and the pastoral historian will find this collection of nineteenth-century farm structures of much interest. It is lo-

cated on the 450-acre/182-hectare Burden Research Plantation, which was given to Louisiana State University by Ione Burden and her brother Steele Burden. The museum comprises a group of (mostly) original buildings assembled from the delta area (beginning in 1970) to simulate a small regional sugarcane plantation of the last century. Only the Blacksmith's Shop, the Sugarhouse, and the Acadian House are partially reconstructed.

The museum is divided into three contiguous sections: (1) the Barn, a large contemporary building (1972) adjacent to the parking lot and now housing a vast, and often fascinating, collection of artifacts, tools, and vehicles; (2) the Working Plantation, the major grouping of buildings and one presided over by the cypress-framed Overseer's House (c. 1835), with detached kitchen, slave cabins, Blacksmith's Shop, and Sugarhouse deployed around the green in front; (3) the Folk Architecture, with a Negro Country Church (c. 1870), a Pioneer Cabin (c. 1810), and a reproduced Acadian House. The church interior is particularly interesting. Altogether a major statement of rural plantation life of over a century ago.

Open Mon.–Fri. 8:30–4 by appointment, except university holidays; telephone (504) 766-8241

---

5 **The LSU Union** (1960–61)
Louisiana State University
Tower Drive
Baton Rouge, Louisiana

DESMOND-MIREMONT & ASSOCIATES, MATHES, BERGMAN & ASSOCIATES, WILSON & SANDIFER, ARCHITECTS

The exterior of the Union was designed to fit comfortably with the earlier buildings. It utilizes the same cornice height and colors, while maintaining a quietly regional yet structurally logical lineup of concrete columns, with exterior walls set back from eave edge in Louisiana fashion. The Union is surrounded by live oaks—a "memorial grove"—and the architects purposefully elevated the major rooms to enjoy this spinney. On the inside there is animation of spaces, levels, and movement, and this carries through on all three floors. It is, in other words, a very three-dimensional interior, one that works well and is fun to use. The building houses cafeteria, dining room, auditorium and conference rooms, game rooms, bookshop, and ballroom, with a

1,315-seat theater attached at right. Structure throughout is of concrete with columns on a 24-foot/7.3-meter grid. There are a few structural exaggerations, but the detailing, especially the use of colors, and the lighting are good, while the interlocking and the variety of spaces are excellent—as is the circulation. Desmond-Miremont were the prime designing architects.

Open during school year

---

6 Houmas House (1840)
W off LA 44 onto LA 942, just NW of
Burnside, Louisiana

A classic Louisiana mansion of brick stuccoed, with six two-story Tuscan columns across the front (note spacing) and five on either side. Second-floor galleries encircle the house while the whole is topped by an unexpected cupola. Spared during the Civil War because of its upriver location and because its then-owner was an Irishman and thus a British subject, the plantation was successfully active throughout the

nineteenth century. It went on to become, indeed, the country's largest
producer of sugar. However, much of the land was sold when a subsequent owner died in 1899, and Houmas—named for a southern Louisiana Indian tribe with a reputation for bravery—fell on sad days. Then
in 1940 it was purchased by the late Dr. George B. Crozat, who spent
twenty-five years lovingly restoring the house (cleverly concealing contemporary amenities) and establishing the garden which extends almost to the Mississippi River. On the interior the stairway especially
should be noted. The good doctor then refurnished it with proper—
and very choice—period pieces, and it was opened to the public by his
heirs in 1970. Attached to the house at the rear stands a small dwelling from the end of the eighteenth century, while out in front are two
hexagonal *garçonnières* which served as simple accommodations for
sons of the family (i.e. garçons) and travelers.

*Tours daily Nov.–Jan. 10–4; Feb.–Oct. 10–5, except major
holidays: admission*

7 Court House and Lawyers' Row (1840)
Court House Square
Clinton, Louisiana

J. S. SAVAGE, ARCHITECT

This simple but diverting Greek Revival building, square in plan, carries an unexpected "plantation" dignity. Surrounded by two-story-high, unfluted Doric columns (of brick stuccoed), the building's peripteral or columnar girdling provides some sun and rain protection—plus chiaroscuro. Its hip roof is topped by an octagonal cupola. Within are municipal offices which have been in continuous use since the Court House was finished; it is one of the oldest surviving in the state. (The Claiborne Parish Court House at Homer, 1860, is highly similar.)

Be sure to note the droll parade of five small Greek "temples" on the north border of the square. Called Lawyers' Row, they were erected at roughly the same time as the Court House, and were occupied by lawyers of such distinction that they were reputedly consulted by colleagues from all over the state. The buildings make a delightful

backdrop for the Court House. Unfortunately the same cannot be said for the other sides of the square. The Court House itself was thoroughly restored in 1936.

Open during office hours

---

8   Ashland-Belle Hélène (1841)
off LA 30: 2.5 miles/4 kilometers SE of Geismar via LA 73 from US 61; 6 miles/9.7 kilometers NW of Darrow via LA 22 from US 61
between Darrow and Geismar, Louisiana

JAMES GALLIER, SR., ARCHITECT

A plantation near the edge of the Mississippi which has had more than its share of troubles. However, happily to report, it is recovering from almost total neglect—aided several times by Hollywood, which has restored part of it for sets. Although all is still not in order, the house and grounds form a peculiarly nostalgic, proud remembrance of a vanished era. Entirely surrounded by a peristyle of twenty-eight square Doric columns or piers, eight to a side—and square in plan itself—the

house states its case with conviction. Much of this positiveness stems from its heavy entablature and its "invisible" roof which seem to propel the hard-edge colonnade at the observer. It is illuminating in this regard to compare Ashland with the more delicate Oak Alley in Vacherie (q.v.), also square in plan and surrounded by twenty-eight round columns (not piers) and with high hip roof and dormers. The rotundity of Oak Alley's columns forms less of a "barrier" than do piers, while the receding geometry of its prominent roof tends to pull one on. Belle Hélène has great strength; Oak Alley great grace. Surviving—but just—the house is being slowly restored; the exterior has recently been completely rehabilitated. The inner furnishings are sparse, but the house with its 20-foot/6.1-meter-wide galleries and 30-foot/ 9.1-meter-high piers is still a stalwart number.

Open daily 9–4, except holidays: admission

---

9 Madewood Plantation House (1846–48)
Bayou Lafourche, on LA 308, 2 miles/3.2 kilometers S of Napoleonville, Louisiana

HENRY HOWARD, ARCHITECT

A large Greek Revival house magisterially pedimented with six two-story Ionic columns to produce one of the most powerful "temple" facades in the state. This is closely "protected" by two small *tempietti* which echo the mansion's lines and add geometric cadence to the whole. Their cornices match the height of the veranda deck which stretches across the portico, as, of course, do the angles of their own small pediments. Note, too, the delicate wood railing of the gallery. There is a handsome balance here which is saved from dryness by the rhythm of the small dependencies and by the fine detail work (especially in the capitals). The roof and floors of the mansion were reputedly framed by, and the pediments enclosed in, cypress wood from the plantation—hence the name of the house—with walls of brick stuccoed ranging from 18 inches/46 centimeters (inner) to 24 inches/61 centimeters (outer). Fortunately protected from destruction at the time of the War Between the States, the house had a succession of subsequent owners but rarely with deleterious results. In 1964 it was purchased by the Harold K. Marshalls, who have since carried out a complete restoration. It is now owned by their son, Keith C. Marshall.

The windows go all the way to the floor—as is the bayou custom—for greater ventilation. The central hall divides the house into two halves, with graceful stairs at the end; like the other rooms, including the ballroom, the hall is well attended to. Many of the furnishings today are of the Marshall family which lives at Madewood.

Open daily 10–5, except holidays: admission

---

10 Melrose Plantation (late 18th/early 19th century)
17 miles/27 kilometers S of town on LA 493
near Natchitoches, Louisiana

A collection of upstate plantation buildings as unusual architecturally as they are sociologically. Known until 1875 as Yucca Plantation, the group of buildings was probably managed (but not owned) by a freed black female slave who successfully controlled it—and her own numerous slaves—for the last quarter of the eighteenth century. Upon being freed by her French common-law husband she and her sons were

given the land now known as Melrose Plantation. The title was recorded in the name of one of her sons. Although little is known about "Marie Therese," the ex-slave entrepreneur—who was born (1742) nearby and known as Coin-Coin to her African mother—it is possible that her admiration for things African was influential in the design of several of the earliest buildings. The African House (c. 1800), which measures 39.9 x 35.7 feet/12 x 10.8 meters, is a one-and-a-half-story brick structure with an enormous overhang on all four sides. Though the wooden Ghana House of more recent construction is a modest affair of squared logs, they both make a unique contribution to our architectural development because of their suggestions of African background. Yucca House, the first plantation building (c. 1796)—built and owned by Marie Therese's son—is a simple hip-roofed, one-story, verandaed regional example. The more ambitious Melrose House dates from around 1833, and probably was built by Marie Therese's grandson. The central part is of brick over *bousillage* on the ground floor with cypress above; it has front and rear galleries and a hip roof in the typical "raised cottage" style. Octagonal abutments of wood were added at each end around 1900. Melrose complex is listed in the National Register of Historic Places. Natchitoches (Nak'-a-tosh) is the oldest town in the Louisiana Purchase and contains a number of buildings of interest.

Open daily except Mon. and Wed. 2–4:30: admission

---

11   Shadows-on-the-Teche (1831–34)
217 East Main Street (LA 182) at Weeks
New Iberia, Louisiana

One of the greatest Louisiana town houses open to the public, the Shadows provides us with a slightly eclectic, up-country mansion of a wealthy Delta planter. Being town-oriented, a street facade provides the main entrance, rather than the one facing the bayou. (Compare the earlier Virginia plantations, where the water approach was paramount.) The house is divided vertically into seven well-proportioned bays by eight stuccoed brick Tuscan columns (with high bases and thin capitals), and emphasized horizontally by its second-floor veranda or gallery, and, above, by an unusually triglyphed cornice (which encircles the house): an interplay is set up which is most satisfying. Three dormers and two inset chimneys add their own touch. The cor-

nice, incidentally, may well have been changed in later years, for the well-publicized watercolor by Adrian Persac, dated 1861, shows a much fuller, more routine, entablature. The two end bays are screened from top to bottom by green-painted wood blinds and lattices to conceal the outside stair behind the north bay (there is no stair at the other). This architectural sleight-of-hand, which also knits the entire front more compactly together, is thought by some—probably apocryphally—to stem from a Spanish edict taxing inside stairways. The Bayou Teche facade of the Shadows is less enticing than the front, having a simple loggia inset at the upper floor over a three-arched service area. The former steamboat landing lies only a few hundred yards beyond the beautifully landscaped antiformal grounds.

The interior is highly compartmented, and there is no inside hall—a reflection of the no-hall raised cottage plan early popular in Louisiana. The present dining room, for instance, which occupies the center of the lower floor, is reached only via the front porch or the back service loggia. This room may have been the drawing room originally, with the dining room in the corner at right. The upper floor, which contains the present drawing room as well as the bedroom, is also without interior hall, the veranda providing access.

The house was commissioned and basically designed by David Weeks, who unfortunately died just after moving in. James Bedell was the master builder who put it together. However, it remained in the family, undergoing a few ups and many downs, until Weeks Hall, the great-grandson of the builder, began restoration (partially achieved) of both house and grounds in 1922. Before his death in 1958 Mr. Hall generously gave the mansion, including all the furniture and appointments plus an endowment, to the National Trust for Historic Preservation. The interior presented an authentic, unspoiled ensemble, although further restoration (fortunately aided by countless—some say forty thousand—original documents) was needed. The National Trust, having completed full restoration (1961) to the antebellum era, is maintaining house and grounds with its noted solicitude.

Open daily 9–4:30, except Dec. 25: admission

12 The Vieux Carré (1721–1856)
**Canal and North Rampart Streets, Esplanade Avenue, the
   Mississippi River**
New Orleans, Louisiana

The Vieux Carré at one time was a delightfully unspoiled enclave in a busy, busy city. It had been fashioned over several centuries by local cultures (French and Spanish), shaped in part by local weather (i.e. heat and humidity), and molded of local materials (brick and cypress). Its commerce was seemly, its signs and notices couth. It constituted one of our great and unspoiled urban heritages.

The French Quarter, as the Vieux Carré is more popularly called, is, of course, still there and the major impact is still delightful. However, official lassitude and commercialism have sullied much that is genuine in this unique area. (Fortunately the city has declared a moratorium on any more new hotels in the Vieux Carré.)

For the diligent, though, there are still great charms and unexpected delights to be found. Among these pleasures are: the domestic scale and overall sense of ensemble; the rows of one-story nineteenth-century-vernacular wooden houses set at right angles to Orleans, Burgundy, and Dauphine Streets (among others—and possibly Haitian-derived); the balconied two- and three-story houses directly lining many streets in the Continental fashion, almost dripping with ironwork, their filigreed galleries miraculously supported by the thinnest of pipestem columns; the unexpected open vistas, the closed views (such as the back of the cathedral seen at the end of Orleans Street), and

then an occasional glimpse into an inner courtyard; the ubiquitous—
generally delicious—smells, the unexpected sounds, the changing tex-
tures; and finally the green pasture of Jackson Square, now a National
Historic Landmark. All these, and more, are among the Quarter's
delights.

The *quartier,* which in its early days formed the entire original city,
was laid out in 1721 in the customary military grid by Le Blond de la
Tour, the French governor's chief engineer, and supervised by Adrien
de Pauger, a Royal Engineer. After the fall of Quebec (1759) the
town was enclosed by a rampart (hence the current street name).
These fortifications were completely rebuilt (c. 1791) by the Spanish,
who had taken over in 1762, a gift of Louis XV to his cousin Charles
III of Spain. The plan centers on the Place d'Armes (1720), the present (Andrew) Jackson Square (replanned and renamed in the
1850s), and this in turn was, and is, dominated by the Cathedral of St.
Louis. Built—also by de Pauger—in 1724–27, the church burned
(with much of the town) in the great fires of 1788 and 1794. (It was
rebuilt 1789–94 by Gilberto Guillemard, a French architect in the
service of Spain.) The somewhat disjointed facade we see today, with
its ambitious steeples, is the work (1851) of the French-born, Beaux-
Arts-trained J. N. B. de Pouilly. (The cathedral is open Mon.–Sat.
9–5, Sun. 1–5.) To the left of the church stands the Cabildo
(1795–1847), and to the right the Presbytère (1791, 1813, 1847), the
former the finest Spanish-designed—perhaps more properly Spanish/

Latin American-designed—secular building in the country. It and its near-twin, the Presbytère, were heavily burdened by the prominent Mansard roofs added to each in 1847, but they still make a rare, representative pair. The Cabildo was originally built as the City Hall. In 1967–69 its much altered interior was restored as closely as could be determined to its appearance in 1803 at the time of the transfer of Louisiana to the United States. It is part of the Louisiana State Museum (open Tues.–Sun. 9–5: admission). The architects of the restoration were Maxwell & Lebreton and Richard Koch and Samuel Wilson, Jr.

Extending on either side to frame the square are the three-and-a-half-story, deep red Pontalba Buildings (1849–51), with shops on the ground floor and residences above. These row houses (made into apartments by the WPA in the 1930s) were commissioned by the Baroness de Pontalba as a speculative venture, with plans and specifications from James Gallier, Sr., and exterior design and some changes by Henry Howard. Their building was undertaken to anchor the area, because the center of fast-expanding New Orleans was then moving across Canal Street, and its residences into the Garden District and the Esplanade. The combination of the need for more room plus the semiostracism by the Creoles (i.e. old families) of the "new" Americans, who moved in energtically following the Louisiana Purchase (1803), provided, ironically, the salvation of the French Quarter. It was bypassed and left largely untouched until the depradations after World War II. The Baroness' "failure" was the Vieux Carré's blessing.

The galleries on the Pontalba Buildings are of cast iron, made in New York City, and were among their first large-scale use in New Orleans. (Galleries, as opposed to balconies, extend completely over the sidewalk.) The city had, of course, a tradition of wrought-iron balconies going back to the early French days. Wrought-iron "outrigging" had become so popular—both for sun protection and decoration— that they were often added to previously balcony-less houses. Samuel Wilson, the distinguished New Orleans architect and historian, feels that the best examples were made in the 1790s by Marcellino Hernandez. The first galleries, Mr. Wilson feels in quoting Cabildo records, date from 1789 when Don Joseph de Orue y Garbea petitioned that "in order to give more beauty and comfort to a house he intends to build . . . he intends to build it with a porch on the edge of the sidewalk, and far be it from obstructing the traffic of pedestrians, said porch will afford protection in time of rain and strong sun" (*Magazine of Art,* October 1948). Wrought iron held sway until the 1830s–40s, when the cheaper and more ornate cast iron gradually superseded it.

These buildings and this square constitute the formalism of the Vieux Carré: its unique pleasures—and there are many along its maze of streets—are even more rewarding. Savor them at a stroll, with eyes and ears receptive and nose twitching.

Even if the Mississippi River, which occasioned the Vieux Carré's location and which forms its southeast border, cannot easily be reached because of the intervening six railroad tracks, at least the proposed elevated highway across this vital "outlet" was killed—but only after enormous efforts by concerned citizens. The resulting possibility is that eventually a complete water's edge rehabilitation will take place and the "lost" river incorporated again as an essential ingredient of the area. The first move toward this goal was taken in 1976 when the "Moon Walk" was constructed over the tracks to provide limited access to the river's edge. Connected by broad steps with Jackson Square, the 12-foot/3.6-meter-wide, wood plank Walk extends some 420 feet/128 meters along the levee. Benches and planters alternate to provide a fine promenade, with steps at midpoint which descend to the river's edge. Pressure-treated pine was used for construction. The project was named in honor of former mayor Moon Landreu; Cashio & Cochran Associates were the designers. There are also suggestions for a double-armed extension of the whole riverbank area to provide levee promenades along the Mississippi, with hotel and parking facilities to absorb the present crunch on the seventy-five blocks of the Vieux Carré.

---

13   Madame John's Legacy (1726–28/1788)
632 Dumaine Street
New Orleans, Louisiana

Madame John's is an adaptation of a type probably more often seen in the country than in town. It is of the typical French raised cottage style (compare Parlange in New Roads), with veranda across both its 41-foot/12.5-meter-wide front and back, the whole topped by a steep dormered roof. Although the early house, built by a French sea captain, did not survive the fire of March 18, 1788, its reconstruction—according to building contracts—commenced within weeks, using most of the plan and some of the salvageable materials. It is thus safe to assume that the dwelling we see today is basically similar to the earlier: the burned-out inhabitants did not have time for changes. However, it should be pointed out that the street-side *galerie* originally went around three sides to face the garden-patio which once stood to the left. It is likely, too, that the dormers were added later. The house was meticulously restored (1972–73) by F. Monroe Labouisse III and the Louisiana State Museum, which owns it, and was reopened to the public in 1975. It contributes an excellent souvenir of the intriguing French period of early American architecture. Madame John's name, incidentally, comes from *Tite Poulette,* one of the perceptive short stories of New Orleans' George Washington Cable.

Open Tues.–Sun. 9–5, except holidays: admission

14 Pitot House (1799–1800)
1440 Moss Street (take Orleans Avenue NW to Moss, then R)
New Orleans, Louisiana

The Pitot House is another of the few remaining representatives from France's American "colony" which stretched from Canada to the Gulf of Mexico. It once commanded a 30-acre/12-hectare plantation along the Bayou St. John. As is true of much Gulf architecture, a West Indies influence can be seen in its design. (Though the French-born James Pitot himself emigrated from Haiti during the slave uprisings, he did not buy the country retreat which bears his name until 1810. Pitot, incidentally, was the "first democratically elected mayor" of New Orleans.) The lower floor of the house with its masonry base and columns supports an airy second level with a sun-shielding, outdoor-living *galerie* or piazza surrounding three sides with jalousies giving added weather protection. The walls are of typical French post-and-brick construction covered with plaster where protected by the galleries and wide ship-lap siding where exposed. The regional and cultural responses are excellent. The house was threatened in 1962 as the site

was needed for a school, but the Missionary Sisters of the Sacred Heart, then the owners, gave it to the Louisiana Landmarks Society, which had it moved (1964) a block away. It was then completely restored by architects Koch and Wilson (1976), an 1830 drawing by a French artist helping greatly in restoration. The interior is simple and airily furnished. Note the punkah attached to the ceiling, the precursor of the electric fan.

Open Thurs. 11–4, group tours by appointment: admission.
Telephone: (504) 482-0312

---

15   The Louisiana Cemeteries—St. Louis #1 (1789) and #2 (1823)
St. Louis Street at Basin Street
New Orleans, Louisiana

The New Orleans cemeteries rank high among the world's burial grounds for their sculptural fascination. They are not as grandiose as the Monumental (*sic*) Cemetery in Milan and they pale beside the Tombs of the Caliphs east of Cairo, but in the United States they stand apart. Their vaults also stand several feet (a meter or so) off the ground because just below the turf lies groundwater. But they are elevated with a spectrum of enclosure that boggles the visitor. The experience is not macabre, and this functional funerary phantasmagoria should be seen by all. Although most of the jam-packed vaults, like most houses, display little or no individual merit, their collective silhouette, almost a miniaturized skyline, works wonders. Some of the New Orleans tombs are the work of highly qualified architects, among them de Pouilly, whose work was mentioned for the cathedral, the Freret brothers, James Gallier, and Benjamin Latrobe.

Many of the early cemetery grounds—which are largely treeless—were enclosed by "wall vaults." Measuring some 12 feet/3.6 meters high and 9 feet/2.7 meters thick, their outer faces form a protective peripheral ring along the street, while on the cemetery side multilevel columbaria (also called *fours* for their resemblance to French ovens) open on the vaults' faces. These "ovens" were generally rented—mostly to the less affluent—either for a specified number of years or in perpetuity. If the rent did not come through the bones were pushed into the back, the coffin remnants burned, and the vault re-rented! Inasmuch as there is no stone near the Mississippi Delta area, many of the vaults and the columbaria are of brick stuccoed and whitewashed. However, a number—obviously for the wealthy—are of stone, or have

a stone facing, some of which was imported from as far away as France. In addition to masonry, the wrought-iron work also should be noted for this at times attains great delicacy. The St. Louis Cemetery #2 stands near #1 at St. Louis Street and North Claiborne. There are others of note throughout the city as well as in several towns to the south.

Open daily Mon.–Sat. 9–5, Sun. 1–5, except holidays

16 Gallier Hall (1853)
St. Charles Avenue at Lafayette Square
New Orleans, Louisiana

JAMES GALLIER, SR., ARCHITECT

A surprisingly rich Greek Revival building. Built originally as the Municipal Hall, it was changed to the City Hall three years after completion. The sculpture in the pediment is not the world's most imaginative and the frieze around it tends to the lush side, but otherwise its Ionic

portico carries itself with style. The whole marble-fronted building was completely restored in 1969–70, the interior being transformed into offices and its great rooms rented for cultural events and receptions. It is now called Gallier Hall, for once a municipal building named for its architect.

Open Mon.–Fri. 9–4, except holidays

17   Gallier House (1857–60)
1132 Royal Street
New Orleans, Louisiana

JAMES GALLIER, JR., ARCHITECT

Almost all of the nineteenth-century New Orleans town houses are closed to the public; however, this residence and the adjacent erstwhile commercial building (1832) are not only open, the house was designed by one of the famous Louisiana architects. (Gallier was born in England but brought to America at age five.) The double-width com-

mercial unit, which was occupied by a bottling plant for years, and the house are externally similar. Each has the distinctive New Orleans street-facing gallery (8 feet/2.4 meters wide), upheld by the slenderest of cast-iron columns, columns which here erupt into a fantasy of iron grillwork on the balcony level and eave. When continued by adjacent buildings, these verandas create an "arcade" which provides shade in sunshine and an umbrella in the rain. Moreover the galleries extend the "protection" of the house so that the pedestrian feels he has an "association" with the street. Note the rustication of the ground floor of the residence and its elaborate entry. The interior of the commercial building has been remodeled into a museum with particularly instructive displays of the architecture of the region and of Gallier Jr. (including his drawings).

The house and backyard garden have been completely restored by Richard Koch and Samuel Wilson, Jr., with Christopher Friedrichs helping with the garden. Take a look at the advanced-for-the-day plumbing arrangements, including both hot and cold running water and a patented toilet. The colors and wallpapers are all authentic, with the furnishings typical of the nascent Victorian fashionable in the 1860s when the Galliers lived there. The restoration (1970–71) was made possible by the Ella West Freeman Foundation, and the house opened to the public in 1971. Be certain to go out onto the balcony and survey the street, itself notable for its cast-iron parade.

Open Mon.–Sat. 10–4:30, except holidays: admission

---

18 615 Howard Avenue Building (1888–89)
Howard Avenue at Lee Circle
New Orleans, Louisiana

H. H. RICHARDSON, ARCHITECT

Richardson, one of the country's greatest architects, was born 65 miles/105 kilometers north of New Orleans but—due in part to the Civil War—this is his sole building in the South. (Richardson, after five years in Paris, thought postwar northern opportunities greater—not to mention that he had a Boston fiancée.) The building's plans were

originally submitted in a competition for a library in Michigan, which was never built, but HHR then readily—and questionably considering the difference in climate—used them for the city's Howard Memorial Library. Though completed three years after his death (by Shepley, Rutan and Coolidge) it is one of the most elegant of Richardson's famous series of modified Romanesque buildings.

The magnificent geometry seems sharper here and the details more incisive than in his similar work in Massachusetts and Vermont, even though this is hard to discern under the thick green vines which blanket the building. Note, for instance, the controlled "ferment" of the projected semioctagonal tower versus the half-round entry arch next to it, both pulled together vertically by the triangle of the roof pediment. The geometry continues' with a powerful slash of windows which is terminated by the corner tower. Incidentally, both the dark sandstone and its master stonecutter came from Massachusetts. When the library was transferred to Tulane University (1941), the building served a variety of office functions. Since 1972 it has been occupied by Kullman Lang Inman & Bee, attorneys.

Can only be seen from street

The **Confederate Memorial Hall** (1889–90), 929 Camp Street, which abuts the former library, was designed by Thomas Sully. It is open Mon.–Sat. 10–4, except holidays: admission.

---

19   John Hancock Building (1960–62)
St. Charles Avenue at Calliope Street
New Orleans, Louisiana

SKIDMORE, OWINGS & MERRILL, ARCHITECTS

SOM's first essay (1951) with wraparound sun-screening—probably the first large-scale use in the United States—was for New Orleans' Pan-American Life Insurance Company at 2400 Canal Street. The John Hancock Building shelters the same general type of activity in a second-generation wraparound, with increased know-how and refinement evident. Much of Hancock's subtlety comes from the use of precast concrete "louvers" for the sun grid (instead of aluminum as at PALIC), plus the addition of a slender horizontal sun shade which gives both greater sun protection and keener scale relation as it plays

off against the thick floor slab. Would that more buildings in New Orleans and elsewhere were so protected from the sun. Be sure to note the Hancock terrace with its dolmen fountain by Noguchi.

Lobby open during office hours

---

20 Parlange (c. 1750)
**c. 8 miles/13 kilometers N off US 190 on LA 1 or LA 78, or on
  LA 1, 6 miles/9.7 kilometers S of**
New Roads, Louisiana

Parlange was built only thirty-two years after Bienville founded New Orleans (1718), so gives us an informative index of early domestic architecture in Louisiana. (This finds a climax eighty to a hundred years later in the great Mississippi River plantations.) Parlange's architecture is an excellent example of the French-influenced raised cottage style or "early Louisiana type." Moreover it has been lived in continuously, inhabited, *mirabile,* by descendants of the same family for eight generations. The house is built of stuccoed brick on the ground floor for the usual protection against water and dampness, and the circular columns which help support the gallery that surrounds and "protects" the house are also of brick. (Their original, wedge-shaped form-

works still exist. There was no stone in the Delta region for the stone-trained French builders.) The upper part of the house was constructed of cypress and moss packed together with clay and stuccoed, a technique known as *bousillage,* literally "bungled" or "botched."

The exterior of the dwelling needs attention. Comfort has triumphed over "purity" in that part of the veranda has been screened, the front stairs were probably inside the gallery originally, the roof at the rear was extended in the middle of the last century, and the formal garden in front has disappeared. Still, Parlange provides as nostalgic a picture as is to be had of that unfortunately vanishing species of French culture in the U.S.A.

The interior reveals some fine detailing (note, for instance, the fanlights over the windows). However, as little has been removed from the house for well over two centuries, its inner spaces are so crowded they are difficult to grasp—though the effort is recommended. For years only minimum upkeep could be made, but after World War I the family was able to spruce matters up somewhat. Note the unusually steep, French-influenced hip roof—its height precisely equals that of the two floors—and the two dovecotes in front.

Open daily 9–5, except Dec. 25: admission

21   D. C. Reeves Elementary School (1969)
North 1st Street, c. .5 mile/.8 kilometer N of US 190
Ponchatoula (near Hammond), Louisiana

DESMOND-MIREMONT-BURKS, ARCHITECTS

A very low-budget school lifted above the ordinary by the sensitive disposition of its separate units and its friendly scale. Its freestanding "pavilions" of local materials, set between carefully preserved moss-laden oaks and pines, and connected by covered walks, are each surrounded by peripheral porches—in the approved, logical, and appealing Gulf idiom. Here the porches can double as open-air teaching spaces. There are two clusters of classrooms (eighteen total), and separate buildings for library, administration, and cafeteria-auditorium. Refreshingly understated. Andrew Gasaway was associate architect.

Grounds open during school hours

22   San Francisco Plantation (1853–56)
on LA 44, 2.5 miles/4 kilometers W of
Reserve, Louisiana

"This improbable assemblage of Gothic, Classic and miscellaneous Victorian architectural elements is Louisiana's best known fantasy in architecture" (John Desmond, FAIA, in *Louisiana Architect,* January 1968). Obviously influenced in design by the Mississippi riverboats which once steamed past its front door—the river then without levee— San Francisco is a racy maverick among Louisiana plantation houses. Measuring 70 feet/21 meters wide by 60 feet/18 meters deep, and dominated by an almost outrageous "cornice" (which largely camouflages the setback top floor), the exterior combines the paradox of being both filigreed and weighted. It is surrogate Greek Revival attempting the Victorian.

After a stroll around its "Corinthian" porch (note the cast-iron capitals), take a look inside where sumptuosity awaits. The drawing room, in particular, literally glows, its cornice and its cypress ceiling being exquisitely painted. (The identity of the artist and even the date of this painting have never been verified. Its attribution to Dominique Canova and/or his pupils is not authenticated. Moreover the suggestion that the unfinished top floor was to have been a ballroom is unfounded.)

Mr. and Mrs. Clark Thompson leased the house from 1954 to 1974 and undertook much basic preservation. In 1973 ECOL, the Louisiana division of Ingram Oil Company, purchased the extensive plantation as the site for an oil refinery, giving the house (1975), with funding for its restoration, to the San Francisco Plantation Foundation. In 1976 Marathon Oil purchased the refinery from Ingram, generously continuing funding the work on the house until its completion in 1977. The extensive (several-million-dollar) restoration was carried out by Koch and Wilson, Architects, coordinating their three-year work with interior specialists and archeologists. It is a National Historic Landmark (1974) which uses the dates 1849–50 for its construction. Later research favors 1853–56.

Open daily 10–4, except major holidays and Mardi Gras: admission

---

23 Oakley (c. 1799)
Audubon State Commemorative Area
on LA 965 via US 61, 4.5 miles/7.2 kilometers E of
St. Francisville, Louisiana

Oakley stands out as a sizable residence of backcountry persuasion, distinguished by its lofty, louvered porches, which were reputedly contemporary with the original construction. Possibly influenced by West Indian prototypes—after all, de Soto from his base in Havana discovered the Mississippi River in 1541—the house is one of the earliest users of large-scale fixed louvers or jalousies for shielding its airy verandas. It rests on the usual locally fired brick base with two stories of clapboard above. The dwelling—purchased by the state in 1947—has been carefully restored and its early Federal furnishings brought together by the joint effort of the Daughters of the American Revolution and the National Society of the Colonial Dames of America in the State of Louisiana. Be certain to see the outbuildings behind.

The 100-acre/40-hectare park is a memorial to John James Audubon, who painted in this colorful Feliciana area in 1821—and also was tutor to the young daughter of the house. The plantation is administered by the Louisiana Office of State Parks.

Open Mon.–Sat. 9–5, Sun. 1–5, except holidays: admission

---

24 Rosedown Plantation and Gardens (1834–35/wings 1844)
c. 1 mile/1.6 kilometers NE of town at fork of LA 10 and US 61
St. Francisville, Louisiana

Of all the Louisiana plantations which are open to the public, the gardens at Rosedown are the most extensive and varied and the house and grounds among the best-maintained. The gardens in spring are doubly effective because the bright colors of their azaleas and camellias, etc., find a perfect background in the moss-dripping trees, in particular the allée of forty live oaks which frame the approach to the dwelling. Although the mansion itself—now a museum-house—is not uncommonly

distinguished, combining on the exterior a slight amalgam of influences, it is elegantly furnished within. It was almost continuously lived in since built until 1956 when it was purchased by the Milton Underwoods, who carefully restored the building and opened it to the public in 1964. More than 80 per cent of the furnishings belonged to the original builder. In addition to the main house there are outbuildings, even including a doctor's office, at the rear which are worth investigating. Be sure to explore the several gardens. The flower plot (at right) is based on the geometry of the parterres at Versailles. The statuary was purchased in Italy by the original owners. George M. Leake of New Orleans was the restoration architect. The interiors were by McMillen of New York, and the landscape architect of the restoration—more than ably aided by Mrs. Underwood—was Ralph Ellis Gunn of Houston. The original designer is not known.

Open Mar.–Nov., daily 9–5, Dec.–Feb., daily 10–4: admission

25   Acadian House Museum (1765)
Longfellow Evangeline State Commemorative Area
off LA 31, just N of
St. Martinville, Louisiana

Cypresses, pines, and a monumental live oak, all heavy with Spanish moss, make a marvelously regional setting for this Creole raised cottage. Though of small stylistic significance, the house, its outbuilding, and its grounds provide an informative and romantic vignette. The Acadian area of Louisiana was named for its French-Canadian settlers —locally the Cajuns—who were forced from Acadia, Nova Scotia, in the mid-eighteenth century when they would not swear allegiance to the British who had captured the area. They still are a group apart, speaking today a French patois. (Louisiana at the time of the Acadian migration was, as mentioned earlier, French, and its churches were administered—until 1763—by the diocese of Québec, which is why this far-off land was chosen for resettlement. During the French Revolution, the early Acadians were joined by many titled French families.)

The house in the Longfellow Commemorative Area (formerly State Park) has the usual masonry lower story, with upper floor and a half framed in cypress with moss and mud walls clapboarded, all put together with pegs in place of nails. (It is, thus, as mentioned, a Creole-type dwelling, not Nova Scotia Acadian.) In plan it is a room and a half deep with a gallery across the front and, until the 1850s, one also across the rear when it was enclosed for added rooms. The state purchased the dwelling in 1931 and restored it, opening it to the public as a museum in 1933.

Be sure to see the Acadian Craft House, also in the park. Note the chimney construction (notched wood and mud), and the steep stair to the boys' room in the attic. The little house is a reproduction of the one-front-room version of the Creole-Caribbean cottage that was adopted in Louisiana by the Acadians. The house type is now known as "the Cajun cabin."

Open daily Mon.–Sat. 9–5, Sun. 1–5, except holidays: admission

---

26 Oak Alley (1837–39)
on LA 18, 2.5 miles/4 kilometers W of
Vacherie, Louisiana

GILBERT JOSEPH PILIÉ, ARCHITECT

Much of the Classic Revival—that pristine but sometimes desiccated style which hypnotized American architects for roughly the first half of the nineteenth century—would not be entered in a functionalist's notebook. Its visual rewards were often great, it certainly stood for law and order, but too many buildings, especially in the North, were strait-jacketed into temple formations. Oak Alley, however—like many of its type throughout the South—is a superbly logical, semi-Greek Revival answer to the problems of its specific environment. An enormous (70 feet/21 meters square) parasol of a hip roof, supported by twenty-eight two-story Tuscan columns, protects the house from merciless sun and lashing rains. Its double galleries are so wide that windows can be kept open almost all the time while in fair weather each veranda forms an open-air living room. In front, spaced a precise 80 feet/24 meters apart as they advance to the Mississippi, stretch the unbelievable oak trees (twenty-eight in number like the columns), which understandably changed the name of the house from Bon Sejour—and which antedate the mansion by at least a century.

The thick brick stuccoed walls of Oak Alley are painted pink as are the columns (also of brick)—proper mates to the fern-covered trees (*Polypodium incanum*). The dwelling, like most great houses in the South, fell on more than hard times following the Civil War, and early in this century it was deserted and in danger of falling apart when Mr. and Mrs. Andrew Stewart purchased it (1925) and began a restoration (really a renovation) under the direction of the late Richard Koch, FAIA, who did much work in rehabilitating Louisiana's magnificent architectural inheritance. George Swainey was the builder of the house, not the architect as sometimes claimed. Though the interior furnishings do not match the quality of the outside and its setting—what could?— this remains one of our greatest estates. As Clarence J. Laughlin wrote concerning southern Louisiana plantations, "There is in many of them an architectural feeling as close to being truly indigenous as anything that can be found in the United States—not omitting New England" (*Architectural Review,* June 1947).

Open Mar.–Oct., daily 9–5:30; Nov.–Feb. 9–5, except major holidays: admission

Michigan

Sault Ste. Marie 19

Mackinac Island 14

Mackinaw City 15

Midland 17 •

• Muskegon 18

Troy 21

Bloomfield
Hills 1

Warren 22

Lansing ■

Southfield 20 •

Grosse Pointe
Farms 12

Kalamazoo 13 •

• Marshall 16

Dearborn 2

Detroit 3–11

MICHIGAN

The buildings in boldface type are of general interest. The others are for the specialist.

Bloomfield Hills

1 **Cranbrook Academy of Art** (1941–43)—Eliel Saarinen

Cranbrook School for Boys (1927)—Eliel Saarinen

Kingswood School for Girls (1933)—Eliel Saarinen

Institute of Science (1933)—Eliel Saarinen

Dearborn

2 **Greenfield Village** (17th–19th century)

Detroit

See also Bloomfield Hills, Dearborn, Grosse Pointe Farms, Southfield, Troy, and Warren

3 The Skyscrapers of Griswold Street (early 20th century)

Michigan Consolidated Gas Company—Minoru Yamasaki & Associates

Guardian Building—Smith, Hinchman & Grylls

Buhl Building—Smith, Hinchman & Grylls

Ford Building—Daniel Burnham

Dime Building—Daniel Burnham

City National Bank—Smith, Hinchman & Grylls

4 **Albert Kahn and the General Motors Building** (1920–22)—Albert Kahn Associates

5 Northland Shopping Center (1954)—Gruen Associates

6 **McGregor Memorial Conference Center** (1958)—Minoru Yamasaki & Associates

7 **Reynolds Metals Company Building** (1959)—Minoru Yamasaki & Associates

                      8 Lafayette Park (1956–63)—Mies van der Rohe
1300 Lafayette East (1963)—Burkhardt & Straub
                      9 Blue Cross/Blue Shield Service Center (1970–71)—Giffels & Rossetti
                   10 Center for Creative Studies (1974–75)—William Kessler & Associates
                   11 **Renaissance Center** (1973–77)—John Portman & Associates

Grosse Pointe Farms   12 Grosse Pointe War Memorial (1910)—Charles A. Platt

Kalamazoo   13 **General Headquarters of the Upjohn Company** (1961)—Skidmore, Owings & Merrill

Mackinac Island   14 **Grand Hotel** (1887)—Mason & Rice

Mackinaw City   15 **Fort Michilimackinac** (1715–20/ reconstructed 1959–   )
Mackinac Bridge (1954–57)—David B. Steinman

Marshall   16 Honolulu House (1860)

Midland   17 **First United Methodist Church** (1954) —Alden B. Dow

Muskegon   18 **St. Francis de Sales Church** (1964–66)—Marcel Breuer and Herbert Beckhard

Sault Ste. Marie   19 **Tower of History** (1967–68)—Rafferty Rafferty Mikutowski & Associates

Southfield   20 IBM Office Building (1977–78)—Gunnar Birkerts and Associates

Troy   21 K mart Corporation International Headquarters (1970–72)—Smith, Hinchman & Grylls

Warren   22 **General Motors Technical Center** (1951–56)—Eero Saarinen & Associates

1 Cranbrook Academy of Art (1941–43)
500 Lone Pine Road (1.1 miles/1.7 kilometers W of US 10)
Bloomfield Hills, Michigan

ELIEL SAARINEN, ARCHITECT

Architecture, waterscaping, sculpture—a triumphant triumvirate. The main mall at the Cranbrook Academy of Art is not only a wonderful example of campus planning, it is one of the highlights of American architecture in the early 1940s. It was also one of the first educational institutions in this country to eschew the threadbare neo-Colonial and the Collegiate Gothic. Eliel Saarinen (1873–1950), who designed the Cranbrook buildings for the farsighted George G. Booth, came to this country from his native Finland in 1923 upon winning the second prize in the famous Chicago *Tribune* Competition (which many thought his

design should have won). His impact on our architecture and architectural education was significant, while the achievements of his late son, Eero (1910–61), are legendary (see Index). At Cranbrook Eliel was helped by the Swedish-born Carl Milles (1875–1955), who collaborated with the elder Saarinen in the water design of the mall, and who did all the sculpture there. Milles stayed for twenty years as the Academy's resident sculptor. The buildings at Cranbrook, with a sensitive spatial relationship between units, a quietly civilized brick simplicity, and a splendid emphasis on craftsmanship, recall the best of Scandinavia and Finland of that period. Whereas formalism (especially that of the museum and library at the head of the mall) is present, the Academy grounds and its museum are very worth a visit. As Ian McCallam thoughtfully put it in his book *Architecture USA* (Architectural Press, London, 1959) Cranbrook is "one of the first important inroads made by a European architect on the American scene since Colonial times."

The nearby **Cranbrook School for Boys,** *photo below* (520 Lone Pine Road—1927), the **Kingswood School for Girls** (885 Cranbrook Road —1933), and the **Institute of Science** (Institute Way—1933) all show the Northern Countries' tradition of feeling for and respect for massing and site, one highlighted close up by many inventive, even playful details.

Grounds and museum open Tues.–Sun. 1–5, except holidays: admission

2   Greenfield Village (17th–19th century)
     **SW from Detroit on US 12 (Michigan Avenue), S on Southfield
         Expressway, SW on Village Road**
     Dearborn (Detroit), Michigan

A sometimes curious mixture but an always rewarding microcosm of
Americana, mostly of the eighteenth and nineteenth centuries, with a
commendable emphasis on early industrial laboratories and workshops.
The layout is extensive—it covers 260 acres/105 hectares—with almost a hundred buildings to be seen. Each is an original structure
(some partly restored) moved to this site. The focus is on the buildings which housed almost every facet of life in the United States, with
emphasis on those of the last century. However, our European background is not forgotten. There are, among other foreign examples, a
watchmaker's chalet from Switzerland and an early-seventeenth-century
house from Gloucestershire. Public buildings, stores, schools, a church,
and numerous houses—from the log cabin to Henry Ford's birthplace—are properly grouped to form a village.

But the unique contribution of Greenfield Village lies in its highly impressive collection of industrial shops. All of these are important in the historical development of invention and industry in this country. They range from single buildings, such as the small shed where the first Ford car was put together, to the Wright brothers' cycle shop, to the eight-building Menlo Park Compound where (when it was in New Jersey) most of Thomas Alva Edison's pioneering work was done. (Edison was a close friend of Mr. Ford.) Most of the workshops and laboratories at Greenfield are in working order, and for the mechanically and industrially inclined visitor they and their equipment and machinery afford a unique insight into this vital element of our country's growth. Further exhibits can be seen in the nearby Henry Ford Museum (incongruously housed in a replica of Independence Hall), which harbors major collections of American Decorative Arts, Furniture, and, appropriately, a grand collection of some two hundred automobiles. Don't miss.

Open daily, summer 9–6, winter 9–5, except Jan. 1, Thanksgiving, Dec. 25: admission

---

3   The Skyscrapers of Griswold Street (early 20th century)
Griswold Street from Jefferson Avenue to Fort Street
Detroit, Michigan

ARCHITECTS AND DATES AS NOTED

Three blocks of Griswold Street, beginning at Jefferson Avenue (opposite the Civic Center), are lined with a series of skyscrapers of note which limn a fifty-year span of high-rise evolution. Walking northerly from Jefferson:

Michigan Consolidated Gas Company (1963), corner of Jefferson (and Woodward)—Minoru Yamasaki & Associates, architects; Smith, Hinchman & Grylls, associates. A twenty-eight-story building, square in plan, which is of interest esthetically and structurally. The approach is graced by two reflecting pools, one with a statue by Giacomo Manzù. On the ground floor there is a particularly airy, 25-foot/7.6-meter-high lobby wrapped in clear glass inset from the edges. At night the lobby glows outward onto four of the city's avenues. Visually the building breaks away from the "standard" curtain-wall approach, being

sheathed with grille-like panels. These panels are two stories high and made of reinforced concrete, their "spandrels" designed with a central projecting ridge and angled sides to frame lozenge-shaped windows. These reach from floor to ceiling but have only a 20-inch/51-centimeter width to dampen acrophobia from the inside. The overall result is a shining white building (85 per cent white quartz aggregate in the concrete) which is only slightly marred by the filigreed cooling tower on top. W. B. Ford Associates were responsible for the interior; Lee DuSell designed the lobby ceiling and elevator doors.

Guardian Building (1929), 500 Griswold—Smith, Hinchman & Grylls, architects. Formerly the Union Trust, this thirty-six-story structure has been too overlooked as a contributor to the architecture of the late 1920s. Its exterior midsection is relatively mild with brick and terra-cotta decoration, but the base and top are rich with basically Mayan-inspired accents. (All exterior ceramics are from the famous Pewabic Pottery of Mary Chase Stratton.) On the inside the design of the main banking floor of the Michigan National Bank is positively refulgent and should by no means be missed. It is one of our great period pieces. Its chief of design was the talented but little-known Wirt C. Rowland.

Across Griswold on the southwest corner of Congress Street stands the twenty-six-story **Buhl Building** (1925), also by Smith, Hinchman & Grylls. Although there are Romanesque (and some Gothic) details, overall the building was most advanced. Its chief contribution can be seen in its Latin-cross plan which eliminated the relatively dark and airless light courts characteristic of most high buildings of its time. Moreover its exterior is of verticality unimpeded by Classic cornice. William E. Kapp was the principal designer.

Daniel Burnham contributed two early high-rise structures to the street, the curiously unsatisfactory eighteen-story **Ford Building** (1909), 615 Griswold, and the far-better-coordinated, U-shaped, twenty-three-story **Dime Building,** 719 Griswold, of a year later. Both show the Classical details favored by the chief of construction of the famous 1893 World's Columbian Exposition in Chicago, but their main bodies reveal straightforward steel-framed cages. Neither, incidentally, is mentioned by Thomas S. Hines in his excellent biography *Burnham of Chicago* (Oxford University Press, 1974).

The dominant of the group is the forty-seven-story **City National Bank** (ex-Penobscot Building) (1928), 645 Griswold—Smith, Hinchman & Grylls, architects. Its symmetrically built-up massing with studied breaks and setbacks is reminiscent of the contemporary work also popular in Chicago. These setbacks were in part occasioned by the building's pre-air-conditioning date. Corner windows are useful for natural ventilation; central air conditioning tends to simplify both plan and profile. Note the Indian head over the arched entrance. Wirt C. Rowland was chief of design.

   Smith, Hinchman & Grylls, it should be added, conduct "the oldest, continuously operating architectural and engineering practice in the United States." They celebrated their 125th anniversary in 1978—having commenced in 1853—and are still going strong.

Buildings open during office hours

---

4   Albert Kahn and the General Motors Building (1920–22)
West Grand Boulevard between 2nd Avenue and Cass Street
Detroit, Michigan

ALBERT KAHN ASSOCIATES, ARCHITECTS

The late Albert Kahn (1869–1942) arrived in the United States as an eleven-year-old in an impoverished family and though never undergoing further schooling in his adopted land he eventually made an enor-

mous impact on it. For he developed in his Detroit office innovative factory concepts and startling planning efficiencies which help make this city—and this country—the motor capital of the world. Some feel, indeed, that Detroit might well have not become the Motor City if it had not been for those two contemporary geniuses Albert Kahn and Henry Ford. Kahn's greatest work was in industrial building, and in this field—which had been spurned by other architects until World War II—he was the first to demonstrate to tough industrial executives that the space-organizing ability of a perceptive architect brings an essential talent to major plant planning. This was a field previously left completely to engineers. He was so successful that he not only won Detroit and much of the nation, he built several billion dollars' worth of factories—reportedly some five hundred—in the U.S.S.R. in the late 1920s and early 1930s. Kahn's 1905 plant for the Packard Motor Company—in which he was helped by his engineer brother—was the first of concrete in the field; his Pierce-Arrow factory in Buffalo (1906) introduced the novel one-story concept for a giant-scale production facility whose plan in effect diagrammed an assembly line, the whole properly day-lit by skylights; his famous Rouge Plant (1917–22) for Henry Ford was probably the single most impressive industrial installation in the country; and in 1937 he built an airplane assembly building for Glenn L. Martin with clear floor area of 300 x 450 feet/91 x 137 meters. His most elegant single structure was the 1937 Half Ton Truck Plant for Chrysler, now changed.

Almost all of Kahn's great industrial buildings have been so altered since erected—or are not open to the public—that little of his personal contribution can now be seen. However, this General Motors Building —the largest corporate office block built at its time—is not only unchanged on the exterior after more than a half century of use, its restrained Classical touches were modest in an era when most city buildings were encrusted with every imaginable frosting of architectural sleight of hand. (It must be added that Albert Kahn's architectural predilections for domestic work were strictly historicist.) The General Motors Building is one of the important skyscrapers of its time. Always well kept up, in 1970 it underwent extensive renovation to maintain it in top condition.

In 1978 General Motors Corporation announced a four-year joint private and public revitalization of the residential neighborhood—the six-block New Center—which adjoins its world headquarters. The master plan is by Johnson, Johnson & Roy.

Lobby only open to the public during office hours

---

5 Northland Shopping Center (1954)
Eight Mile Road at Northwestern Highway and Greenfield Road
Detroit, Michigan

GRUEN ASSOCIATES, ARCHITECTS

The enclosed, air-conditioned shopping mall has largely replaced the earlier concept of an open-air aggregation of shops deployed around a major department store—such as this one. Thus Northland, that granddaddy of all large shopping centers, sadly is no longer what it was. Look, though, at (1) its variety of spatial experiences, both horizontal and vertical; (2) its accessibility with its unvexed understanding of layout, including parking; (3) its profusion of trees, shrubs and flowers; (4) its complement of "fun" sculpture, fountains and murals; (5) its strict control of signs and graphics; and (6) its underground truck servicing. If Northland's prime is past it contributed greatly as a paragon of a pioneer.

Open daily except Dec. 25

---

6   McGregor Memorial Conference Center (1958)
Wayne State University
Ferry and Second Avenues
Detroit, Michigan

MINORU YAMASAKI & ASSOCIATES, ARCHITECTS

A gem set in an immaculate garden, a memorial, in the finest sense of the word, to its donors, Mr. and Mrs. Tracy W. McGregor. It is used both by the university and by civic, cultural and educational groups. The two-story (plus basement) building is dominated by its full-height central hall and lounge which bisects the mass into two sections. This is topped by a translucent ceiling which, with its glass end walls, suffuses the interior with a radiant quality of natural light. Along each side of the hall on both levels is a maximum of eight conference, discussion, and/or meeting rooms, arranged so that they can be combined or separated to accommodate from ten to three hundred people. Dining room and kitchen on the lowest level can feed up to five hundred. The hall-lounge itself tends to be overfaceted in detail for a small area, but it is alive spatially, especially from the upper level. Colors and furnishings throughout are excellent, highlighted by the white marble floor, turkey-red carpet, and black leather Barcelona chairs by Mies van der Rohe. From the outside there is a slight lack of articulation at each end caused by the hall dividing the building into halves with its roof-high angled glass ends separating them.

Overall, however, McGregor has that elusive quality so rarely seen in today's architecture, a sense of style. At night the building glows. The understated Japanese garden and L-shaped pool with three "islands"—all designed by the architect—wrap around two sides of the building, complementing the architecture, and creating quiet retreats on a crowded urban campus.

Open Mon.–Fri. 1:30–4, except holidays

7　**Reynolds Metals Company Building** (1959)
16000 Northland Drive, off Northwestern Highway
Detroit, Michigan

MINORU YAMASAKI & ASSOCIATES, ARCHITECTS

Reynolds Metals was one of the early corporate *palazzi*. While its exterior may now seem dated by its cross-hatching of aluminum screening, its interior possesses a spirited quality of space and light. This combined office and showroom, which lies just across the highway from Northland Shopping Center (q.v.), consists of an elevated box containing two floors of offices atop an inset entry-showroom floor, the whole planned around a central court or light well. This latter is

roofed by ninety-one pyramidal, translucent skylights upheld by tetra-hedral trusses. Light thus flows in from the ceiling as well as from the periphery of the exhibition floor. Access balconies for the office levels open onto the court. Structure and office partitions are based on a 5-foot/1.5-meter module: construction is of waffle concrete.

On the exterior, the upper two floors are wrapped in a gold anodized aluminum grille (note that the two sections do not touch), projected 5 feet/1.5 meters from the outer walls, where the grille acts as a gilded sun shield and substantially reduces air-conditioning load. The rings of this brise-soleil were imaginatively cut from extruded aluminum pipe 10 inches/25 centimeters in diameter. The building rests on a low po-dium originally with reflecting pool. A hundred-seat auditorium is lo-cated in the basement. Not only a successful building, it brought back "some of the richness of facade and roof line that went out when the modern movement came in" (*Architectural Forum,* May 1957).

Reception floor open during business hours

8   Lafayette Park (1956–63)
Lafayette Avenue between Rivard and Orleans Streets
Detroit, Michigan

MIES VAN DER ROHE, ARCHITECT

Among the most important (sometimes pro, sometimes con) middle-
to upper-income urban rehabilitations in the United States is the
Lafayette Park development, a sizable (78-acre/32-hectare) flatland,
largely within walking distance (.5 mile/.8 kilometer or so) of downtown Detroit. The Park is surrounded by major streets, but—and here
lies its greatest contribution—it is basically penetrated only by short
service roads. Moreover in the center there is a 19-acre/7.7-hectare
park, with a school and small shopping center at one end and places
for active games at the other. However—and herein lies its weakness
—in spite of a high level of architecture, there is a lack of focus, a lack

of a spontaneous, communal center, which is unfortunate. (Compare Queen Anne Village at Reston, Virginia, and its magnetic core.) Lafayette Park seems more of an aggregation of self-focused, individual buildings than a planned community; one returns to one's slot—either horizontal or vertical. This lack of communality results directly from a planning concept which mechanistically checkerboards—at right angles only—every building, with little spatial hierarchy or buildup.

The architectural realization of Lafayette Park, however, is of high, occasionally excellent, quality, in the hard-drawn, Miesian tradition, balancing three twenty-one-story apartment blocks with two-story town houses and one-story row or terrace houses. Such a mixture is commendable from several points of view, although it is possibly questionable to have so many low buildings on such expensive land. The one-story terrace houses (186 altogether), each with small walled yard, are particularly inviting—and very popular. Note that they rest on a low (3–4 feet/.9–1.2 meters) earth berm, with natural grade recesses or cuts for the automobiles (one per unit), so that the cars almost disappear visually between the projections of the terraces.

The most dominant buildings are, of course, the high-rises which offer apartments from efficiencies to those with two and sometimes three bedrooms, each with lavish window expanse. The views outward are spectacular. The Pavilion Apartment, 1 Lafayette Plaisance, which was the first built (340 units), has a small commissary and other service shops on its ground floor with swimming pool alongside. The twin Lafayette Towers, of 300 flats each, flank a 370-car garage atop which is a terrace with their own pool. They are similar to the Pavilion, but more open on the grade floor (having no shops), hence "lighter" on the ground. All three have a concrete structure clad with aluminum. Although the complex tends to the rigid side in both planning and architecture for many of its inhabitants "it is the only place in the world to live" (*The Detroiter,* July 1975). The adjoining shopping center (1963) was designed by King and Lewis. Ludwig Hilberseimer was planning consultant.

Across Lafayette Avenue rises the handsome **1300 Lafayette East** (1963), a 30-story luxury apartment block containing 336 units with two floors of commercial space. It was designed by Burkhardt & Straub.

Grounds open daily

9   Blue Cross/Blue Shield Service Center (1970–71)
Lafayette, St. Antoine and Chrysler Freeway
Detroit, Michigan

GIFFELS & ROSSETTI, ARCHITECTS

The Blue Cross/Blue Shield Center makes a fine addition to the eastern edge of Detroit's central business district. Its affirmative exterior focuses on a sunken forecourt which adds to urban pleasures. The east and west exterior walls of the twenty-two-story skyscraper are blank against the sun, with sharply recessed strips of windows activating the north and south facades. Its reinforced concrete piers taper properly as their load lessens (their angle echoed in the low mastaba mass of the adjacent Blue Shield Building). The tall and low units frame two sides of the sunken plaza onto which the basement-level cafeteria opens. This sheltered, landscaped spot forms an agreeable extension of the building proper and a welcome retreat from the hurly-burly about.

Grounds open daily, lobby during business hours

10   Center for Creative Studies (1974–75)
John R Street at Kirby (behind Detroit Institute of Arts)
Detroit, Michigan

WILLIAM KESSLER & ASSOCIATES, ARCHITECTS

The Center for Creative Studies College of Art & Design is an independent, accredited undergraduate arts college authorized by the state
to give Bachelor of Fine Arts degrees in a series of disciplines concerned with the visual arts. Tracing its origin back to 1906 and the Society of Arts & Crafts, the college has dramatically established itself in
this new facility. The building is adjacent to the Detroit Community
Music School—with which it has recently merged administratively—
and lies a block away from the Detroit Institute of Arts (1927—Paul
Philippe Cret and Zantzinger, Borie & Medary, architects) and the
University/Cultural Center.

The Center's structural system is based on precast concrete components. Its "column collars" which receive beams and develop prominent bay modules recall childhood Tinkertoys, but there is nothing ju-
venile about the building. The bays are 32 feet/9.7 meters square, and,

as is obvious, are freely flexible both horizontally and vertically. There is, thus, an alive positive/negative three-dimensionality about the building, with solids alternating with the see-through and the walk-through. The "plaza" approach and entry were designed as a forum, so that students and visitors alike could look into the ground-floor studios (though more could have been made of this as the dining area takes up two bay widths). Inside on the upper levels this visual interaction is further developed. Altogether the Center forms an admirably flexible workshop for 350 students with expansion possible in several directions. Robert M. Darvas & Associates were the structural engineers.

Reception area open during school year

---

11   Renaissance Center (1973–77)
East Jefferson at Brush Street
Detroit, Michigan

JOHN PORTMAN & ASSOCIATES, ARCHITECTS AND ENGINEERS

This crystal quincunx might well be the most stimulating event, physically and psychologically, that ever happened to a less than stimulating city. Renaissance Center is sparking the renascence of downtown Detroit: no small achievement. And this rebirth, it should be added, is just what its fifty-one backers, led by Henry Ford II, set out to do. For Detroit's central business district was edging into atrophy as a reflection of both a cruel social situation and the usual flight to suburbia. Though most American cities have similar problems, Detroit synthesized them, and only an extraordinarily daring, ebullient—and risky—leap would help matters. Whether the self-consciously detached "fortress" concept was the best answer we shall never know. The fact remains that it works. Some 25,000 people per weekend often visit it to dine, shop, and look. And RenCen has already generated much new building. Though these partially siphon tenants from older CBD structures, it is pertinent to add that most of the older ones also are doing well.

The Renaissance Center complex is composed of four 39-story semioctagonal, steel-framed office towers "protecting" the 73-story, 1,400-room Detroit Plaza Hotel—the world's tallest—of glass and concrete. These five structures, the hotel sheathed in bronze reflective glass, the office blocks in tinted glass curtain walls, rest on a 4-level podium containing over 70 shops, 4 movie theaters, and parking ac-

commodations for 6,000 automobiles. Two cylindrical, glass-enclosed elevator shafts append opposite sides of each office tower. The Center edges the Detroit River with Windsor, Ontario, across the water. Its concept of closely grouped multiple buildings with mirror walls that play games with darting sunbeams is a product of one of the most pyrotechnic minds in today's architecture. John Portman first startled the world with his breathtaking Hyatt Regency in Atlanta (q.v.). He then expanded across the country, sometimes with an emphasis on acrobatics, but always worthy of study. Architectural futurism attends Detroit's Renaissance Center (and Portman's Los Angeles Bonaventure Hotel—q.v.), and the use of glass in both might be excessive, but the image is potent.

The hotel lobby spaces in RenCen shoot upward for eight stories, then radiate three-dimensional tentacles horizontally. (Note, for a detail, the role which the spiral stairs add in the swirl of dimensions.) Yet with its many intimate retreats and lounges overlooking its "lake," the hotel's public areas maintain human scale. It should be added that some spaces can be confusing, redundancy is not unknown, and the atmosphere of endless balconies dripping vines can become insistent, but excitement lies here and excitement is a useful attribute if you run a hotel. On top there are two levels of cocktail lounges with the usual revolving restaurant above. It is pertinent to keep in mind the "explosive" quality of the interior versus the smooth skin geometry of the outside. Renaissance Center was privately financed.

Detroit was desperate for a spark of hope. It now has one. Moreover it is attracting conventions and suburban corporations that had long spurned the city. Significantly, Renaissance Center Phase II is also under way: ground was broken (1979) for its twin, adjacent, twenty-story office towers by John Portman & Associates. They are scheduled for completion in 1981.

There is an obvious need to knit the Center into the fabric of the area, and in the process let us hope that the 1902 "Roman" dollop across the street, known as the Wayne County Building (John and Arthur Scott, architects), will be remembered. And if, as anticipated, middle- and upper-income apartments are created along the lovely riverbank, the city's population mélange, civic concern, and tax balance would be far healthier.

Hotel always open: stores open Mon.–Sat., office buildings during business hours

12   Grosse Pointe War Memorial (1910)
Russell A. Alger, Jr., House
32 Lake Shore (Cadieux Road exit S off IS 94, S on Lake Shore)
Grosse Pointe Farms, Michigan

CHARLES A. PLATT, ARCHITECT

Charles Adams Platt (1861–1933) was known, above all, for his elegant houses, grandly conceived but rich without ostentation. The Russell Alger mansion typically fits this pattern. Properly set back from the main road and edging Lake St. Clair on the southerly side, it enjoys privacy and a view of Canada across the water. The most prominent feature of the facade is, of course, the projected central bay with its sixteenth-century Italian-inspired entry. (The power of Giulio Romano's Palazzo del Tè of 1534 is hinted.) Note that its richness is transferred upward by the window framing directly above the door to the circular bull's-eye opening in the pediment. A quiet, semi-

Mediterranean quality characterizes the rest of the house. The most notable feature of the interior is the richness of the ceilings in the main room. Used for a time as a branch of the Detroit Institute of Arts, the dwelling was given by Mrs. Alger to the Grosse Pointe War Memorial Library Fund in 1949 and renamed the Grosse Pointe War Memorial. The adjacent William Fries Auditorium (1962) provides banquet and ballroom facilities and is named for the donor. The buildings are much used by the community.

Open Mon.–Sat. 9–9, except holidays

---

13   General Headquarters of the Upjohn Company (1961)
**Portage Street, c. 2 miles/3.2 kilometers SE of town beyond
    airport**
Kalamazoo, Michigan

SKIDMORE, OWINGS & MERRILL, ARCHITECTS

Administrative Hesperides (by the Chicago office of SOM), the basic philosophy of which was to make every office as tied to nature as possible. This marriage to environment begins before one enters the building, first with several man-made ponds that form an intermedium between nature and architecture, then with formalized water via a large rectangular pool—complete with three landscaped islets—alongside the entrance of the building. As one enters and ascends by escalator to the main floor, one is greeted by a large (150 feet/46 meters square) planted open court off the reception area. Six smaller courts (all but one 50 feet/15 meters on a side) are placed throughout so that each work space, executive or otherwise, looks outward onto the pleasant surroundings or adjoins an intimate courtyard with pool. The progression of spaces from open nature to private garden is sequential. It is a concept that flows with inner space and easy intercommunication. Partly one story in height (at rear), but largely two (front and midsection), the 432-foot/132-meter-square building is covered by one flat roof with wide overhang on all four sides to give weather and sun protection. The chevron pattern of the overhang reflects (strongly) the space-frame structure of the roof. All service functions, including cafeteria, are located on the lower floor, all offices on the upper. Bruce Graham was partner in charge of design; the landscaping was by Sasaki & Associates.

Visitors welcome to reception area during business hours

---

14   Grand Hotel (1887)
Mackinac Island, Michigan

MASON & RICE, ARCHITECTS

Not many hostels of that ebullient *fin de siècle* period of wooden magnificence today remain in the United States. (See, also, the Hotel del Coronado near San Diego, California.) It is therefore encouraging to report that not only is the 260-room Grand Hotel at Mackinac in top physical condition, it is thriving. Architecturally its basic plan forms an extended rectangle—with what must be the longest porch in the world (800 feet/244 meters) across its front. And if the building itself is not overly distinguished stylistically, it does possess grandeur, and it unequivocally states an era. Though the interior has been respectfully modernized, the exterior is still as originally built, and there

are few spectacles to equal its three-story veranda, stretched to infinity, overlooking the Mackinac Straits. Much of the island is a 2,000-acre/809-hectare state park, so the adjacent hotel's setting and its gardens have been well preserved. Moreover no automobiles are allowed. Unique—and listed in the National Register of Historic Places.

Open mid-May to mid-Oct.

15 Fort Michilimackinac (1715–20/reconstructed 1959–) Mackinaw City, Michigan

Architecturally and historically, this reconstruction of an early-eighteenth-century French fort—plus, outside its walls, several typical houses of the period—provides us with a revealing collection of early French activity in the upper midriff of the continent. The reconstruction of the palisaded fort and its inner buildings, the earliest of which dates from 1715, was meticulously researched and undertaken with all the technology of contemporary archeology. It is a project which is still continuing, as can be seen from mid-June to late August.

From the architectural point of view, the primary interest lies in the

techniques of primitive wood construction, among them the *poteaux,* or vertical posts, driven into the ground, a process of speedy enclosure but one of limited life-span. The *poteaux* technique was also used for dwellings. (Compare the more permanent horizontal log construction on stone foundation, introduced into North America by the Swedes in 1638.)

The squarish fort, which measures roughly 320 x 360 feet/98 x 110 meters, was built to ensure the safety of the French fur traders and priests who had long been active in the area. It has both a land and a water gate. The main buildings within the palisade are a barracks, the commanding officer's house, a church, two traders' houses, and a storehouse. All buildings rest on their original foundations, but their aboveground appearance is partially conjectural (especially that of the church). Within, they have all been carefully furnished of the period.

With the tiny "village" outside, the reconstructed fort gives us a fascinating insight not only into building techniques in a rough frontier, but in the pivotal French and English confrontations in this part of North America, issues which were not resolved until France, in defeat in the French and Indian Wars, ceded Canada to Great Britain in 1763. Architecture and history are explained in both guided tours and in full descriptions, plus, in the church, a sound-and-light presentation.

Open mid-May to mid-June 9–5, mid-June to Labor Day 9–8,
Labor Day to mid-Oct. 9–5: admission

The **Mackinac Bridge,** visible from the fort, was designed by David B. Steinman and built 1954–57. Its main span is 3,800 feet/1,158 meters —third only to the Golden Gate Bridge in San Francisco and the Verrazano-Narrows in New York City (q.v.). However, its overall length from anchorage to anchorage is 8,614 feet/2,626 meters and its 552-foot/168-meter-high towers make it "the largest suspension bridge in the world."

16   Honolulu House (1860)
Fountain Circle, 107 North Kalamazoo Avenue
Marshall, Michigan

This fetching dwelling was built by Abner Pratt, who had been United States Consul to Hawaii (1857–59) but was forced by the illness of his wife to return to Michigan. He therefore built this scaled-down replica of his beloved house in Honolulu, bequeathing the mainland one of our few Island-influenced dwellings. The front is dominated by a high gallery, atop a stone half basement, which extends from one end to the other (77.5 feet/23 meters) and rises as an "observation tower" in the center. The frolicsome, triple-scrolled brackets upholding this porch, and echoed around the eaves, are almost worth the trip them-

selves. The walls, strangely, are of sandstone covered with vertical boards and batten. On the interior impressive grandeur holds forth from the entrance hall—note the curved stair and the ceiling decoration—to the elaborately painted rooms on either side. Note, too, the fancifully molded plaster cornices. Tropical woods, mostly teak, ebony, and mahogany, abound, although some were painted over (with more than abandon) later in the century (1883), when the murals that once depicted Hawaiian landscapes were, unfortunately, also painted out. The house was variously occupied until 1951. At that time it was purchased by a local benefactor who sold it (1961) to the Marshall Historical Society and made into a museum-house.

The Society also publishes a list of other buildings of interest in this architecturally rewarding and preservation-minded town.

Open mid-May to Oct., Mon., Wed.–Fri. 1–4, Sat.–Sun. 12–5: admission

---

17 First United Methodist Church (1954)
MI 20 (Jerome Street) at West Main Street
Midland, Michigan

ALDEN B. DOW, ARCHITECT

Alden Dow has designed many fine churches, but this welcoming, nature-loving example, though one of his earlier, is still one of the best. Note the strong outpouring of light from a large concealed roof window over most of the sanctuary. On either side of the nave are outdoor gardens, with a pool on the southeast side. The planting helps screen the nave windows from distracting activity along the street. The architect sought to expand the church outward in a "growth beyond ourselves," hence the openness over the sanctuary and through the sides.

Open Mon.–Fri. 9–5:30, Sat. 9–12

---

18   St. Francis de Sales Church (1964–66)
2929 McCracken Avenue (W from town on Sherman Boulevard or
   Norton Avenue)
Muskegon, Michigan

MARCEL BREUER AND HERBERT BECKHARD, ARCHITECTS

Its trapezoidal front wall—a "banner"—splays out laterally as it rises, while at the same time leaning backward; its two side walls are double-curved in paraboloid sections; and its back, also a trapezoid, splays in toward the top, and leans in. Structure was the driving force of design, and as Breuer has said, "Church architecture, at its best, is always identical with the structural logic of the enclosure" (*L'Architecture d'Aujourd'hui* #108, 1963). The strength of the exterior is carried through within, where we find a walled-in, virtually windowless (except for skylight) nave of great power. The spatial effect on entering under the low balcony, then encountering the lofty nave, is effective, as is the relation of the freestanding balcony to the church.

The sanctuary is brilliantly understated, with an uncluttered high altar, resting on a low red brick podium, and with a plain concrete ciborium or canopy cantilevered from the rear wall. The sacramental altar (with bright colored betonglass in the ceiling of its niche) lies off-center and above and is reached dramatically by sixteen unrailed steps. The choir is asymmetrically placed at left in front of the organ. The nave, which seats 972 (with 231 in the balcony), slopes downward in theater fashion. As the prime source of all lighting, natural or artificial, comes from either the roof skylights or from ceiling fixtures placed between the beams, a stern atmosphere results, but the solidity of solid concrete encircling one offers protection and comfort against the outside world. A walled open atrium forms an excellent introduction to the church, with the narthex sheltering the baptistry in the center and confessionals along the side. The rectory stands at the rear.

Open daily

---

19   Tower of History (1967–68)
Shrine of the Missionaries
326 East Portage Avenue
Sault Ste. Marie, Michigan

RAFFERTY RAFFERTY MIKUTOWSKI & ASSOCIATES, ARCHITECTS

The problem of the monument in an ethos of antimonuments taxes architectural imagination. However, it has been solved here with great skill. Though the tower will eventually serve also as a detached church tower (when funds materialize for the church to be built at its foot), it

also stands as an independent work. Tower, church, and a museum are part of a Shrine of the Missionaries complex, commemorating the early priests, almost all French Catholics, who served this then wild area over three hundred years ago. The architects who designed this observation post realized that a single massive tower of whatever shape would of itself be no more exciting than a single massive tower. They therefore took two large and near-identical parallelograms, the taller 210 feet/64 meters high, plus a slightly smaller third parallelogram, grouped them into a triangular formation, left the spaces between the three largely open, and laced them together at the top with multilevel viewing platforms. The injection of the horizontals into the verticals produces energetic interpenetration. The main observation deck is glass-enclosed but the four others are open. All give panoramic vistas of the famous Soo Locks, the world's busiest—and one of the state's leading tourist attractions—plus a good slice of Canada, and, of course, the scene of the activities of the seventeenth-century missionaries. Because the tower has viewing platforms both enclosed and open, staggered in height and varied in both orientation and size, the visitor experiences spatial enjoyment which is almost totally absent from most gazebos. It stands as sculpture in its own right—sculpture for use, it should be added. George E. Rafferty and Richard J. Rafferty were partners-in-charge; Frank Kacmarcik was religious consultant. The firm was earlier known as Progressive Design Associates.

Open July–Aug., daily 9–9; late May–June and Labor Day–Oct., daily 9–6: admission

---

20   IBM Office Building (1977–78)
2445 Northwestern Highway at Nine Mile Road
Southfield (Detroit), Michigan

GUNNAR BIRKERTS AND ASSOCIATES, ARCHITECTS

A highly innovative, fourteen-story office block the design of which was basically energy-conservation-generated. This is apparent from a

distance in that the two sunniest sides—south and west—are bright, reflective anodized aluminum, while the north and east are deep gray fluorocarbon-painted aluminum. The building thus refracts a substantial amount of sun load. (Although the energy savings via color are probably only slight, the conservation message is clear.) Note that two of the diagonal corners are curved while the other two are outlined in slender blue vertical panels. Color notes are perked up on the north side by the red entry. The design of the building's wall section and its fenestration was intensely concerned with heat load and loss. Working with computers and Joseph R. Loring & Associates as mechanical engineers, the architects evolved a "sill reflector" section whereby a continuous, curved stainless steel sill reflects sun- and sky-light through clear thermal glass (set at a 55° angle outward) onto a reversed curved inner reflector of white metal. The two complementary curves were plotted to bounce daylight into the office space at approximately the same degree with either a high summer sun or low winter one. Fluorescent fixtures, hidden at the top of the inner reflecting shield, supplement outside light when needed. The angled glass gives a 2.3-foot/66-centimeter-high, eye-level strip of window for additional light and views out. Though the wall section which evolved is obviously more expensive than a routine curtain wall, the architects expect the energy savings (both in heating and air conditioning) to pay for the design in less than ten years. This imaginative result might well give rise to new thinking regarding fenestration in high-rise buildings. It is fully occupied by IBM.

Lobby open during office hours

21　K mart Corporation International Headquarters (1970–72)
3100 West Big Beaver Road at Coolidge Highway (N from Detroit
on IS 75 to Big Beaver Road, then W)
Troy, Michigan

SMITH, HINCHMAN & GRYLLS, ARCHITECTS

The exterior of the K mart Headquarters tends purposefully to the quiet side with its service-and-elevator towers of "mahogany" masonry blocks, its horizontal bands of bronze mirror glass, and its vertical panels and framing of weathering steel. The scale, moreover, is excel-

lent, with the eighteen "towers" forming a changing silhouette on the 30-acre/12-hectare suburban site about 18 miles/29 kilometers north of downtown Detroit. Though the exterior might be termed somber, the interiors, especially the three-and-a-half-story lobby, are full of light, art, and space. The steel-framed building serves as world headquarters for all of K mart's vast operations (from needlework to real estate). For maximum flexibility the complex is divided in checkerboard fashion into thirteen modules 100 feet/30 meters square, connected by three major diagonal halls. Some modules stand free except for corner communications, others abut; height varies from two to four stories. Well-planted open courts separate many modules and spruce up the connecting corridors' outlooks. The reticent entry was placed at the second level so that most vertical movement would be via the stairs —one up, one down. The brooding bronze head in the entry court is by Michael Aryton. Having 1,800 to 2,000 employees with few outside free-time options, there are full in-house amenities including a 600-seat cafeteria. The first phase of expansion took place in 1978–79, the "notches" of some corners accommodating additional service towers. William R. Jarratt was project manager; Charles T. Harris, project designer; Johnson, Johnson & Roy, Inc., landscape architects.

Lobby open during business hours; public tours at 2 P.M. weekdays

22   General Motors Technical Center (1951–56)
Mound Road, just N of Twelve Mile Road
Warren (Detroit), Michigan

EERO SAARINEN & ASSOCIATES, ARCHITECTS

A profound interrelation between architecture, landscaping, and waters
—both still and active—forms the dominant impression of this
magnificent layout. (Cf. Cranbrook Academy in Bloomfield Hills.)
There is a partnership here between forty-one buildings and nature
(some of which is man-fashioned nature) which has earned the Center
the sobriquet of an industrial Versailles. The second impression recog-
nizes the businesslike efficiency, colorful positiveness, and flexibility of
its individual buildings. There are six major groups on this campus:
Design Staff (with dome), Engineering Staff, Manufacturing Development, GM Research Laboratories, Environmental Activities Staff, and
Technical Center Service Section, all with several subunits. The central
restaurant building, one of the best from the design point of view,
stands between Engineering and Manufacturing Development. The low
structures (three floors maximum) are deployed about a rectangular
22-acre/8.9-hectare lake, approximately 1,800 feet/549 meters

long by 550 feet/168 meters wide, embellished by four islets containing weeping willows. The lake acts as a spine for the layout, and in addition to giving orientation and visual pleasure serves as a water recirculator for the Center's air-conditioning system. The feeling of orientation is highlighted and the basic horizontality of the complex energized by the elegant, three-legged stainless-steel-clad water tower which rises from the waters. Its upward thrust is repeated by the fountains, particularly when their computerized "ballet"—designed and programmed by the late Alexander Calder—erupts. Landscaping and trees (some 13,000 altogether—75 men are required to maintain the grounds) have been imaginatively used to shield cars from view and sun from cars.

The technically advanced buildings are almost all of curtain-wall construction (porcelain panels over a fireproof core), with a basic 5-foot/1.5-meter module throughout. The pungent end walls, however, are of brightly colored glazed brick, a Saarinen innovation inspired by ancient Assyrian (i.e. Gates of Ishtar) tiles. The Technical Center was begun under Eliel Saarinen, but the present version was developed by Eero Saarinen after his father's retirement, then death in 1950. An influence from Mies van der Rohe is apparent. Smith, Hinchman & Grylls were associate architects-engineers; Thomas D. Church was landscape architect. Though only the reception building and the Design Staff and Research Laboratories lobbies are open to the public, a sightseeing bus circles the entire grounds. The trip is much recommended for its architecture, its waters, and—by no means least—its corporate progressiveness.

Conducted tours June–Labor Day, 10–5: telephone (313) 575-0334 for schedule

Mississippi

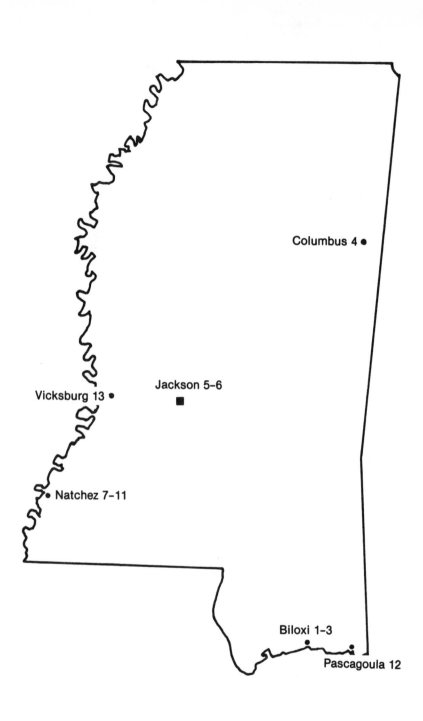

Columbus 4 ●

Jackson 5-6
Vicksburg 13 ● ■

● Natchez 7-11

Biloxi 1-3
●
Pascagoula 12

MISSISSIPPI

The buildings in boldface type are of general interest. The others are for the specialist.

Biloxi

1 **Beauvoir** (1850–52)

2 Broadwater Beach Marina (1965)—
T. M. Dorsett, Jr.

3 Biloxi Public Library and Cultural Center
(1976–77)—MLTW/Turnbull Associates
City Hall (1904)—Stuart Evans

Columbus

4 **Waverley Plantation** (c. 1852)

Jackson

5 State Office Complex (1970–72)—
Barlow & Plunkett
State Capitol (1903)—Theodore C. Link

6 Dormitories and Library, Tougaloo College
(1971–73)—Gunnar Birkerts & Associates

Natchez

7 Connelly's Tavern (c. 1798)

8 **Rosalie** (1820–23)—James S. Griffin

9 **D'Evereux** (1836–40)

10 **Stanton Hall** (1851–57)—Thomas Rose

11 **Longwood** (1860–62)—Samuel Sloan

Pascagoula

12 Old Spanish Fort (c. 1721)

Vicksburg

13 Old Court House Museum (1858–61)

1   Beauvoir (1850–52)
200 West Beach Boulevard
c. 5 miles/8 kilometers W of Biloxi on US 90
near Biloxi, Mississippi

Beauvoir is a relaxed example of the function-bred raised cottage found along the Gulf Coast and the lower Mississippi where the problems of flooding, dampness, and insects are always a threat. Following the usual response, the elevated basement is of masonry, with cypress-built house above, surrounded by porch or gallery on three sides. In addition to shielding the dwelling from the hot sun, the piazza provided in the cool of the evening the most popular living "room" in the house. Shaded by live oaks and a scattering of cypress and cedar it directly faces the Gulf—and was among the very first to do so.

Within, the basically square front section can be widely opened to catch even the suspicion of a zephyr, while the 15-foot/4.6-meter-high reception hall which runs down the middle acts as a breezeway. In the past this area often doubled as a banquet hall, extending, as it does, from the front entry to the rear service porch. Connecting onto the

central hallway are the front and rear parlors to the left of the entrance and two bedrooms to the right. Their frescoes have recently been restored. Two additional bedrooms occupy the left (northwest) corner at the rear, matched by a wing on the opposite side containing dining room and pantry. Connecting doorways and triple-hung windows almost anticipate the "open plan" so favored today. The dwelling is flanked by twin cottages, the east one of which was used as a plantation office and also a study-schoolroom (now the Library Cottage), while the western dependency (enlarged) was used for guests.

Occupied by Jefferson Davis after the former President of the Confederacy retired (1877), the house remained in the family until 1902 when Mrs. Davis sold the estate to the Mississippi Division, Sons of Confederate Veterans. It was operated by the state as the Mississippi Confederate Veterans Home 1903–55. In 1940, in accordance with Mrs. Davis' earlier-expressed wishes, it was turned into the Jefferson Davis Shrine and opened to the public as such the following year, having been properly restored, and with many of the original furnishings recovered and others duplicated mostly with a Victorian motif. A Davis museum occupies the basement. House and cottages were reputedly designed by James Brown, the original owner. The shrine is owned and operated by the Mississippi Division, Sons of Confederate Veterans.

Open daily 8:30–5, except Dec. 25: admission

2   Broadwater Beach Marina (1965)
opposite Broadwater Beach Hotel on US 90
Biloxi, Mississippi

T. M. DORSETT, JR., ENGINEER

At last a marina which does not grind out an endless series of ungainly boat shelters. Three sides of this "square" of water on the Gulf of Mexico are framed by airily roofed slips, while the piers on the fourth are uncovered. Thus the largely enclosed marina establishes an entity. The boat shelters which border and frame it are constructed of slender, prefabricated concrete sections with a shallow arch profile to shed the rain and set up a minuet around the lagoon. The entry, toilet, and wash pavilions at three corners, and the marina restaurant—all in wood—are folksy in detail, but the general concept and the boat um-

brellas are highly imaginative, aided by the landscaping and light
standards. There are 136 berths altogether, 110 of which are covered.
All are equipped with fresh water, electricity (110–220 volts) tele-
phones, and television connections.

Open daily

Hurricanes have done much damage to the lovely Mississippi coast,
but their batterings are nothing compared to the continual devastation
occasioned by the selfish hand of man. Slashed by highways and made
sleazy by haphazard zoning and commercial developments, the state's
entire coastal area needs immediate action to prevent it from degen-
erating into a gulfside slum.

3   Biloxi Public Library and Cultural Center (1976–77)
217 Lameuse Street
Biloxi, Mississippi

MLTW/TURNBULL ASSOCIATES, ARCHITECTS

The Biloxi Library is deceptively simple, almost diffident on the exterior. However, within one is rewarded by unfolding spaces and evanescent light. The building reaches out to embrace an entry court (Bicentennial Plaza), its one-story height setting an inviting atmosphere. The left wing protects the freestanding Creole cottage (c. 1836) which was the town's first library (1900) and which has been restored by Nicholas H. Holmes, Jr. (1976). The far (i.e. back) side of the building, with its entrance to the Cultural Center, is marked by a 65-foot/20-meter-high "observation tower" where boldness of angles, spatial penetrations, and even improbability introduce one to the main

hall. Its stair leads to the second-floor exhibition space and 120-seat assembly room.

The space of the library interior—the main public area—is accented in plan by the open arms of the Y-shaped plan and by the sharply canted ceiling which rises from low entry to high point over the cylindrical control desk and the mezzanine above. The right arm of the Y is devoted to the children's wing (with some noise factor), with the extensive adult section to the left. A domestic, armchair atmosphere overlooking the garden in front was sought in the reading areas. Daylight comes from sizable banks of windows and from roof monitors which are concentrated over the top-lit control cylinder then run along the ridges of the roof. The light colors of the interior are based on white and grays with light blue ceiling and numerous touches of purple. The furniture, especially the laminated oak tables and the Windsor chairs, is direct and handsome. William Turnbull was project architect; TAG, The Architects Group, were associates.

Open Mon.–Wed. 9–8:30, Thurs.–Sat. 9–5:30, except holidays

Directly facing the library stands the ambitious granite and marble U. S. Court House and Custom House, now the **City Hall,** designed by Stuart Evans in 1904 and restored in 1960.

---

4   Waverley Plantation (c. 1852)
   N from Columbus c. 5 miles/8 kilometers on US 45, W on MISS
       50, c. 10 miles/16 kilometers from
   Columbus, Mississippi

The geometry of this too-little-known plantation house recalls the negative/positive countervail of the south front of Inigo Jones' Queen's House (1617–35) in Greenwich, England. The contrast of inset porch and two-story Ionic columns with the planar sides is excellent. The porch becomes a delicate gallery on the upper level. On the more startling side the house is topped by a massive octagonal cupola. The cupola forms, indeed, an extension of the core of the building, its 35 feet/11 meters width being that of the entrance loggia and the central hall. Within, the similarly octagonal hall erupts 65 feet/20 meters to the top, with three tiers of delicately balustraded balconies (also eight-sided) lightening the way. Twin circular stairs pirouette alongside.

Two rooms per floor flank this stupendous open "entrance salon" which also doubled as a ballroom. There are master bedroom and parlor on the west side of the first floor, dining room and library on the other, with four identically sized bedrooms above.

The house was built by George Hampton Young when he acquired the plantation, which at that time comprised 50,000 munificently successful acres (20,234 hectares). The Civil War ended this prosperity, and when the last of the builder's sons died in 1913, the mansion stood empty, and was occasionally vandalized until Mr. and Mrs. Robert Allen Snow, Jr., purchased it and 20 acres/8.1 hectares of land in 1962, whereupon they began its diligent restoration. Fascinating. The house is a National Historic Landmark.

Open daily 9–5, except Dec. 25: admission

NOTE: Year-round tours in Columbus can also be arranged by appointment: contact the Chamber of Commerce, Box 1016, Columbus, Miss. 37901. A yearly house Pilgrimage also takes place, usually the first week in April.

5   State Office Complex (1970–72)
High Street at President
Jackson, Mississippi

BARLOW & PLUNKETT, ARCHITECTS

An efficient, dignified, well-detailed government complex comprising the twenty-story Walter Sillers State Office Building and the low mass of the State Supreme Court. These stand at opposite ends of a slightly elevated plaza with, imaginatively, the air-conditioning machinery neatly—and anonymously—housed between, along with a row of seven flags and well-designed lamp standards. No historic trappings, fortunately, are to be seen. Ample parking is provided beneath the podium. Construction is of precast concrete on a 5-foot/1.5-meter module.

The **State Capitol** (1903), scaled down from its prototype in Washington, lies directly facing. It was designed by Theodore C. Link, who was also known for his famous Railroad Station in St. Louis.

Reception areas open during office hours

6   **Dormitories and Library** (1971–73)
    Tougaloo College
    **County Line Road (W off Tougaloo exit of IS 55), c. 9 miles/14
        kilometers N of**
    Jackson (Tougaloo), Mississippi

GUNNAR BIRKERTS & ASSOCIATES, ARCHITECTS

The early (1965–66) plans for a total but phased rebuilding of
Tougaloo College, which Birkerts Associates evolved from a complicated set of conditions, will probably never materialize. However, the
first stage of two dormitories and adjacent library forms an auspicious
beginning. Birkerts initially had proposed a spectacular three-level
scheme on the sloping site, with roads and parking on the first level,
groups of varied-length classrooms oriented north and south on the
second, topped by fingers of dormitories airily propped in space above
and at right angles to the academic grouping, the dormitories resting
on pilotis which would absorb the grade fall-off.
    In this initial phase much of the aerial effect can be seen in these

two dormitories, one for men, the other for women. It should be pointed out that propping the buildings on stilts grew from the weak subsoil conditions of unstable clay which demanded bell-bottom concrete piers of considerable depth on which to place the buildings. Moreover, across the low west end of the site stands an undistinguished two-story classroom building (1959) which visually and physically blocks the sweep of the rolling, well-treed landscape. Therefore to prevent any feeling of lateral enclosure by this compromised situation, Birkerts boldly cantilevered the dormitories in space. Chief among other benefits is ground (and transportation) freedom, while the sense of privacy and "liberation" in the bedrooms is of course enhanced. The result almost suggests a train of Pullman cars on a trestle, but the space games are stimulating.

The reinforced concrete supporting piers are paired 12.2 feet/3.7 meters apart and 30 feet/9.1 meters on center, with modules of two and three bays making up the groups of dormitory rooms for a total length of 210 feet/64 meters. Access to each is by means of an open passageway suspended under the two floors of rooms, with three sets of stairs, one at the center, two near the ends, leading to clusters of double bedrooms and lounges. (On the interior, emergency doors connect the full building length in case of fire.) At the uphill entry only a few steps lead to each underslung passerelle but at the far end the stairs are several platforms high. The rooms cantilever approximately 9 feet/2.7 meters on either side of the supporting piers, lending an untethered freedom to the dormitories. The abrupt cutoff of their far ends, however, tends to leave them momentarily poised in space. Their walls are of prefabricated, natural color, concrete panels fabricated on the Waldschmidt System of Hamburg, Germany. They are striated in texture with unusual but effective square windows surrounded by a circular "frame" painted to indicate lounges versus bedrooms. (Early studies had strip windows.)

The L. Zenobia Coleman Library, centered between the two dormitories, and close to the old administration building on the crest of the rise, had a lateral space problem inasmuch as its entrance (near top) was at a major walkway. To keep the library from bifurcating the campus, the uphill corners were left open (see photograph) so that the building forms an inviting horizontal pedestrian pivot, while its vertical setbacks create two-story "pavilions" with play of spaces and dramatic structural expression. The construction employs the same deep, belled foundation piers used in the dormitories. On these were erected an ingenious series of prefabricated piers, prestressed beams, and panels— developed by the architect—which permit Tinkertoy flexibility and options, with speed of erection and economy. The library bay size, like that in the dormitories, is 30 feet/9.1 meters square. Efficiency and inner spaces are excellent.

Tougaloo, a small, basically black college, stressing a liberal arts curriculum, has made an impressive start with these three buildings. Let us hope that it will be able to carry out more of its exciting plans.

Grounds and library open during school year

---

7 **Connelly's Tavern** (c. 1798)
   Jefferson and Canal Streets
   Natchez, Mississippi

A good two-story vernacular tavern on a hill overlooking the Mississippi, first built as a residence for James Moore. Its full-length porches, one above the other, make this one of the few Spanish-influenced—perhaps more properly Spanish West Indies-influenced—buildings in the state. (Spanish troops under de Gálvez had captured Natchez in 1779, holding it until 1798.) The porches, being on the western side, provide

sun protection and also afford an excellent view of the river and distant Louisiana. In plan, the taproom fills much of the ground floor, with bedrooms above. The tavern was used as a school, then a tenement, until purchased in 1934 by the Natchez Garden Club, which has fully restored and authentically refurnished it. It was made a National Historic Landmark in 1975 and is listed as the House on Ellicott's Hill.

Open daily 9–5, except Dec. 24–25—by tour only during Pilgrimage: admission

---

8   Rosalie (1820–23)
100 Orleans Street
Natchez, Mississippi

JAMES S. GRIFFIN, ARCHITECT

An unusual, late Georgian house, with a hint of Charleston in the overall and a touch of Federal in details. One is greeted by an ample portico of four Tuscan columns projecting gracefully from the main fa-

cade on Orleans Street, while the entire garden side is spanned from end to end by a double porch with six columns. The fence surrounding the house is of heart cypress, its pickets held by slots, not nails. Picturesquely situated near the site of old Fort Rosalie, built by the French (1716) to command the Mississippi, the house still surveys the river from its 200-foot/61-meter-high bluff which made Natchez a favored location for military reasons as well as those of flooding and health. The plantations were in the river-irrigated lowlands, but the mansions were clustered on the heights, giving the city its unique character. (Cf. the great spread-out Louisiana plantations and those in Virginia and the Carolinas.) The front portico mentioned resembles several in the area (Auburn and Arlington, built in 1812 and 1816 respectively, and each only open at Pilgrimage, are two), but note that the brick behind the portico is stuccoed and painted white at Rosalie, an effect which provides bright porches on two levels both in front and back. The dwelling escaped damage during the Civil War shelling of the town—it was later occupied (1863) by a considerate Northern general and his wife and staff—hence has come down to us in reasonable shape. After the death of the heirs of the second owners, who had purchased it and its furnishings in 1857, the house was acquired (1938) as a shrine by the Mississippi Society of the Daughters of the American Revolution. It has been richly refurbished—note especially the double parlors with their French chandeliers—and beautifully maintained.

Open daily 9–5, except holidays: admission

NOTE: Natchez contains in a small area the finest collection of antebellum houses in the country. The annual Natchez Pilgrimages, in October, March, and early April, enable one to see approximately thirty that are otherwise closed to the public. Inquire at Stanton Hall, Natchez, for details, or write Pilgrimage Headquarters, Box 347, Natchez, Miss. 39120.

---

9 D'Evereux (1836–40)
off US 61/84 (D'Evereux Drive), c. 1 mile/1.6 kilometers NE of Natchez, Mississippi

D'Evereux, the most pristine, the most elegantly gracious Greek Revival house in the state, is also one of the most totally satisfactory anywhere. Of compact design, it has almost a temple quality with its

pedimented front and six carefully fluted Doric columns. (Note, too, the small, feathery wrought-iron balcony.) A like number of columns, but unfluted and supporting a full-width upper veranda, line the back or garden side; facing south, the veranda was—and is—a much-used open-air "room." The building's sides are relieved by simple pilasters, with a quiet entablature encircling all. An observation cupola, surrounded by a wooden balustrade, tops the hip roof. The four downstairs rooms (the only ones open to the public because the family lives in the house) have been superbly restored, and are marked by great refinement. Note, especially, the crystal chandeliers. Supposedly all dimensions in the house are divisible by three, from the number of columns to their height (24 feet/7.3 meters) to the dimensions of all rooms—an early precursor of Le Corbusier's "modulor."

The house, like so many throughout the South, fell on difficult days after the Civil War until purchased in 1923, when partial restoration was undertaken. In 1962 it was acquired by the T. B. Buckles and returned to its magnificent early condition. James Hardie (also spelled Hardy) is generally credited as being the architect. One of the great American mansions.

Open Mon.–Sat. 9–5, except Dec. 25: admission

10   Stanton Hall (1851–57)
401 High Street between Pearl and Commerce
Natchez, Mississippi

THOMAS ROSE, ARCHITECT

Stanton Hall since its completion has been held to be "the most pala-tial house in Natchez." Its opulence is immediately apparent as one draws up to the prominent portico, where four Corinthian-inspired col-umns with cast-iron capitals and a cast-iron rail around the porch and upper veranda seek to impress the visitor. They do. Note the careful "wrapping" of the columns by the continuous grillwork on the upper gallery. Even the knobs on the front door—like most of the other hardware—are silver-plated on brass. The interior is not only rich in detail but in spaces. The mind reels at the long hall which bisects the house and is not even broken by stairs, and at the conjunction of the music room with parlor to make a ballroom 72 feet/22 meters in

length. The dining room is 40 feet/12 meters long and boasts two marble mantelpieces. The furnishings, obviously, had to live up to this three-dimensional excitement. (In spite of legends to the contrary, most of the furnishings were American.) There is sumptuousness here, or as the *Mississippi Free Trader* (April 5, 1858) described it: "The edifice is an immense symmetrical brick pile, the work of those eminent brick-masons, Messrs. Reynolds and Brown, stuccoed to a snowy whiteness by those long-established and celebrated stucco-plasterers, Messrs. Price and Polkinghorn. The work-box, of the highest elegance of finish and tasteful pattern, was executed under the supervision of Captain Thomas Rose—Mr. John A. Saunders being his experienced and faithful, as well as skillful, foreman. The painting and rich oak ingraining was done under the direction of Mr. John Wells, so famous for the high finish of his work . . . The grand front to the south presents a pure Corinthian facade, and might well be taken for a purely Grecian temple."

Stanton represented the end of a period, and, as it happened, an epoch.

Following the Civil War, the house underwent gradual deterioration, at one time serving as a school, until the Pilgrimage Garden Club bought it in 1938 and carefully restored and redecorated every inch with Natchez and other museum quality antiques. The French mirrors and the chandeliers are original. Stanton Hall now serves—in addition to its own special attractions—as an information center for all houses in the Natchez area. The club also runs the first-rate Carriage House Restaurant on the grounds of the estate which encompass a city block in size. The building is a National Historic Landmark.

*Open daily 9–5, except Dec. 24–25—by tours only during
Pilgrimage: admission*

---

11 Longwood (1860–62)
**W off Lower Woodville Road, S from J. R. Junkin Drive (US 65
    By-Pass)**
Natchez, Mississippi

SAMUEL SLOAN, ARCHITECT

The never-finished Longwood—construction stopped when its Philadelphia workmen hastened home at the start of the Civil War—is the most impressive (and the largest) of the few remaining houses that

were inspired by the architectural philosophy of Orson Squires Fowler. Fowler had been a successful phrenologist who preached that the "spherical" or the octagonal was the most logical plan for a house, and in 1848 wrote an influential book on the subject—*A Home for All*—which went through many printings. Though his geometry never approached Boullée's (1728–99) fantastic proposal for a 500-foot/152-meter-high spherical tomb for Newton, Fowler's persuasive arguments found some echo, almost a hundred years later, in Buckminster Fuller's hexagonal Dymaxion House of 1927, and, of course, in Fuller's geodesic domes, which reached a climax in the 250-foot/76-meter-diameter sphere at the Montreal Expo '67. Maybe we have underrated Orson Squires Fowler. (Octagonal plans were, of course, well known in the history of architecture, San Vitale in Ravenna—526–47—being one of the first great examples.)

In 1860 Dr. Haller Nutt commissioned Samuel Sloan—"one of the most distinguished of early American architects" (Henry F. Withey in his *Biographical Dictionary of American Architects* [*Deceased*], Hennessey & Ingalls, 1970) to design Longwood: would that it had been finished. To compound the tragedy, Dr. Nutt died in 1864. Although only the basement level had been fully enclosed, it and the two main floors are still in excellent condition. If the six-story dwelling (basement, three main floors, solarium, and observatory—all crowned by an onion dome or an East Indian *amalaka*) had been completed, the towering central hall, which runs through the house, would have been staggering, for Dr. Nutt had planned an elaborate system of mirrors to reflect sunlight even down to the basement level. He also had anticipated the use of solar heat in winter, and planned to ventilate the house in summer by drawing cool air in from the lower level and exhausting it at the top. In plan all thirty-two major rooms open onto both the central hall and exterior loggias so that there are two exits plus cross ventilation in each.

S. P. Cockerell's Sezincote (1805) in Gloucestershire and John Nash's famous Royal Pavilion at Brighton (1815–22) might have influenced Messrs. Nutt and Sloan to produce what could be termed a "Moorish-Tuscan" mansion. Paul Norton, the distinguished architectural historian, writes that Nutt was familiar with Oriental architecture and once went to "Egypt with his family mainly to observe the growing of cotton" (*The Arts in America, the 19th Century,* Scribner's, 1969). In any case Longwood is one of the most fascinating houses in the country. Fortunately it was purchased (1968) by the Kelly E. McAdams family, whose McAdams Foundation generously gave it and 5 acres/2 hectares in 1970 to the Pilgrimage Garden Club, which is gradually restoring it, having acquired 82 acres/33 hectares of additional land as protection. Unique—and since 1970 a Registered National Historic Landmark.

Open daily 9–5, except Dec. 24–25—by tours only during Pilgrimage: admission

---

12 Old Spanish Fort (c. 1721)
4602 Fort Street, 5 blocks N of US 90
Pascagoula, Mississippi

The De la Pointe Outpost or Fort, built by the French and captured by the Spanish, has largely disappeared except for the carpenter's shop. Even this service building had walls almost a foot and a half (46 centimeters) thick—largely made of timbers and crushed oyster shells—the better to withstand Indian attack. Though the other buildings in the

compound have, as mentioned, vanished, this almost pathetic-seeming structure—recently a farmhouse—has considerable value to the specialist as one of the few remaining fortified buildings in the Mississippi Valley. Charles E. Peterson, FAIA, of the National Park Service, and the genius who "invented" HABS, the Historic American Buildings Survey, says that it is "a great archeological curiosity and a unique survival from the earliest period of Gulf Coast Colonization." It is now in the good hands of the Jackson County Historical Society and is listed in the National Register of Historic Places.

Open daily 9–5, except Dec. 25: admission

---

13   Old Court House Museum (1858–61)
Cherry Street at Grove and Jackson
Vicksburg, Mississippi

Squarish in plan, oriented by the compass, the old Warren County Court House is embraced by four well-projected porticos. There are four 30-foot/9.1-meter-high Ionic columns on the north and south sides, and six on the east and west. An octagonal lantern topped by an

open bell tower rises above this ambitious mass. The interior has been converted to a museum, one primarily concerned with the War Between the States, a grim share of which tragedy took place at the building's base. Note the four small structures standing at the diagonals: originally cisterns for fire protection, they were later converted to offices. Used as a courthouse from 1861 to 1939, when a new one was built, the building was saved from destruction in 1946 by the Vicksburg and Warren County Historical Society. It should be noted that although William Weldon is listed as the architect in some sources, the museum itself has no precise record of this attribution. There is even a theory—again without documentation—that the courthouse was designed "by a slave named Jackson." However, it is certain that William Weldon and his brothers George and Thomas were the builders.

Open Mon.–Sat. 8:30–4:30, Sun. 1:30–4:30, except holidays: admission

North Carolina

Greensboro 15–16   Hillsborough 17   Edenton 9–12

Winston-Salem 30   Chapel Hill 6

Research Triangle Park 25   ■ Raleigh 22–24   Pettigrew State Park 21

Asheville 1

Fontana Dam 13   Charlotte 7–8   Fremont 14   Bath 2

Mount Gilead 18   New Bern 19–20   Cape Hatteras 5

Beaufort 3–4

Wilmington 26–29

NORTH CAROLINA

The buildings in boldface type are of general interest. The others are for the specialist.

Asheville	1 **Biltmore House and Gardens** (1891–95)— Richard Morris Hunt
Bath	2 **Historic Bath** (mostly 18th century) St. Thomas Church (1734–c. 39) Palmer-Marsh House (c. 1744) Bonner House (c. 1830)
Beaufort	3 **Old Burying Ground** (1731–early 20th century) 4 **Beaufort Historical Association Complex** (mid-18th–mid-19th century)
Cape Hatteras National Seashore	5 **Cape Hatteras Lighthouse** (1869–70)
Chapel Hill	6 **North Carolina Blue Cross/Blue Shield** (1971–73)— Odell Associates
Charlotte	7 **Mint Museum** (1835–40) —William Strickland 8 Presbyterian Home (1966–68/1974)—J. N. Pease Associates
Edenton	9 **The Cupola House** (c. 1725/1758) 10 St. Paul's Episcopal Church (1736–60) 11 **Chowan County Court House** (1767) 12 **Barker House** (c. 1782)

Fontana Dam

13 **Fontana Dam** (1941–45)
—Tennessee Valley
Authority

Fremont

14 Charles B. Aycock House
(1840)

Greensboro

15 Burlington Corporate
Headquarters (1971)—
Odell Associates
Ciba-Geigy Corporation
Building (1967/1970)—
Odell Associates

16 **Governmental Center**
(1968–73)—Eduardo
Catalano

Hillsborough

17 The Old Courthouse and
Museum (1844–45)—
John Berry

Mount Gilead

18 Town Creek Indian Mound
(c. 1550–1650)

New Bern

19 **Tryon Palace Restoration**
(1767–70/1952–59)—
John Hawks

20 **Stevenson** (c. 1805), **Jones**
(1809), **and John Wright
Stanly** (1780) **Houses**

Pettigrew State Park

21 Somerset Place (c. 1830)

Raleigh

22 **North Carolina State
Capitol** (1820–24/1833–
40)—William Nichols,
William Nichols, Jr., Town
& Davis, David Paton

23 J. S. Dorton Arena (1952–
53)—Matthew Nowicki
and William Deitrick

24 **State Legislative Building**
(1961–63)—Edward
Durell Stone

Research Triangle Park

Wilmington

Winston-Salem

25 **Burroughs Wellcome
Company** (1970–72)—
Paul Rudolph

26 **Orton Plantation Gardens**
(c. 1725/1840/1910)

27 **Burgwin-Wright-Cornwallis
House** (1770)
St. James' Episcopal
Church (1839)—Thomas
U. Walter

28 **The Bellamy Mansion**
(1857–59)—Rufus F.
Bunnell
Zebulon Latimer House
(1852)

29 Hoggard High School
(1967/1969)—Leslie N.
Boney

30 **Old Salem Restoration**
(1766–1830/1950–   )
Museum of Early Southern
Decorative Arts (1965)

1 Biltmore House and Gardens (1891–95)
W off US 25, c. 2 miles/3.2 kilometers S of
Asheville, North Carolina

RICHARD MORRIS HUNT, ARCHITECT

There is not another house in the U.S.A. which unfurls wealth in a more princely fashion than George Washington Vanderbilt's Biltmore, all 250 rooms and 780 feet/238 meters of it. There is no other which approaches it in size. Even Hunt's other "vacation houses" for the Vanderbilts at Newport, Rhode Island—The Marble House (1892) and The Breakers (1895, q.v.)—seem almost modest beside it, while the Loire châteaux on which Biltmore is based are amiable transatlantic peers. Mr. Hunt did not spend nine years studying, working, and traveling in France in vain. It should be added that Mr. Vanderbilt himself had more than a cursory interest in architecture in addition to a smart array of languages.

For some observers there is a lack of coordination in the main facade as it peers across its smooth green parterre, double-lined with trees. This is largely because the central entry dominates the adjacent elements with its pronounced projection and richness instead of coordinating with them. Most prominent is the stair attached to the left of the front door, basically a copy, here glazed and reversed, of the famous Francis I double-spiral, towered stair at Blois (c. 1525).

However, it is on the interior that Biltmore staggers, particularly the incredible six-story-high (75 feet/23 meters) Banquet Hall with its barrel-vaulted ceiling hovering over all. Beautifully proportioned and acoustically excellent, this baronial refectory is embellished with thrones, tapestries, halberds, rugs, ad infinitum, with a triple fireplace emblazoning the end. The smaller but even more lavish library, which holds some twenty thousand volumes, mostly rare, seemingly often read, is also not to be missed. But visit all the rooms open to the public—each as originally furnished: there will never be another house like it.

The landscaping was laid out by Frederick Law Olmsted, who among other great works designed New York's Central Park (q.v.). Chauncey Delos Beadle took over the grounds after Olmsted's death in 1903, having begun with him in 1890. He stayed on at Biltmore for sixty years. The approach road which Olmsted and Beadle plotted from gate to house is serpentine and highly effective, taking one through the closeness of the forest then bursting onto the esplanade. A series of garden terraces escort one from the formality of the mansion

to the freedom of nature with a progression that well merits study. In addition to the Italian garden next to the house, there is a 4-acre/1.6-hectare walled garden in the English style, plus rose garden and azalea gardens beyond.

Although only 11,000 out of the 125,000 acres (4,452 of 50,586 hectares) of the original estate remain—much of it having been generously given to the government as part of Pisgah National Forest and some of it sold—the house itself stands as built and furnished. It was opened to the public (by Vanderbilt heirs) in 1930. The Music Room, strangely never finished with the rest of the house, was completed in 1976 under the skillful guidance of Alan Burnham, FAIA, a longtime student of Hunt's work.

Open daily 9–5, except major holidays: admission

2 Historic Bath (mostly 18th century)
NC 92, 16 miles/26 kilometers E of Washington
Bath, North Carolina

The collector of villages will find in Bath—population 225—an almost untouched microcosm of eighteenth-century Americana in the South. The oldest incorporated town in North Carolina, founded in 1705, it lies between two creeks which flow into the Pamlico River, thence into the many-fingered, romantic—historically and visually—Pamlico Sound. (Walter Raleigh's ill-started ventures of 1585–87 on Roanoke Island—carried out by Grenville and White—were on the northern edge of Pamlico; Blackbeard the Pirate was said to have been in cahoots with Governor Eden in Bath itself, and was eventually killed, in 1718, at Ocracoke Inlet at the entry to the sound. More recently the Wright brothers made another kind of history at Kitty Hawk, near the juncture of Pamlico and Albemarle sounds. Cape Hatteras angles the barrier reef between Pamlico Sound and the Atlantic.)

Bath was near the first Post Road (1738–39) from New England to Charleston and Georgia, giving it not only importance but architectural communication. The earliest settlers were from Virginia—the region was called Albemarle before it was designated North Carolina (1691), while the lower section of the state belonged to South Carolina until 1712. There was thus a crosscurrent of architectural (and other) influences, both North and South, molding the area. Though architectural heroics will not be found in Bath, the whole is greater than its parts.

St. Thomas Church (1734–c. 39), Church Street at Craven, is simplicity itself, a brick rectangle in form with walls 2 feet/.6 meter thick, and, since a storm in 1905, towerless. Its front is marked by unusual white memorial plaques around the door, surmounted by a prominent relieving arch built in the wall. Note the cypress shingles put on during the recent restoration instead of the more usual ersatz. The interior, which is full of ancient mementos, is plain with white plaster walls, dark tie beam, and two windows flanking the simple (but questionably detailed) natural wood retable. The whole church has been enthusiastically restored by the congregation.

The nearby **Palmer-Marsh House** (c. 1744) on Main Street provides a strongly scaled local example of domestic work in the mid-eighteenth century. Built, it is thought, by Michael Coutanch, a Frenchman who

was born on the Isle of Guernsey and lived in Boston before coming to Bath, it is one of the oldest dwellings still standing in the state. Like the church, it has been recently restored (by the Beaufort County Historical Association) and deeded to the state, which maintains the house. The most notable feature of the exterior is a 17-foot/5.2-meter-wide, 4-foot/1.2-meter-thick chimney at the east end, "split" at the top with windows between its twin flues. The kitchen in the basement is also worth a look. The pyramidally peaked, square outbuilding is the reconstructed smokehouse. On the grounds are live oaks well over two hundred years old.

The **Bonner House** (c. 1830), Main Street at Front, on the point overlooking the water, though built much later, furnishes us with another good example of the backcountry "Federal" of the area. Restored by the Oscar S. Smith family, it has been given to the Historic Bath Commission.

Buildings open Tues.–Sat. 10–5, Sun. 2–5: admission to houses

3   Old Burying Ground (1731–early 20th century)
Ann Street between Turner and Craven
Beaufort, North Carolina

Beaufort is a small, ancient (founded in 1709), little commercialized fishing village. It lies only a few miles from Cape Lookout National Seashore (1966) on North Carolina's famous Outer Banks and on the south is adjacent to Morehead City's bustling industrial port. Among its treasures is this moss-draped graveyard almost weary with age but still extending a gracious invitation to explore and even to reminisce. Deeded to the town in 1731, this plot a block northeast of Front Street —the business section—is full of unusual tombs, some with explanatory legends. "All the graves in this older area are facing east so that the occupants might face the rising sun on Judgment Morn," to quote the local guide. One of the most startling of these graveside commentaries concerns the Robert Chadwicks, who rescued a young Chinese cabin boy, converted him to Christianity (c. 1880), with pride sent him to Trinity College (now Duke) and then to Vanderbilt Theological Seminary, and in time bought him a ticket to his native China to set up shop as a Methodist missionary. There Charlie Jones (Soong), more correctly Soong Yao-ju, eventually married and in the proper course of events fathered six distinguished children—among them Mme. Chiang Kai-shek. If it had not been for Beaufort's Chadwicks it might well have been a different world. But more important than individual graves or the adjacent church (1854, remodeled 1897) is the encompassing atmosphere of tombs and trees, of man and nature, which develops the cemetery's haunting coupling of nostalgia with impendence.

Open daily 9–5

4   Beaufort Historical Association Complex (mid-18th–mid-19th century)
Turner Street between Front and Ann
Beaufort, North Carolina

There are over a hundred century-old buildings in Beaufort, and its energetic Historical Association has so far purchased and restored six of them. Two open to the public are the Joseph Bell House (c. 1767) and that of his grandson Josiah (c. 1825). Both express Carolina seashore vernacular with pronounced influence from the West Indies in their double porches or piazzas. Both were probably built by ship's carpenters. The older house stands colorful in its original barn red while the latter, spatially less encumbered, is in a mustard color. They are nicely

furnished and both have restored gardens. The J. Pigott House (c. 1830), which serves as a summer art gallery, Courthouse (1796), Old Jail (c. 1829), and Apothecary Shop (c. 1859), all furnished, complete the complex. Hampton Mariners' Museum is located next door. An Old Homes Tour on the last weekend in June enables the visitor to see other buildings as well.

Open year round, Mon.–Sat. 9–5, Sun. 2–5, except major holidays: admission

5 Cape Hatteras Lighthouse (1869–70)
Cape Hatteras National Seashore, North Carolina

The famous Hatteras light is at 193 feet/59 meters the tallest in the United States; but transcending mere measure, it is the world's most superb example of three-dimensional, functional graphics. Its spiraling bands of black and white polarize the quiet horizontality of its gloriously desolate setting. It stands an unmistakable beacon by day as well as by night: contemporary sculpture from sea or land. The earliest

light on the cape was built in 1798 but was severely damaged in the Civil War. When the present lighthouse was constructed it stood 1,500 feet/457 meters from the surf. Then erosion threatened it and in 1935 it was deactivated and replaced by a steel-framed light about a mile away. However, when the beach was stabilized by steel pilings and sandbags, the light was refurbished—it had been vandalized—and recommissioned (1950) with a new 250,000-candlepower beacon.

The tower sits on a "Classical" octagonal base of carefully quoined granite, the shaft itself (of brick stuccoed) spiraling smoothly upward to its bracketed, black metal top. (The 165-foot/50-meter light at St. Augustine, Florida, built in 1874, was modeled directly on it.)

The Hatteras Lighthouse area forms the country's first National Seashore (1937), here a 70-mile/113-kilometer stretch of ocean, barrier reef, and sound—the Outer Banks. It is one of seven such seashore parks which Congress authorized in 1937, at least one of which is still not open. (A number of other seashore sites recommended by the National Park Service first in 1935, then in 1955 "with highest priority," were sloughed off by an indifferent Congress, and, of course, snapped up, at least in part, by developers and industry.) The famous Pharos of

Alexandria (283–246 B.C.) at a legendary height of 200–600 feet/ 61–183 meters—greatly doubted—might have been higher; several European lights were more daringly engineered; but in the annals of world pharology none can touch the graphic dynamism of this North Carolina outpost which surveys the well-known graveyard of the Atlantic.

Open mid-June–Labor Day, daily 9–6; rest of year 9–5, except Dec. 25

6   North Carolina Blue Cross/Blue Shield (1971–73)
Chapel Hill-Durham Boulevard (US 15/501), 2 miles/3.2 kilometers E of
Chapel Hill, North Carolina

ODELL ASSOCIATES, ARCHITECTS

Geometric immoderation might be seen in this rhomboidal, elevated, and cantilevered Service Center, but it is carried through with purpose, clarity of form, and fine landscaping. The angles of its long mirror-glass facades—the south at 45° "earthward," the north at 45° "sky-

ward"—evolved from careful studies to minimize solar heat load in summer and to admit the low warming sun in winter. The west end also projects outward to reduce late afternoon sun heat. Considerable energy savings are reported. Wind-tunnel tests were carried out on a scale model in an aero-space laboratory to determine if adverse wind conditions would result from the shape; they do not. The ground level is unenclosed except for central reception area and cores for structural support and vertical circulation. Thus when one approaches the building (the road comes from the north) there is a sweep of sunny space through and under, while from the nearby highway the building seemingly floats on its low ridge. A programmed fountain rises from an ovoid pool which contains symbolic sculpture (suggestive of computer parts). On the far side are twin stainless "wind" sculptures which emphasize the "throughness" of the elevated building and act as foils to its mathematics. They were designed by Scopia Inc. of St. Louis. The entire 38-acre/15-hectare site has been carefully landscaped, with parking lots for the company's 900-plus employees bermed and largely hidden by trees.

The three office floors of the 500-foot/152-meter-long, 100-foot/30-meter-wide building are virtually column-free. Basic layout consists of offices (enclosed) near the center with secretarial pools along the windows. The light from the south wall has worked well, but it was found advisable to install thin metal blinds behind the double glazing of the north to control sky glare. No draperies are necessary. The space-frame steel structure is upheld by six equispaced cores, producing cross-braced structural-utility bays of 23 feet/7 meters width alternating with office bays 62 feet/19 meters long. A floor for services and staff dining is underground. Expansion was anticipated.

Tours Friday at 2:30, grounds open during office hours

---

7   **Mint Museum** (1835–40)
    **501 Hempstead Place, NE off NC 16 on Colville Road, then R on
       Eastover Road**
    Charlotte, North Carolina

WILLIAM STRICKLAND, ARCHITECT

In the earlier part of the nineteenth century the Charlotte area was the largest producer of gold in America. The descriptive folder of the museum states that "There were, at one time, between 75 and 100 mines

within a 20 mile [32 kilometer] radius of Charlotte. One . . . had a main shaft 350 feet [107 meters] deep, and 3,500 feet [1,070 meters] of levels." So that the ore could be minted near the source, Congress in 1835 commissioned William Strickland to design a U. S. Branch Mint. Strickland was earlier the country's leading exponent of the Greek Revival as evident in his Second Bank of the United States in Philadelphia (q.v.) and his Capitol in Nashville (q.v.). Here, however, he edged toward the Federal Style in his flattish, centrally pedimented facade. The building was partially destroyed by fire in 1844, but was rebuilt two years later, it is thought as Strickland designed it (except perhaps for piazzas in the rear). In use as a hospital during the Civil War, minting having stopped in 1861, the building was employed as a federal assay office from 1867 to 1913. Old Mint then was utilized for various civic functions until threatened (1932) by the expansion of the downtown post office. Concerned citizens banded together and had it moved to its present site—which was donated—in the southern section of the city. Since 1936 it has served as a museum of the arts, the interior properly remodeled for this purpose. The relaxed, almost domestic scale of the exterior is highlighted by the 14-foot/4.3-meter wing-spreaded eagle in the pediment.

Open Tues.–Fri. 10–5, Sat.–Sun. 2–5, except holidays

8   Presbyterian Home (1966–68/1974)
Sharon View Road, off US 74 on SE edge of
Charlotte, North Carolina

J. N. PEASE ASSOCIATES, ARCHITECTS

Church-affiliated housing for the elderly has proliferated greatly in the
past years, and some of this work, like the present example, has attained a high quality of architectural design. This Presbyterian Home
is situated on 22.5 acres/9.1 hectares of wooded, rolling land on a residential edge of the city. The first six-story building initially took in
110 residents. Plans were drawn, however, so that this number could
be expanded by erecting a similar building which was carried out in
1974. The occupants make "donations" for their quarters, accommodations which range from a single bedroom for one person to bedroom
and living room with kitchenette for two, each unit on a 14-foot/4.3-
meter-wide module 20 feet/6.1 meters deep. Groups of ten to twelve
bedrooms (some single, some double) open onto a central smallish
lounge, with a larger lounge in the center. Variations of sizes and jux-
tapositions of rooms develop a "staggered" outline which keeps the
scale from being too insistent. Many of the apartments have substantial balconies. A fully equipped infirmary is attached.

Lobby and grounds open daily

9   The Cupola House (c. 1725/1758)
408 South Broad Street between King and Water Streets
Edenton, North Carolina

Edenton, on Albemarle Sound, explored by a Jamestown party in
1622, settled about 1660, incorporated in 1722, is one of the oldest
towns in the state, and like Bath (q.v.) on Pamlico Sound, grew up because of its protected-from-the-Atlantic port location. Some of North
Carolina's first buildings were erected here; fortunately several dating
from two hundred and more years ago still exist. Edenton's most distinguished is the so-called Cupola House though esthetically ill-served
by the topping which gives it its name and which jars its facade.
   "The design of the house is one of the most striking essays in the
Jacobean style in America" (T. T. Waterman in Johnston and Waterman's *The Early Architecture of North Carolina,* University of North
Carolina Press, 1947). The Jacobean Style in England evolved out of
the Elizabethan under James I (King 1603–25), and, largely under the
influence of Italian Mannerism, introduced an almost Baroque approach to design, especially ornament. On the exterior of The Cupola
House this is manifest in the unusual framed and bracketed overhang,

and in the broken eave pediment mentioned above which is reflected
by the angles of the porch, which was possibly added later. The
double-hung windows, instead of casement, are thought to be the
earliest of this type in the state. The cupola, almost ludicrously out of
scale, dates from the house-building proper, influenced by Williamsburg.
It is certainly one of the earliest domestic cupolas in the Colonies, those
in New England, with few exceptions, not appearing until later.

The real richness of this strange house, however, lies inside. It
possesses interiors of such quality that the Brooklyn Museum purchased (1918) the finest rooms on the ground floor. (These have been
scrupulously restored.) Note especially the library and drawing
room with their vigorous mantels which almost burst their small
confines with their energy. The library door, too, is outstanding. (This
interior woodwork dates from 1756–58 when the house was sold, and
was subsequently remodeled by the new owner.) The stair is original,
and leads to several excellent rooms on the top floor. A highly unusual
house, Jacobean in transition to the Georgian, curious without, unfet-
tered within. It is a National Historic Landmark.

Open Tues.–Sat. 10–4:30, Sun. 2–5: admission

---

10   St. Paul's Episcopal Church (1736–60)
South Broad Street (US 17) at West Church
Edenton, North Carolina

An unpretentious example of Village Georgian, surrounded by its cemetery, and another of the prides of Edenton. Though the transition from brick tower to shingled steeple is not altogether satisfactory, note at the other end the rare, semicircular apse laid with all-header bricks. This latter is an influence from Virginia. The barrel-vaulted interior is engaging except for the anachronistic Victorian window in the chancel. In difficulty after disestablishment, the church was first restored in 1806–9. Damaged by fire in 1949, it has since been completely renovated and welcomes all to its nave and its amiable grounds.

Open daily 8–5

---

11   Chowan County Court House (1767)
East King Street at Court
Edenton, North Carolina

A small but skillfully proportioned two-story courthouse which Waterman calls "perhaps the finest Georgian courthouse in the South." Its discreetly projecting and pedimented central bay, the relation of this three-windowed bay to the one-windowed (per floor) sides, the prominently modillioned cornice and pediment, and a competent cupola

atop the hip roof make a nicely taut building. In front, a bowered village green slopes down to Edenton Bay and the Sound. The courtroom on the ground floor is still in use, and in addition to court work accommodates a variety of public meetings. Note the apsidal bay at the rear on which stands the portentous judge's chair. The second floor contains an unusually tall (13 feet/4 meters) and sizable (30 x 45 feet/9.1 x 14 meters) white-pine-paneled Assembly Room, reputedly the largest in the Colonies at that time. This served for town festivities, banquets, and similar gatherings. Its painted paneling rises to the ceiling to meet its cornice.

Having been in constant use the Court House is in excellent condition. The brick stringcourse across the front was formerly painted white, as were the lintels over the windows. Authorities attribute the design of the building to one Gilbert Leigh, a local man who originally came from Williamsburg. The influence of the Virginia Capitol is evident. Outstanding—and a National Historic Landmark.

Open Mon.–Fri. 9–5, except holidays

---

12   Barker House (c. 1782)
bottom of South Broad Street
Edenton, North Carolina

The Barker House, now serving as a Visitors' Center with helpful audiovisual program, stands at the end of South Broad Street (an extension of US 17) overlooking Albemarle Sound. A comfortable dwelling of the late eighteenth century, it is marked by twin chimneys and the double porches (added later) typical of the North Carolina coastal region. It was moved in 1952 to this panoramic site, restored, and, in addition to the Visitors' Center, now serves as headquarters for Historic Edenton and its museum. Useful information on the area is available. Mrs. Barker, incidentally, presided over the "Edenton Tea Party" (October 25, 1774), forswearing the use of tea as a protest against British repression. This is held to be "the earliest known instance of political activity on the part of women in the American colonies."

Open Tues.–Sat. 10–4:30, Sun. 2–5, except holidays: tours of town—fee—from here

---

13   Fontana Dam (1941–45)
NC 28
Fontana Dam, North Carolina

TENNESSEE VALLEY AUTHORITY, ARCHITECTS AND ENGINEERS

The Fontana Dam occupies one of the most wildly natural sites of the TVA system. The approach, particularly from the nearby Tennessee border, is guaranteed to impress: one winds in and out of wonderful scenery, accompanied by a playful river, then edges around a sharp abutment of hills to confront a 480-foot/146-meter-high dam—the tallest east of the Mississippi River—sculpting a valley as it rises dizzily above. From the top the scenery unfolds to show some of the most glorious mountainscapes in the eastern part of the country.

TVA's well-known concern for integrating engineering in the countryside is everywhere evident. One of the unusual features of Fontana is the absence of a visible overspill; spillways are out of sight at the east end near the Visitors' Building so that no interruption impairs the majestic 2,365-foot/721-meter-long barricade. Overspill is carried to the riverbed by enormous tunnels (34 feet/10.4 meters in diameter) in the mountainside, with deflectors at the bottom to throw the water up and out to neutralize its force so that its head will not erode the bed of the Little Tennessee River. A Visitors' Building stands at the east (open daily), adjacent to the incline railroad which transports one

down to the powerhouse. The powerhouse itself is a reasonable concrete building (superfluously clad in limestone), with three generators
which are turned by the pressure of waters originating 377 feet/115
meters on the other side of the solid mass of concrete. A cantilevered
roadway across the top of the dam enables one to enjoy the views on
both sides.

14   Charles B. Aycock House (1840)
c. 2 miles/3.2 kilometers E of US 117 and S of NC 222
Fremont, North Carolina

The restored birthplace of Governor Charles B. Aycock represents a
typical farm in eastern North Carolina in the mid-1800s. In addition to
the frame house in which Aycock was born (1859), there are four
original farm buildings and a restored one-room school (1870, and
moved to this site) with further restoration to come. None of the structures originally witnessed a paintbrush, and an invisible chemical pre-

servative has been used to provide protection while maintaining the early idiom. Note that the kitchen and dining room are separate from the house. The simple furnishings are mixed original and period.

Open Mon.–Fri. 9–5, Sun. 1–5, except holidays

15 Burlington Corporate Headquarters (1971)
**Friendly Road at Hobbs Street, c. 3 miles/4.8 kilometers WNW of
   downtown**
Greensboro, North Carolina

ODELL ASSOCIATES, ARCHITECTS

A startling headquarters building which combines several of the latest architectural fashions—a steel exoskeletal frame and mirror glass (here topaz-colored), plus a four-story core of executive offices which is suspended from roof trusses that rest on the six-story exoskeleton.

The two lower floors of this central block are occupied by the personnel office. A service wing partially surrounds the tall building with flourishing landscaping in the courts.

Odell Associates designed the **Ciba-Geigy Corporation Building** (formerly Burlington Industries Research Center) (1967/1970), 8 miles/ 13 kilometers west of Greensboro on IS 40, between Guilford and Sampson roads. This is composed of several loosely joined but well-articulated units, tied by fountains and penetrated by gardens, the whole resting easily on a slight rise adjacent to the Interstate.

Grounds and reception area open to public during business hours

---

16 Governmental Center (1968–73)
Greene Street at Sycamore (between Washington and Market)
Greensboro, North Carolina

EDUARDO CATALANO, ARCHITECT

The demands of civic dignity for the new are reinforced by the classic sobriety of the adjacent Old Guilford County Court House (1918, Harry Barton, architect). The resulting U-shaped grouping, with the

old Court House forming the right leg, the new Court House the center, and the Municipal Office Building the left leg, forms a good adjunct to downtown Greensboro. The old has been used and respected yet the new was not compromised.

Both city and county functions are economically housed together. The three units, aided by a fall-off in grade, are elevated above a two-level, four-hundred-car, partially underground garage common to all. A Governmental Plaza and a well-planted sunken garden (which also provides additional access to the garage) serve as central focus. With this large court and the substantial setback of the buildings from the street, the city has been effectively opened up and new vigor given to midtown development.

The larger of the two new buildings, the County Court House, stretches as mentioned across the top of the group. Its plaza level contains the functions most used by the community, while the second and third floors are filled with courtrooms (all purposefully windowless) with an exterior periphery of offices. The design of the individual courtrooms—one evolved with the cooperation of the North Carolina Bar Association—is unusual inasmuch as these squarish chambers place the judicial benches on a diagonal to "improve the audio-visual contact between judges, witnesses, jurors and attorneys." The top floor of the Court House will accommodate future expansion, while the lower floors contain records and miscellaneous offices.

The Municipal Office Building is of greater interest architecturally, combining a development of interior spaces and light which is climaxed by a large skylit "garden" containing three hardy scheffleras (*Brassaia actinophylla*). Overlooking the garden and propped on piers in the middle of the structure—with exhibition room underneath—stands the City Council Chamber. This is an informal room which also serves for other civic and community activities including regional exhibitions. The two floors below the plaza are occupied by the Police Department, while the upper three levels are filled with municipal offices. The third floor is open to criticism in that its window area (the vertical slots) is on the meager side. The unusual structure, which is prefabricated, is based on a specially designed lineal-coffered precast system, entirely flat in its soffit—its first institutional use at this large scale. Altogether, Greensboro has a fine new complex which has given downtown its first urban space. Peter C. Sugar was associate architect to Catalano, while McMinn, Norfleet & Wicker were local associates. Deborah Forsman was structural engineer.

Open during office hours; plaza always open

17 The Old Courthouse and Museum (1844–45) South Churton Street (NC 86) at East King Hillsborough, North Carolina

JOHN BERRY, ARCHITECT-BUILDER

The facade of the Orange County Historical Museum—until 1953 the Orange County Court House (and the third on this site)—is almost invisible behind stands of trees, but one soon discovers a neatly pedimented, two-story Greek Revival building which will interest the specialist. Four properly spaced Doric columns delimit its porch, while brick pilasters line its sides. The whole is bound by a continuous and well-detailed entablature with the roof topped by a cupola of less distinction. The large courtroom, which almost fills the second floor (note corner fireplaces), has been turned into a regional museum (1957) depicting the development of Orange County, including a hypothetic diorama of an Indian village which flourished nearby in the seventeenth century. It is pertinent to note that the second story of many early courthouses was used as the courtroom because the roof trussing enabled the top floor to be free of partitions or supports. The ground floor and basement are occupied by county offices.

John Berry, as the plaque outside proclaims, was a well-rounded "Builder, Architect, Legislator, Humanitarian." The museum was established in 1957 as an outgrowth of the two hundredth birthday of the town in 1954. It was designated a Historic American Building by the Department of the Interior in 1963.

Open Tues.–Sun. 1:30–4:30, except holidays

---

18 Town Creek Indian Mound (c. 1550–1650)
N off NC 73 on County Road 1160, 5.5 miles/8.9 kilometers E of Mount Gilead, North Carolina

Indians have of course been indigenous to what is now North Carolina for millennia; the first European to comment on them apparently was De Soto in his dispatches of 1540. And when John White in 1591 saw

the word CROATOAN carved on a tree in the Raleigh-sponsored Roanoke Settlement—and found no survivors—it seemed obvious that the first English attempt at colonization of the New World ended with the Indians in control. Tantalizingly some experts in linguistics have traced a sprinkling of English words in the eastern Siouan dialects, suggesting the possibility that this famous Lost Colony—perhaps only the females—was merely abducted, not dispatched.

In central (Piedmont) North Carolina the Creek, a Muskogean-speaking people of Pee Dee Culture, were widespread, having moved into the area—displacing the "native" Siouan-speaking people—in the mid-fifteenth century. Coming from as far west as Alabama, the Creek were probably familiar with the Mississippian Temple Mound culture. The mound at Town Creek is of modest height and dimension with a simple "temple" atop, the whole surrounded by a palisade of sharpened logs. Used as a "fortified" refuge and ceremonial and burial center, it was reconstructed beginning in 1936. No one lived within the compound except for the priests in charge: note the reconstructed priest's dwelling.

Properly separate today stands an instructive Visitors' Center. This State Historic Site is administered by the Office of Archives and History. (Descendants of the Cherokee who escaped banishment from westernmost North Carolina to Oklahoma in 1830 are still found in the mountains.)

Open Tues.–Sat. 9–5, Sun. 1–5, except holidays

19 **Tryon Palace Restoration** (1767–70/1952–59)
George Street at Pollock, 1 block S of US 17 (Broad Street)
New Bern, North Carolina

JOHN HAWKS, ARCHITECT

New Bern—named by 1710 Swiss settlers—possesses in Tryon Palace
the most significant Colonial restoration in the United States after
Williamsburg (Portsmouth, New Hampshire, with more but less signal
buildings in its Strawbery Banke, q.v., not excepted). The ambitious
restoration of Governor Tryon's palace is due to the energy and resources of Maude Moore (Mrs. James Edwin) Latham, who was born
in New Bern and who from early childhood had wanted to rebuild the
state's first "permanent" capitol. The superb result involved the complete rebuilding and furnishing of the palace and its flanking buildings.
(The stable adjunct to the west was structurally sound after the 1798
fire which destroyed the main building, and though the east dependency survived the fire, it "at some unrecorded time . . . disappeared.") In addition to the rebuilding of the house, the extensive gar-

dens—today one of the delights of the place—had to be carefully replanted. The problem was further complicated by the fact that fifty-four houses, which for 150 years had naturally encroached on the old domain, had to be removed by the state, which by then had title to the area.

The restoration, like that at Williamsburg, was not conjectural. It was built on the excavated foundations of the eighteenth-century buildings, with the aid, unbelievably, of the architect's original drawings, which were found in New York and London. The whole project has been sumptuously carried out, from house, to furnishings, to gardens. The refurnishing of the palace was enormously simplified by a precise inventory—discovered in England in 1953—made for Governor Tryon in 1771 when he was appointed Royal Governor of New York and left New Bern. (The furnishings of the governors of the Colonies were their personal properties and went with them when they were transferred.)

Tryon Palace derives, as would be expected, from Palladio, interpreted by John Hawks via James Gibbs's *A Book of Architecture* (1728). Plate 63 of his book shows a very similar dwelling with raised two-story centrally pedimented block attached by quadrants to flanking two-story dependencies. The use of quadrants—the most graceful of hyphens—was puzzlingly rare in the American Colonies, Mount Airy near Richmond (private) and Mount Vernon (q.v.) being the only two surviving prominent examples. Hawks was brought from England by Governor Tryon to design and supervise the building of his "palace." The guidebook claims that Hawks was "the first professional architect to remain in America," but little is known of his subsequent activities except for two houses in New Bern of which the John Wright Stanly House (1780, q.v.) is open to the public. (Peter Harrison, 1716–75, Yorkshire-born, is generally considered our first "professional" architect.) In any case Mr. Hawks with the usual books turned out a more than distinguished building.

As one approaches the palace, one notes the 1741 English wrought-iron gates: they are probably the most elegant in the country. A second gate (of little interest) and a wrought-iron fence enclose the semiovoid "compound" of the palace, the main building flanked by stable dependency at the right, with kitchen and office at the left (east). The royal coat of arms of George III stands colorfully forth in the pediment. The roof parapet on either side of the pediment was rare for its time. Most of the lower floor of the palace is given over to "official" rooms, that is Government House, climaxed by the Council Room in the southeast (far left) corner. This also doubled as a ballroom. In addition to fine furniture and chandeliers, several kings and a queen supervise affairs of state from their canvases. The State Dining Room, adjacent to the Council Room, is equally rich. It should be noted—as the tour hostesses point out—that all of the mantels and much of the molding (chair railing, etc.) came from a series of eighteenth-century English mansions either direct or via antique dealers. Even the brass locks were found abroad. In spite of the resulting lack of consistency, all of the interior was restored to its period of greatness. The upper floor formed the Governor's Residence and, like the lower, has been meticulously restored and beautifully furnished. Note, on going upstairs, the skylight which Hawks used to illuminate the interior.

In addition to seeing the house—informed hostesses escort one through and guidebooks are available—the visitor should explore the elaborate series of gardens which occupy much of the grounds. These range from intricate geometrical compositions, to kitchen gardens, to "wildernesses" found on each side of the smooth and ample South Lawn which once rolled down to the Trent River. The outbuildings, too, should not be missed, for they have been just as carefully restored as the mansion. Note the several "blind" windows in these dependencies. Perry, Shaw, Hepburn & Dean of Boston, who restored Williamsburg, were the restoration architects for Tryon Palace. It might indeed be "The Most Beautiful Building in the Colonial Americas" as the brochure proclaims: Hugh Morrison adds—from studying the drawings before the rebuilding—"Beyond question the finest house in North Carolina, and perhaps in any of the Colonies" (*Early American Architecture,* Oxford University Press, 1952).

Open Tues.–Sat. 9:30–4, Sun. 1:30–4, except holidays: admission

---

20 Stevenson House (c. 1805), **611 Pollock Street**
Jones House (1809), **Pollock at Eden Street**
John Wright Stanly House (1780), **307 George Street**
New Bern, North Carolina

In addition to the stellar attraction of Tryon Palace, New Bern possesses a number of enlightening houses, mostly of wood, which date from the end of the eighteenth century and into the early nineteenth. Three of these are neighbors of the palace. The **Stevenson House** stands immediately east of the palace entry, a clapboarded building of two and a half stories which was purchased (1957) by the Tryon Palace Commission and thoroughly restored by them (1964–66). On the homely side on the exterior (note the captain's walk), it has fine Federal furnishings within.

Another Palace Commission dwelling is the **Jones House,** just west down Pollock Street. This is used as an official guesthouse and, though not open to the public, is worth a look at the exterior of the house and at the garden. The house displays the typical North Carolina, Caribbean-influenced "piazzas." Considerable West Indies trade was shipped from New Bern and other Carolina ports and these verandas obviously reflect this. They are, incidentally, almost never found in Virginia. Mary Mix Foley in her admirable book *The American Home* (Harper & Row, 1979) feels that a French influence via South Carolina Huguenots can be seen in these "galleried" dwellings.

The **John Wright Stanly House,** probably designed, as mentioned earlier, by John Hawks after he had finished the palace, is the most accomplished of these dwellings. Its flush wood siding, wrought-iron balustraded hip roof, quoins, and pedimented entry and first-floor windows lend it patrician distinction. A Northern architectural influence is apparent, which is perhaps not surprising as Mr. Stanly made his fortune in shipping along the Atlantic seaboard. The house was moved to this site just down George Street from the palace in 1966, shorn of later additions including dormers and door transom (it had been used as the town library with apartments for the previous thirty years) and fully restored (1972). The exterior with its oyster-colored walls is superb as are the two gardens (Richard K. Webel, landscape architect). The interior with great refinement of paneling and detail, its furnishings

reflecting the 1780–1820 period, is also of very high merit. Waterman in his aforementioned *The Early Architecture of North Carolina* terms it "the finest of the period in the state."

Like Tryon Palace itself, the three houses mentioned were restored through the foresight and generosity of the late Mrs. James Edwin Latham, and, also like the palace, most of the architectural restoration was under the direction of Perry, Shaw, Hepburn & Dean, with William G. Perry and Conover Fitch, Jr., in charge.

Open—except as noted—Tues.–Sat. 9:30–4, Sun. 1:30–4, except holidays: admission. Get map at Chamber of Commerce, 211 Broad Street

---

21   Somerset Place (c. 1830)
7 miles/11.3 kilometers S of US 64 at Creswell
Pettigrew State Park, North Carolina

The house at Somerset plantation falls more in the category of upper-bracket low-country tradition than that of a mansion of architectural

distinction. However, the dwelling and the numerous outbuildings (some still in the process of restoration) give an excellent idea of the size and complexity of large-scale farming operations in this region early in the last century. The plantation began in the 1780s as a 100,000-acre/40,469-hectare cooperative for raising rice. Much of the land was swamp and had, with great difficulty, to be drained. The grandson of the principal founder was willed the plantation and around 1830 began constructing the house we see today (or reconditioning an earlier building), adding many more outbuildings, new canals, and effecting a shift from rice to corn as a cash crop.

The house—which grew through the years—was used primarily as a winter home, heat and mosquitoes prompting summers in the North. Note the proliferation of double-decked porches (added after 1830)—typical of the Carolina coast as we have seen—to shade the dwelling by day and afford refreshing sitting places in the breezes of dusk. (Moreover the second level was more apt to be free of plant- and ground-loving mosquitoes.) T-shaped in plan, the house had fourteen rooms, enough to accommodate numerous guests, many of whom stayed for a month. Sliding doors could throw the two parlors together but there is no major salon.

After the War Between the States the family was forced to sell the plantation, the house eventually becoming vandalized. Acquired by the federal government in the 1930s, it was transferred to the state as Pettigrew State Park, and a careful restoration of the house undertaken. In 1969 the renewed plantation was opened to the public. Although few of the furnishings are original all are of the 1850 period. Somerset Place is administered by the Division of Archives and History of the Department of Cultural Resources.

Open Mon.–Sat. 9–5, Sun. 1–5, except holidays

---

22 North Carolina State Capitol (1820–24/1833–40)
Union Square, Fayetteville Street, Mall, and Hillsborough Street Raleigh, North Carolina

WILLIAM NICHOLS, WILLIAM NICHOLS, JR., TOWN & DAVIS, DAVID PATON, ARCHITECTS

Wayne Andrews in his handsomely illustrated *Architecture in America* (Atheneum, 1960) calls this "the most distinguished of all our state capitols." Situated at the center of important crossroads in the ap-

proved fashion of the day, and occupying only the small center section of its square, the North Carolina State Capitol is not only commanding urbanistically, its architecture is of great interest. The history of the building is curious. The initial structure was a two-story State House on this site constructed between 1792 and 1796. Architect-builder William Nichols, the State Architect, vastly expanded this core in 1820–24, adding two wings to make a cross plan, a third floor, and a domed rotunda to contain a treasured statue of Washington (in Roman armor) sculpted in 1820 by the famous Antonio Canova. In June 1831 Nichols' building burned to the ground (Washington's statue was also destroyed), and William Nichols, Jr., as agent for his father (who then worked in Alabama and Mississippi), was retained to devise plans for a replacement, keeping the cross plan but making it larger. Young Nichols had completed the initial plans and then was succeeded in August 1833 by the more experienced Ithiel Town of New York's Town & Davis, who significantly refined the Nichols proposal. (Ithiel Town, incidentally, was probably the best engineer in the country at that time, inventing and patenting, 1820, the much-used Town lattice truss for wooden bridges. The royalties from this helped him when architecture was depressed.) In 1834 Town & Davis, having completed design work, hired David Paton, a young Scot who had worked for Sir John Soane in London, to supervise construction for the state. Paton not only supervised, he made numerous changes on the interior (the outside walls of gneiss had been largely completed), with, it is pertinent to note, some design consultation (1836–37) with William Strickland. From this mixture of talents evolved the building we see today.

North Carolina's Capitol adds a solid note to the Greek Revival with its sturdy, cruciform dimensions of 160 x 140 feet/49 x 43 meters, and its well-detailed porches on east and west fronts with Doric columns above a sharp-edged rusticated "basement" and low copper dome floating above the central rotunda. A restraint bordering on dryness characterizes the interior of the central rotunda, but the second-floor gallery is boldly cantilevered over the lower hall. The Senate Chamber is not well knit, but the semicircular House of Representatives' hall with two-story Corinthian-derived columns comes out handsomely. The columns and details on both Senate and House were copied from specific Greek temples but some liberties were obviously taken. In a more up-to-date fashion the Supreme Court Chamber (gallery added c. 1858) and the State Library were designed in the Gothic Style.

The grounds encircling the Capitol are particularly herbaceous, bursting with over twoscore varieties of trees, almost all native to the state, and all carefully identified. In front an unusually composed, realistic statue by Charles Keck (dedicated in 1948) presents the three Presidents North Carolina has given the nation: Andrew Jackson, James K. Polk, and Andrew Johnson. (A duplicate of Canova's Washington was installed in the rotunda in 1970.) While the building's functions have been taken over by the new Legislative Building one block north (q.v.), the Capitol continues to house the offices of the governor and secretary of state. The legislative chambers and former Supreme Court Chamber and State Library are intact and open to the public. The whole building was restored for the Bicentennial and is now being properly refurnished.

Open daily Mon.–Sat. 8:30–5:30, Sun. 1–6

23   J. S. Dorton Arena (1952–53)
1025 Blue Ridge Boulevard W of city on State Fair Grounds
Raleigh, North Carolina

**MATTHEW NOWICKI, ARCHITECT, WITH WILLIAM DEITRICK;
FRED N. SEVERUD, ENGINEER**

The architects took two enormous and opposing concrete arches, raised the arc of each at a 22° angle to the ground, abutted their open ends, and elevated their juncture on two low triangular supports. (This deceptively extended their thrust lines—compare Mies van der Rohe's Barcelona chair.) They then stretched cables between the arches to create support for the roof and for lateral stability and thus designed our first stressed-skin roof system. It is a brilliant concept. Moreover Nowicki—who died in a plane crash before construction began—and Deitrick plotted the seating arrangement to create the greatest number of places toward the center, and to reflect this undulation of seats both inside and out. The resulting elliptical, column-free "great room" measures 221 feet/67 meters long by 126 feet/38 meters wide and contains 5,500 permanent seats and 4,400 portable ones. Agriculture, industry, and commerce are its chief users. In 1979 a thorough renovation and updating was carried out by engineers Buffaloe, Morgan & Associates. The arena is listed in the National Register of Historic Places.

Open during events

24 State Legislative Building (1961–63)
Halifax Street at Jones, Salisbury, and Wilmington
Raleigh, North Carolina

EDWARD DURELL STONE ASSOCIATES, ARCHITECTS

The new State House—a block from the Capitol—solves its difficult problem of official "monumentality" and current "democracy" in formal terms but with welcoming scale on the exterior and some good spaces within. The 340-foot/104-meter-square building rests on a low, non-authoritarian podium which "levels" the uneven site and permits a large parking garage in half of the basement floor. A continuous colonnade of square, marble-clad columns frames the two main floors of the building on all sides, the third partial floor projecting upward in the middle in a Greek-cross plan with an open-air garden at each corner. At entry level a brace of fountains set in wide bowls occupies the corners in front of the main facade. The scale of the exterior, as mentioned, is humanistic.

One is not prepared, however, on stepping inside the front door to confront abruptly a magisterial flight of vivid red carpeting which cheers visitors to the third floor. (Elevators are available.) The ground floor is taken up by individual offices which completely line the building's periphery, with a variety of committee rooms placed in the inner core. The second floor houses the Senate Chamber (circular) and the larger House of Representatives (square), with, again, individual offices along the outer walls. A library and services take up the central area. Four interior courtyards, two stories high and capped with skylights, penetrate the State House near its corners, injecting space and light into the two working floors. The third floor—the only one open to the public—is given over to the upper half of the two legislative chambers, plus an auditorium and small snack bar. Here one can enjoy views of both Senate and House via their upper-level galleries, gaze down upon the waters and trees of the central rotunda court which rises from the second floor, and stroll out to enjoy the rooftop "gardens" and the view. The strongly patterned pyramidal ceilings of the top floor are insistent, but spaces, play of light, and planting are fine. The furniture was designed by the architect; Edward D. Stone, Jr., and Richard C. Bell were the landscape architects; Holloway-Reeves were associate architects.

Open June–Aug., Mon.–Fri. 8–5; Sept.–May, Mon.–Fri. 8:30–5:30, Sat. 9–5, Sun. 1–5

---

25   Burroughs Wellcome Company (1970–72)
3030 Cornwallis Road
Research Triangle Park, North Carolina

PAUL RUDOLPH, ARCHITECT

The Burroughs Wellcome headquarters is one of the most dazzling administrative complexes in the country. Firmly astride the top of the most prominent ridge in Research Triangle Park, it forms a "man-made extension" and marches down the slope with a series of splayed-wall, articulated units. Faint recollections of Zoser's Stepped Pyramid at Saqqara (c. 2800 B.C.) and of the Mayan work in Mexico and Guatemala come fleetingly to mind, but this is no exercise in historicism. Burroughs Wellcome is a hardheaded look at establishing a major research institute with flair and flexibility within a realistic budget.

Two of Paul Rudolph's chief concerns in architecture involve the psychology of space and movement through buildings and the play of

natural light in them. In both of these he has—as what perceptive architect has not?—been influenced by the work of Frank Lloyd Wright and Le Corbusier. Rudolph is also in this day of increasing mass production concerned with multiples, that is similar forms put together in such rhythmic fashion that the banality of the base unit vanishes in the orchestration of the whole. All of the above are present here. Space excursions will be seen even in the smaller dimensions of the laboratories, where, as elsewhere in the building, rigidity evaporates in canted planes and in the absence of the right angle. Three-dimensional enclosure and dramatic lighting reach a climax of progression in the towering lobby. The flood of natural light in the outer offices and laboratories is controlled by a clerestory and "outrigging" of baffles so that the effect illuminates the room, but the source (direct sun) is little evident. Inward-slanting bands of windows provide a direct view outward for the occupants. Artificial light is equally well handled. Rudolph's employment of similar units or modules multiplied to create a building finds imaginative exposition at Burroughs Wellcome. The lozenge-shaped elements interact up and down the slope, coalescing to form the total fabric of the building as the building itself grows from the hill. There is expressionism here, and in spots suggestions of the arbitrary, but the results are very spirited.

Reception lobby and grounds open to visitors during business hours

26   Orton Plantation Gardens (c. 1725/1840/1910)
   **W across river on US 17/74/76, S on NC 133 18 miles/29
       kilometers**
   near Wilmington, North Carolina

Orton is a nostalgic witness of an era long past: in the spring it is one
of the most glorious spots in the United States. The only survivor of
several score of plantations that once lined the Cape Fear River, the
plantation and its house evolved over many years. The first building
was a small (c. 60 x 75 feet/18 x 23 meters) one-and-a-half-story
house dating from around 1725. Timber and its by-products such as
turpentine formed the basis of the economy of the area then. Following Independence, and with the need for supplying the British navy no
longer important, rice was introduced and the nineteenth-century fields
of Orton eventually stretched for some 6 miles/9.6 kilometers along
the tidal waters of the Cape Fear River which were so vital to its cultivation. The quality of the cereal grass grown along this river—the
northern limit of the rice belt—attained such renown that it was used
as seed rice throughout the South. In 1840, with growing affluence, the
old house was expanded to two stories and, this being the peak of the
Greek Revival period of architecture, a properly gabled, sharply detailed portico with tall Doric columns (of cement on brick) was added
to the river (east) side. After the War Between the States (when, for-

tunately for its preservation, the house was used as a hospital by Northern troops), and with the consequent abolition of slavery and the absence of capital, rice could be grown only with difficulty and Orton languished.

Later in the nineteenth century the house was restored, then in the early part of this century it was purchased by the James Laurence Sprunt family, who still own it and who added the two side wings (1910—designed by Kenneth M. Murchison) and the chapel (1915—a memorial to Mrs. Luola Sprunt), also extending the gardens. A further expansion of the gardens was undertaken in the early 1930s, largely under the direction of R. S. Sturtevant, the landscape architect. Mr. Sturtevant, and the late Churchill Bragaw who succeeded him, created a relation of house to garden to river of masterful unity, establishing a series of paths to strengthen this mutual interrelationship. The approach provides tantalizing snatches of columns. As one comes nearer, the house reveals itself on one side while the broad marshscape—the previous rice fields now a wildfowl sanctuary—opens to the right, climaxing with the distant river. Close at hand are paths which meander through live oaks with Spanish moss, pause by the brown but clear waters of a cypress swamp-lake, and cross a lagoon which once led to the river that furnished the main access to the house until as late as the 1920s. The parterred Scroll Garden, visible from a small bridge, injects a formal note to counterpoint the hedonistic nature. In between are vistas and, in season, millions of azaleas and camellias alternating with a variety of other plants (note the Chinese wisteria) and flowers: 12,000 acres/4,856 hectares of another world. Go in spring if possible, but go.

Gardens open daily 8–5, except Dec. 25: admission—house not open

---

27 Burgwin-Wright-Cornwallis House (1770)
224 Market Street at 3rd
Wilmington, North Carolina

A North Carolina "city" house, lifted well above the ordinary by the quality of its detail, by its magnolias and richly restored garden, and its three-story kitchen and neat well house behind. Spared during the Revolution by being commandeered as Lord Cornwallis' headquarters (1781), the house was purchased (1937) by the National Society of the Colonial Dames of America in the State of North Carolina to use

as their state headquarters. It has since been thoroughly restored and furnished and opened to the public.

Note, on approaching, the double-decked piazza with Ionic columns, well-turned balusters, and elaborate Palladian door, the entry accented by roof pediment. (The double-verandaed porch and the south wing were added before 1848 by Thomas Henry Wright.) Inside, the most elaborate chamber is the second-floor Great Room, or supper room, with good paneling and an unusual inner wall divided into five bays. A museum room in the basement contains a variety of collections. The Burgwin-Wright-Cornwallis House gives fine insight into the Wilmington of two hundred years ago—one of the few trophies remaining. (Note also the "vented" wall along the street.)

Open Tues.–Sat. 10–5, also Sun. 2–5, Mar. 15–Apr. 15: admission

Directly across 3rd Street stands **St. James' Episcopal Church** (1839, transept 1879—open daily), designed by Thomas U. Walter, who later achieved fame when finishing the Capitol in Washington. It is a good example of the Gothic Revival.

---

28 The Bellamy Mansion (1857–59)
Market Street at 5th
Wilmington, North Carolina

RUFUS F. BUNNELL, ARCHITECT

The Bellamy Mansion marks the end of both an architectural and a social era. Magisterial with its two-story Corinthian columns on its corner site, prodigal in Classical detail, it has also a hint of the new Italianate style in the roundheaded coupled windows on the second floor and the non-Classical cupola on the roof. (Observe, too, the cast- and wrought-iron gate and fence and the marvelously rich front door.) The Classical Revival as architectural expression was dying when the house was built, while the Civil War killed off the South's wealth even

when it spared its sons. (The house was used as Military Headquarters for the Commanding General of the Union Occupation Forces.) Built for a prominent doctor, the house stayed in the family until acquired (1971) by the non-profit, charitable Bellamy Mansion Inc., which is seeking funds for its total restoration and refurnishing. Although structurally sound, it is in need of considerable attention, particularly the interior which was injured by fire (1973). With moderate investment, the house could be restored to the landmark status its architecture merits.

At present can only be seen from street: restoration in progress

Of related interest is the not-distant **Zebulon Latimer House** (1852), 126 South 3rd Street. (Open Tues.–Sat. 10–5, Sun. 2–5, except holidays: admission.) Built a few years before the more imposing Bellamy Mansion, it shows clearly the Italianate vogue mentioned above. Stylistic schism took over the nation in the mid-nineteenth century and the Classical Revival phased out. Note, however, the semi-Classical front porch across the Latimer dwelling. The house's interiors have been furnished with Empire and Victorian pieces. The property was purchased by the Lower Cape Fear Historical Society Inc. in 1967 and now serves as their headquarters. The Society, founded in 1956, is doing much supportive work in preserving the architectural heritage of

this ancient (1740) and picturesque port city. In this they are helped
by the Historic Wilmington Foundation Inc., which provides a revolving fund for the preservation and restoration of important buildings.
Together they are responsible for the creation of the Wilmington Historic District, now listed in the National Register, which encompasses much of downtown. Tours of the Historic District can be
taken from Thalian Hall (1858), Princess Street between 3rd and 4th.
(Tours Tues.–Sat. 10–5, except major holidays and Christmas–New
Year's week: admission.)

29   Hoggard High School (1967/1969)
   NC 132 at Shipyard Boulevard
   Wilmington, North Carolina

LESLIE N. BONEY, ARCHITECT

With ample, flat land, the architect has produced a splendidly zoned
school separated into logical components. These include semidetached

gymnasium-auditorium at the left, directly accessible from the street; administration, library, and basic classrooms in a two-story-with-courtyard central block; and a wing containing the noisy and/or odoriferous functions of music, vocational shops, cafeteria, and kitchen in a one-story group at the right, separated by a Fine Arts Courtyard. The unusual projections at the windows hide unit air conditioners and serve as a shadow-casting design feature. The windows, two per classroom, can be opened in pleasant weather, and are laterally sun-screened by projecting fins. The courtyards and the open forum at the gym double for outdoor dramatics, rallies, art shows, and, that essential educational ingredient, socializing. Separate traffic patterns are maintained for service, bus, and student parking. The capacity of the school was doubled (1969) with the addition of a new wing. The school has been so successful that it was used as a prototype for another high school built in 1976.

Grounds and reception area open during school hours

---

30 Old Salem Restoration (1766–1830/1950–   )
Old Salem Road (US 52/NC 8) at Academy Street, just S of IS 40
Winston-Salem, North Carolina

The followers of Jan Hus (1369–1415) were the vanguard of Protestant dissenters (i.e. pre-Martin Luther). Having had their troubles in Bohemia for several centuries, they finally established a Moravian refuge in the New World. Moving first to Georgia (1735), they left five years later when the English-Spanish struggle over Florida threatened their pacifistic life in Savannah. They settled—as did others from Germany and what is now Czechoslovakia—in Pennsylvania, creating a flourishing headquarters in Bethlehem (q.v.). In 1753 a small group went southward to inspect further lands for new refugees, having been offered a sizable tract by the Lords Proprietors of North Carolina, who admired their diligence and wanted to build up the center of their holdings. Finding the land to their satisfaction, the group bought 98,985 acres/40,000 hectares in the state's rolling Piedmont. Large numbers of Moravians moved here, augmented by refugees from Europe. Among them were a carefully selected group of expert craftsmen for this was to be primarily a product as opposed to a farming community.

The early pioneers settled in villages (Bethabara, Bethnia, etc.) near

the present Salem, intent on planning and building a new town later. With their dedication to hard work these "Brethren" soon developed one of the most unusual towns in eighteenth-century America. They called it Salem, which is derived from the Hebrew word for "peace" (actually it is *shālōm,* the Arabic *salaam*). The town was commenced in 1766, being meticulously laid out by Christian Gottlieb Reuter, a surveyor and planner, working with strict "liturgical" instructions from Friedrich Marshall in Bethlehem. Marshall gave important mandates as to how the town should be planned, even to the size of lots and the nature of the buildings which were to frame the town's open square. All land, incidentally, belonged to the church, and was leased year by year to tenants. (The church, indeed, ran almost everything from prices of goods to the arrangement of marriages.) Both in plan and architecture the town of Salem reflects the Central European background of most of its citizens. The theme of the plan was a square, largely (and closely) framed by the principal buildings, transversed across the bottom by the main street. There was a rigidity of organization (but not so much of space) rarely seen in the Colonies, where growth and focus, even around the town centers, was more casual. (Compare Oglethorpe's 1733 plan of Savannah.) The architecture also reflected Continental traditions, employing at first half-timbering (*Fachwerk*) with the same red brick infilling seen throughout Central Europe.

The Single Brothers House, Main Street at Academy, the first part of which was finished in 1769, is probably the best example of German half-timber-and-brick architecture in this country. (Before restoration it had been completely clapboarded in 1825—as had several others. The 53-foot/16-meter-long brick second part, built in 1786 and attached at the south, tends to the dull side.) Other buildings of architectural importance are: the Miksch Tobacco Shop (1771), built of logs clapboarded, standing immediately north of the Single Brothers House (note the tile roof and the "manufactory" at the rear; interiors good); the Boys School (1794) across the street, now serving as a museum; and, to the south and still on Main Street, the John Vogler House (1819), which shows less Germanic influence due to its late date (good restored interiors), and the Tavern (1784), built of brick —the first in the settlement—the year an earlier *Fachwerk* tavern burned. With many inventories as guidance the Tavern has been restored to the 1800 era; an 1816 annex has been adapted for use as a restaurant. It is interesting to note that the corresponding buildings which the Moravians earlier constructed in Pennsylvania were largely of local limestone, it being so freely available there. Actually as building progressed in Salem it too became more "regional" and less European because of the availability of almost limitless wood and good clay.

Salem, which merged with the bustling Winston in 1913, fell on sad days following World War II, and urban blight sullied the old community. After a survey by concerned citizens in 1949, Old Salem, Inc., was chartered the next year by the state, $3,500,000 was raised (later almost doubled), and a long-term process of restoration undertaken. "In only fifteen years Old Salem, Inc., has acquired control of sixty-four separate properties—five by gift, fifty-two by purchase, and seven by lease. Ninety-four nonconforming structures have been demolished or removed from the area, and twenty-two buildings have been restored, five of which are now open to the public" (Ralph P. Hanes, Chairman of the Board of Trustees, Old Salem, Inc., in *Antiques,* July 1965). Current (1980) figures are: 111 properties acquired, about 100 non-conforming structures removed, 60 buildings restored or reconstructed on their original sites. Nine of these are now open to the public. Main Street is the prime focus of the restoration—a process which continues—with the Single Brothers House, mentioned above, being the most prominent. The houses which have been put back in their original shape are rented as an important source of revenue. Altogether Old Salem is one of the most revealing "ethnic" restorations and one of the finest town museums in the country, and all concerned with its creation should be very proud, for the task was not an easy one. Perry, Shaw, Hepburn, Kehoe & Dean of Boston were the initial architects, but later work has been carried out by Old Salem itself.

Open daily, Mon.–Sat. 9:30–4:30, Sun. 1:30–4:30, except Dec. 25: admission. Tours from Reception Center

At the south end of Main Street stands the **Museum of Early Southern Decorative Arts** (open Mon.–Sat. 10:30–5, Sun. 1:30–4:30, except Dec. 25: admission), not an official part of the restoration, but its fifteen period rooms, ranging in date from 1690 to 1820 (and all reconstructed), will be of interest to those in its field. It was opened in 1965.

Ohio

Painesville 19

Kirtland 17

Bowling Green 3

Cleveland 11–13

Akron 1

Tallmadge 21

Van Wert 23

Canton 5

Bellville 2

Zoar 24

Sidney 20

Troy 22

Columbus 14–15

Brownsville 4

Dayton 16

Marietta 18

Chillicothe 6

Cincinnati 7–10

OHIO

The buildings in boldface type are of general interest. The others are for the specialist.

Akron	1 **Edwin J. Thomas Performing Arts Hall** (1971–73)—Dalton, van Dijk, Johnson & Partners and Caudill, Rowlett, Scott
Bellville	2 **Bandstand** (1879)—Abraham Lash Bandstand (1975), Medina
Bowling Green	3 Wood County Court House (1893–96)—Joseph W. Yost and Frank L. Packard
Brownsville	4 **Flint Ridge Museum** (1968)—E. A. Glendening
Canton	5 Central Plaza (1963)—Tarapata-MacMahon Associates
Chillicothe	6 **Adena—The Thomas Worthington House** (1806–7)—Benjamin H. Latrobe
Cincinnati	7 **Taft Museum** (c. 1820)
	8 **Plum Street Temple** (1865–66)—James K. Wilson
	Cathedral of St. Peter in Chains (1845/1957)—Henry Walter
	City Hall (1888–93)—Samuel Hannaford & Sons
	9 Cincinnati Union Terminal (1929–33)—Fellheimer & Wagner
	10 **Riverfront Stadium** (1968–70)—Finch-Heery
	Suspension Bridge (1856–67)—John Augustus Roebling
Cleveland	11 **The Cleveland Arcade** (1888–90)—John M. Eisenmann, George H. Smith

12 **Blossom Music Center** (1967–68)—
   Schafer, Flynn & van Dijk

13 Metropolitan Campus of
   Cuyahoga Community College
   (1968–69)—The Outcalt-Guenther
   Partners

Columbus

14 **State Capitol** (1839–61)—Henry
   Walter et al.

15 Wyandotte Building (1897–98)—
   D. H. Burnham & Co.

Dayton

16 **Old Court House** (1847–50)—
   Howard Daniels

   Plaza (1974)—Lorenz Williams
   Lively Likens & Partners

Kirtland

17 **Kirtland Temple** (1833–36)

Medina (See Bellville)

Marietta

18 **Rufus Putnam House** (1788)

Painesville

19 **James F. Lincoln Library** (1966–
   67)—Victor F. Christ-Janer &
   Associates

Sidney

20 **People's Federal Savings & Loan
   Association** (1917–18)—Louis H.
   Sullivan

   Memorial Building (1875)

   Shelby County Court House (1881)
   —G. Maetzel

Tallmadge

21 **First Congregational Church** (1822–
   25)—Lemuel Porter

Troy

22 **Miami County Court House** (1885–
   88)—Joseph Warren Yost

   Safety Building (1972)—Hart-
   Ruetschle-Hart

Van Wert

23 Van Wert County Court House
   (1874–76)—Thomas J. Tolan &
   Son

Zoar

24 **Zoar Village State Memorial** (early
   19th century)

1 Edwin J. Thomas Performing Arts Hall (1971–73)
Center Street at Hill
Akron, Ohio

DALTON, VAN DIJK, JOHNSON & PARTNERS AND CAUDILL, ROWLETT, SCOTT, ARCHITECTS

The Thomas Performing Arts Hall—the first phase of an ambitious cultural complex for both the University of Akron and the city—faces on Center Street and lies just across an important bridge from downtown. The architects realized that the hall would gain by day as well as by night (when, of course, most performances are held) if it could tap a share of the business community using this thoroughfare. Thus by day one passes a multiterraced, richly landscaped introduction to a provocatively angled concrete building, while by night floods of warm light pour out from its great glass front, revealing the structure within. The latter is an almost irresistible attraction, particularly when animated by crowds during intermission. (This glass, incidentally, is thick plate, end-butted to eliminate mullions.)

The program for the Thomas Hall called for facilities which could accommodate a wide variety of events, and instead of building several

separate units it was decided that it would be better and less expensive to produce one that was highly flexible. The result is an auditorium which can be almost immediately adjusted in seating capacity from 900 to 2,400 or 3,000. The computer-controlled means of effecting these changes lies in the extraordinary ceiling made up of 3,600 acoustically dampened steel plates in seven random shapes suspended in catenary "loops" over both audience and stage. Sections of the ceiling can be raised or lowered to meet the size desired, while the counterweights in the form of twenty-seven lead-filled chromed steel cylinders are cabled to the lobby to double as excellent abstract sculpture. Very imaginative. The main floor of the auditorium is divided by change in level into orchestra and grand tier with a "floating" balcony above. The ceiling can be lowered so that it covers only the 900 seats of the orchestra. "Acoustical dynamics"—in metal instead of traditional concert hall wood—and "seating geometry" have been combined with architectural shape (11° sidewall splay) for sophisticated theater design, technically brilliant and acoustically excellent. There is, however, a visual "presence" of the tentlike ceiling with its prominent joints. The treatment of the sidewalls and the merger of auditorium with stage are very good, as is the lighting. The lobbies are enjoyably capacious, the front part embellished, as mentioned, with the tension "sculpture" of the chromed counterweights. Covered automobile access and underground garage are commendable.

Charles E. Lawrence was chief of design. George C. Izenour, the theater consultant, and Dr. Vern O. Knudsen, the acoustician, have been working together for some fifteen years. They and the architects have produced here one of the most advanced theater/concert halls to be seen.

Open for performances

---

2   Bandstand (1879)
Public Square off Main Street
Bellville, Ohio

ABRAHAM LASH, ARCHITECT

Though not the most momentous shelter in Ohio, this village bandstand (just south of Mansfield) recalls nostalgically a time when entertainment came from the community, not to the community via air-

waves and cable. The pavilion's exuberant Victorian and Eastlake detailing also conjures the innocence of a long-vanished era of architecture. As the *Richland Star* wrote of its dedication: "The benediction was offered and a volume of music broke upon the air, which continued loud and long. We are pleased to note the excellent manner in which Mr. Bell performed this part in calling the people to order and introducing the speakers and also the tasty and orderly method in which the ceremonies were performed" (September 18, 1879). Measuring 20 feet/6.1 meters in both diameter and height, it may well be the best bandstand in the country. Pure delight. Both Bandstand and Town Hall (1876) are registered National Historic Sites.

An identical **Bandstand** was erected in Medina, Ohio, in 1975, adding a fine accent to Courthouse Square and a complement to the Medina County Court House (1873—T. D. Allen, architect: the Greek Revival original building dated from 1841). Ron Kohanski and Henry Chambers were the architect-supervisors of the new bandstand. Their most difficult task was to find woodworkers today who could turn out such delicate tracery! The Medina stand was the gift of the Letha House Foundation. Band concerts are generally held on Friday evenings during June and July.

3   Wood County Court House (1893–96)
East Court Street between Summit and Prospect
Bowling Green, Ohio

JOSEPH W. YOST AND FRANK L. PACKARD, ARCHITECTS

Those with a fondness for a Romanesque Revival courthouse in the
fashion made rampant by H. H. Richardson toward the end of the last
century will find here a stalwart specimen. Its low, bowed entrance
"porch" is highly unusual in utilizing a projected flattish arch, flanked
by two octagonal turrets, to frame the entry. Behind, a square attached
tower shoots upward—to oversized clocks—with a contemporary front
door in its base. The granite stonework is brawny, with carved relief as
contrast which is especially intricate around the door. Note the stairway, columns, and stained glass within.

Open during office hours

4 Flint Ridge Museum (1968)
IS exit 55 eastbound, 56 westbound, off OH 668, 3 miles/4.8 kilometers N of
Brownsville, Ohio

E. A. GLENDENING, ARCHITECT

Flint was the major stone for Indian arrowheads and scraping knives, and this ridge was the most prized source in the Midwest. Mined for probably ten thousand years, the area was so useful that it became neutral territory for all tribes. The area's wares were exported as far away as the Atlantic Coast. This small museum, set in a 525-acre/212-hectare memorial park (open daily), was carefully placed on top of an actual pit, dramatically lit by a baffled skylight, and made startlingly realistic by two sculpted figures depicted at work inside. Around the pit and its "manikins" are grouped well-organized displays, lit by artificial light, showing the geology of the region, flint characteristics, and Indian life. Because of its parklike setting, wood (cedar) was used throughout the building.

In addition to the pit and surrounding exhibit areas, there is an information desk and office, toilet facilities, and an outdoor lecture area. A well-keyed museum, one of four by the same architect for the Ohio Historical Society, all depicting phases of Indian culture in the area.

Open Mar.–Nov., Tues.–Sun. 9:30–5; Dec.–Feb., Sun. only 9:30–5: admission

---

5 Central Plaza (1963)
Market Avenue at Tuscarawas Street
Canton, Ohio

TARAPATA-MacMAHON ASSOCIATES, ARCHITECTS; JOHNSON, JOHNSON & ROY, LANDSCAPE ARCHITECTS

Well-designed information, exhibition, and refreshments kiosks; trees and flowers, flags and fountains have transformed "an asphalt meadow" into an urban oasis. This is a move which almost every city must

make if it is to stem even partially the flight from downtown. In addition to the information-exhibition building and a year-round cafe, there is a winter ice-skating rink. Though this well-paved town center is small in size (160 x 500 feet/49 x 152 meters) and strictly budgeted —over three quarters a gift of the local Timken Foundation (whose bearing works are the city's chief industry)—Central Plaza is a tribute to private enterprise working for public good, as well as being a fine example of urban uplift. Largely because of it, more than $20 million worth of new building and remodeling has been generated in this area.

6 Adena—The Thomas Worthington House (1806–7)
W out Allen Avenue Extended, off OH 104
Chillicothe, Ohio

BENJAMIN H. LATROBE, ARCHITECT

Dominating a hill northwest of the town, and itself almost dominated by oaks, elms, and magnolias, the Worthington house and garden make a handsome team. Considering building conditions at the beginning of the nineteenth century in this part of Ohio—it was called Northwest

Territory until 1803 when Ohio became a state (with Chillicothe its first capital)—the mansion represents an impressive achievement. Benjamin Latrobe, who was at one time architect of the Capitol in Washington, designed the house, having met Colonel Worthington when the latter was serving as Ohio's representative. As Talbot Hamlin points out in his biography of Latrobe (Oxford University Press, 1955), the plan of the house with its projected wings resembles that of "Old West" at Dickinson College in Pennsylvania which Latrobe designed in 1803. The results here, built with local sandstone, walnut, and slate, are commendable, though proclaiming a certain rusticity. The house became a State Memorial in 1946—the gift of the daughters of the late owners—and has been restored to its early-nineteenth-century condition, as have the numerous outbuildings and the gardens.

Open Apr.–Oct., Tues.–Sun. 10–5: admission

---

7   Taft Museum (c. 1820)
316 Pike Street at 4th
Cincinnati, Ohio

The Taft Museum was built as the residence of Martin Baum, with James Hoban of Washington fame thought by some to be its architect or at least a consultant. The house also recalls Jeffersonian principles of proportion. (Some attribute the house to Latrobe but this is not borne out by Hamlin.) Now almost surrounded by manufacturing and commercial buildings near downtown Cincinnati, the house—transformed into a museum—and its gardens provide an agreeable urban retreat. Its architectural ambitions attain elegance, with two-story central block and lower wings at either side, and an unusual play of oval lights in the central section. A positively scaled, well-projected Tuscan portico marks the entry, giving a Greek Revival touch to the Federal Style building. The entire house is of white-painted wood.

The interior, having been converted to a museum in 1932, has no original or Taft furnishings left but has been carefully decorated with antique printed cottons and satins of the period of the house itself. The museum's collection of Duncan Phyfe furniture (c. 1820) is one of the most representative in the country. The former second-story ballroom should also be noted, particularly the six enormous windows which lead onto the rear balcony—and which from the back make the house suggest Mississippi Delta plantations. The garden at the rear was laid out in 1949 by Henry Fletcher Kenney. The house and its art, given to the citizens of Cincinnati with an endowment by the Charles Phelps Taft family, is a top example of its period, while the art collection readily matches the quality of the architecture.

Open Mon.–Sat. 10–5, Sun. and holidays 2–5, except Thanksgiving and Dec. 25

---

8   Plum Street Temple (1865–66)
8th Street at Plum
Cincinnati, Ohio

JAMES K. WILSON, ARCHITECT

Relatively restrained "Saracenic" on the exterior but a glorious outburst of Middle Eastern and Gothic architectural motifs and influences within, the Isaac M. Wise Temple (to use its other name) is one of the few of its "style" remaining in the United States. Having been beautifully maintained—the exterior was recently cleaned and the 1,400-seat interior restenciled—it is an outstanding monument; would, only, that it were open more frequently. There is little "formal" archi-

tectural tradition for designing a synagogue, and as with churches, early temples in the United States followed the various architectural fashions (Georgian in Providence, Greek Revival in Charleston, etc.). However, in the mid-nineteenth century, a mantle of details of vaguely Moorish origin cloaked most temples. At Plum Street they abound and even include minarets—but all with a context of extraordinary homogeneity. The famous Rabbi Wise (1819–1900), who founded Reformed Judaism in this country—and had a hand in the temple's design —claimed the Alhambra as its inspiration. It is one of our great religious buildings, both outside and in. It is, of course, listed in the National Register of Historic Places.

When the temple is paired with the Roman Catholic **Cathedral of St. Peter in Chains** (open daily) directly opposite, one enjoys a diverting Judeo-Christian seesaw of architecture. (The latter dates from 1845, portico 1855, heavily restored in 1957—Henry Walter, original architect.) Talbot Hamlin called it "one of the handsomest and most monumental of Greek Revival churches in the United States" (*Greek Revival Architecture,* Oxford University Press, 1944)—a judgment with which not all of us will agree.

Open only infrequently: telephone Wise Center for information—
(513) 793-2556

Take a look also at the Richardson-inspired **City Hall** (open during business hours) on the northwest corner at 801 Plum Street (1888–93—Samuel Hannaford & Sons, architects). A rich crossroads.

---

9 **Cincinnati Union Terminal** (1929–33)
W end of Ezzard Charles Drive
Cincinnati, Ohio

FELLHEIMER & WAGNER, ARCHITECTS

Railroad passenger stations in the U.S.A. trace almost a century-and-a-half career, reflecting through the decades a valuable, giant-scaled mirror of architectural and spatial development. As the railroads themselves prospered many outdid themselves to take care of and impress their passengers. The Cincinnati Union Terminal—finished in the

Depression years—was one of the last moments of glory in this cavalcade. Little of substance in the field was built after it. (The sizable Los
Angeles Union Station, finished in 1939, was the last of the great de-
pots.) That the Cincinnati station is even standing today, passenger
operations having ceased in 1974, is a tribute to stouthearted preservationists, local and nationwide.

The building itself climaxes an elevated plaza and drive with a monumental semicircular front. Measuring 200 feet/61 meters in diameter,
it is "the unchallenged giant of station portals" as the late Carroll L.
V. Meeks put it in his splendid book *The Railroad Station* (Yale University Press, 1956). Its apsidal entry forms one of the highlights of
the Art Deco movement, keyed by a band of murals by Winold Reiss
wrapping the semicircle of the room. Numerous decorative touches, including even the terrazzo paving, brighten the rest. The enormous entrance exedra leads, with unexpected diminution—almost a spatial
siphon—onto a lengthy, slightly arched, concourse which spans and
which once gave access to the tracks below. .

Its rail functions having ceased, as mentioned, and a science museum
having failed, the future of the terminal was uncertain until January
1979. In that month an agreement was signed with a developer to
renovate the building into a "glamour shopping mall," with some hundred stores, a suitable number of restaurants, and entertainment facilities. Remodeled, it opened in August 1980. Paul P. Cret was architectural adviser for the exterior of the building; Colonel Henry M.
Waite, structural engineer.

Open daily

---

10   Riverfront Stadium (1968–70)
2nd Street, US 52 at Suspension Bridge
Cincinnati, Ohio

**FINCH-HEERY, ARCHITECTS (OF HEERY & HEERY AND FINCH,
ALEXANDER, BARNES, ROTHSCHILD & PASCHAL)**

With ingenuity and technical bravura the architects have shoehorned
an imposing multipurpose stadium between the Ohio River and downtown Cincinnati. Railroads had to be moved, seawalls and floodgates
erected, ramps over highways built, and adequate parking provided, all
under extreme conditions of site and soil problems. Some $15 million
was spent in non-stadium outlay.

The Riverfront convertible football/baseball arena rests easily on its involved underpinnings, its white-painted steel vertical structure (the ringing columns) contrasting with the horizontal, precast concrete seats. Circular in form (700 feet/213 meters in diameter), the stadium develops a pared "crown" for the Queen City, enhanced by the light peripheral construction, the expressed "bowl" of seats, and the outward cantilever of the top edge. The sometimes conflicting requirements of baseball and football—for one, baseball needs some 150,000 square feet/13,936 square meters of playing ground, football only about 90,000 square feet/8,361 square meters—have been resolved at Riverfront by making the lowest rank of seats movable, developing a capacity of 56,062 for football and 51,730 for baseball. These "layers" of seats have each been brightly color-coded (red, yellow, green, and blue), setting a rainbow scene visually as well as facilitating finding one's place.

The stadium rests atop a basically rectangular plaza which in turn forms the roof-deck of the triple-tiered garage for almost 3,000 cars (with open parking nearby). Since the stadium is immediately adjacent to the central business district, an elaborate bridging for pedestrians ties stadium to the downtown. Many people can walk to the ball game. Moreover the extensive covered parking under the arena is used daily by the business community. The Riverfront Stadium constitutes an imaginative solution to a particularly tough problem. It is also a key element in the revitalization of downtown Cincinnati. (Which is why the stadium was located on this expensive site instead of the suburbs.) Prybylowski & Gravino were the civil and structural engineers.

Open for events

Be certain to take a look at the husky **Suspension Bridge** adjacent. Designed and built by John Augustus Roebling (1856–67), it combines
suspension cables with Howe trusses for stiffening, a "searching out"
approach later refined (i.e. omitting trusses) by Roebling in the
Brooklyn Bridge (q.v.). Its 1,057-foot/322-meter span was the longest
in the world when built.

11   The Cleveland Arcade (1888–90)
401 Euclid Avenue, and Superior Avenue
Cleveland, Ohio

JOHN M. EISENMANN, GEORGE H. SMITH, ARCHITECTS

The Cleveland Arcade forms a mid-block urban nexus between two
major avenues: in design it is unparalleled in the United States. (See
also The Arcade of 1827–28 in Providence, R.I.) Not only does it provide a protected pedestrian link between two downtown thorough-
fares, it mediates—joyfully—the change in level between them. In
early-nineteenth-century Europe, skylighted arcades (as opposed to
covered sidewalks) began to grace Paris, London, Milan, and Naples
as smart meeting and shopping locales—so successfully, it might be
added, that all are still going strong. Cleveland was influenced by them
and by a direct example in Toronto. With this distinguished lineage, it

furnishes us with a perpetual urban lesson, one particularly suitable in a lakefront city buffeted by wintry gales. The constituent fact of the arcade's excellence lies, first, in its breadth of conception—at 290 feet/88 meters long, 60 feet/18 meters wide, and 104 feet/32 meters high, only the Galleria Vittorio Emanuele II in Milan (1867) is longer (but not quite as wide or high)—and, secondly, in the excellence of its design.

Lightness and air characterize the interior, with a subtle scale buildup lending it character. Note that as the arcade rises it steps backward in tiers with successive floors, admitting thus the maximum of sunshine. Because of the 12-foot/3.7-meter change in level between the two outside avenues, there are two main "streets" or shopping levels in the arcade (providing for scores of shops), with the third level via its step-back forming a secondary one. The two upper floors are primarily for professional and office use. With the setbacks of the floors establishing a horizontal emphasis and the skylight-capped roof attracting the eye upward, an energetic horizontal/vertical activity results. Note, too, that none of the floors is precisely treated like the one below.

One of the chief structural problems concerned trussing the glazed roof so that the usual tie rods—which would have detracted enormously from the inner lightness—could be dispensed with. Eisenmann, who had been trained as an engineer and had studied in Germany, developed a trussed arch, supported on knee braces, which transmits the roof load to the outer masonry walls, a solution so daring that only a bridge-building firm—the Detroit Bridge Company—would undertake it. The span of the three-hinged arches is 49.9 feet/15.1 meters with 23 feet/7 meters rise. The supporting columns and beams are of cast iron, the intricately detailed railings of wrought iron. (Note the beam-end beasties: they once held incandescent bulbs in their mouths.) In actuality the arcade is part of a complex which created two nine-story office buildings (on the upper side) with the five-story arcade separating them—and bringing light and revenue into their midst. Thus the arcade itself is almost swallowed up when seen from either street, while its own Romanesque arched entrances lean to the heavy side. All of which intensifies the contrast when one steps within (preferably from the angled Euclid entry—modernized in 1939) and encounters its inspired light and lightness. A success from its opening day, Cleveland's arcade is still one of the country's greatest urban achievements. In 1979 the skylight was reglazed and the arcade thoroughly renovated and updated mechanically.

Open daily

---

12 Blossom Music Center (1967–68)
from Cleveland (c. 30 miles/48 kilometers): c. 5 miles/8 kilometers S of exit 12 of Ohio Turnpike (IS 80) on OH 8, then 2 miles/3.2 kilometers W on West Steels Corners Road
from Akron (c. 8 miles/13 kilometers): N on OH 8, then 2 miles/3.2 kilometers W on West Steels Corners Road
Cleveland-Akron, Ohio

SCHAFER, FLYNN & VAN DIJK, ARCHITECTS; R. M. GENSERT ASSOCIATES, STRUCTURAL ENGINEERS

The Blossom Center's structure is based on a stupendous, obliquely angled steel arch (400 feet/122 meters span, 200 feet/61 meters rise), its spread-out legs buttressed underground against enormous concrete footings and its sharply inclined frame upheld by ten exposed steel col-

umns (inclined to meet the arch at approximately 90°). From the upper section of this arch and its supports are hung one end of a series of trusses; these horizontal members then extend to rest on columns at the open end to uphold a low conic roof. Under this great umbrella, which is partially open on the two sides and fully so across the back, are 4,642 seats, an orchestra pit for 110 musicians, and a broad stage which will also accommodate a 110-person orchestra, 200 choir, plus children's choir. The stage proper has variable wings so that its size and acoustic reflection can be geared to the renowned Cleveland Orchestra—which uses Blossom as its summer home—down to a soloist or small jazz group. Offices, Green Room, dressing rooms, and services are located behind and below stage. The Center's 526-acre/213-hectare site was carefully chosen so that the auditorium could "expand" outward and upward on the hillside in a dished fan shape that provides 10–12,000 additional seats under the stars, a delightful spot, incidentally, for a preconcert picnic. The covered concert hall was designed with extra-wide peripheral aisles so that rain would be no problem. In keeping with the Center's bucolic setting, the control gates and ticket offices are placed out of sight, along with the extensive parking lots.

The steel trusswork of the roof has twenty-one "small" pipe trusses instead of the eleven larger ones which the architects would have preferred, but economics prohibited this expensive simplicity. (The longest truss spans 175 feet/53 meters.) Economics also leave their mark on the weathering steel of the great arch and its supporting columns, which should have been sandblasted to a uniform color. These, however, are small details of a great concept. The architecture and engineering are of a very superior order, the shell is totally at home in its unspoiled setting, acoustics (amplification is almost never needed) and sight lines are superb (even on the hillside): hall and hill are one. Peter van Dijk was chief of design; Pietro Belluschi served as consultant to the client; Heinrich Keilholz and Christopher Jaffee were the acoustic consultants. The Center was named for the Blossom family of Cleveland, who have generously supported the Cleveland Orchestra and this brilliant shell. Schafer, Flynn & van Dijk are now known as Dalton, van Dijk, Johnson & Partners.

Open mid-June–Sept.: for schedule of performances write
Severance Hall, Cleveland 44106, or telephone (216) 231-7300

---

13   Metropolitan Campus of Cuyahoga Community College (1968–69)
Community College Avenue, Woodland Avenue at 30th Street
Cleveland, Ohio

THE OUTCALT-GUENTHER PARTNERS, ARCHITECTS

A six-thousand-student, two-year commuter college on the southeast edge of downtown Cleveland which offers several key architectural lessons. In spite of its size and an inevitably crowded site, simplicity of both concept and scale were generators of its design: its layout is immediately and comfortably graspable. The major campus buildings are elevated on and frame a block-sized "podium" with extensive parking (essential for a non-dormitory college) along sections of the periphery. This platform is skillfully interrupted toward the center by a "sunken" (i.e. ground-level) forum, where trees, planting, and a fountain not only enliven the scene but give the campus an essential, spontaneous core and a pleasant inward focus. About this center are grouped several major buildings, including the library and student union, with a covered walk surrounding the forum on three sides. Other buildings on the podium are grouped about smaller courts. Walks connect them all, with planting boxes injecting touches of nature. The design of the main building develops a slight layer-cake cast with alternating continuous bands of tan concrete, deep red brick, and stretches of glass, and some of the details are heavy (railings), but this is quibbling. The overall architecture is very good, and the concept excellent. John A. Rode was partner-in-charge. The Outcalt-Guenther Partners are now known as Rode, Kaplan, Curtis, Woodward.

Campus open daily

---

14   State Capitol (1839–61)
High, Broad, State, and 3rd Streets
Columbus, Ohio

ARCHITECTS AS NOTED

Although it required seven architects (four designing, three consulting), twelve governors, and twenty-two years to design and complete this state house, the effort was not in vain. Low-haunched, compact, and powerfully molded, with conviction showing on all sides and the top, the Capitol forms a virile member of the Greek Revival élite. In spite of its modest two-story height, it is 504 feet/154 meters long by 184 feet/56 meters wide, and thus fills with suitable authority its city block, marred only by the 1901 annex at the back. The limestone building is crowned—refreshingly—by a substantial cylinder instead of a dome. Because the porches on each of its four sides are recessed, the

entablature slashes around the building as an unbroken force, binding and compacting the mass into a sturdy block. This solid rectangularity then plays against the cylindrical drum above, with even the low triangular pediment above the main entry adding a geometric touch. A drum, incidentally—and fortunately—was demanded by the legislators because of disagreement about and the expense of the once-intended dome.

The design of the Capitol was begun with a competition which was won (1838) by Henry Walter of Cincinnati. The officials, however, were not wholly satisfied and got Alexander Jackson Davis, the apostle of Greek Revival, to consult with Walter, whom they kept as resident architect. The cornerstone of the Walter-Davis plan was laid in 1839. But all was not settled: W. R. West replaced Walter, who retired, in 1848, while Nathan B. Kelly took over in 1854, to be replaced by Isaiah Rogers in 1858 (apparently Kelly's interiors were too romantic). Rogers, a well-known architect of the period, was aided by consultations (1856) with two of the country's great designers, Thomas U. Walter and Richard Upjohn, whose advice, obviously useful, primarily concerned the size and nature of the drum. The exterior of the building, in spite of the tribulations of its construction, came off magnificently. The interior, because of them, and because of the multiplicity of the hands which touched it, is less satisfactory. But all in all the building is one of our great capitols, and one of our few with a distinctive personality.

Rotunda open Mon.–Fri. 8–5, Sat.–Sun. 9–4:30

15 Wyandotte Building (1897–98)
21 West Broad Street
Columbus, Ohio

D. H. BURNHAM & CO., ARCHITECTS

The small and little-known Wyandotte Building displays bays of windows which practically ripple across its facade. The west front of the eleven-story building is more rhythmic than the north as its windows are spaced 1-1-2-1-1, but any way one looks at it, this is still a fine token of its time. In serious danger of demolition, the structure was purchased (1978) by a group of businessmen known as the KRV Company, which was organized to effect the building's complete rehabilitation. Recalling the joint work of Burnham & Root (see Index), the Wyandotte forms a good member of the Chicago School of high-rise design.

Lobby open during business hours

16   Old Court House (1847–50)
NW corner of 3rd and Main
Dayton, Ohio

HOWARD DANIELS, ARCHITECT

Ralph Adams Cram called this august Greek Revival courthouse "the finest thing of its kind in America" (Dayton *Evening News,* September 6, 1923). It is lifted above the ordinary by its setback corner location, tawny limestone walls, unfluted Ionic columns, and its unique "scallops" bitten off the two rear corners. These indentations functionally reflect the shape of the great oval courtroom which fills the rear third of the structure. Its civic functions long ago (1884) superseded by a larger building, the Old Court House was in danger of destruction, but preservationists and the energetic Montgomery County Historical Society saved it. Beginning in 1973, the building was then transformed into a "living museum" of the area and its history.

Its Greek Stylistic derivation supposedly stems from a copy of James Stuart and Nicholas Revett's famous book *The Antiquities of Athens*

(1762), which a local dignitary possessed, a copy of the plate showing the Thesion being sent to the architects invited to compete for its commission. Mr. Daniels, the winner, used only the temple front (and changed the Doric columns to Ionic), with the sides pilastered instead of becolumned (to admit proper light and air), and, as mentioned, took logical bites out of the rear corners. He also put a coffered Roman dome over the two-story courtroom. The building itself is of solid masonry (even the original roof was of stone until it leaked too much); only the window sashes and inner doors are made of wood (the outer doors are metal). The vaulting of the basement is of interest, as is the spiral stair to the visitors' gallery of the courtroom. Very impressive of its kind.

Open Tues.–Fri. 8:30–4:30, Sat. 10–4, except holidays

The previously hemmed-in building was "liberated" on one long side and back by a richly patterned **Plaza** in 1974 by architects Lorenz Williams Lively Likens & Partners, making the Old Court House a more contributory member of Dayton's resurgent downtown.

---

17   Kirtland Temple (1833–36)
9020 Chillicothe Road (OH 306) at Joseph Street
Kirtland, Ohio

An unusual religious building, especially on the interior. It is the only temple belonging to the Reorganized Church of Jesus Christ of Latter-day Saints (which is legally separated from the Salt Lake City Mormon Church). Moreover it is the only Mormon-built temple which can be entered by the public for religious services. (In Utah Mormon temples are restricted to members of that faith in good standing.) Architecturally the exterior of the Kirtland church, which was built of local stone stuccoed, unskillfully combines several motifs. There are Gothic Revival windows in the facade along with a semi-Palladian opening, while above the cornice almost everything, including the tower, bespeaks the Colonial.

It is on the interior of the two auditorium or "court" floors that the interest lies. At each end of both of these floors rise four-tiered seats for pulpit and priests. Each of the three upper levels contain three rows of seats for priests (eighteen per room), reflecting the RLDS's hierarchy of spiritual and temporal leaders, Aaron and Melchizedek. In front of the three-rowed banks stands the pulpit with a table which

can be raised for the sacrament. The boxed pews in the center of the auditorium can be changed to face either direction. This double-ended concept is rare in religious architecture. Note, too, the rich detailing (mostly adaptations of the Greek Revival) of the pulpits, and the quality of daylight within the courts. The second floor was used primarily as a school and for priesthood education, while the top half-floor (with the dormers) provided meeting rooms. The pews accommodated four hundred. It is claimed—in a church bulletin—that the inspiration for the building, including basic interior dimensions ("fifty-five by sixty-five feet [c. 17 by 20 meters] in width thereof, and in the length thereof"), was divinely inspired: however, the exterior actually measures 59′1″ by 79′3″.

Open daily 9–6: donation

---

18 **Rufus Putnam House** (1788)
Campus Martius Museum
Washington and 2nd Streets
Marietta, Ohio

Marietta rises at the confluence of the Ohio and Muskingum rivers, along the edge of the Northwest Territory which was ceded to the United States in 1783 by the Treaty of Paris. In that year a hardy

group of New Englanders, most of them reportedly boatbuilders from Massachusetts, set forth to size up the 1,800,000 acres/728,000 hectares of land they had just bought as the Ohio Company of Associates. In early 1788 under the leadership of Rufus Putnam they crossed the Appalachians. When the necessary number of flatboats and pirogues were ready they floated down the Ohio River from Pennsylvania. General Putnam laid out the town, naming it for Marie Antoinette in gratitude for French help in the Revolution—in which the general had distinguished himself. His house was one of the first constructed, forming part of the wall of the stockade. It is the earliest known dwelling still extant in Ohio. Roughly used in later years, Putnam's sturdy dwelling was saved in 1932 when the Campus Martius Museum was being built and the house was incorporated (on its original foundations) in the new building. In 1966–72 it underwent meticulous structural restoration and refurnishing with original pieces and artifacts from the Putnam and other families.

The result is a fine bit of New England-influenced architecture constructed on an active Indian frontier. Mr. Putnam—shortly afterward the surveyor general of the United States—added four additional rooms to the early house and these are shown in the restoration by framing, not enclosure.

Open Mon.–Sat. 9:30–5, Sun. 1–5, except major holidays:
admission

---

19   James F. Lincoln Library (1966–67)
Lake Erie College
Mentor Avenue (US 20) just W of midtown
Painesville, Ohio

VICTOR F. CHRIST-JANER & ASSOCIATES, ARCHITECTS

Behind a screen of miscellaneous nineteenth-century buildings, promising new developments of Lake Erie College are taking place under the
direction of Victor Christ-Janer. The most important is this library,
seemingly made of carefully piled, gigantic, metal packing cases. These
windowless, cubistic forms exert a fascination that pulls one on.
Within, exterior solidity transmutes into spatiality, and a series of vis-

ual excursions on several levels generates a maze-like setting for books and study.

This labyrinthine series of spaces off of spaces—the smaller ones being retreats for quiet study—gives us one of the two chief contributions of the building. The other is in the lighting, both natural and artificial. The most direct source of illumination pours from a series of boxed ceiling skylights—"earth-sky relatedness"—ringed with artificial light (to maintain the same direction), one of the skylights poking two stories deep into the small chapel. The second source of illumination rises from a peripheral band or collar of horizontal "windows," through which reflected light arrives. This is made possible by cantilevering the aluminum panel walls beyond their structural frame, and glazing the gap at the bottom between panel and wall. At night, the reverse obtains, and bright bands of inner light pour over the exterior. This imaginative use of aluminum (all walls are of this material on a concrete base) rightly earned for the architect the coveted R. S. Reynolds Memorial Award in 1967. All the trees on the site were scrupulously preserved, thus it is questionable that the library did not open up more to its felicitous setting. The only intimation of the outside from within comes through its glass doors. See also the nearby Lincoln Commons (1960), by the same architect, and the earlier dormitories.

Open daily except major holidays

---

20   People's Federal Savings & Loan Association (1917–18)
SE corner of Ohio and Court Streets
Sidney, Ohio

LOUIS H. SULLIVAN, ARCHITECT

A jewel of a bank, one of the great Sullivan's last works. His familiar arch—which he first used to acclaim in his Transportation Building at the Chicago World's Fair of 1893—here graces the north-facing narrow end of the bank, with sculptured ornament of unbelievable intricacy greeting the customers. (Sullivan almost undoubtedly picked up this arch motif from Moroccan gates he saw in publications while a student at the Paris École des Beaux-Arts—cf. the Bab el-Khemis at Meknes.) This is a broadly decorated facade compared to Sullivan's earlier bank at Grinnell, Iowa (1914—q.v.), with its huge splash of concentrated ornament. At Sidney the strong cornice belting, poly-

chromed arch, gryphons, wiry lettering, and the low belt course which ties all together, produce an overall richness. The long side of the building—possibly Sullivan's finest wall and the bank's most coordinated feature—parades a line of opal-glass windows, elevated to throw natural light deep onto the banking floor. The details of the terra-cotta sculpture echo the delights of the facade.

The interior is austere, indeed a bit flat, compared to Sullivan's banks at Owatonna, Minnesota (1908—q.v.), and the one at Grinnell. However, he makes a compelling feature of the vault door (probably the first time this was done), setting its intriguing mechanism behind a glass wall. (Cf. Skidmore, Owings & Merrill's Manufacturers Hanover Bank in New York of 1953.) Sullivan also used indirect lighting (in the vases) and an early form of air conditioning. Both interior and exterior of the Sidney bank have been beautifully maintained. Sullivan himself considered it one of his finest buildings. This rebuffed idealist, the "father of modern architecture," died tragically a few years later (1924), without work, and largely without friends.

Open during business hours

The **Memorial Building** (1875), facing the bank, is reminiscent of the perfervid Philadelphia work of Frank Furness (see Index) but is chopped up on the ground floor by the Chamber of Commerce. The brave Union soldier in the niche of the pediment faces the fair female atop the Second Empire **Shelby County Court House** (1881) on the green opposite, G. Maetzel, architect (who designed several other courthouses in Ohio).

21 **First Congregational Church** (1822–25)
115 Tallmadge Circle
Tallmadge (Akron), Ohio

LEMUEL PORTER, ARCHITECT

Here, immediately northeast of Akron, is a complete Connecticut village green with a complete Connecticut Late Colonial village church. It is no accident, for this northeastern section of Ohio, from the Pennsylvania line to beyond Sandusky (two thirds across the state) and up to Lake Erie, was the famous Western Reserve—land "reserved" for settlers and soldiers from Connecticut when that state gave up (1800) its pretension to the whole Northwest. Moreover, Mr. Porter, the architect-builder, was born in Waterbury, Connecticut. There are numerous towns in the Reserve laid out in similar New England fash-

ion with Tallmadge at the Reserve's southern edge the most imposing. The town, with its eight radiating roads, was originally planned as a religious community, with the church at the intersection of the highways. It soon went secular.

The church itself, which measures 56.5 x 44.5 feet/17.1 x 13.5 meters, would be a capable but unremarkable example in the East, but here it illumines an architectural episode that reflects an important part of the state's heritage. The shallow portico, with four hand-carved, stretched, Ionic columns (of solid walnut), is highly competent, similar in form to several in Connecticut. The tower rises behind and in plane with the front edge of the columns, encountering a bit of difficulty higher up as its square form meets the octagonal open belfry. The heavy oak frame of the church, sitting on a stone foundation, is enclosed by white clapboarding, all materials coming from local quarries and forests. The former wood shingles on the roof were cut from a single chestnut tree. The interior has the "standard" plan with U-shaped balcony around three sides, here with a circular low domed ceiling that reaches to the side walls.

In 1849 the interior was "modernized" and ill-treated but in 1925 for the church's centennial, it was restored. In 1975—for its 150th anniversary—the building was put in pristine condition by the Ohio Historical Society. The Society had acquired the church in 1972, when the congregation built a new and larger house of worship, and it now operates the old.

Contact custodian to visit

---

22 Miami County Court House (1885–88)
West Main Street at South Plum
Troy, Ohio

JOSEPH WARREN YOST, ARCHITECT

Troy's courthouse proffers bifurcated whimsy of astounding ingenuity. The three-story building, whose four facades are similar in size and treatment, resembles in color and texture—and perchance even in architecture—a gigantic square of gingerbread. Atop this cavorts a cornucopia of white temples and domes of Classical and would-be Classical inspiration, the whole surmounted by a raised drum and central dome, topped by the statue of Justice. Nestled between four corner

domed "attics" peak four richly pedimented (and half-hidden) temples, their triangulations adorned with greenish copper figures, that on Main Street upholding five books of law. This marvelous building is only marred by horizontal metal awnings.

Open Mon., Wed., Fri., during office hours

Although a few county offices still occupy the Court House, most of the county administrative staff, including the Sheriff's Department and Jail, is now housed in a consciously quiet three-story **Safety Building** adjacent. It was designed (1972) by Hart-Ruetschle-Hart, with John F. Ruetschle partner-in-charge.

---

23 Van Wert County Court House (1874–76)
121 East Main Street
Van Wert, Ohio

THOMAS J. TOLAN & SON, ARCHITECTS

The lofty, projected symmetry of the Van Wert facade was unusual at a time when most courthouses in the Ohio and Indiana area consisted of spread-out bulks crowned with a central, and often near-invisible,

tower. However, Thomas Tolan and son Brentwood boldly made their rich tower the entrance itself, and echoed its form and elements in the flanking corner pavilions. Several other Ohio courthouses of the late 1860s and the 1870s have central projected entries, but this Second Empire example stands out because of its tripartite composition and scale buildup, plus its overall cohesion. Though the results are obviously Main Street-oriented, with the lengthy office section behind backed up against the facade, overall the building establishes a firm and colorful presence. The proliferation of white limestone quoins and framings of the openings gives vertical contrast to the white horizontal basement and to the white mid-building banding, with both shining against the red brick of the walls and the gray tiles of the Mansard roof. The interior, refurbished in 1970, is of secondary interest. Fortunately the building is highly regarded locally and is well maintained. Understandably, both Thomas and Brentwood Tolan were the architects for a number of Ohio and Indiana courthouses.

Open during office hours

24   Zoar Village State Memorial (early 19th century)
on OH 212, SE of Fort Laurens
Zoar, Ohio

Zoar, like Old Economy and Ephrata in Pennsylvania (q.v.), was settled early in the last century (1817–18) by a German religious sect
known as the Society of Separatists of Zoar. Its organization was based
on communal life and property and, for eight years—1822–30—
celibacy, primarily to free women for fieldwork. By 1835 this perpetu-
ally at work community of some five hundred souls was self-supporting
in most necessities. In that year it built the Number One House, otherwise (and erroneously) known as the King's Palace, for the aged
though used by others as well. It is now a well-furnished museum. Toward the end of the century (1898) the community was dissolved because of bickering, out-of-date farming and industrial methods, and a
too-restrictive life for the young. It was made a State Memorial in

1933 and a restoration program was inaugurated by the Ohio Historical Society in 1966.

Though no architecture of distinction will be found—most of the early individual houses being log-based—the folklorist and ethnic historian will get an insight into an early period of the state. Note, too, the restored half-timber Tinsmith's Shop: straight out of the Black Forest whence emigrated the early Zoarites. The unusual geometry of the garden, one of the most interesting features at Zoar, represents the New Jerusalem, its design inspired by the Book of Revelation, 21st chapter: "It had a great, high wall, with twelve angels, and on the gates the names of the twelve tribes of Israel were inscribed; on the east three gates, on the north three gates, on the south three gates, and on the west three gates." A tall Norway spruce near the center stands for the "tree of life" with twelve junipers in a circle about it, the space between representing heaven. "Twelve straight and narrow paths" lead from "heaven" to the world about.

Open Apr.–Oct., Wed.–Sun. 9–5, except holidays: admission

South Carolina

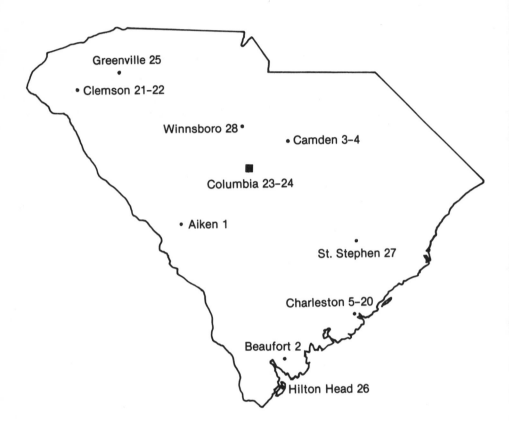

Greenville 25

• Clemson 21-22

Winnsboro 28 •

• Camden 3-4

Columbia 23-24

• Aiken 1

St. Stephen 27

Charleston 5-20

Beaufort 2

Hilton Head 26

SOUTH CAROLINA

The buildings in boldface type are of general interest. The others are for the specialist.

Aiken

1 Owens-Corning Fiberglas Plant (1960)— The Bechtel Corp.

Beaufort

2 Bay Street Houses (mostly 19th century)

Camden

3 "Historic Camden" (18th–19th century)

4 **Bethesda Presbyterian Church** (1820–22)— Robert Mills

De Kalb Monument (1825)—Robert Mills

Charleston

5 St. James Episcopal Church (c. 1713–19) at Goose Creek

6 **Drayton Hall** (1738–42)

7 **Boone Hall Plantation** (18th century/ 1843/1935)

8 **St. Michael's Church** (1752–61)—Samuel Cardy

9 Heyward-Washington House (c. 1770)

10 City Hall (1800–1)—Gabriel Manigault

11 **Joseph Manigault House** (c. 1803)— Gabriel Manigault

12 **Nathaniel Russell House** (1808–9)

13 **The Fireproof Building** (1822–26)—Robert Mills

Hibernian Hall (1839–40)—Thomas U. Walter

14 **The Urban Scene and "The Charleston House"** (late 18th/early 19th century)

15 Edmondston-Alston House (1828–29/ 1838–39)

16 **Middleton Place House and Gardens** (1741–   ) **and Magnolia Gardens** (1830–1850s)

Cypress Gardens (1920s)

17 Main Building, College of Charleston
(1828–29/portico and wings 1850–51)
—William Strickland; Edward B. White
18 **St. Philip's Church** (1835–38/1848–50)
19 **Market Hall** (1840–41)—Edward B.
White
20 **Charles Towne Landing Exposition Park**
(1970)—Harlan McClure; Synergetics Inc.

Clemson

21 Hanover House (1714–16)
22 **Keowee Toxaway Visitors' Center** (1969–
78)—Freeman, Wells & Major

Columbia

23 **Robert Mills Historic House and Park**
(1823–25)—Robert Mills
Hampton-Preston House (1818)
24 **U. S. Post Office** (1964–66)—Lyles,
Bissett, Carlisle & Wolff

Greenville

25 Textile Hall (1964–66/1969/1977)—
J. E. Sirrine & Co.

Hilton Head

26 **Sea Pines Plantation** (1959–   )—Sasaki
Associates

St. Stephen

27 St. Stephen's Episcopal Church (1767–
69)

Winnsboro

28 **Fairfield District Court House**
(1822/1844/1939)

1   Owens-Corning Fiberglas Plant (1960)
on SC 215, 3 miles/4.8 kilometers E of town
Aiken, South Carolina

THE BECHTEL CORP., ENGINEERS

Form was largely dictated in the design of this Fiberglas yarn installation, but color was optional and the options were well picked up.
The first element of the plant is the white 150-foot/46-meter-tall
"batch" house, which receives the dry bulk raw materials by rail. Via
electronic monitoring, it then dispatches these in aerial "feeders" to the
parallel lineup of furnaces where the strands are produced. These enormous furnace units are of light blue aluminum, topped by full-length,
clamshell ventilators, a vivid salmon in color. A one-story manufacturing facility processes the fibers which arrive from the furnace. Very
effective, even from the road.

*Not open to the public but can readily be seen from either US 78
or SC 215*

2 Bay Street Houses (mostly 19th century)
Bay Street
Beaufort, South Carolina

Bay Street has a well-bred lineup of properly fenced and verandaed
homes, primarily from the nineteenth century. Though most of them
are private they well merit a stroll. Generally clapboarded, with vague
Federal and/or Greek Revival overtones, and raised above dampness
by a brick basement, they all enjoy a view of the nearby Broad River.
The oldest visitable by the public is the **John Mark Verdier House**
(1795–1800), 801 Bay Street. (Open Wed.–Sat. 11–3, except holidays: donation.) The dating of the house is uncertain, the National
Register giving c. 1790. Recently fully restored and with good Adamesque interiors, it is owned by the Historic Beaufort Foundation
which bought the dwelling from the Beaufort Museum in 1968. The
most imposing building is the **George Parsons Elliott House** (c. 1840)
at 1001 Bay Street at Charles (open Mon.–Fri. 10–3, except holidays:

admission), a three-story mansion of considerable richness within, especially in its plasterwork. It was saved in the Civil War by being commandeered as a Union hospital, then saved again in 1965—and beautifully restored and furnished—by the Bank of Beaufort. In 1975 the house (formerly known as the Holmes-Hall House from its post-Reconstruction owners) was transferred to the Beaufort Preservation Society. None of the architects are known.

Open as indicated

---

3 **"Historic Camden"** (18th–19th century)
   South Broad Street (US 521), c. 1 mile/1.6 kilometers S of
   Camden, South Carolina

Camden, founded in 1733, is one of the state's most ancient towns. It seeks to re-create via "Historic Camden" part of the village which

stood on this site shortly after Revolutionary times. The beginnings thus far are modest but they include the **Cunningham House** (c. 1835), at one point enlarged from two to four rooms, and now serving as tour headquarters; the white clapboarded **Craven House** of around 1789—good interiors; and two more simple structures, the **Bradley Log House** (c. 1800)—note chimney—and the **Drakeford Log House** (c. 1812). It is hoped to enlarge the restoration substantially but even in this initial phase, which was dedicated in 1970, it gives a good idea of the simple Piedmont houses of almost two hundred years ago. It should be added that all buildings are original structures restored to their former pristine conditions.

Open June–Labor Day, Tues.–Sat. 10–6, Sun. 1–6; rest of year Tues.–Fri. 10–4, Sat. 10–5, Sun. 1–5, except holidays: admission

---

4   Bethesda Presbyterian Church (1820–22)
502 De Kalb Street (US 1)
Camden, South Carolina

ROBERT MILLS, ARCHITECT

One of the most delightful small Greek Revival churches in the country. Sitting back on its green lawn from the main street in Camden—the church faces directly on US 1—it is doubtful that one will encounter a finer religious building on that thoroughfare from Madawaska, Maine, to Key West, Florida. The church, one of the earliest examples of the Greek Revival in the state, is curiously double-ended, with an excellent four-column Tuscan portico facing the avenue, and a three-column (solid on axis!) portico at rear, now the main entry. (Mills himself made no mention of a rear portico, and its design makes it unlikely that he had anything to do with it.) The avenue facade is distinguished by a large, arched, framed recess, stuccoed and painted white, with two roundheaded, shuttered doors (rarely used) on either side. Originally this recess was of plain brick with a white arch over its top and over the two doors. A small rectangular plaque, also white (again, originally of plain brick), is placed above each door, and is repeated atop the five windows along the sides. The entrance end is unusually complicated by twin flights of external stairs which meet and then double back as they rise to the gallery above, with the two main

doors placed under their landings. Six doors in one small church seem
redundant, but the two at front were probably primarily for ventilation.
The church is topped off by what Mills termed "a neat" spire.

The interior, which was restored in 1937, is white, chaste, and a little dry, and, as Mr. Mills wrote, "is so arranged that the floor and
pews rise as they recede from the pulpit, giving every advantage to the
audience in seeing and hearing." Mills also added, "it is far easier to
harm, than to benefit church architecture in the making over" (H. M.
Pierce Gallagher, *Robert Mills,* Columbia University Press, 1935).
The chancel wall is marked by repetition of the framed recess seen on
the facade and by the recesses of the two flanking doors. The central,
raised pulpit is reached by twin flights of curved stairs. The five windows on either side carry out the round-head motif seen in front.

Note, also, the **Monument** to De Kalb (1825) on the avenue front
of the church which Mills also designed. (General Johann De Kalb, a
German-born hero of the American Revolution, was killed [1780] in
the Battle of Camden.)

Open daily

5 St. James Episcopal Church (c. 1713–19)
  **c. 15 miles/24 kilometers N of Charleston via US 52 or 78; just
  N of branching of 52 and 78 turn E .6 mile/1 kilometer on
  Polaris Facility Road, then .4 mile/.6 kilometer S at 1st fork
  near Charleston (Goose Creek, Berkeley County), South Carolina**

Difficult to find, this venerable church in a primitive country setting is
well worth the expedition. With its pink stuccoed brick walls, white
quoins and woodwork, and jerkin-head roof the exterior is highly unusual among early (or even late) Colonial churches. (It should be mentioned that 1708 and 1711 have also been given as dates for its construction.) Note the elaborate, large-scaled door with pelican in the
pediment nourishing her young with blood from her breast in the fashion approved by the Society for the Propagation of the Gospel (whose
emblem it is). The interior is dominated by an extraordinarily elaborate chancel, its sanctuary wall, or reredos, being vigorously, even
baroquely, molded in stucco and brightly painted. The pulpit with its
freestanding axial position and prominent sounding board almost
speaks by itself. (Note the hatchment of the Izard family above.) The

pulpit totally eclipses the altar. The entry end of the church, in contrast, is naively simple.

Many of the early settlers in Charleston and its environs were Englishmen from the Bahamas and Barbados, while the "Goose Creek Men" were, supposedly, largely Barbadians, with some Huguenots. There is, thus, in this pastel-colored, stuccoed masonry church a touch of West Indies background. The church lapsed into disuse for much of the nineteenth century—it was spared destruction in the Revolution because the coat of arms of George I was still behind the pulpit. The earthquake of 1886 caused grave damage. Makeshift repairs were made from time to time, but not until 1955–60 was a complete restoration and a strengthening of the foundations carried out. It was repainted in 1973. St. James was founded and built by Francis LeJau (1665–1717), a Huguenot who fled his native France to safety in England where he became eventually a Canon of St. Paul's Cathedral in London. He was sent to South Carolina by the Society for the Propagation of the Gospel in large part "to cater to the desire of the French population." He lies buried near the altar.

See adjacent caretaker to visit: donation

---

6   **Drayton Hall** (1738–42)
9 miles/14 kilometers W of city on SC 61
near Charleston, South Carolina

Drayton Hall, according to the late Henry Francis du Pont, founder of the Winterthur Museum, is "the greatest house in America." Of the three superb Ashley River plantations it alone is standing. It is moreover unbelievably unchanged from the day it was built except for the disappearance of its two dependencies or flankers, which were built fifteen years after the main house. (The houses of nearby Magnolia Gardens and Middleton Place were barbarically burned by federal troops.) No plumbing will be found within Drayton's rooms, no electric wires chase through its walls. Even the paint in the Great Hall is only the third coat. Saved from destruction in the War Between the States by being used as a smallpox hospital, this glorious relic of another era is now safely under the protection of the National Trust for Historic Preservation.

Designed roughly at the same time as the great James River houses (and a century before the Louisiana and Mississippi plantations),

Drayton, even more than its Virginia peers, draws heavily on the precepts, as interpreted by British architects, of Andrea Palladio. This can be seen in its basic layout of main dwelling and dependencies, the latter, as mentioned, long vanished, and in its strictly canonical architectural treatment. (One dependency was destroyed in the earthquake of 1886 and the other in the hurricane of 1893.) The twin stairs on the land (now main approach) side, somewhat awkwardly flanking a door to the raised basement, lead up to a handsome, semi-inset, double-decked porch with stone columns, Tuscan below, Ionic above. The whole is topped by a trim pediment that breaks from the entablature. As Professor Frederick D. Nichols points out, this portico—the first two-story one in the South (possibly the Colonies)—is almost precise from Palladio's Villa Pisani of 1555 (*Antiques,* April 1970). The river front has no porch but is flush with its continuous, straight-line cornice enlivened by a pediment (perching a bit nervously on the eave), whose angles are echoed by two of the three central windows (one is arched) and the virile door framing. Divided stairs with wrought-iron balustrade escort one to the ground. Both facades are organized into 10-foot/3-meter bays, the land-side porch filling three with two bays on either side for a two-three-two rhythm. The house measures 70 feet/21 meters across and is 52 feet/16 meters deep. The Mansard roof has a delicate break in angle (called a bellcast)—which lends lightness to the mansion's profile—topped by a narrow vertical rise and a lower (nearly invisible) hip with substantial chimneys on either side. Behind the entries are the Great Hall in front and the Stair Hall on river side, each superbly paneled. *Antiques* magazine (the aforementioned issue of April 1970) calls the latter "the finest in America." The dining room opens off the Great Hall with boxed stair to the kitchen (post-1893 hurricane) in the basement. All rooms in the house are fully paneled with very rich fireplaces, in general taken from handbooks. (The mantel in the first-floor drawing room, which had been added around 1800, was stolen in 1972.) The mansion had been slightly vandalized but is now undergoing complete restoration. Fortunately Drayton Hall was acquired by the National Trust for Historic Preservation (1974) and opened to the public in 1978.

Open daily, tours 10–3, except major holidays: admission

---

7   Boone Hall Plantation (18th century/1843/1935)
   **c. 6 miles/10 kilometers NE of Charleston, N off US 17/701 on
      Long Point Road**
   near Charleston (Mount Pleasant), South Carolina

The unforgettable aspect of this still working, 738-acre/298-hectare plantation is the .75-mile/1.2-kilometer avenue of live oaks smothered with Spanish moss that leads to the mansion. This allée ranks high among the "streets" of this country, epitomizing the approach to a Deep South plantation, and constituting a monument to its owners, who could scarcely have grasped what magnificence over a century of maturation would bring. While the plantation itself dates from the end of the seventeenth century—the grant to Major John Boone is dated 1681—the present owner's attribution of 1743 as the date of the allée is questioned by experts. Samuel Gaillard Stoney's *Plantations of the Carolina Low Country,* Carolina Art Association, 1964, states that the Horlbeck family, which had purchased Boone Hall in 1817, "set out the avenue to the house and marked it with a marble slab stating it was planted in 1843."

Alongside the oak avenue are the remains (also probably early to mid-nineteenth century) of a line of nine slave houses of an original twenty-seven. The mansion itself was completely rebuilt in 1935. Only its lower floors are open to the public. The nearby cotton-processing buildings and dock have been restored and are now used as a gift shop and snack bar.

Open Mon.–Sat. 9–5, Sun. 1–5, except holidays: admission

---

8 St. Michael's Church (1752–61)
80 Meeting Street at Broad
Charleston, South Carolina

SAMUEL CARDY, PROBABLE ARCHITECT

St. Michael's and its neighbor St. Philip's (q.v.), and Philadelphia's Christ Church (q.v.), are three of the Colonies' great churches of the mid-eighteenth century. All three derive from English prototypes with inspiration primarily from the architecture of Christopher Wren and James Gibbs. The tower of the steeple of St. Michael's rises in line with the entry wall of the church à la Gibbs—as opposed to Wren who "attached" towers outside the fabric. The design of the lovely, much-copied, triple-stage, octagonal steeple on square base certainly hints of Wren's St. Bride, Fleet Street, London (1680), whose slender 227-foot/69-meter-high steeple has four octagonal stages on a square tower. However, the designer of the well-knit St. Michael's is not posi-

tively known, though the church feels that "Samuel Cardy is the likeliest candidate for architect." This conclusion is further seconded by Mr. Gene Waddell, director of the South Carolina Historical Society. Cardy is also mentioned by HABS (Historic American Buildings Survey) as probably being responsible for the design, while almost all agree that Cardy undertook construction and supervision of the church. The attribution by some to Peter Harrison of Rhode Island is thus very insubstantial.)

St. Michael's is rightly admired for its monumental Roman Doric portico (the present one being rebuilt after the earthquake of 1886), and this was long considered the first of its great size to grace any church in the Colonies. (The first English church with a freestanding portico with giant columns was probably London's St. George's, Hanover Square, 1712–24, by John James.) However the argument can be well advanced—and it is thought sustained—that the triple porticos at the west end of the nearby St. Philip's built in 1723, though destroyed by fire in 1835, were almost exactly rebuilt (except for degree of projection) in 1835–38, making them the first by almost thirty years. As St. Michael's former historiographer put it, "It is clear that the architect for St. Michael's intended to copy St. Philip's in the way of porticoes and out-do St. Philip's in the way of the tower." (Which he certainly did.) The columns and walls of St. Michael's are of brick stuccoed and painted white, with the tower rising, as mentioned, flush with the front wall, directly behind the portico. (The steeple's high arcade level offers a fine panorama of the city.)

The interior—changed only a bit through the years (1772, 1905)—is daringly trussed from wall to wall, there being no intermediate supports. (The interior of Nicholas Hawksmoor's St. Alfege, Greenwich, England, 1712–14, has been mentioned as inspiration and is similarly spanned.) The nave, which measures 70 feet/21 meters long by 51 feet/16 meters wide, tends to be restless, contrasting the white plaster of ceiling and walls with the heavy cedar of the galleries which encroach upon the nave with their low broadness upheld by one-story supporting columns. Highlighting the insistence of this dark wood in the nave is the freestanding, octagonal pulpit, the massive cap of which rises above the gallery on the side. Backing this up stands the chancel, renovated and restenciled in 1905, and resplendent in almost Byzantine glory. The Victorian glass of the Palladian chancel window (1893), like that on the side aisle, is anachronistic to the eighteenth-century spirit of the church. (Such glass gives the same infelicitous effect in several Greek Revival churches and a Greek Revival synagogue also in Charleston.) The organ, some pipes of which are original, stands in the case initially made for it in 1768 by Johann Snetzler and imported from London. The eight bells in the steeple were also from London (1764), sent back there during the Revolution, returned, then sent to London to be recast following their smashing during the Civil War. Be sure to see the cemetery adjacent with delicate wrought-iron gate (1838) by J. A. W. Justi.

Open Mon.–Fri. 9–5, Sat.–Sun. 9–12, except holidays

---

9   Heyward-Washington House (c. 1770)
87 Church Street
Charleston, South Carolina

The typical Charleston "double house" has a central hall with only two rooms per side. Thus each room is on a corner for maximum ventilation with the hall acting as a form of wind tunnel. The Heyward House (Washington, of course, slept there) gives us an excellent example of this functional planning with a facade which suggests a hint of Philadelphia as well as of Charleston. In 1929 it was purchased by the

Charleston Museum and after complete restoration—it had been used as a bakery in previous years—and then complete and elegant refurnishing, opened to the public. Note the bold use of color, which was traced to the original paint and the rich furniture, most of which had been locally made. The Holmes bookcase by Thomas Elfe is one of the masterpieces of Charleston as well as of American furniture. The garden at the rear should also be seen.

Open daily 10–5, except holidays: admission

10 City Hall (1800–1)
80 Broad Street at Meeting Street
Charleston, South Carolina

GABRIEL MANIGAULT, ARCHITECT

Built in 1801 as The First Bank of the United States, then in 1818 changed to the City Hall, the building now serves for offices and on the second floor houses an excellent portrait gallery (in the City Council

Chamber). The building has undergone several ups and downs. It is thought by some historians that the exterior was originally livelier, with a play of bright pilasters against red brick walls, walls which were later covered with stucco. The interior, too, has suffered because of a change of function. It is to be hoped that it will be restored to its Federalist integrity and beauty.

Open Mon.–Fri. 9–5, except holidays

11   Joseph Manigault House (c. 1803)
350 Meeting Street at Ashmead Place
Charleston, South Carolina

GABRIEL MANIGAULT, ARCHITECT

At the beginning of the nineteenth century Joseph Manigault was one of Charleston's wealthiest men, and his brother Gabriel (1758–1809)—a rice planter and politician by profession—was the city's "best-known amateur architect." This house which he designed was

built in an area then known as Wraggsboro on a lot given Joseph by the family of the brothers' mother, Elizabeth Wragg. An unusual feature is the pedimented circular gatehouse (porticoed on inner side), the edge of which shows at left in the photograph. The two-story porch across much of the facade was incorrectly restored. Gene Waddell, Director of the South Carolina Historical Society, writes that "An early sketch has since turned up, and it shows that the original porch had six columns with irregular spacing."

It is the interior, however, which shows the greatest architectural achievement. The wide entrance hall finds a climax in the graceful cantilevered circular stair which fills the far end, abetted by a sparkling chandelier. Gabriel Manigault became interested in architecture while studying law in London, and apparently the then newly fashionable Adam Style impressed him. Though it is dubious that he introduced the style to Charleston, Adam delicacy can be seen throughout all major rooms, the dining room being exceptionally fine. Note the elaborate cornices, arches, doorways, mantels, and fireplaces.

The dating of 1790, sometimes used for the house, has been found to be incorrect. Charleston—and the rest of us—are fortunate that the dwelling still stands, for it had been abused for years (boarding house etc.), and until 1935 a filling station occupied one corner of the lot (which corner the Standard Oil Company of New Jersey gave to the rehabilitation).

The house was restored (1942) by the late Albert Simons, FAIA, and although few of the present furnishings belonged to Mr. Manigault, all are of the early nineteenth century. Since 1933 the house has been owned and operated by the Charleston Museum. It was designated a National Historic Landmark in 1974.

Open daily 10–5, except holidays; last tour 4:30: admission

---

12 Nathaniel Russell House (1808–9)
51 Meeting Street
Charleston, South Carolina

High among the elegant town houses of the United States stands the Russell mansion in Charleston. Outside and particularly within, the house exults in style. Set in a tree-girt lot with garden about it, the building enjoys more space than most along the historic streets of its area. Its narrow end faces the road, and this facade is marked by an

energetic play of verticals and horizontals. The three very tall windows
of the second (i.e. main) floor are set in recessed red-brick arches with
white keystones; the thinness of these windows, their tight recessed
framing, and the keystones all emphasize verticality. Then prominent
white lintels atop the windows and a narrow white stringcourse set up
a horizontal motion aided by a subtle double-brick stringcourse above.
Finally, the three topmost windows push upward only to be countered
by the almost heavy horizontality of the parapet across the top. A light
wrought-iron balcony, which breaks out in a semicircle before each of
the second-story windows, pirouettes across the front (note Russell's
initials in the center one). At left projects an angled, four-sided bay,
also with balcony. The plan reflects the Charleston "single house" (i.e.
one room deep).

On entering one is swept, almost before realizing it, to the floor
above by a "flying" stair of mahogany that coils upward to the third
floor without touching a wall: a rare technical and esthetic achievement. The rooms on the second floor—where the main living areas
were placed to catch more breeze and light, and to avoid the damp and
mosquitoes—are radiant with a flood of daylight from windows that
virtually touch the floor, the half-circle balconies outside enabling
them to be opened safely. Many elements reflect the New England
(Rhode Island) background of Mr. Russell. Originally, it should be

pointed out, the large windows had external shutters. The atmosphere of space and light is magnificent, as can be seen especially in the ovoid drawing room, or music room, opposite the ovoid stairway. The use of ovals for room shapes is very Adamesque, while the lavish decoration epitomizes the Adam-inspired Federal Style then coming into fashion. From fireplaces to doors to cornices both design and workmanship are exemplary. Used among other causes as a boarding school, then a convent school at the end of the last century, and again as a home for many years, the house was purchased (1955) by the Historic Charleston Foundation, aided by many friends, as its headquarters. Upon being sumptuously restored, it was opened to the public the following year. Although the architect is not known, the house numbers among the very great.

Open Mon.–Sat. 10–5, Sun. 2–5, except Dec. 25: admission

---

13 The Fireproof Building (1822–26)
100 Meeting Street at Chalmers
Charleston, South Carolina

ROBERT MILLS, ARCHITECT

The advantage of having so much timber at times proved to be an architectural liability to the American colonists, certainly in crowded cities, where the threat of fire was high. Most large communities, even as early as the late seventeenth century, outlawed any but stone or brick construction in town, at least for the outside walls. However, it took more than 150 years after earlier troubles with fires to construct the country's first structure for the fireproof storage of records, Charleston's County Record Building. Though it has been nicknamed the Fireproof Building since the time of its construction, Mills himself always referred to it as the Fireproof Office. Mills also convinced the city to surround the building with a small park to act as a firebreak as well as add more light and air.

As the structure had to accommodate a number of state agencies, easy inner circulation was necessary. The nearly square plan was therefore divided into three banks of barrel- and groin-vaulted, squarish rooms separated by two barrel-vaulted longitudinal corridors. A skylit stairhall illuminated the middle, while the hall also served to stimulate a flow of air from bottom through skylight. Even the original casement

windows and shutters were made of iron. The reason that only two of
the three floors are fireproof is that the top floor was initially rented
out for private offices, later to be used for personnel but not for the
storage of important official records. The upper walls are of masonry
but roofed with a wood truss. Actually only four of the rooms are *totally* fireproof (and without fireplace), the two end ones in the center
bank of the lower floors. The others, however, lag not far behind in in-
cendiary security.

The Fireproof Building is the most noted, still standing structure
which Mills designed for his native town even though what we now see
was watered down from his original design which had clean-cut pediments over its two Doric porticos (one at each end, as Mills was
wont), instead of the awkward parapet which now tops the building;
fluted columns instead of dull stuccoed ones; and graceful curved twin
stairs. (The stairs were replaced after the famous 1886 earthquake—
when part of the pediment also fell off—but these apparently were the
only damages the building suffered.) Moreover some of the changes
might well have been carried out by John George Spidle, a local
Charleston architect who was hired to supervise construction when
Mills was away. Though good, the building is not an esthetic triumph
—due to its straying from Mills' drawings—but it is very definitely a
technical triumph. It now houses the South Carolina Historical Society.

Mills, who, as mentioned, was born in Charleston (1781), and early educated there, was one of the country's first native-born, adequately trained architects, with Hoban, Jefferson, and Latrobe all helping his education. He was also an accomplished engineer, climaxing his career with the Washington Monument in the nation's capital—q.v.

Open during business hours

Though closed to the public, take a look at the gate and exterior of **Hibernian Hall** (1839–40) across Meeting Street (105): designed by Thomas U. Walter. It is a fine example of Ionic Greek Revival.

---

14   The Urban Scene and "The Charleston House" (late 18th/ early 19th century)
S of Broad Street between Ashley and Cooper Rivers
Charleston, South Carolina

On Charleston's triangle of land formed by the meeting of the Ashley and Cooper rivers stretches an unparalleled regional response to urban living. Meandering down Church Street, Legare (pronounced la-GREE), Tradd, or Meeting—to name only a few—the visitor, especially on foot, will encounter urban felicity of the highest order. Moreover this patrician region has not been spoiled by commercial development or exploitation. Then too, the Civil War left most of the once comfortably-off citizens financially prostrate so that they could not afford late-nineteenth-century architectural excursions.

Since 1931 this twenty-block, 144-acre/58-hectare delight has been "protected" by a city ordinance, and in 1966 the entire area was declared a Registered National Historic District. (A Society for the Preservation of Old Dwellings had been founded in 1920.) By 1966 the boundaries incorporated 412 acres/166 hectares, and in 1975 this was increased by 377 acres/152 hectares. While preservation zoning is practiced today by over a hundred cities, the 1931 Charleston action was the first of its kind. (The first legal historic zoning was that of the Vieux Carré—q.v.—in New Orleans.) It should be added that in the area south of Broad Street relatively little restoration has been necessary: most of the houses are basically as they stood 150–200 years ago even if they lacked paint; they were not rehabilitated as was much of Savannah nor rebuilt as, for instance, was most of Williamsburg.

Broad Street itself serves as the northerly edge of the domestic Historic District, in addition to being the financial and commercial spine

of the city. (Though the Ansonborough area and Harleston Village lie to the north of Broad—and both are very fine—these are largely rehabilitated sections of the city. As mentioned the area south of Broad Street has been largely untouched for well over a century.) Because of this street's own considerable values, the Broad Street Beautification Committee was organized by its tenants and owners, and working with the Historic Charleston Foundation, commenced (1968) an ongoing volunteer upgrading project according to a master plan. Many buildings have been refurbished, unsightly signs removed, utility wires taken down, and trees planted.

The houses in Charleston form a unique solution to sun and rain, dampness and heat—and occasional floods, hurricanes, and earthquakes. Though surprisingly packed together each manages a private garden, generally in the back. This clustering possibly stems from similar "town house" groupings frequently found in the Caribbean, especially Barbados, with which early Charleston was very familiar. Before the Revolution many English settlers, including the Middletons (1678) and Draytons, came to the Carolinas from this semitropical part of the world, and after it a number of Royalists went back. Another factor leading to urban tightness was that the city had walled fortifications until the early 1700s, and in the East Bay commercial sections many people lived over stores until around 1800. The most intriguing—and the most functional—of the Charleston houses is the so-called "single house" which is a single room wide for greater ventilation. The rooms extend onto double-deck porches which measure about 10 feet/3 meters wide, forming piazzas for open-air living. In general they grace the south or westerly sides and were often added to older dwellings. Galleries in various forms are, of course, not unknown in Europe. However, the eagle-eyed, peripatetic Carl Feiss, who knows most of the Western Hemisphere and every street in Charleston, writes (in a personal letter) that "I know of no prototype anywhere in Europe or Latin America (for the verandaed 'single' house). So I suggest without a qualm that it is a Charleston invention. Why not? And curiously enough Savannah architects and builders were so jealous of Charleston that stupidly they refused to be influenced as also did the rest of the American South." The West Indies domestic influence mentioned above was logically echoed in Charleston, where ground, insect, and flood conditions are largely similar. This led to the use of masonry for the lower floor even if the upper two are of wood. Generally this base was stuccoed for greater protection against ground moisture.

Almost all of the lots in this "peninsula" area of the city are fenced, many handsomely (note the ironwork on their gates). Most houses have their narrow end to the street, and the typical front door, often of distinguished design, somewhat startlingly opens onto the non-enclosed piazza and not the front hall. In back of the houses are (or were) the outbuildings containing kitchens, in many cases, plus erstwhile stables and servants' quarters. Gardens for both flowers and vegetables fill much of the remaining open space and the city is famous for them. *Quaint Old Charleston* (Legerton & Co., 1965) mentions that "Two of our best known flowers are named after Charleston people. The gardenia was named by Linnaeus after Dr. Alex Garden, and the poinsettia was named after Dr. Joel Poinsett, who introduced the flower from Mexico."

It is gratifying to note that an enlightened group of citizens and politicians is determined that "historic" Charleston will not be allowed to become commercialized. The Preservation Society of Charleston, the "Charleston Ordinance" of 1931, the work of the Historic Charleston Foundation in buying up old houses, renovating them, and reselling them with controls, all of this is inspiring, and inevitably involves dedicated work. Only recently were the above groups able to block an Interstate which the highway engineers wanted to run through a key historic area.

Above the "peninsula" area lies the Ansonborough Development (Hasell, Meeting, George, Laurens, and East Bay streets), which was sponsored by the Historic Charleston Foundation. This was one of the first neighborhood preservation-restoration projects in the country. Since 1958 over 120 houses, mostly from the mid-nineteenth century, have been rehabilitated. This work continues. The 1974 Inventory and Historic Preservation Plan for the city was in large part the work of the aforementioned Carl Feiss, the noted architect and planner, who has been a consultant to the city since 1965.

With the exception of several "museum houses" described in the text, all homes in the historic peninsula of Charleston are closed to the public except during spring and fall tours. They can, however, be seen from the street. For tours in March and April contact Historic Charleston Foundation, 51 Meeting Street, telephone (803) 723-1623; for tours in October contact The Preservation Society of Charleston, 147 King Street, telephone (803) 722-4630

15   Edmondston-Alston House (1828–29/1838–39)
21 East Battery
Charleston, South Carolina

Many Charleston houses are self-effacing on the exterior while often
opulent within. It is also true that most of them are surprisingly closely
packed along the city's delightful streets. The Edmondston-Alston
House breaks out of these conventions. Though it occupies a narrow
site it enjoys a sparkling sweep of Charleston harbor and distant Fort
Sumter, and its self-assured, almost regal, and regional, exterior is
matched by its internal appointments. The three-story stucco-on-brick
house was built by Charles Edmondston with low-pitched roof and
with porches or piazzas on the first and second floors along the southern side. In 1838 Colonel William Alston purchased the dwelling for

his son, Charles, who then added the third-floor piazza and the balustrade around the top, with the family coat of arms decorating the center of this parapet. In all probability the cast-iron balcony in front of the tall second (main) floor windows replaces one of wrought iron which fell and was destroyed in the earthquake of 1886. The interior with elaborate and often inventive woodwork (all original) has been described by the authoritative Albert Simons as "between the Adam and Greek revival" stylistically. The furnishings give full documentation of almost a century's occupation (until 1920) by the Alston family. Part of the dwelling was opened as a museum house in 1973; the owners occupy the third floor, which remains private. One of the rare Charleston-bred houses open to the public and one with a more than rewarding view.

Open Mon.–Sat. 10–5, Sun. 2–5, except Dec. 25: admission

16 Middleton Place House and Gardens (1741–   )
Magnolia Gardens (1830–1850s)
E off SC 61, NW of Charleston (Magnolia is about 12 miles/ 19 kilometers from downtown, Middleton 3.5 miles/5.6 kilometers farther along)
near Charleston, South Carolina

These two gardens off the same road northwest of Charleston are, in season, among the greatest to be seen. Even in late summer, Middleton will stir the soul, but from February to April, when first the camellias and then the azaleas are in bloom, both of these plantations will leave the beholder stunned by nature's poetry with plants, trees, lawns, and waters.

Middleton was begun in 1741, and thus forms the country's oldest landscaped gardens still in existence. Its 65 acres/26 hectares were formally organized, more so than at Magnolia, with enormous parterres stepping down to the Ashley River. Several pools are appropriately situated, with the Reflection Pool measuring 664 feet/202 meters long. The whole is carefully related to the mansion. Reputedly it took one hundred men ten years to lay it out.

Unfortunately the main house and the north flanker were destroyed (1865) during the War Between the States, only the battered south wing remaining. The repair of this "Gentlemen's Guest Wing" was

carried out in 1870, adorned with what Hugh Morrison termed "anachronistic Flemish gables" (*Early American Architecture,* Oxford University Press, 1952). The ends indeed resemble the Jacobean influence evident at Bacon's Castle (q.v.) in Virginia, built some two hundred years earlier. It is possible that the rehabilitation sought to recall "the old fashioned" main house, which was built before 1741, the rebuilding using an ancient drawing which has since disappeared. (The flankers were added around 1755.) In any case the exterior is puzzling for one dating from the last half of the nineteenth century. (King Street in Charleston has some Dutch-Jacobean gabled houses.) The interior, opened to the public in 1975, is well worth seeing, being furnished with many original Middleton furnishings. The well-stocked stableyards are nearby. The property is administered by the non-profit Middleton Place Foundation.

The gardens boast uncountable camellias—introduced to Middleton in 1783 by André Michaux, a French botanist: three of the four original plants are still alive. Azaleas and other flowers abound, while the enormous live oaks, veiled with Spanish moss, add a mysterious dream quality to the landscape. After years of almost total neglect the parterres and gardens were signally restored primarily through the efforts of the J. J. Pringle Smiths—Mr. Smith was a Middleton descendant—earlier in this century. The Garden Club of America, in celebrating the two hundredth anniversary of Middleton, called it "the most important garden in America." Lunch is served in the restaurant (open Feb.–Nov., daily 12–3).

Magnolia Gardens has an ancient horticultural history inasmuch as the first garden and house on the site were created in 1672. Both have long since vanished. Most of the present garden was laid out in the 1850s, part in 1830. As at Middleton, the house was wantonly destroyed during the War Between the States. The gardens have been brilliantly restored, and there are, among other flowers, some five hundred *varieties* of camellias. The layout is more romantic than Middleton, with a number of lakes, including several lined with bald cypress with their typical "knees"; their waters have been made almost black from the tannic acid of these roots. Altogether a dream, or as the literature proudly proclaims in quoting John Galsworthy, "the most beautiful garden in the world."

The *Taxodium distichum* buff will find at **Cypress Gardens** a satisfying quota (160 acres/65 hectares) of this wonderful tree, which is best seen by rowboat. The gardens, laid out in the 1920s and amplified by azaleas and other flowers, were generously given to the City of Charleston in 1963. Located approximately 24 miles/39 kilometers north of town, 4 miles/6.4 kilometers east off US 52, they are, however, only open Feb. 15–May 1, 8 A.M.–sunset: admission. The lake was originally used as a freshwater impoundment for cultivating rice.

Middleton House and Gardens open throughout year daily 9–5;

house open Mon.–Sat. 10–6, Sun. 2–6: admission; Magnolia
Gardens open only Feb. 15–May 1, daily 8:30–5:30: admission

---

17   Main Building, College of Charleston (1828–29/portico and wings
  1850–51)
  66 George Street at St. Philip Street
  Charleston, South Carolina

**WILLIAM STRICKLAND, ARCHITECT; ADDITIONS BY EDWARD B.
WHITE**

Strickland's Main Building (now completely rehabilitated and known
as Harrison Randolph Hall) was a simple, pedimented affair, transformed into an imposing late Classic Revival example by White's enormous portico. (The entire structure sustained some damage in the
1886 earthquake.) The pink stucco, added about 1840, is a good foil

for the thick greenery about it. Note, too, Edward White's Gate Lodge of 1850, and the somewhat tangled Library of 1854–56 by George Edward Walker.

The college, founded in 1770 and chartered in 1785, has done a remarkable job in its recent major expansion. Until 1970 it was a small, private institution with three to four hundred students on a limited campus. In that year it was made part of the state's higher education department with a projected enrollment of five thousand. Working closely with the local community in a once-fashionable but later bypassed neighborhood known as Harleston Village, the college has bought up a series of buildings (more than 120 to date). Many are eighteenth- and nineteenth-century houses of latent architectural distinction; seventy-five have been thoroughly rehabilitated and a score of insignificant ones removed. There are plans for further acquisitions, plus the building of several new facilities, none of the new ones to be higher than Randolph Hall. The domestic scale of the neighborhood is thus being maintained and the whole of Harleston Village infused with quiet vigor and a feeling of renascence. A series of architects has been retained, working under the Advisory Committee on Area Preservation, and with Edward Pinckney Associates coordinating and providing site planning and landscaping. The monumental portico on the north front of Randolph (1976) was designed by Simons, Mitchell, Small & Donahue.

Guide booklet available in Main Building during office hours

---

18 St. Philip's Church (1835–38/1848–50)
146 Church Street between Queen and Cumberland
Charleston, South Carolina

On the exterior St. Philip's bears more than a casual relationship to St. Michael's, also in Charleston (q.v.), each with roughly similar spires (St. Philip's is 201 feet/61 meters high) and each with a prominent portico. Their resemblance is no coincidence inasmuch as both were, as usual, strongly influenced by eighteenth-century London prototypes primarily the work of Wren and Gibbs. St. Philip's, as is obvious, has three identical Tuscan pedimented porches embracing the base of its tower. (The tower partly disappears into the corpus of St. Michael's, as we have seen.)

However, on the interior the two churches are startlingly dissimilar: St. Philip's is more coordinated architecturally and more airy, with a parade of opulently topped two-story Corinthian columns (very Gibbsian) supporting arches which uphold the roof and plaster-vaulted nave (the lateral ceilings are flat). The interior is thus woven into a unity of verticals and horizontals, arches and vaults. Moreover the galleries are ranged only along the two sides tying into the column midpoints. (There is a modest organ and ex-choir gallery, however.) St. Michael's, on the other hand, tends to produce a layered or stratified space, its flattish ceiling (supported by unseen trusses) hovering over the entire nave width, while its U-shaped balcony establishes a strong horizontal as it rests on its one-story columns.

The first St. Philip's—the first Anglican church in the Carolinas—was built of wood in 1681 (ironically on the site now occupied by St. Michael's), but by the early eighteenth century it proved inadequate and was replaced (1710–23, final touches 1733) by one on the plot where the present church stands. This burned in 1835 but was almost immediately rebuilt largely to the design of its predecessor but with some changes, including the chancel, made by Joseph Hyde, its architect. The steeple—much improved over the original—was added in 1848–50 by Edward B. White. The chancel was expanded in 1921 following another fire.

It is provocative to note that the 1723 building, according to the folder entitled *History of St. Philip's Church* in quoting Dr. Dalcho's *History of the Church in South Carolina,* had "three porticos before the west, south and north doors." This, of course, is some thirty years before the building of St. Michael's, which, it has been long claimed, had one of the first monumental porticos in the Colonies. An ancient print of the 1723 St. Philip's shows the three porticos almost precisely as they are today, the exception being that the earlier ones do not project as much and are topped by an ungainly tower. Moreover McCrady's *A Sketch of St. Philip's Church* (1901—p. 38) states concerning the 1838 building that "in regard to its external sittings, the *new* differs not greatly from the *old* building [his italics]. The three characteristic porches, north, south and west, were repeated, each with four columns supporting entablature and pediment." It would thus seem without question that not one but three monumental porticos appeared in Charleston in 1723 on the second St. Philip's Church.

Open daily 9–5

---

19   Market Hall (1840–41)
188 Meeting Street at Market
Charleston, South Carolina

EDWARD B. WHITE, ARCHITECT

Mr. White, who, as both architect and engineer, designed many of Charleston's buildings (including, as mentioned, the steeple of St. Philip's Church—1850, q.v.), produced this toylike Roman Doric "temple," which today stands wistfully puzzled by the sweep of traffic at its feet. The inspiration for its facade was probably the Temple of Fortuna Virilis (100 B.C.) in Rome, but with Doric instead of Ionic columns. Note the appropriate (for a market) alternation of ox skulls and rams' heads in the metopes: they also grace its counterpart in Rome. This jaunty Classic Revival building with a fine double stair has been used as a Confederate Museum since 1899. Stretched out behind

with a ripple of arches that picks up those of the rusticated basement of the elevated "temple," is the old market. Much of this has recently been restored into a series of shops.

Open Mar.–Oct., Wed. and Fri. 1–3, Sat. 10–4, except holidays

---

20   Charles Towne Landing Exposition Park (1970)
   **c. 6 miles/9.7 kilometers NW of downtown via IS 26, then, at
      marker, 2.7 miles/4.3 kilometers SW on SC 7 and SC 171
   Charleston, South Carolina**

**HARLAN McCLURE, ARCHITECT; SYNERGETICS INC., STRUCTURAL
ENGINEERS**

The three hundredth anniversary of the founding of South Carolina by the British was celebrated by the state in 1970. In 1526 the Spanish had sent an expedition of five hundred men, women, children, slaves,

and animals from San Domingo in the West Indies to settle a spot near the present Georgetown, but disease, revolt, hostile Indians, and bad weather drove them back after a few months. French efforts at settlement (1562)—mostly to counter Spanish influence in Florida—also aborted. But the British group, fortified by the English in Barbados, who comprised almost half the population, set up and maintained a community which succeeded from the beginning. Then ten years after the first village was begun, the settlement moved to a more strategic and healthful location across the Ashley River to the spot where it joins the Cooper. Both rivers were named for Lord Ashley (Anthony Ashley Cooper), one of the eight Lords Proprietors of the province.

The Charles Towne Landing—the original settlement—has been given a spritely, imaginative group of pavilions whose exhibits vividly recall conditions of the earliest days there. Four medium-sized pavilions form an introductory, service, and administrative core, with a theater (too inconspicuously placed) behind them. The climax is the striking open-air Exhibit Pavilion. Resting on a low podium and surrounded by a moat, this see-through, airy space-frame (subsequently braced) sets a wonderfully inviting note. Its elaborate exhibits are almost all underneath its terraced platform, with clever viewing "wells" offering snatches of the displays below. A sweeping spiral ramp provides access to and egress from this lower hall which is marked by effective exhibition techniques. Good show. On the grounds there is even a 1670 "Experimental Crop Garden," while just offshore is anchored the *Adventure,* a reproduction of a typical seventeenth-century trading ketch.

Open Apr.–Sept., Mon.–Sat. 9–6, Sun. 9–7; Oct.–Mar., daily 9–5, except Dec. 24, 25: admission

21   Hanover House (1714–16)
South Palmetto Boulevard
Clemson, South Carolina

Now located on the south edge of the campus of Clemson University, this simple, clapboarded house was dismantled (1940) and moved here from its original site across the state in Berkeley County. Otherwise it would have disappeared when Lake Moultrie was enlarged by the damming of the Santee River and its waters raised as part of the hydro development there. Hanover House is not an elaborate dwelling but it is one of importance in showing the advanced state of the art at this early date. Note the beaded-edge clapboards,. the fine old brick chimneys, and the shingled, bell-cast, Mansard roof. (An 1895 photograph shows a full-length porch across the front as an extension of the roof.) The house has been carefully restored and authentically

furnished in the simple fashion of its period. It was built by Paul de
St. Julien, a French Huguenot.

Open Tues.–Sat. 10–12, 1–5:30, Sun. 2–6, except holidays

---

22   **Keowee Toxaway Visitors' Center** (1969–78)
     Duke Power Company Nuclear Station
     W from Clemson on US 123, N on SC 130 8.3 miles/13.4
        kilometers near junction with SC 183
     near Clemson, South Carolina

FREEMAN, WELLS & MAJOR, ARCHITECTS

Responsive man working in an unspoiled setting has produced an
enlightened regional development. The Duke Power Company created
this project to generate electric power from a variety of complementary

sources. In addition to its hydro installation and pump storage facility, the project includes one of the nation's major nuclear generating installations. Lake Keowee and Lake Jocassee, whose waters are necessary for cooling as well as for power, were created by damming two rivers. Jocassee is higher than Keowee so that a "pumped-storage" transfer can be used to "recycle" the water by utilizing other Duke System generation at late-night, off-peak hours. The waters of the lower lake are lifted to the upper so that at peak periods they can turn the dynamos in the lower Keowee. There is, of course, an energy loss in this cycling —about three kilowatt-hours' output to produce two—but power at peak periods is so much more valuable that the interchange is economical.

The Oconee Nuclear Station is composed of three reactor units in cylinders 190 feet/58 meters high (plus 30 feet/9.1 meters underground) and 120 feet/37 meters in diameter. The turbine-generator building attached to them is 800 feet/244 meters long and 200 feet/61 meters wide. The Visitors' Center commands a panoramic sweep of much of the layout including Lake Keowee and its backdrop of the Blue Ridge Mountains. The building itself, of reinforced concrete, is strong in general form but mannered in detail. The interior contains offices, a meeting room, and an exhibit "The Story of Energy" which is imaginatively organized and well worth studying.

The overriding importance of Keowee Toxaway lies not in its individual units, though these are good, but in the concerned ecology which introduces a mammoth industrial installation to a lovely mountain setting and does so with respect to nature. The lakes, incidentally, are open to the public for picnicking and sailing.

Open Mon.–Sat. 9–5, Sun. 10:30–6, except holidays

---

23   Robert Mills Historic House and Park (1823–25)
1616 Blanding Street between Pickens, Henderson, and Taylor
     Streets
(entrance on Henderson)
Columbia, South Carolina

ROBERT MILLS, ARCHITECT

Robert Mills (1781–1855), as mentioned in the description of The Fireproof Building in Charleston, was South Carolina's most noted architect. He was also one of the nation's most distinguished designers in

addition to being a highly talented engineer. His most renowned work is the Washington Monument (q.v.) but in Pennsylvania, he also designed what was at the time the longest single-span bridge in the world. (See H. M. Pierce Gallagher's *Robert Mills,* Columbia University Press, 1935.) Mills's domestic output was limited, so that this Federal-Greek Revival mansion he designed for Mr. Ainsley Hall is particularly valuable. That it exists at all is due to the efforts of the Historic Columbia Foundation which, at the last moment, saved the property (1962) from becoming one vast parking lot. Upon reconditioning and refurnishing, the Ainsley House was opened to the public (1967) and totally restored as the Robert Mills Historic House and Park for the state's Tricentennial of 1970.

The mansion, which is of brick, rests on a white-painted raised "basement" with a squarish two-story dependency (reconstructed) on either side. The dwelling's two facades differ markedly, that on the north—the main entrance—carrying the usual pedimented two-story portico, here with four slender Ionic columns; that to the south or garden side having a distinctly original seven-arch, projected colonnade across the entire front, with smaller brick arches, flush with the edge, at the lower level. The south front is further distinguished by an intriguing arched "niche," almost a small exedra, which accommodates the twin doors from the twin drawing rooms on this side.

The building, incidentally, was never used as a residence by Mills or anyone else. Shortly after completion it was sold (1829) to the Old

Columbia Theological Seminary, which occupied it for almost a hundred years. Thus, although the interior was structurally intact, but needing much repair, the furnishings have had to be collected from various sources in recent years. The restoration of the house and the reconstruction of the two dependencies (on their old foundations) was carried out by Simons, Lapham, Mitchell & Small of Charleston and Reid Hearn Associates of Columbia.

Open Tues.–Sat. 10–4, Sun. 2–5, except major holidays, including last two weeks in Dec.: admission

Directly across the street at 1615 Blanding stands the **Hampton-Preston House** (1818—open Tues.–Sat. 10–4, Sun. 2–5, except major holidays, including last two weeks in Dec.: admission). It will interest the specialist both outside and in.

---

24   U. S. Post Office (1964–66)
Assembly Street at Taylor
Columbia, South Carolina

LYLES, BISSETT, CARLISLE & WOLFF, ARCHITECTS

A difficult, 9-acre/3.6-hectare lot with a drop-off of 40 feet/12 meters has been keenly analyzed by the architects to produce a four-level, local post office and state mail distribution center of efficiency and distinction. The site was chosen for both interstate highway and rail proximity, with a track extension actually being incorporated in the design of the building. Thus, the railway post office cars can enter directly for loading and unloading and the mail not require a truck transfer. Highway mail trucks also use this lowest level and its docks. The second level, bridged like the bottom one by a ramp from Taylor Street, accommodates city delivery trucks and first-class mail distribution.

Both of the lower decks are of reinforced concrete. The main, or third, floor is attached to Assembly Street by an attractive plaza, and forms the public level of the post office operations. This can also be reached directly by car (from Taylor), and offers short-term parking on its elevated platform. This floor and the one above, which is filled with postal office space, form a smart, colonnaded rectangle of bronze and dark-tinted glass, one well set off by good landscaping and street furniture. In addition to providing an advanced technical facility, the new post office distinctly upgrades its downtown area. Lafaye, Fair & Lafaye were associate architects.

Open during office hours

---

25 **Textile Hall** (1964–66/1969/1977)
Exposition Avenue, S of intersection IS 385 and SC 291
Greenville, South Carolina

J. E. SIRRINE & CO., ARCHITECTS-ENGINEERS

With a West Hall measuring 600 x 250 feet/183 x 76 meters and a 38-foot/11.5-meter link connecting this with an East Hall 240 x 400 feet/73 x 122 meters, this mammoth one-story-and-mezzanine building still manages to bring off a no-nonsense flair. This is due first to the quality of the three, slightly overlapping, concrete "umbrellas" that step down from building to road, and, second, to the line and scale of the freestanding covered walk that stretches along much of the front.

Textile Hall Corporation is a non-profit group, primarily concerned with the development of the textile world, but also dedicated "to advance and encourage the cause of religion, literature, science and art." Every two years it stages a huge Southern Textile Exposition of the

latest machinery and developments in the field which has made such an impact on the region.

Because of the building's great size and its relative infrequency of use, economy of construction played an omnipresent role. While a strict budget is not apparent on the outside, the interiors are spartan, being basically undivided exhibition space—which is their purpose. The interior is so vast that it is divided into "avenues" and "streets"— seven of the former, seventeen of the latter. Construction is of poured-in-place concrete columns with prestressed concrete girders and single tees. The exterior is of red brick. In 1969 a two-story addition was made adjoining the original building at the south end, and in 1977 a one-level addition added to this.

Primarily open during expositions

---

26 Sea Pines Plantation (1959–   )
at S end of US 278
Hilton Head Island, South Carolina

**SASAKI ASSOCIATES, MASTER PLANNERS, LANDSCAPE
ARCHITECTS, ARCHITECTS; VARIOUS INDIVIDUAL ARCHITECTS**

The important lesson of Sea Pines Plantation does not lie in its build-ings, though they are generally reasonable, but in its land usage and planning. These shine like a beacon among bulldozer developers. All of the natural loveliness of this island, which lies roughly halfway be-

tween Beaufort, South Carolina, and Savannah, Georgia, was preserved to the last bush. Moreover even the birds and wildlife have a permanent refuge here, with 1,600 of its 5,200 acres (647 of 2,104 hectares) being a game sanctuary. With this love of land and premise of preservation in mind, the developer, Charles E. Fraser, got hold of two people important to the success of planning and controlling this "plantation." The first of these was Hideo Sasaki, then chairman of the Department of Landscape Architecture at Harvard, for the overall planning; the second was Dr. Myres McDougal of Yale, who drew up restrictive land covenants so that almost complete design control could be exercised over all building by an architectural review committee.

The Plantation—which has not been without some start-up troubles —is laid out for approximately 2,200 homesites with about one quarter of these planned for year-round retirement living. The majority of the lots face or have some view of the ocean or Calibogue Sound and the Intracoastal Waterway; others face onto one of three golf courses. Harbor Town provides an excellent marina and boating center, a waterfront inn, a community and cultural center. The houses and public buildings, which were designed by Sasaki Associates and other architects, several of whom have offices on Hilton Head Island, vary from the first-rate to the folksy. One of the most inventive, and ecologically sympathetic, residential areas is The Treetops, a group of 308 town houses in a forest, most of which are perched above grade and are interconnected by a 13-foot/4-meter high boardwalk. Balsley, Balsley, Kuhl were the landscape architects for these 21 acres/8.5 hectares. Hilton Head's concern for land usage and the respect for nature and wildlife could scarcely be better.

Open daily: get map from Chamber of Commerce near entry

---

27   St. Stephen's Episcopal Church (1767–69)
Church Street on SC 45, .5 mile/.8 kilometer E of US 52 on SC 45
St. Stephen, Berkeley County, South Carolina

St. Stephen's is a surprisingly sophisticated church both for its time and its place, a place once made wealthy by indigo. Note its multicurved "Jacobean" gable ends—recalling Bacon's Castle (q.v.) in Virginia—its gambrel roof which "returns" across both ends, its unusual brick Tuscan pilasters and its roundheaded windows and doors. A topside heaviness freights the small nave beneath its elaborate roof, but the detailing of the walls and their Flemish bond brickwork reveals

high competence. Though the church is usually locked, a reasonable impression of the interior can be had by looking through the unshuttered windows at chancel end. The tray ceiling, as would be expected from the outside, follows the line of the roof. A remarkable "sunburst" atop a Palladian window in the center of the chancel wall, with a heavily framed plaque on either side, highlights the interior. After the collapse of the indigo market following the Revolution, the St. Stephen area, its plantations, and this church were largely abandoned. In time prosperity returned—first because of rice cultivation, then cotton, and finally, a rounded farming and timbering activity. Francis Villepontoux and A. Howard are generally credited as designers-constructors. In 1957 an extensive restoration was completed and St. Stephen's is now an active mission church with regular Sunday services.

Generally locked but key available nearby; services on Sun.

28 Fairfield District Court House (1822/1844/1939)
South Congress Street (SC 321) at Washington Street
Winnsboro, South Carolina

ROBERT MILLS, SUPERVISING ARCHITECT

The small town of Winnsboro (population c. 3,500), located some 24 miles/39 kilometers north of Columbia, possesses in this Greek Revival courthouse one of South Carolina's most puzzling buildings. Though its designer is not known, according to the South Carolina Department of Archives and History, it was built "under the direction of Robert Mills." (Mills was "State Engineer and Architect" from 1820–30.) The original core (1822) was enlarged across the back in 1844, but it took until 1939 for the curved flying stair—almost certainly not designed by Mills—to be installed. At the same time the entire building was completely renovated. Though none of the elements of the facade are of themselves distinguished, the tympanum being amateurish, as indeed are the Roman Doric columns, the overall effect is graceful. The stairs sweep up to the large courtroom which occupies the upper floor; though of minor architectural interest, it is worth a look. The remainder of the building is filled with routine civic offices. Some authorities feel that one Thomas Harmon (who altered Mills's Court House of 1823 at Kingstree, S.C.) was probably the designer of the Winnsboro building.

Open during office hours

Tennessee

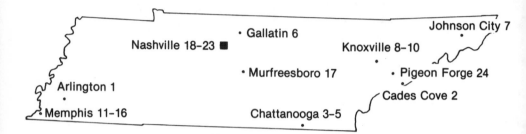

Arlington 1

Memphis 11–16

Nashville 18–23 ■

· Gallatin 6

· Murfreesboro 17

Chattanooga 3–5

Knoxville 8–10

Johnson City 7

· Pigeon Forge 24

Cades Cove 2

TENNESSEE

The buildings in boldface type are of general interest. The others are for the specialist.

Arlington
1 Arlington Developmental Center (1968–69)—Mann & Harrover, with Eason, Anthony, McKinnie & Cox

Cades Cove
2 **Cades Cove Historic District** (19th century)

Chattanooga
3 **Cravens House** (1856–66)
4 **The Chattanooga Choo-Choo** (1906–8/1973) —Donn Barber
5 **Hunter Museum of Art Extension** (1974–75) —Derthick & Henley

Gallatin
6 **Cragfont** (1798–1802)

Johnson City
7 **Rocky Mount Historic Site** (1770–72)

Knoxville
8 William Blount Mansion (1792–94) Craighead-Jackson House and Garden (1818)
9 **TVA, Norris Dam** (1933–36) **and the Bull Run Steam Plant** (1962–66)—Tennessee Valley Authority
10 Clarence Brown Theatre for the Performing Arts (1968–69)—Bruce McCarty & Associates

Memphis
11 **The Noland Fontaine House** (1870–73)— M. H. Baldwin & E. C. Jones James Lee House (1843/1853/1873)
12 **Mallory-Neely House** (1852/1883)
13 First National Bank (1962)—Walk Jones, Mah & Jones
14 Fire Station (1967)—A. L. Aydelott & Associates
15 Luther Towers, Housing for the Elderly (1970–71)—Walk Jones & Francis Mah; William J. LeMessurier & Associates Barry Homes (1970)—Waik Jones & Francis Mah

16 Commercial & Industrial Bank (1970–72)—
Gassner-Nathan-Browne

Murfreesboro   17 Oaklands (c. 1825/1830/c. 1850)

Nashville   18 **The Hermitage** (1818–19/1831/1834–36)
Tulip Grove (1836)
19 **State Capitol** (1845–59)—William Strickland
20 **Belle Meade** (1853–54/1880s)
21 **The Downtown Presbyterian Church**
(1849–51/1881–82)—William Strickland
22 The Parthenon (1896–97/1920–31)
23 Lewis House and Morgan House (1966–67)—
Brush, Hutchison & Gwinn

Pigeon Forge   24 The Old Mill (1830)

1 Arlington Developmental Center (1968–69)
N off IS 40 at Airline Road, then W on Milton Wilson Road
Arlington, Tennessee

MANN & HARROVER, WITH EASON, ANTHONY, McKINNIE & COX, ARCHITECTS

Arlington is a sobering complex situated on a 600-acre/243-hectare site roughly 25 miles/40 kilometers northeast of Memphis. It was designed to take care of the mentally retarded of all ages but with emphasis on children. Remedial help is held paramount; custodial care is available when necessary. The planning philosophy worked out between staff and architects stipulated a series of independent "home" units loosely dispersed over the slightly rolling landscape, all grouped around a central school with no vestige of the institutional. The basic unit is a cluster or "neighborhood of cottages," one cluster comprising four cottages, each of which accommodates 32 ambulatory patients

(128 altogether). These are grouped in square, somewhat rigid formation and focused inward onto central "play" and recreation courts.

Each of the cottage groups, of which there are eight altogether, develops a "home" feeling with which its charges can identify. However, it does seem like excessive crowding to put eight mentally handicapped patients into one tight room, and there are four patient wards per cottage. Intensive-care patients are accommodated in two separate units directly behind the administration building. Interiors are simple, sturdy, and bright, a far cry from the philosophy that was once (?) basically concerned with "urine-resistant flooring and escape-proof windows" (*P/A,* August 1965). The roof angles seem repetitive but as a whole the complex is sympathetic. Roy P. Harrover was partner in charge of design, assisted by Robert B. Church, III.

Tours available Mon.–Fri. 8–4:30: contact volunteer services at (901) 867-2921

---

2   Cades Cove Historic District (19th century)
Great Smoky Mountains National Park
c. 7 miles/11 kilometers SW of TENN 73 on unnumbered road
    just E of Townsend
Cades Cove, Tennessee

The unspoiled atmosphere and the sylvan beauty of this cove with its nineteenth-century farms exert a bucolic spell. The site, isolated in the Great Smokies, is an upland valley, some 2,000 feet/610 meters high, 5 miles/8 kilometers long by 2 miles/3.2 kilometers wide. Its community at one time consisted of approximately one hundred families, who had little contact with the "outside" world until paved roads in the 1920s made it reasonably accessible.

The early settlers, the first arriving in 1818, cleared the land and built a series of log structures for their homes, barns, churches, stores, and mills. Many of these are still standing, some in operation by descendants of the original settlers. Limited farming is still carried out (supervised by the National Park Service) to keep the area historically accurate and to prevent the land from reverting to forest. An 11-mile/18-kilometer-long Loop Road takes one by many buildings and farm groups. Some require a small but worthwhile hike. Most of the original structures have been rebuilt or restored. Several appropriate to

the time and the need have been brought in from more distant areas of the Park. One of the most unusual pioneer settlements, it has been a National Park since 1930. A self-guiding auto tour book is available.

Open daily sunrise–sunset

3 Cravens House (1856–66)
Lookout Mountain, off TENN 148
Chattanooga, Tennessee

A simple, architecturally unpretentious but beautifully situated house built for Robert Cravens, a pioneer industrialist. Nearly demolished in the Civil War, it was rebuilt on its original foundations immediately thereafter. It is now part of the Chickamauga and Chattanooga National Military Park. There is more history than architecture here, but

it is a recommended trip. Once sadly deteriorated, beginning in 1956 the house was carefully restored outside and in by the Association for the Preservation of Tennessee Antiquities.

Open mid-Feb.–mid-Dec., Tues.–Sat. 9–5, Sun. 1–5: admission

---

4 The Chattanooga Choo-Choo (1906–8/1973)
South Market Street between Alabama and 14th
Chattanooga, Tennessee

DONN BARBER, ARCHITECT OF ORIGINAL STATION

The problem of utilizing major railroad stations now that passenger traffic is minuscule has been "solved" in most places by demolition. However, imagination of a high order came to the rescue in Chattanooga. Its two-level terminal with magnificent brick arched entrance has been transformed into an inn and an imposing series of restaurants, utilizing the domed station lobby (85 feet/26 meters high) as the main

dining room. Other dining rooms—note the frothy Palm Terrace—and shops set a merry scene. Moreover, a nostalgic lineup of stationary Pullman cars serves as forty-eight posh family hotel suites (two per car), and a new three-story, 202-room Hilton Motor Inn (designed by architect Klaus Peter Nentwig) adjacent to the tracks supplements the Pullman accommodations.

The entire transformation has been carried out with close regard for the old building by the Chattanooga Choo-Choo Company, a private enterprise composed of twenty-four local business leaders. The enormous brick arches at entry and trackside are firmly intact, the 68 x 82-foot/21 x 25-meter waiting room is restored to its original condition, its steel-supported dome—one of the world's largest—now hovering over diners. The decor purposefully emphasizes the Victorian, and does so with zest. The Choo-Choo on Track 29 dates from an 1880 prototype and was in active service until the mid-1940s. The central tracks have been removed to make a garden complete with gazebo, the landscaping hemmed by original train sheds. Altogether the restoration is a delightful, and instructive, use of an imposing and sturdily built station, one that will appeal to all, train fan or not. (It is one of the city's main tourist attractions.)

Donn Barber's architectural expertise began at Yale, continued at

Columbia, and was polished at the Paris Beaux-Arts (1898), where, reputedly, the young man won an Institute competition for "a railroad station for a large city." Not unexpectedly, the Chattanooga Choo-Choo has been a very active influence in the urban renewal of the area. It is listed in the National Register of Historic Places. (An extensive model railroad pike by the Chattanooga Model Railroad Club is located on the second floor of the station.)

Open daily

---

5 Hunter Museum of Art Extension (1974–75)
10 Bluff View Avenue
Chattanooga, Tennessee

DERTHICK & HENLEY, ARCHITECTS

Designing a major addition to a museum that is much older is always difficult. In this case the addition was to a 1904 red brick Colonial Revival mansion. When the site is a narrow one dropping precipitously

into the river, difficulties are compounded. The architects have met the problem of paying architectural respect without architectural imitation and have capably shoehorned their new building into several levels of limestone bluff. The scale of the all-concrete exterior welcomes; a colorful Calder stabile (1963) draws one on; and the curved end of the auditorium (reflecting the portico of the house) adds to the geometry of the front. Though on entering there is little hint of the dramatic panorama of the Tennessee River below, the gallery areas offer spatial rewards on two levels, including some vistas out onto the river, and one thoughtful vignette of the mansion. The exhibits in these areas are basically temporary as opposed to the fine permanent collection (mostly American) in the well-reconditioned main house. The two have internal communication. The sculpture garden, which occupies the roof of the new building and the lawn of the old, enjoys stunning views of river and countryside, plus a first-rate wrought-iron fence by Albert Paley (1975) which joins the two buildings. The Hunter Museum School, located on the lower level, offers instruction in many branches of the arts and forms a very active adjunct to the museum. This is supplemented by lectures and recitals in the auditorium at entry which seats 176. The house and grounds were given to the Hunter Art Gallery in 1951 by the Benwood Foundation.

Open Tues.–Sat. 10–4:30, Sun. 1–4:30, except major holidays: donation

---

6   **Cragfont** (1798–1802)
off TENN 25, c. 6 miles/10 kilometers E of
Gallatin, Tennessee

Cragfont is a stalwart T-shaped rural mansion situated atop a hill where it surveys the countryside in all directions. Its ashlar walls with prominent joints were built with stones from local quarries, while its timber was hewn in the nearby forest. The masons and carpenters who constructed it were imported, one understands, from Maryland, the birthplace of General James Winchester who commissioned the house. Note the added-on star-studded tie rods which firmly sustain the lateral walls. In the rear of the simple Georgian block projects a wing with upper and lower galleries on either side. The gable ends of the dwelling are so filled by the out-sized chimneys that they are windowless. The interior shows the same rugged simplicity as the outside, a generous

hall and stairway to the second floor dividing it down the middle. The house suffered various indignities from assorted inhabitants until it was purchased by the state in 1959, restored and appropriately furnished by the Association for the Preservation of Tennessee Antiquities.

Open mid-Apr.–Oct., Tues.–Sat. 10–5, Sun. 1–6: admission

---

7 **Rocky Mount Historic Site** (1770–72)
The Cobb-Massengill Home
**on US 11E, 19 and 411, c. 6 miles/10 kilometers NE of Johnson
   City and SW of Bristol**
near Johnson City, Tennessee

A good example of trans-Appalachia log vernacular, its two-pen plan including a dogtrot or breezeway. In the late nineteenth century it was covered with weatherboards (clapboards) for greater weather protection and to create higher architectural status for the then-owner's nubile daughters (*Tennessee Historical Quarterly,* Summer 1966). The result is that the underlying dressed log structure of white oak is still surprisingly sound. The well-appointed dining room is located behind

the dogtrot, with freestanding kitchen, completely rebuilt, beyond it. The paneled Great Room is unexpectedly accomplished for this remote area (until 1790 part of North Carolina), with furnishings throughout being of the period. The state purchased the house in 1959, restored it, and opened it to the public in 1962. A new memorial museum of brick stands adjacent.

Open Apr.–Oct., Mon.–Sat. 10–5, Sun. 2–6: admission

---

8 William Blount Mansion (1792–94)
200 West Hill Avenue at State Street
Knoxville, Tennessee

The Blount Mansion was one of the earliest frame houses constructed west of the Blue Ridge in the newly opened "Territory South of the River Ohio" (also known as the Southwest Territory) of which William Blount was the first governor. Saved from threatened demoli-

tion by a statewide group in 1925—primarily the Daughters of the American Revolution—both house and garden have been expertly restored, although it was not until 1960 that all work was completed. The result is a simple cream-colored weatherboarded house whose rooms are well fashioned and furnished. A parlor was added in 1794. The horizontal pine paneling in the bedroom and that in the kitchen and law office, the latter two in rear, are outstanding of their period. Alden Hopkins, landscape architect of Colonial Williamsburg, then his assistant Donald Parker, were responsible for the gardens which the Knoxville Garden Club maintains.

Open all year Tues.–Sat. 9:30–5, also May–Oct., Sun. 2–5, closed holidays: admission

The brick **Craighead-Jackson House and Garden**—the Visitors' Center to Blount Mansion (same hours, joint admission)—also merit a look. Built in 1818, restored and opened to the public in 1966, the Craighead-Jackson House shows a new generation of architectural sophistication. Both houses are operated by the Blount Mansion Association.

9 TVA, Norris Dam (1933–36) **and the Bull Run Steam Plant**
   (1962–66)
   NW from Knoxville on IS 75 to US 25W to Claxton School, then
   SW c. 2 miles/3.2 kilometers on marked road; c. 15 miles/24
   kilometers from
   Knoxville, Tennessee

TENNESSEE VALLEY AUTHORITY, ARCHITECTS AND ENGINEERS

TVA has changed the face of much of the southeast overwhelmingly
for the better, and its success has spawned similar developments not
only in this country but in many of the developing nations of the
world. It is rightly upheld as an example of what can be done to up-
grade a region. This once-depressed, erosion-ravaged section of Appalachia was not even "developing" forty to fifty years ago. It was mori-
bund, with a per capita income, unbelievable as it now seems, of
around $168 per annum in 1933 and with only 3.5 per cent of its
farms having electricity. (Tennessee's per capita income in 1979 was
over $6,500.) It can be said, indeed proclaimed, that TVA was largely
instrumental in saving the South, for it provided inexpensive power
which attracted industry and raised employment, its twenty-nine dams
helped control flooding, and its stabilized rivers provided transportation. And however history will judge the atomic bomb and atomic
energy, they were created in nearby Oak Ridge because of the power
capacity of TVA.

The earliest sources of TVA energy were river-based, but when the
full water-power potential of its seven-state region had been harnessed,
the Authority—to keep up with the growing demand for electricity—
augmented this source with steam, as here at Bull Run and at Paradise,
Kentucky (q.v.). By 1978 TVA had increased its generating capacity
100 per cent over its pre-1968 level, primarily with nuclear plants, of
which Browns Ferry in Alabama is the first of seven anticipated. No
more sizable dams are planned.

Though electric power, flood control, and year-round navigation are
TVA's chief concerns, "community development" and recreational use
of its waters are of increasing moment.

Norris Dam on the Clinch River off IS 75 and US 441, about 21
miles/34 kilometers NNW of Knoxville—center of TVA's operations
—was the first to be constructed (1933–36), and it was here that a

momentous breakthrough in architectural philosophy occurred. The earliest design proposals for the powerhouse and non-dam facilities were in a so-called "Colonial Style" when David Lilienthal, TVA's first director, asked Roland Wank (1898–1970), who had been retained as town planner for the expansion of Norris, "to take a look." Wank took a look for two weeks, came back to Mr. Lilienthal and said, "This is the way I think it should be," and then outlined the sparse, powerful, unencumbered, dateless lines which have made TVA design the great exemplar in architectural-engineering terms. Wank, fortunately, got the job as chief of design (1933–44), producing a superlative series of structures from power plants to gantry cranes. Norris Dam itself was a good beginning but the work of the next eleven years was finer.

The Bull Run Steam Plant (1962–66), like most of its confreres, rises above routine industrial force with coordinated strength and basic simplicity of line. It is dominated by an 800-foot/244-meter-high chimney (equal to a seventy-story building), anchored by its power-house (950,000-kilowatt capacity), and tethered to the land by the giant covered conveyors. These feed it coal at over 5 tons/4.5 metric tons per minute from a 123-foot/37-meter-high silo, and though the complex is not as overwhelming as the coal-fired plant at Paradise with

its hyperbolic cooling towers, it is still very powerful. The lake formed
by the Melton Hill Dam supplies the 400,000 gallons/1,818,435 liters
of water a minute needed for cooling. On design terms, Bull Run rees-
tablishes TVA's reputation for excellence, a reputation that had
slipped a bit following Wank's departure. As with most of its under-
takings, Bull Run was designed and constructed by the Authority's
forces. The chief engineer during the early developing period was
Arthur E. Morgan. In brief it can be said that TVA is "the world's
boldest venture in regional reconstruction" (*The Architectural Review,* London, June 1943).

Visitors welcome daily, 9–5, except major holidays

---

10   Clarence Brown Theatre for the Performing Arts (1968–69)
University of Tennessee
1714 Andy Holt Avenue
Knoxville, Tennessee

BRUCE McCARTY & ASSOCIATES, ARCHITECTS

The Clarence Brown Theatre is one of the most architecturally accomplished buildings on the University's campus. Though the setting was made difficult by grade fall-off and by the adjacent and previously existing small Carousel Theatre, the site has been handled to emphasize the identity of the theater. It is separated by trees from the avenue and well tailored in brick and concrete. The rounded corners of the brick auditorium and stage house are countered by the sharp-edged concrete canopy and ticket offices with a lineup of multiple-globe street lights adding their touch. The interior of the lobby across the front is not as gracious as one might like, due primarily to the treatment of the concession stand, but the wide lobbies on either side welcome as they step down the grade and open outward to paved terraces for fine-weather intermissions.

The auditorium (by far the finest part) is full of atmosphere and sparkle, its red continental seats arced to the stage while overhead a series of down-lights add bright accents against the black ceiling. Between each two rows of lights are the service catwalks, which are virtually invisible to the audience and hence offer many options in the placing and adjusting of spotlights. The auditorium, which seats 600, has a 60-foot/18-meter-wide adjustable proscenium with two side stage extensions. The 43-foot/13-meter-deep stage offers considerable flexibility with two hydraulic lifts and provision for up to 39 rigging sets. A Laboratory Theatre with 120 seats (and separate entry) is incorporated in the building, along with the usual backstage services. The firm is now known as McCarty, Bullock, Holsaple, Inc.

Open for performances

---

11 The Noland Fontaine House (1870–73)
680 Adams Avenue
Memphis, Tennessee

M. H. BALDWIN AND E. C. JONES, ARCHITECTS

A jaunty Victorian mansion, fully restored outside and in, and not only open to the public but available for luncheons, receptions, and meetings. Substantially constructed of handmade brick by Amos Woodruff with walls 14–16 inches/36–41 centimeters thick, the house comprises a main floor for the sitting room, music room, and kitchen, four bedrooms on the second, and four more on the third with windows nudging the tiles on the Mansard roof. The proper Victorian

tower—a "retreat" within—projects loftily above. The detailing throughout merits scrutiny from the quoins, to the rich porch at left, to the elaborate terra-cotta trim on the main openings, to the cast iron cresting the ridge. The interior is also grandiosely attended to. Note the ceiling in the stair hall (of hammered tin in imitation of carved plaster), the frescoed ceiling in the parlor, and the carvings and cornices of a more than liberated hand. Furnishings of the period, some original, set the proper tempo.

Open daily 1–4, except holidays: admission

The adjacent, gingered **James Lee House** (1843/1853/1873), at 690 Adams Avenue, was saved from the bulldozer through the generosity of Miss Rosa Lee, the last of the family to live there. Miss Lee had also purchased (c. 1930) the Fontaine House and established the James Lee Memorial to house the Memphis Academy of Art. The Depression curtailed most activities, and in 1958 it seemed likely that both houses would be torn down since new facilities for the Academy had been built. The Association for the Preservation of Tennessee Antiquities stepped in and was eventually able to acquire funds to preserve and restore the Fontaine House which was opened in 1964. The Lee House will be opened upon completion of restoration.

12   Mallory-Neely House (1852/1883)
652 Adams Avenue
Memphis, Tennessee

The Victorian Village Historic District of Memphis, and the not-distant Mallory-Neely and Fontaine and Lee Houses (q.v.) comprise one of the nation's finest collections of mid- and late-nineteenth-century dwellings. Nine of the residences and outbuildings have been designated a historic district and are listed in the National Register of Historic Places (1972). Though most of these period houses are private, the three mentioned are open to the public and well merit exploration. The Mallory House underwent a substantial change in 1883 when James Columbus Neely purchased it and added a third floor—and his name. He also changed the facade to incorporate the then fashionable "Tuscan" central tower. Note its carefully dissimilar, strangely gabled flanks. The result today is on the hoary side with purplish stucco covering, or more or less covering, its brick walls. One might, indeed, be

tempted to pass it by: don't, for the interior, almost untouched for a hundred years, is one of the Victorian prides of America. (The exterior is scheduled for early rehabilitation.) The drawing room in particular is sumptuous almost beyond belief, while the parlor and dining room are not far behind. The colored Tiffany glass in the front door is possibly unsurpassed, while the French window (1883 renovation) on the stair-landing facing it is almost as fine. Moreover the house has been continuously lived in until the present (now with caretakers). The furnishings are all of the Victorian period.

The dwelling and carriage house behind were given (1972) by the children of the late Mrs. Barton Lee Mallory (née Neely) to the West Tennessee Chapters of the Daughters, Sons, and Children of the American Revolution. A new slate roof has been recently installed to protect the fabric of the house, and the capable hands of Yeates/Gaskill/Rhodes Inc., restoration architects, are working on the exterior as funds materialize. One of the finest of its period to be seen.

Open daily 1–4, except holidays: admission

---

13   First National Bank (1962)
165 Madison Avenue
Memphis, Tennessee

WALK JONES, MAH & JONES, ARCHITECTS

A pure, meticulously detailed twenty-three-story skyscraper, a building which in large measure launched the remarkable downtown renaissance of Memphis. The bank, impeccably furnished, occupies the first three floors of the squarish tower. Set back from the street, the main entrance offers a miniplaza with trees and fountains. The building can be illuminated at night by fluorescent tubes placed at each window head. In spite of refinement of both design and furnishings, the bank was inexpensively built.

Open during business hours

---

14   Fire Station (1967)
Union Avenue at South Front Street
Memphis, Tennessee

A. L. AYDELOTT & ASSOCIATES, ARCHITECTS

An efficient, functional fire station serving downtown Memphis from its site overlooking the Mississippi River. The structural frame is of reinforced concrete with walls of precast masonry panels. A design element which lends invitation to the building can be seen in the glass en-

closure of much of the equipment floor. With the overhead glass doors usually open the sensation of immediate availability is underscored, while the glass on the side enables the passerby to examine the powerful equipment within. Street and building are thus cleverly interlocked.

Always open

15 Luther Towers, Housing for the Elderly (1970–71)
274 Highland Road between Poplar and Central Avenues
Memphis, Tennessee

WALK JONES & FRANCIS MAH, ARCHITECTS; WILLIAM J. LeMESSURIER & ASSOCIATES, STRUCTURAL ENGINEERS

Combining capable design with a highly advanced systems technique of prefabricated concrete components, this housing for the elderly commands double attention. The use of large-scale prefabricated building elements in the United States lags lamentably behind that of Europe (including virtually all of Eastern Europe), yet this inevitably is the direction which architecture and engineering must take if we are to house tomorrow. This example demonstrates with skill and economy the advantages of technological expertise, here brilliantly developed by Francis Mah and William LeMessurier, the well-known Boston engineer. The Mah-LeMessurier System (MLS) is one which may, at last, rank with or even exceed European developments.

It lies beyond the scope of this guidebook to go into technical details, but in brief the MLS as used here is based on components of cubelike, open U-shaped service cores (8 feet/2.4 meters high and 8 feet/2.4 meters square)—the dimension being determined by bathtub plus chase. The related components are prestressed double-T floor beams (8 feet/2.4 meters wide, 38.5 feet/11.7 meters long), beams (14 inches/36 centimeters square, 24 feet/7.3 meters long), and wall panels. The "secret" of the system is that the cores (seen here as the windowless projections) act as structural columns and are post-tensioned together along with beams, wall panels, and floor double tees. The prefabricated elements form, in effect, a post-tensioned space-frame. Grooves in the walls of the cores receive the prefabricated wall panels. The cores contain all bathrooms and mechanical chases and venting, and the kitchens, correspondingly, are placed adjacent. The resulting "box," beam, and panel system can be fabricated by any well-equipped manufacturer. Dimensions are flexible and can be changed to meet specific needs. Post-tensioning of these components is carried out by means of hydraulic jacks on every third floor, threaded rods being incorporated in each core, or "structural activity module," for this purpose.

Luther Towers uses the MLS cores on the periphery to create a very progressive addition to the Memphis skyline. It was sponsored by the Lutheran Services of Tennessee with FHA subsidy. Its 196 apartments accommodate 236 low-income elderly on 13 floors, the apartments divided into efficiencies and 1-bedroom units. Some rigidity in plan can be seen in that the solid-wall service cores occupy more than a third of the outside periphery, thus compromising flexibility in the location and size of the windows. However, Luther Towers is only the first of one of the most exciting new directions of American prefabrication. It has accomplished much as a pioneer. As LeMessurier says, "We learn something new about this system every day" (*Architectural Record,* April 1971).

Reception area open daily

Barry Homes (1970), 255 North Lauderdale Street, designed by the same architects, is very similar. Its 300 low-income units are housed in a fourteen-story tower.

---

16   Commercial & Industrial Bank (1970–72)
200 Madison Avenue
Memphis, Tennessee

GASSNER-NATHAN-BROWNE, ARCHITECTS

An imaginative downtown bank which attracts polite attention on the exterior by its triangular profile, while extending considerable welcome within via its four-story Garden of Eden entry. Its herbaceous introduction, well laid-out horizontally, almost envelops one spatially, its shrubs providing color while its trees almost touch the yellow welded steel space-frame. In spite of the extra cost involved, it is probably safe to say that the money invested has yielded ample returns. The skylight of

7,000 square feet/650 square meters angles to provide light to the bank's four general floors with a terraced executive floor above. Bank officers' desks line the edge of the bower, while check-cashing, etc., takes place just behind, the tellers arranged so that they can also serve drive-in customers at rear. The space in the top triangular peak is filled with the utilities. Construction is of poured-in-place reinforced concrete. William J. LeMessurier Associates were the structural engineers; Robert C. Green & Associates landscape architects with Robert Dingwald horticultural consultant.

Open during business hours

---

17   Oaklands (c. 1825/1830/c. 1850)
N end of North Maney Avenue from US 70S
Murfreesboro, Tennessee

Three conjoined houses, one in front of the other, comprise Oaklands. The earliest is a four-room pioneer cottage with detached kitchen; the second is of brick; and the last, from the 1850s, and our main concern,

also of brick and the largest of the three. Its early Victorian brackets and roundheaded door and central window—with a hint of the Romanesque Revival—were given a porch (perhaps a few years later) with arched headings which leap-frog across and extend the front. To judge from an early facade drawing, the house had been on the prim side before this addition. The interior has been well restored, with furnishings following the three periods of its growth, the work being carried out by the Oaklands Association which acquired the dwelling in 1959, the city having purchased it two years earlier to keep it from destruction. A valuable revelation of the architectural development of Tennessee throughout half of the century.

Open Tues.–Sat. 10–4:30, Sun. 1–4:30, except major holidays: admission

18 The Hermitage (1818–19/1831/1834–36)
c. 12 miles/19 kilometers E of city off IS 40, take Old Hickory exit near Nashville, Tennessee

The first house, other than a cabin, which Andrew and Rachel Jackson occupied (and almost undoubtedly designed themselves) was built in 1818–19. It was a "comfortable but unpretentious" square brick dwelling. When Andrew Jackson was installed as the nation's seventh President in 1829 the residence—to meet new demands—was considerably enlarged and renovated (1831), two wings being added, one containing a dining room reputedly capable of seating one hundred guests. A fire in October 1834 destroyed much of the interior of the house but left most walls intact. Rebuilding was almost immediately undertaken but changes were introduced, the most prominent of which was the erection of a Greek Revival two-story portico of quasi-Corinthian columns with cast-iron leaves across the front. (Note that this is in effect a screen across the old gabled end—as can be clearly seen at rear.)

Jackson died in 1845, and in 1856 the property, which included 500 acres/202 hectares of land, was purchased by the State of Tennessee; however, following the Civil War it was seriously neglected. In 1889 the Ladies Hermitage Association was formed to "beautify, preserve, and adorn" the residence and tomb, a task which they have carried out admirably. Many of the furnishings were saved from the fire, hence are original, with others added as necessary. The entry hall with Dufour wallpaper of *The Adventures of Telemaque* (c. 1823) is particularly

fine. Note the well-kept grounds, including the tree-lined, guitar-shaped driveway (1837), the nearby log cabin where the Jacksons once lived (1804–19), and Rachel's Church (1823). (Jackson's wife died nine years after the couple moved into The Hermitage but her contribution can be seen in the garden layout.)

Nearby stands **Tulip Grove** (1836), a Greek Revival-influenced house built for Jackson's nephew who was also his private secretary. The entire group is under the careful supervision of the Ladies Hermitage Association.

Open daily 9–5, except Dec. 25: admission

---

19 State Capitol (1845–59)
N off Charlotte Avenue between 6th–7th Avenues
Nashville, Tennessee

WILLIAM STRICKLAND, ARCHITECT

Masterfully utilizing a thrust of elevated land (the highest in the city), and boldly conceived to be observed on all four sides, the Tennessee Capitol ranks with the finest, and most original, in the nation. The perceptive Paul F. Norton, on the other hand, considers it "Strickland's

worst monument" and "ludicrous" (*The Arts in America, The 19th Century,* Scribner's, 1969). Porticos with eight Ionic columns and blank pediments—atop a rusticated Doric basement—fill and climax the two gable ends, with flat porticos of six similar columns projecting to break the midexpanse of the two sides. The influence of Athens' Erectheon is strong. Loftily, perhaps too loftily, perched atop the roof and serving in lieu of the traditional dome, sits a rusticated square tower base surmounted by a circular lantern (total height 170 feet/52 meters). Its design was inspired by the oft-used Choragic Monument of Lysicrates in Athens (335 B.C.), including the base (but with eight columns instead of six, as Agnes Gilchrist points out in her estimable book *William Strickland, Architect and Engineer,* Da Capo Press, 1969). The well-windowed Capitol places the House of Representatives with its two lateral galleries across the north end of the building (offices under the galleries), while the Senate shares the south end with the State Library, both the same size, a substantial lobby filling the middle. The building measures 238 x 109 feet/72 x 33 meters.

The talented Strickland (see Index for his other works) died in 1854, when the Capitol had already received its first legislative session, but before the completion of many details, including the tower (1855), and the terraces five years later. Appropriately he was buried in the north wall of the building which climaxed his distinguished career. Strickland's son, Francis, supervised completion of the work from 1854–59. In 1960 a major restoration was made of the entire area.

Daily tours on the hour, 8–4, except holidays

20   Belle Meade (1853–54/1880s)
Harding Road and Leake Avenue, c. 6.5 miles/10.5 kilometers SW of downtown
near Nashville, Tennessee

The history of Belle Meade covers a large share of the nineteenth century. The property, comprising some 5,300 acres/2,145 hectares, was purchased in 1807 by John Harding, who erected the log cabin mentioned below. In the 1820s a two-story, one-room deep brick house was put up. To this some ten years later were appended a kitchen building and breezeway. In 1853 a fire destroyed much of the brick dwelling, but rebuilding was commenced by General William Giles Harding, John's son, who had a sound knowledge of civil engineering and who very likely contributed to the new design. Harding was possibly able to incorporate the back and two side walls of the burned building in the new house. In the 1880s internal changes were carried out of which the most notable is the downstairs hall. The porte cochere was also a possible result of the 1880s work. In any case the

result is an elegant, largely Greek Revival house. Its external highlight is the porticoed facade of Tennessee limestone which presents a highly refined lineup of six slender Doric piers with narrow pediment angled above. The interiors, particularly the hall stair, are richly corniced and well furnished. The design of the house is frequently ascribed to William Strickland but the attribution is on stylistic grounds for no documentation has been found. The enormous smokehouse, carriage house, and stable (1890s) are not to be missed. (Belle Meade was at one time a great thoroughbred horse farm.)

Be sure to see the log cabin nearby, built in 1807 (actually rebuilt following an Indian attack and burning). Its two parts, each the length of conveniently handled logs, are separated by a dogtrot. The cabin once served as a stop, Dunham's Station, on the Chickasaw Trail, later the famous Natchez Trace. Acquired by the state in 1953, house and grounds are administered by the Association for the Preservation of Tennessee Antiquities.

Open Mon.–Sat. 9–5, Sun. 1–5, except major holidays: admission

---

21   The Downtown Presbyterian Church (1849–51/1881–82)
Church Street at 5th Avenue
Nashville, Tennessee

WILLIAM STRICKLAND, ARCHITECT

Pause but briefly to take in the pharaonic entry and the exterior towers of this relic inspired by the land of Mosaic bulrushes; save your strength for the interior. For within, the Downtown Presbyterian unveils the most engaging extant Egyptian Revival interior to be seen in this country. Although perhaps more suited to *Aïda* than infant baptism or even corporate worship, it is a design of such power as to place it high among the various revivals that characterized most American architecture of the last century and almost half of this. (It might also be kept in mind that Egypt is mentioned in the Old Testament more than any country except the Holy Land, hence this Christian adaptation of Egyptian architecture is not too farfetched.)

The hypostyle "halls" of massive Egyptian columns and lotus-bud capitals à la Karnak—both in relief and in painted perspective—that frame the chancel are daringly conceived and boldly painted. The win-

dows along the two sides each carry the proper cavetto cornice, while overhead painted clouds once wafted by.

However, it must be brought out that the two end "walls" seen today framing the sanctuary were not designed by—or at least not put in by—Mr. Strickland, but are additions dating from 1881–82. At that time "the church underwent a major redecoration to bring a richer Egyptian flavor to the interior. The Egyptianesque colors, patterns, scenes and symbols were added to the auditorium" (James A. Hoobler in an article in the *Tennessee Historical Quarterly,* Fall 1976). Because the church records for those years have been lost, it is not known who was responsible for the design, but Strickland's influence was certainly strong.

Measuring 80 x 136 feet/24 x 41 meters, the nave and balcony accommodate 1,300. The church was called The First Presbyterian until 1955 by which time most of the congregation had moved to the suburbs. It is now known as The Downtown Presbyterian Church. Strickland had timidly used the Egyptian Revival in his Mikveh-Israel Synagogue (1822–25) in Philadelphia, a building long demolished (see Gilchrist), but this Nashville example sings with conviction.

Open irregularly except for services: inquire

22 **The Parthenon** (1896–97/1920–31)
Centennial Park
SW on West End Avenue, NW on 25th Street
Nashville, Tennessee

"The Athens of the South" could, of course, do no better to celebrate the state's centennial in 1897 than to reproduce the Parthenon to house its Gallery of Fine Arts. Constructed in short order in plaster and lath—William C. Smith was surrogate architect—it became such a well-loved "friend" that in the late 1920s work began on replacing it in permanent form. This new building was to be a copy (restored) to the precise millimeter of Messrs. Ictinus and Callicrates' masterpiece in Athens (built 454–438 B.C.), except that a special café-au-lait concrete was used instead of Pentellic marble. This change of material is virtually the only difference between old and new except for a flat site in Nashville instead of an acropolis. There is curvature of the stylobate (on which the columns rest), entasis (the subtle vertical curve) of the columns and proper intercolumniation (i.e. closer together at corners). Moreover the sculpture in the pediments of the original (much of it now in the British Museum) stands fully restored here.

Nashville's Parthenon continues to serve as a museum with up-to-date art galleries in the basement. It also brings into sharp focus the question of whether or not the Parthenon in Athens in its present roofless, lonely-columned splendor is not more appealing to our space-conscious age as a ruin than as it appeared over 2,400 years ago when it was a near-solid sculptured block. Hart-Freeland-Roberts were the architects in charge of reconstruction (1931) with William Bell Dinsmoor consultant. It is listed in the National Register of Historic Places.

Open Tues.–Sat. 9–4:30, Sun. 1–4:30, except holidays

23   Lewis House and Morgan House (1966–67)
Vanderbilt University
Pierce Avenue between 24th and 25th Streets
Nashville, Tennessee

BRUSH, HUTCHISON & GWINN, ARCHITECTS

Twin 11-story apartments for married students, with 120 units (12 per floor) each, the first of a group of 4. Apartments vary from efficiencies to two-bedroom. By leaving the ground floor largely open, the architects have achieved not only a see-through spaciousness, but a popular sheltered communal area, used by children in inclement weather and groups of families for cook-outs. The long sides (163 feet/50 meters) of the buildings are protected from excess sun by 2-foot/.6-meter-deep, freestanding egg-crate grilles, and, as one walks by, constantly changing impressions develop between white concrete grilles and dark brick spandrels and base. The fire stairs project 4 feet/1.2 meters beyond the end walls, enabling a glazing strip to be inserted so that a light-spill floods out at night. Orderly and comely, the buildings were also very inexpensive.

Grounds and lobbies open during school year

---

24   The Old Mill (1830)
1 block NE of US 441, center of
Pigeon Forge, Tennessee

Not limited to producing flour from whole wheat, rye, cracked wheat, and buckwheat, plus cornmeal and grits, the Old Mill generated electricity for the village (population c. 1,400) until 1930. Taking its power from the Little Pigeon River (and standing about 7 miles/11 kilometers downstream from Gatlinburg), the mill presents a direct structural expression of the jobs best done by masonry versus those by wood. Its 24-foot/7.3-meter undershot wheel transmits its forces to two imported French buhrstones for grinding, a process which still continues. The building is nicely supported on 40-foot/12-meter-long poplar beams which rest on stone piers. The 120-foot/37-meter dam was originally of wood but was replaced by concrete in 1906.

Tours Apr.–mid-Nov., Mon.–Sat. 8–6: admission

Virginia

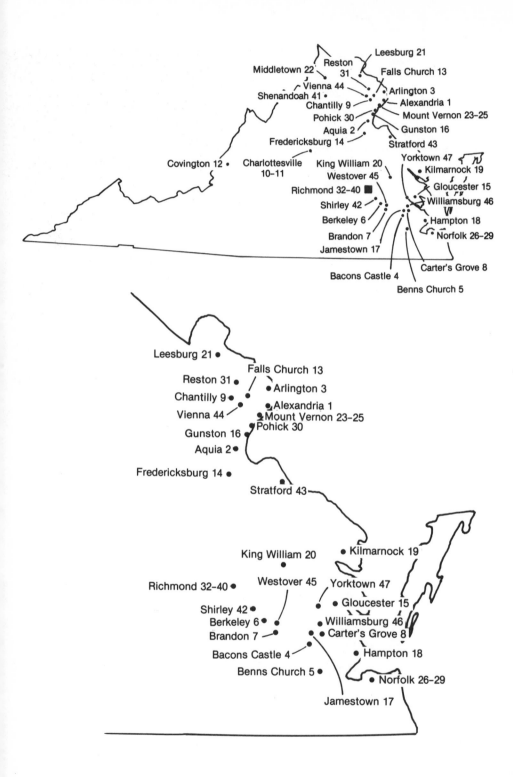

Leesburg 21
Reston 31
Middletown 22
Vienna 44
Shenandoah 41
Chantilly 9
Pohick 30
Aquia 2
Fredericksburg 14
Covington 12
Charlottesville 10–11
King William 20
Westover 45
Richmond 32–40 ■
Shirley 42
Berkeley 6
Brandon 7
Jamestown 17
Bacons Castle 4
Benns Church 5

Falls Church 13
Arlington 3
Alexandria 1
Mount Vernon 23–25
Gunston 16
Stratford 43
Yorktown 47
Kilmarnock 19
Gloucester 15
Williamsburg 46
Hampton 18
Norfolk 26–29
Carter's Grove 8

Leesburg 21 ●
Falls Church 13
Reston 31 ●
Arlington 3
Chantilly 9 ●
Alexandria 1
Vienna 44
Mount Vernon 23–25
Pohick 30
Gunston 16 ●
Aquia 2 ●
Fredericksburg 14 ●
Stratford 43
King William 20
Kilmarnock 19
Richmond 32–40 ●
Westover 45
Yorktown 47
Shirley 42 ●
Gloucester 15
Berkeley 6 ●
Williamsburg 46
Brandon 7
Carter's Grove 8
Bacons Castle 4
Hampton 18
Benns Church 5 ●
Norfolk 26–29
Jamestown 17

VIRGINIA

The buildings in boldface type are of general interest. The others are for the specialist.

Alexandria	1 Historic Alexandria (18th–19th century) Christ Church (1767–73) Gadsby's Tavern (1752/1792) Prince and Queen Streets
Aquia	2 **Aquia Church** (1751–57)
Arlington	3 Arlington House (1802–17)—George Hadfield
Bacons Castle	4 Bacon's Castle (pre-1676)
Benns Church	5 **St. Luke's Church** (c. 1632–65)
Berkeley	6 **Berkeley Plantation** (1726)
Brandon	7 **Brandon Plantation** (c. 1765)
Carter's Grove	8 **Carter's Grove Plantation** (1750–55/1927–28)
Chantilly	9 **Dulles Airport** (1958–62/1979–82)—Eero Saarinen & Associates; Ammann & Whitney
Charlottesville	10 **The Lawn and Rotunda** (1817–26)—Thomas Jefferson 11 **Monticello** (1769–1809)—Thomas Jefferson
Covington	12 Old Humpback Covered Bridge (1835)
Falls Church	13 **Fountain of Faith, National Memorial Park** (1952)—Carl Milles
Fredericksburg	14 Kenmore (1752–56)
Gloucester	15 **Ware Parish Church** (c. 1693–1715)
Gunston	16 **Gunston Hall** (1755–58)—William Buckland **Ann Mason Building** (1974)—Philip Ives

Jamestown   17 **Jamestown Festival Park Reconstruction**
                          (1607–98/1957)

Hampton   18 Virginia Hall (1874)—Richard Morris Hunt

Kilmarnock   19 **Christ Church** (c. 1732)

King William   20 **King William Court House** (c. 1725)

Leesburg   21 Oatlands (1804–27)

Middletown   22 **Belle Grove** (1794–97)

Mount Vernon   23 **Mount Vernon** (mid-1730s/1757–58/
                          1777–84/1787)
                       24 **Woodlawn Plantation** (1800–5)—William
                          Thornton
                       25 Pope-Leighey House (1940–41)—Frank
                          Lloyd Wright

Norfolk   26 **Adam Thoroughgood House** (c. 1636–40)
                       27 Moses Myers House (1791–92/1797)
                          Freemason Street Baptist Church (1848–
                          50)—T. U. Walter
                          Old Norfolk Academy Building (1840)—
                          T. U. Walter
                          Willoughby-Baylor House (1794)
                       28 Virginia National Bank (1968)—Skidmore,
                          Owings & Merrill; Williams & Tazewell
                          Partnership
                       29 **SCOPE—Cultural and Convention Center**
                          (1971 and 1972)—Williams & Tazewell
                          Partnership; Pier Luigi Nervi

Pohick (Lorton)   30 **Pohick Church** (1769–74)

Reston   31 **Reston New Town and Lake Anne Village**
                          (1965–   )—Conklin & Rossant

Richmond   32 **The Virginia State Capitol** (1785–92)—
                          Thomas Jefferson
                          Governor's Mansion
                       33 Wickham-Valentine House (1812)—
                          Robert Mills
                       34 Egyptian Building (1845)—Thomas S.
                          Stewart

Monumental Church (1812–14)—Robert
Mills

Old First Baptist Church (1839–41)—
Thomas U. Walter

35 Cast-Iron Buildings (late 1860s)

James Monroe's Tomb (1858)

36 Old City Hall (1887–94)—Elijah E. Myers

37 Jefferson Hotel (1893–95/1905)— .
Carrère & Hastings; J. Kevan Peebles

38 **Science Museum of Virginia—ex-Broad
Street Station** (1917–19/1979–81)—John
Russell Pope

39 **Reynolds Metals Building** (1955–58/
annex 1968)—Skidmore, Owings &
Merrill

40 **Philip Morris Factory** (1972–74)—
Skidmore, Owings & Merrill

Shenandoah   41 **Skyline Drive** (1931–39)—U. S. Bureau
of Public Roads

Blue Ridge Parkway

Shirley   42 **Shirley Plantation** (c. 1720/1740/1831)

Stratford   43 **Stratford Hall Plantation** (c. 1725–c. 30)

Vienna   44 **The Filene Center and Wolf Trap Farm
Park** (1968–71)—MacFadyen & Knowles;
Alfredo De Vido

Westover   45 **Westover** (c. 1730–c. 34)

Williamsburg   46 **Colonial Williamsburg Restoration** (1699–
1780/1927–   )—Perry, Shaw & Hepburn;
The Colonial Williamsburg Foundation

Yorktown   47 **Main Street and the Nelson House**
(c. 1711)

NOTE: As many of the churches and plantation houses in Virginia
are not in or near a city, they are (in most cases) arranged geographically by their name; i.e. Aquia Church, Berkeley Plantation, etc.

1 Historic Alexandria (18th–19th century)
Alexandria, Virginia

Alexandria was platted in 1749—with seventeen-year-old George Washington an assistant surveyor—given to the District of Columbia in 1789, and returned to Virginia at the request of its "homesick" citizens in 1846. Having an unusual number of old buildings, the town, again becoming popular after years of doldrums, is a pleasant place for a stroll. A helpful map can be had at **Ramsay House** (1724), 221 King Street at North Fairfax (Open daily 10–5, except holidays).

Christ Church (1767–73) at North Washington Street (Alt. US 1) and Cameron (open winter Mon.–Sat. 9–4:30, Sun. 1–5; summer, Mon.–Sat. 2–5) sits comfortably behind low walls with trees and graveyard adding to the ambience. Though the interior lacks coordination and has suffered numerous changes (pulpit moved from north wall to east end, etc.), it forms a light and airy worship room. James Wren was its designer. (The tower dates from 1818.)

Gadsby's Tavern (1752 and 1792), 134 North Royal Street at Cameron (open Mon.–Sat. 10–5, Sun. 12–5, except holidays), is distinguished for its beautiful woodwork and its ballroom now in the American Wing of the Metropolitan Museum in New York but reproduced accurately here.

Prince and Queen Streets (east of Washington Street) each presents a parade of mostly early-nineteenth-century houses (almost all private) many of which have been restored and imaginatively painted. Though not open to the public, their collective impression and simple planting make for attractive walks.

It is hoped that Alexandria's waterfront will be rehabilitated into a Potomac River National Historic Park. This would add greatly to the pleasures of the city.

Buildings open as indicated

---

2   Aquia Church (1751–57)
**just E of Aquia exit of IS 95 and US 1, c. 3 miles/4.8 kilometers
    N of Stafford**
Aquia Church, Stafford County, Virginia

Almost hidden atop a knoll just off the Interstate and US 1, Aquia Church (pronounced ack-quiah) stands peacefully surrounded by a graveyard and a vast variety of trees. The muffled sounds of traffic seem eons away. The building itself was constructed of red brick with prominent, locally quarried, Aquia Creek sandstone quoins, echoed strongly around the doors. (This was the stone that was also used for the Capitol and the White House.) A certain quaintness characterizes the exterior but within it is of lively cheeriness. The church grows from a Greek-cross plan (like Christ Church near Kilmarnock, q.v.), its all-

white plastered and painted interior producing an impeccable atmosphere. The interior is also thought to be a near copy of a parish church in Overwharton, Staffordshire, England, whence came many of the region's early settlers.

There are two dominants within which attract attention: the pedimented "panel" on the sanctuary wall and the three-tiered pulpit at right known as a "triple decker." The pediment is sharply detailed in white-painted wood with the Ten Commandments, the Apostles' Creed, and the Lord's Prayer in four arched black panels impressively installed above the altar table. (In most seventeenth- and many early-eighteenth-century churches in England and the Colonies these words were part of the architecture because of the scarcity of books. This ordinance stemmed from the 1604 Hampton Court Conference which stated, among other requirements, that "the furniture of a church must include the Ten Commandments on the east wall, with other chosen sentences." Thus Faith, Prayer, and Law—the Apostles' Creed, the Lord's Prayer, and the Ten Commandments—were commonly used.) The pulpit at Aquia, unlike many of the period, is spatially related to the sanctuary by its angled projection and its triple desks, seasonally vested, creating thus good three-dimensional activity. The balusters in the pulpit stairs and in the sanctuary railing are white painted topped by dark walnut rails. The square box pews are low and white with the same dark rails seen in the chancel. The organ and choir are in the gallery over the west door. The flood of natural light via its double row of windows, the top one roundheaded to emphasize from the outside that only one floor exists within (as at Pohick Church, q.v.), is admirable, as is the whole feeling of space. (Inigo Jones' Banqueting Hall in London probably inspired the window arrangement.) Though no longer used, note the well-branched chandeliers.

A few years after its completion the church interior burned (1754), but it was rebuilt three years later by the same "undertaker," that is builder-contractor, a gentleman with the lugubrious name of Mourning Richards, who did the work for 110,900 pounds/50,000 kilograms of tobacco. Though repaired through the years, fortunately no major changes were made. Its upkeep has been noteworthy due to a generous endowment given the church in 1873. James Wren (little or no relation to Christopher) was, some feel, the architect, but this is by no means certain.

Open irregularly on weekdays; services Sun. morning

---

3   Arlington House (1802–17)
The Robert E. Lee Memorial
Arlington National Cemetery, via Arlington Memorial Bridge from Washington, or George Washington Memorial Parkway
Arlington, Virginia

GEORGE HADFIELD, ARCHITECT

Arlington House commands an unequaled panorama of Washington from its hilltop site on axis with Memorial Bridge and the Lincoln Memorial. The vista from its gutsy, primitive Greek temple facade (e.g. the Temple of Poseidon at Paestum, 500 B.C.) extends as far as the Capitol. Backed up against the prominent portico with its chubby Doric columns—possibly the only part by architect Hadfield—stands a smallish house with two lateral wings with arcaded windows in the semi-Federal Style. (The wings were built first, as was often the practice of the time, and finished in 1804. The hollow brick columns, am-

bitiously, are stuccoed and "marbleized" with paint. The dining room and "parlors" (to use the Lee terminology for these main rooms) are simply but pleasantly furnished. Purchased by the government in 1883, restoration was not begun until 1925. It is now administered by the National Park Service.

Open Apr.–Sept., daily 9:30–6, Oct.–Mar., daily 9:30–4:30

---

4 Bacon's Castle (pre-1676)
off VA 10 just NNE of town on VA 617
Bacons Castle, Virginia

The almost legendary Bacon's Castle is now fortunately open to the public for at least part of the year. *Preservation News* (of the National Trust) terms the castle "the sole surviving high Jacobean manor house in America" (January 1974), so it is doubly welcome that it can be seen. The Jacobean was an elusive period of English (hence early Colonial) architecture, emerging largely during the reign of James I (1603–25) but picking up the thread of development begun under his predecessor the redoubtable Elizabeth I. Under James, it moved away

from the transitional Tudor toward greater employment of the newly fashionable Renaissance, especially in details. It never fully established itself, however. What it lacked in finesse it sought to assert in bravura. There are awkward moments in the Jacobean—even the Greek use of *Jakōbos* (i.e. James) seems odd—but it made for a spirited scene in domestic building.

At Bacon's Castle (actually built by a man named Arthur Allen) the two boldly curvilinear gable ends, recalling Flemish work, are topped by three square semidetached chimney flues set on the diagonal and rising with Tudor-Jacobean conviction. Note the unusual cross plan of the house with gabled "porches," a typical medieval feature.

In 1856 the dwelling was substantially expanded to the east by uncongenial additions. Partial restoration took place in 1939–41 but by that time the house had lost much of its native medievalism (the casement windows for example). Also gone is the original roof which some feel was of stone tiles as one of them has been discovered. The interior has been altered but the superb paneling installed around 1740 fortunately remains. Note, also, the two original fireplaces with their heavy wood beams finished with a chamfer and "lambs tongue."

Nathaniel Bacon (1647–76), incidentally, organized the first armed rebellion against British authority (the tyranny of Governor Berkeley) ninety-nine years before Lexington and Concord. His troops' use of Mr. Allen's house in 1676 gave it its subsequent sobriquet. Bacon died during the campaign (of either malaria or poison) but his actions were influential in initiating an "American" consciousness.

Bacon's Castle and 40 acres/16 hectares of land were purchased (1973) by the Association for the Preservation of Virginia Antiquities. As Professor William H. Pierson, Jr., put it, "Bacon's Castle is a milestone in the history of the Virginia Colony" (*American Buildings and Their Architects,* Doubleday, 1970). The National Register of Historic Places dates the house c. 1656.

Open during Historic Garden Week, end of Apr., plus Apr.–Sept., Sat.–Sun. 10–5: admission

---

5   St. Luke's Church (c. 1632–65)
   **VA 10, 4 miles/6.4 kilometers SE of Smithfield, near SW end of
      James River Bridge**
   Benns Church, Isle of Wight County, Virginia

St. Luke's proclaims itself to be, "The Nation's Oldest Standing Church" if we believe local legend, which probably most historians are inclined to do. But even if we use the date of 1682 (favored by only a few), St. Luke's is the oldest church in the United States of Gothic derivation that has come down to us basically as built. Moreover at nearby Jamestown stands the tower of a brick church constructed there in 1639–47, so it would certainly seem probable that St. Luke's was completed around the early-middle seventeenth century. (Incidentally, the nave behind the old Jamestown tower was reconstructed in 1907 for Virginia's Tricentennial.) But when speaking of the age of the nation's churches, it is illuminating to read the late Hugh Morrison in his admirable *Early American Architecture* (Oxford University Press, 1952), who writes that "By 1626 43 churches had been built" by the Spanish in New Mexico. However, none of these survive as constructed, with the probable exception of parts of San Estévan at Ácoma, 1629–41 (q.v.).

The square, "almost Norman" tower of St. Luke's, the stepped Flemish gables, the roundheaded windows with two lancets, its buttresses, the startling interior with its timber trusswork and tie beams and its rood screen, all these elements when put together suggest a medieval south English parish church. There is a primitiveness about it, but the results are ingenuous.

In the late seventeenth century the church was "modernized" on the interior by plastering over the medieval ceiling and, outside, by adding a story and the quoins to the tower. After disestablishment it languished, in 1821 it was reactivated, then in the early middle of the nineteenth century it was semiabandoned, while in 1887 a storm severely injured the roof, causing it to be replaced. In 1953–57, the church was declared a National Shrine. Then following the discovery of crumbling foundations and lower walls, and after four years of research, it was meticulously restored to what its original condition may have been. This was based on contemporary English precedent, with the strange exception of the late-nineteenth-century stained glass instead of clear diamond panes which the first church undoubtedly had. A primitive but illuminating building. As Professor William B. O'Neal points out in his *Architecture in Virginia* (The Virginia Museum, 1968), "St. Luke's is the only *original* Gothic building to have survived in the nation." The National Register of Historic Places gives its date as 1632.

Open 9:30–5 daily; closed Jan.

6 Berkeley Plantation (1726)
S off VA 5, turnoff c. 22 miles/35 kilometers SE of Richmond
Berkeley, Charles City County, Virginia

Berkeley and the nearby Shirley (q.v.) are the most historically authentic plantation houses open to the public along the James River. Carter's Grove and Westover (q.v.) are more elaborate and more impressive, but the aforementioned two have maintained their original layout of separate house and dependencies, hence give us a keener insight into the early-eighteenth-century architecture of this evocative part of the world. Virtually all of the Virginia plantations followed English adaptations of the famous Italian villas of Palladio (1508–80), an architect who probably was the most influential designer in the history of the profession. Palladio's domestic work—and that of those who were swayed by him in England and the Colonies—always sought a dominant structure, often with symmetrically disposed lesser units or wings. These were sometimes attached to the house (in either a straight line or arced in front), and sometimes—generally so in the American Colonies—standing unattached in subordinate positions on either side of the main building.

Berkeley falls into this latter pattern, with a red brick main house of two and a half stories and two-story "dependencies," covered with pinkish stucco, on either side. The original one at the west was occupied by the kitchen and servants' quarters, that to the east was a Bachelor's House and sometimes a schoolhouse, and is now used as the entry pavilion. (Both date from the 1840s, having replaced earlier structures.) Berkeley, like all the plantation houses, was originally approached primarily from the river—at that time the only convenient highway—and the series of broadly stepped gardens connecting the house with the river are still part of the pleasures of the place.

The house itself forms a straightforward rectangle, sturdily proportioned but devoid of embellishment except for the unusual pent, or pediment, roofs across the two gables. Doors and windows are simply notched holes in the English-bond brick walls, the brick pediment over the entrances cutting the stringcourse. The exterior walls are 3 feet/.9 meter thick, while even the inner partitions are 2 feet/.6 meter of solid brick. The interiors, though comfortable, are not overwhelming, the original (and more elaborate) paneling and trim having been replaced at the end of the eighteenth century. After suffering indignities through wars and neglect, then undergoing careless changes, the house was purchased in 1926 and since then has been lovingly restored (1937–38) by the owners as a fully operative plantation. Its land grant dates to 1619.

As noted under Plimoth Plantation Restoration in Massachusetts, Berkeley was the site of the first Thanksgiving, proclaimed when the *Margaret* safely dropped anchor in the James River on December 4, 1619, over a year before the Pilgrims landed. (It might be added that most voyagers gave thanks upon landing safely in the New World.)

Open daily 8–5, except Dec. 25: admission

---

7   **Brandon Plantation** (c. 1765)
    off VA 10 NE on VA 611, immediately E of Burrowsville, then
       5.4 miles/8.7 kilometers to
    Brandon, Prince George County, Virginia

Brandon has the most extensive, the best-kept, and the most beautiful gardens along the James River which are open to the public. The grounds in front and back of the house are close-cropped, well treed on the approach side, open but ordered to the northeast, with the gar-

dens proper lying between the house and the river. Although flowers are seasonally evident, it is the manicured lawns, the organization of the trees, the ancient boxwood, and the flowering shrubs which provide the garden's sophisticated appeal.

The warmly scaled house itself provides us with an unusually articulated and lengthy expanse. The first buildings, which were thought to date from the late 1600s, occupied the site of the present two dependencies. These units were then enlarged and joined by a three-division central block designed, some feel, by young (twenty-two-year-old) Thomas Jefferson. But as Waterman in his *Mansions of Virginia* (Bonanza Books, 1945, p. 366) points out and illustrates, the plan is almost straight from Robert Morris' *Select Architecture* (1757)—a book which Jefferson owned. Fiske Kimball first proposed Jefferson's role in the central bay, writing that "it is not unlikely that he made suggestions for its design" (Fiske Kimball, *Thomas Jefferson, Architect* with New Introduction by Frederick Doveton Nichols, Da Capo Press, 1968). The 210-foot/64-meter-long result almost suggests a symmetrical dance with its two-story dependencies, low hyphens, one-story flanks of house, with two-story central bay. The house and grounds were in sad condition until the present owners' parents, who purchased it in 1926, initiated a complete renovation. Very fine.

Gardens only open to the public: daily 9–5:30, except Dec. 25: admission. House open during Garden Week and to groups by appointment: admission

8 Carter's Grove Plantation (1750–55/1927–28)
SW off US 60, turn off 6.2 miles/10 kilometers SE of
Williamsburg
Carter's Grove, James City County, Virginia

Though the exterior of Carter's Grove has been substantially altered by additions, the house remains one of the nation's most distinguished Georgian examples, while the interior is of the greatest splendor. The mansion originally consisted of a two-story central block, hip-roofed and dormerless, 72 feet/22 meters long, and separated (24.5 feet/7.5 meters) from flanking gable-roofed, story-and-a-half dependencies 40 feet/12 meters long. (The dependencies antedate the main house.) It was the standard plantation pattern so to speak, derived from the usual Palladian-inspired English prototypes. Then in 1927–28 carefully designed hyphens were put in to connect the three detached buildings, while rows of dormers were installed on the main roof, which was then raised 11 feet/3.4 meters to accommodate new rooms on the third floor. The entire operation (plus slate roofing, removal of old porch etc.) was skillfully carried out, and the house is more impressive as a 201-foot/61-meter-long, ground-loving mansion than as three individ-

ual buildings—as a look at old photographs will confirm. It is not as authentic as it was but it is more adapted to twentieth-century living. Carter's Grove is very similar to the earlier Westover (q.v.), which also has been altered by the addition of hyphens, but its facades, which are 8 feet/2.4 meters longer than the latter, lack the subtle refinements seen in Westover's segmental window treatment (their diminution as the floors increase). Moreover the near-identical entries at Carter's Grove are of simple brick, neatly pedimented, and not as enthusiastic as the stone-trimmed doorways at Westover. On the other hand, the recent hyphens at Carter's Grove are far superior, as is its elegant massing.

On the interior, the mansion reaches its impressive peak. Its axially aligned entry "salon" and stair hall have no peer in this country—"the finest room in all Georgian architecture" (Morrison)—while its parade of other chambers is not far behind. Both entry and hall are paneled in locally cut heart pine, which was painted when the house was built, while stairs and balusters are of walnut. The tread nosings are secured with nails concealed with heart-shaped inlay, and the carving of the consoles at the end of each tread is noteworthy. (The stairs from the second to third floor date from the 1927–28 changes.) The impression on entering the hall is of vibrancy, with space pulling one up the stair while the lateral halls attract one through the front rooms. The long corridor effect seen today through and beyond the two riverfront rooms did not exist, of course, before the hyphens were added and the previous windows made into doors. The kitchen dependency (at east) is the oldest part of the house, its back section possibly dating from the end of the seventeenth century.

The conjoined halls, with the suave elliptical arch separating them, are reputedly the work of Richard Bayliss who was brought from England to do the woodwork. David Minitree, a local brickmason, was the contractor-builder, while Richard Taliaferro, some authorities feel, may have had a hand in its overall design. Whoever the progenitor, and whatever we may feel about the changes carried through so few years ago, the house unquestionably is one of the country's greatest. The property was purchased in 1963 by the Sealantic Fund, Inc., upon the death of the owner, and opened to the public the following year. Late in 1969 the Fund (Rockefeller-supported) gave the house to the nearby Colonial Williamsburg Foundation, which wisely doubled the acreage to preserve the estate from intrusion. The terraced gardens— called falling terraces in the eighteenth century—which originally stepped down to the James River, have been reconstructed.

Open Feb.–Oct., daily 9–5, Nov.–Jan., 9–4, except Dec. 25: admission

9 Dulles Airport (1958–62/1979–82)
Exit 12 from Beltway (IS 495), then Dulles Access Road
c. 30 miles/48 kilometers W of Washington, D.C.
Chantilly, Virginia

EERO SAARINEN & ASSOCIATES, ARCHITECTS; AMMANN & WHITNEY, ENGINEERS

Dulles Airport is the most stupendous architectural statement on the North American landscape. It is not only a breathtaking structure, it marked a new era in the analysis of passenger-to-plane logistics, that hitherto curiously forgotten facet of air travel. For at Dulles, the myriad "fingers" of conventional airport design—those endless, wearisome corridors down which thousands eternally trudge—have been eliminated. Instead, the airport bus or cab draws up to the terminal, the passengers walk 150 feet/46 meters maximum to a check-in station on the far side, and there board a mobile lounge which "attaches" to the building. They are then whisked to the plane on the airstrip 1 mile/1.6 kilometers away. No harassment of passenger, no juggling or expensive taxiing of jet planes. The building acts as a brief staging point, not a dumping ground; the "bus is now architecture." It is a beautifully analyzed concept. However, for some the building is disappointing inside.

Dulles is isolated in unprepossessing countryside but the approach to the airport has been so adroitly landscaped—by Dan Kiley—that excitement is generated at a distance and is maintained to the very front doors. The drive is calculated to provide vistas of ever-changing perspectives which end by fully revealing building and tower. The terminal itself is visually dominated by its fantastic suspended roof, its overall shape suggestive of one of Eric Mendelsohn's "imaginary sketches" of 1917. Behind stands the exclamation point of the control tower (by I. M. Pei & Partners), which rises with sculptured authority and pagoda elegance over the Virginia landscape.

As one nears the terminal, one encounters the first problem with which the architect, like so many other architects, had to contend: facing north, the entire entrance side stands in shade almost all day long. Nonetheless the scale of the 65-foot/20-meter-high entry has great power. (It does not, however, provide any weather protection.)

On stepping inside the terminal, early anticipation tends to falter, for the space proclaimed by the exterior largely disappears as the sizable central spine of ticket offices, shops, and services blocks a full

grasp of the inner volume. It is a noble frame with little inner nobility, stupendous engineering which services tend to vitiate. (When under construction the framing and roof were awesome.) Moreover glimpses of the catenary of the roof visually "resting on" the top of this spine are awkward. Nor can one see outward toward the landing area (distant) because the wall for the mobile lounges forms much of the south side of the terminal. The service spine—whatever it might do to the terminal's potentially glorious space—is itself characterized by the late Eero Saarinen's admirable attention to detail. The usual clutter of newspaper stands is cleverly masked behind partitions, the shops are restrained, the stainless steel and leather bench-chairs (by the late Charles Eames) have become classics. But in spite of the above criticism, the room is eminently graspable, bright, and sunny. The pure rectangle of the terminal proper is broken at midpoint by an extension for lounge space and, at its end, a restaurant. As regards surface transportation, note that the passenger's automobile is perfunctorily handled: there are no under-cover facilities. (The middle ramp on the exterior is used by deplaning passengers, the lowest one, really a ground-level road, leads to the parking lot—the ramps thus forming a tiered podium for the building.)

The marvelous structure of Dulles is based on heavily reinforced concrete piers, sixteen per side, 65 feet/20 meters high in front, 40 feet/12 meters at back, and spaced 40 feet/12 meters apart for a total length of 600 feet/183 meters. From edge beams that laterally connect each of the two lines of piers are slung steel cables 1 inch/25 millimeters in diameter, and from these are hung 1,792 precast concrete panels, each weighing 800 pounds/363 kilograms. The thirty-two piers incline outward the better to counteract the roof load. (The "rods" which connect the piers laterally and from which the hammock roof is slung, are, contrary to appearances, not on the upper face or fascia, but at that inner point on the rear faces of the piers just behind the "holes" where piers and roof deck first meet.) The airport thus both thrills—it is unforgettable from a distance at dusk—yet can disappoint within when its "promised" sweep of space does not materialize. But even with the above reservations, Dulles obviously ranks among the great buildings of our time.

Dulles—Update Dulles was planned before the advent of jumbo jets carrying some 350 passengers, and before the need for strict security measures. Both of these conditions have thus somewhat compromised the airport's original flow of operations. In spring 1978 plans were announced for a substantial expansion on the "field" side of the terminal, with Hellmuth, Obata & Kassabaum architects. The gates where pas-

596

sengers originally entered the mobile lounges (e.g. the lower part of the south wall) have been removed at the east half and a 50-foot/15-meter-wide, same-level, six-bay lounge departure station created (1979–80). (This abuts the side of the center projecting wing which houses the restaurant and services.) Baggage handling and mechanical services are placed directly underneath this extension (and below grade), out of sight and weatherproof. A west expansion is planned for 1982. These two lengthy rooms were kept purposefully low so as not to impinge on the profile of the terminal's exterior. In the more distant future the building will be extended linearly by adding bays to each end. New Budd "Planemates," carrying up to one hundred passengers, will supplement the earlier mobile lounges. Both can, of course, deliver and pick up passengers at the several entries of the large planes, not simply through the nose door.

Interstate 66 is currently under construction and will feed directly into Washington. Dulles Access Highway will link to this and when completed (c. 1983) will cut downtown surface commuting time to twenty-five to thirty minutes.

---

10 The Lawn and Rotunda (1817–26)
University of Virginia
Charlottesville, Virginia

THOMAS JEFFERSON, ARCHITECT

For a nation which has few successfully composed urban spaces, the Lawn and Rotunda of Mr. Jefferson's "academical village" offer lessons just as valid today as they were when laid out. For here lies one of the world's great architectural conceptions, probably the finest since Bernini's embracing forecourt to St. Peter's (1656–67). Anyone wanting to savor masterful space handling, let alone every architect and planner, should make his hegira here. The greatest rewards are not for the neo-Classical mold of the architecture, for this, fine though it be, belongs to another era, but for what this architecture does in creating and delimiting three dimensions.

Jefferson was interested in education as an essential element of a democracy—his tombstone inscription ends with "the Father of the University of Virginia"—and when he retired from the presidency (1809), much of his energy was directed toward creating the nation's first non-church university. He sought to mold an educational system

in a "village" with faculty and student body united in closely related buildings. "Corporate humanism" Kenneth Clark called it, one cast architecturally in a "Classic," not Georgian, frame.

The plan of the university takes one to an inner refuge of Lawn and Rotunda (at the closed end) via a short flight of compacted stairs to unfold in a revelation of ordered greenery and buildings. The colonnades along each side allow one to participate in enclosure or move outward to observe it; one can walk enframed by building, by building and trees, or by trees alone. Each option has its rewards. From the south end, the broad terraces of lawn as they step up toward the Rotunda (reflecting the inclined profile of the site) create a descant in the rhythm of the whole, giving an upbeat to the colonnades and pavilions on each side and emphasizing the crowning of the Rotunda. The rows of trees are doubled so that the central open space is bordered with tall trees to create a proper horizontal scale, while a smaller row behind eases the scale to the buildings.

Ten two-story "Pavilions," five to a side, were planned to house classrooms on the lower floors with unmarried professors' quarters above, and with dormitories and dining rooms for students spaced in between. Behind these two rows that frame the "grounds" (not "campus"), and separated from them by gardens with the famous serpentine walls, stood another row for students' quarters interlarded with married professors' quarters. Strangely, Jefferson originally planned that these four parallel rows of buildings be simply thus, four rows with no focus at either beginning or end. However, he had the foresight to get professional architectural advice from both Thornton and Latrobe. Thornton's contribution primarily concerned the arcades and pavilions, while Latrobe, also contributing to building design, immediately realized that a dominant was needed to pull the rows of buildings into a unified composition. He therefore suggested that a substantial domed structure would add enormously to the grouping. This idea appealed to Jefferson, who placed the Rotunda, containing the library and six oval classrooms, across the north end of the Lawn and thereby brought into superb unity the previously uncoordinated rows. Based on Rome's Pantheon—a cylindrical corpus with pedimented porch in front but here at precisely half scale—the Rotunda, Jefferson's "capstone of the University," superintends the great space in front, sending out low lateral terraces across its end to connect the center with the rows of housing. The ten red brick pavilions, it should be noted, are all different—a museum of Classical orders based on actual Roman temples. Their spacing, moreover, is not a static symmetry but a brilliant progression of four, six, seven, eight living units between the five pavilions, those more closely grouped being nearest the closed end.

The Rotunda was heavily damaged by fire in 1895 but was rebuilt with alterations by Stanford White, who took out the second floor to make one larger inner space, and replaced the bulky mid-nineteenth-century addition, which had been attached at north, with a portico to match that facing The Lawn. (McKim, Mead & White also were responsible for the 1896–98 building, White in charge, which unfortunately closes the once open end of the Lawn blocking the vista of the distant mountains.) With Professor Frederick D. Nichols, the Jeffersonian scholar and architect, working with the firm of Ballou & Justice, the Rotunda was completely restored to Jefferson's design for the Bicentennial. Although the pavilions and quarters also underwent some changes through the years, they, too, recently have been restored. One of the nation's greatest architectural experiences yet one strangely without subsequent influence.

Tours from Rotunda Mon.–Fri. at 10 and 11 A.M., *2, 3, and 4* P.M.

---

11 Monticello (1769–1809)
SE of town via VA 53, c. 5 miles/8 kilometers from downtown Charlottesville, Virginia

THOMAS JEFFERSON, ARCHITECT

Thomas Jefferson was the nation's most talented self-trained architect, almost a professional. He had spent five years in France (1784–89) as our Minister there, and during that time he studied as many buildings as his duties would allow. This exposure to architectural sophistication and French visionary design and philosophy gilded his book learning and can be clearly seen in Monticello. Moreover he went out of his way to meet the most distinguished avant-garde architects of his day, Boullée and Ledoux among them. Though smitten by the Classicists, Palladio, and the new French approach to domestic life (the Hôtel de Salm, 1782–89, in Paris was particularly pertinent), Jefferson was no copyist (except, in part, with the Virginia Capitol, q.v.) and, as with his glorious University, he was inspired but not fettered either by what he had seen and sketched, or by the books in his extensive architectural library. Although Jefferson's architectural directions were strictly of Classic inclinations, his taste in gardens ran to the informal English fashion of landscaping then also popular in France.

Upon his return to the States (1789), although his beloved wife and

four of his six children had died (Mrs. Jefferson plus three of the children before he went to France), he began a considerable expansion of his early house and garden, a process that was only partially interrupted when he was President from 1801–9.

At Monticello he was perceptive in his recognition of microclimate, for his "little mountain" provides a site 567 feet/173 meters above the Rivanna River and hence boasts cooler, cleaner air as well as finer views. He was also sharply analytic in his deployment of serving versus served areas (cf. the theories of Louis I. Kahn); and finally a capable tinkerer with building mechanics.

For the basic plan of the "new" Monticello he took the flanking dependencies typical of the Palladian school, but instead of flaunting these wings on the approach side of his hilltop house, he moved the dwelling near the east edge of the judiciously leveled site, on which work had begun in 1768. There he projected his dependencies to make an angled U-shaped plan with house in center but with the two long, parallel utility wings half-tucked into either side of the grade drop-off. Thus services are virtually invisible from the mansion except for their roofs which form low terrace decks, one on the north, its twin on the south, the two connected by passages underground as an extended basement of the house proper. By this means views from the house are open in all directions. Not only is servicing of the house (servants, kitchen, dairy, smokehouse, stables, etc.) accommodated on its own totally separated level, the terraces extend the space of the dwelling outward to smooth the transition of house to gardens (which Jefferson also originally designed and which were properly restored in 1939–40). The terraces, framed by "Chinese" railings, terminate in pavilions, the one at the north once having served as a law office. The ingenious embrace of the West Lawn by the house and its two arms provides one of the meaningful contributions of the overall plan.

In the design of the dwelling itself some ambivalence appears, perhaps inevitably. For this house, this "laboratory" house, was put together, taken apart, and eventually fashioned over a period of forty years! Its site utilization and its incredibly original design are masterful; its scale at times disturbing. On the east (approach) side, two floors masquerade as one (the second-floor window frames touching those below), while on the garden side there is some lack of clarity as to what goes on inside. The porticoed parlor flanked by the dining room and Jefferson's bedroom-study—the three forming the first (i.e. original) section of the house—are of two stories. The six "compressed" rooms of the second floor are largely invisible from the west and the three bedrooms of the top floor are windowless but skylit, with the prominent dome containing one half-round and four round windows. The problem was to coordinate all of these elements into a coherent whole. The purist might have reservations concerning the sometimes awkward result; the rest of us will rejoice in its freshness, even if it is vulnerable. Note that Monticello is a building whose design urges one to perambulate about its circumference (a factor stemming largely from its angled corners perhaps an influence from the Hammond Harwood House in Annapolis, q.v.). It is not fully grasped from a static point.

The interiors are for many the most intriguing parts of the house, particularly for the parade of Roman-inspired details. Almost every room disports an entablature or frieze from an ancient temple via one of the late-eighteenth-century French or English books on the antique. (An excellent account of the house and its evolution is contained in *Monticello* by Frederick D. Nichols and James A. Bear, Jr., published by the Thomas Jefferson Memorial Foundation, 1967, and available at the gift shop at entry.) As Mr. Jefferson wrote, "The Hall is in the Ionic, the Dining Room is in the Doric, the Parlor is in the Corinthian, and the Dome in the Attic. In the other rooms are introduced several different forms of those orders, all in the truest proportions according to Palladio." An education in architecture of the period.

Jefferson died in 1826 in near poverty, partly because public duty had kept him from properly managing his estate, but also because, against his better judgment, he had signed a note for a cousin in 1820 who then went bankrupt, taking Jefferson with him. The house was sold five years later, the furniture even earlier. It was not until 1923 that the house and grounds, which had been reasonably maintained until the mid-nineteenth century, and then allowed to degenerate, were acquired by the Thomas Jefferson Memorial Foundation. The desperate and often frustrating efforts to raise funds for the purchase of the property were spearheaded by the Moscow-born Theodore Fred Kuper. In 1954 total restoration was undertaken, much furniture has been retrieved from descendants, and Monticello's pleasures opened to a grateful public.

Open daily Mar.–Oct. 8–5, Nov.–Feb. 9–4:30: admission

---

12   Old Humpback Covered Bridge (1835)
off US 60, 3 miles/4.8 kilometers W of town
Covington, Virginia

The humpback form of covered bridge was rarely used (being more difficult for horse-drawn loads), and this is one of the few still standing in the U.S.A. It is also the oldest covered bridge left in the state.

Remaining in active service for almost a century (until 1929), it was eventually superseded by a steel span. But concerned citizens and civic groups, particularly the Business and Professional Women's Club, and the sympathetic Virginia Department of Highways, put up matching funds, bought the surrounding property, and saved the old span from destruction. In 1954 it was completely reconditioned (except for tin roof), and now graces a state wayside park just off IS 64 and US 60. A Mr. Venable was supposedly its designer; multiple kingpost trusses were used to span its 100-foot/30-meter length with an 8-foot/2.4-meter rise at center.

---

13   Fountain of Faith, National Memorial Park (1952)
US 29 and 211, 2 miles/3.2 kilometers W of town on Lee Highway
Falls Church, Virginia

CARL MILLES, SCULPTOR

Commissioned as the focal point of the cemetery, this evocative group of figures epitomizes Milles' unrivaled interweaving of bronze and

water. Love, tenderness, joy, aspiration, grief, all find expression in these thirty-eight life-sized figures (most of which were modeled on Milles' friends). But transcending the individual figures, which at times are rigid, rises the ebullient fusion of metal and spray, of solid and ephemeral. The oscillation of the fountains being turned on and off makes one more aware of the quality of the message Milles (1875–1955) sought to give. Obviously descended from his Meeting of the Waters in St. Louis (1940—q.v.), the Fountain of Faith summarizes Milles' contribution to outdoor sculpture and water. It is one of the Swedish sculptor's masterpieces in this country. Note that there are no tombstones jostling across the Park's 96 acres/39 hectares, only names engraved in the memorial walls and plaques set flush in the extensive lawn.

Open daily 9–5

---

14   Kenmore (1752–56)
1201 Washington Avenue
Fredericksburg, Virginia

The walled garden of Kenmore surrounds a house of routine Georgian exterior (except for jerkin-head roof), but do not be deterred by its plainness. For behind these simple brick walls, which some historians feel were to have been stuccoed, and behind its starkly punched windows, are rooms with some of the most ornate and beautiful ceilings in this country. Inspired by English books on the subject (Batty Langley's *City and Country Builders' Treasury* of 1740 is mentioned), and carved probably around 1770, they have miraculously survived over two hundred winters and summers with scarcely a crack. Their allegorical scenes merit detailed study. Note, too, the elaborately carved wood mantels, the plaster overmantels, and the Irish crystal chandelier. In plan, the Great Room—"one of the finest of·its style in the country" (Waterman)—and the library face the distant river on the north side of the house, with, on the south, dining room and office flanking a small, asymmetric entry hall. John Ariss, about whom little is known, is credited by one historian as the designer of the interior, but there is no real evidence that Ariss was responsible for any Virginia house. (Apparently he was paid for the plans of two churches, one of which has disappeared, the other never built.)

Originally a large plantation with the usual two dependencies, Ken-

more dwindled to a single house on a 3-acre/1.2-hectare plot, and was purchased (1922)—to prevent its imminent destruction—by a concerned local group which formed the Kenmore Association. The house was then completely restored and the dependencies reconstructed in brick instead of wood on their original foundations, while the Garden Club of Virginia took charge of the grounds (1929). Refreshments are now served in the kitchen dependency (at left).

Open Apr.–Oct., daily 9–5, Nov.–Mar., Tues.–Sun. 9–4, except Jan. 1–2, Dec. 25–26, 31: admission

---

15   Ware Parish Church (c. 1693–1715)
on VA 3 and 14, 1 mile/1.6 kilometers NE of US 17 and Gloucester, Virginia

A simple, rectangular church, 80 x 40 feet/24 x 12 meters in size, designed with perception and restraint and resting behind a low brick wall in a peaceful cemetery. The two long sides of the church are unusual in that they each parade in sequence four roundheaded windows, a pedimented door, and another window, the latter division clearly

marking the chancel, which itself has two identical windows across the end. The main entrance, set in the gable end opposite, is arched like the windows, its shape emphasized by the Flemish bond brickwork, with an oculus immediately above—the only openings in the wall. Note the locally made brickwork throughout and its thickness. Although the interior has been altered at least twice (1854 and 1902), dignity prevails, while the overall impression is of felicity. Though the National Register of Historic Places dates the church at 1715, other authorities mention 1693–1715.

Open during services: can be glimpsed through windows

---

16 Gunston Hall (1755–58)
4 miles/6.4 kilometers E of US 1 on VA 242 (near Lorton)
Gunston Hall, Fairfax County, Virginia

WILLIAM BUCKLAND, INTERIORS AND WOODWORK

The exterior of this small but ambitious house, which measures 60 x 40 feet/18 x 12 meters, will not startle the observer. The interior, however, never descends to a level less than handsome, and in the

Palladian drawing room achieves the sumptuous. Moreover the box gardens behind the house are worth the trip themselves. George Mason, that famous liberal, had started building Gunston Hall, and, it is thought, had the exterior walls up when he realized that he needed a master-joiner to complete the dwelling properly. As his brother Thomson was then finishing his study of law in England, George asked him to find a skilled man to work as an indentured servant to finish the house. Buckland, who had just completed his lengthy apprenticeship in the Joiners' Guild, was chosen—happily for the future development of architecture in the Colonies—coming to Virginia as an indentured servant, like many before him.

Gunston Hall was his first independent work in a career which reached its climax in the famous Hammond-Harwood House (1774) in Annapolis (q.v.), which he designed as a fully qualified architect. It is astonishing that Buckland, then in his early twenties, could produce such knowledgeable design and detail as the interior of Gunston, but his native cleverness and his access to the usual books turned out a rich result. (He was also responsible for the two unusual porches.) The drawing room, as mentioned above, is the climax of the house, but the dining room, the so-called Chinese Chippendale Room, was more innovative in that it was the first Oriental-influenced example in the Colonies, a style then coming into high fashion in England (influenced by the China tea trade). The central hall like many in the South was often used in hot weather as a living room, as its doors could be opened at both ends, an enclosed "dogtrot" so to speak. The master bedroom was, as usual at that time, on the ground floor with the children's rooms in the half story above—though room usage then was more flexible than today.

Gunston suffered after the Civil War, its kitchen dependency was replaced by an awkward addition, and its other outbuildings demolished, while its famous garden was largely ignored. Mr. Louis Hertle, the last private owner, purchased the house in 1912 and made many improvements; in 1932 he generously willed the estate to the Commonwealth of Virginia. Since then it has been fully restored, while the superb grounds and garden have been put back in impeccable shape under the expertise of the Garden Club of Virginia. Gunston Hall was opened to the public in 1952 under the direction of the National Society of the Colonial Dames of America.

In 1974 facilities for visitors were notably expanded by the **Ann Mason Building,** with Philip Ives as architect. Avoiding specious references to Gunston Hall itself (which stands some hundred yards away), or to the adjacent "Colonial" office block (1957), Mr. Ives took the brick and slate used in the eighteenth-century house, and via skillful scale and well-canted roof lines completed a complex which is both architecturally comfortable with its neighbors yet strictly of its time. (Note, for instance, the freedom displayed by the outsized panes of glass.) The facilities include reception, exhibition space and museum, gift shop, and a 210-seat auditorium with kitchen adjacent, and extensive parking on two sides. Very sensitive.

Open 9:30–5 daily, except Dec. 25: admission

---

17   Jamestown Festival Park Reconstruction (1607–98/1957)
Festival Park
Jamestown, Virginia

The beginnings of the New World—Donne's "suburb of the Old"— were established here in 1607, when three improbably small vessels (reproduced and at wharfside) tethered their bows to the trees and America's first "permanent" English colony came into being. Twelve years later (1619) it was to organize the new world's first representative assembly. The establishment of Jamestown—on an up-river site to avoid attack by the Spanish—proved to be rough going for its

104 men and boys, too many of whom were city gentry who hesitated to get their hands dirty. Moreover the area was plagued by mosquitoes, with at times hostile Indians as a backdrop. During the severe winter of 1609–10, when the first colonists of this commercial, not governmental, expedition had been augmented by two subsequent "Supplies," some 440 out of a population of 500 had died. But reinforcements in May of 1610 gave physical and spiritual infusion, then the introduction of successful tobacco cultivation (by crossing mild seed from Venezuela with strong local varieties) provided a cash crop. Subsequently John Rolfe's marriage to Pocahontas (1614) effected peace with the Indians (at least until the massacre of 1622) and matters took a turn for the better. When a bevy of young "maides" arrived in 1620—the settlement had been a largely masculine semimilitary outpost earlier—the seeds for a permanent colony were planted. Jamestown became the capital of an "empire" which Virginia via James I's expanded Charter of 1609 claimed to the Pacific coast. Most of New England, with its later-arrived Pilgrims, was, of course, Northern Virginia (41° to 45° parallel North).

To celebrate the 350th anniversary of the founding of the town, the original pine-palisaded fort, 420 feet/128 meters on the river side, 300 feet/91 meters on the other two, was reconstructed as closely as archeological research and contemporary descriptions permitted (but on a site near to, not on top of, the original town). Whereas what we see today is thus an offsite reproduction, it was carried out with great care, and the results give us a good impression of this early "architecture." The sixteen buildings reflect medieval English prototypes, modified by available materials. A sturdy, unsquared oak or pine frame (most revealingly expressed in the church interior) constitutes the structure, with walls of mud-daubed grapevines or reeds, and roof of thatch. Well worth a look—and don't forget to inspect the transportation.

Open daily 9–5, except Jan. 1, Dec. 25: admission

18   Virginia Hall (1874)
Hampton Institute
off IS 64 at Tyler County Road, then SW
Hampton, Virginia

RICHARD MORRIS HUNT, ARCHITECT

Richard Morris Hunt (1827–95) was one of our most distinguished nineteenth-century architects, the co-founder of the American Institute of Architects and the designer of a clutch of the country's most stupendous mansions (see Index). Here at the noted Hampton Institute, founded in 1868, Hunt designed Virginia Hall, a multipurpose college building (facing the Ogden Auditorium) containing dormitories, dining room, chapel, and teaching areas. It melds a variety of Victorian, Lombard Romanesque, and almost Hanseatic motifs into a spirited period piece facing the Hampton River.

Grounds open daily

---

19 Christ Church (c. 1732)
3.6 miles/5.8 kilometers SW of Kilmarnock via VA 3, 222, and 646
Kilmarnock, Lancaster County, Virginia

Christ Church rises behind a well-tailored brick wall (restored) with a perfection which ranks it as a strong contender for the handsomest

church exterior in the United States. Its slightly offset arms, 68 feet/21 meters on a side, are topped by four hipped roofs of unexpected slight upturn at the eaves, while its three entries cut precisely into the respective "arms" of the plan. Understated elegance can be seen from the compact overall proportions down to details such as the rubbed brick-on-brick of the entries with Portland stone caps and bases. This masonry was probably not equaled in the Colonies. Note that the main doorway is marked by a delicate segmental (i.e. curved) pediment, while those above the two transept doors are triangular with unusual oval windows above each. The prominently keystoned windows are roundheaded to reflect the main entry. The 3-foot/.9-meter-thick brick walls, set in Flemish bond, are of three colors to give subtle variety.

Within there is such an abundance of natural light that the two windows in the chancel (east) wall do not produce a glare. The four arms of the church are simply but neatly vaulted in white plaster. (Though the east-west and north-south measurements are identical, the north-south transept is 4 feet/1.2 meters off center, which gives the west arm of the church extra length.) A narrow stringcourse runs throughout the interior, aligned with the springing of the roundheaded windows and threading the windows visually together. The Commandments stand forth boldly above the altar, revealing the Protestant importance of the Word, and providing, as we have seen, a form of prayerbook for those who did not possess one. The three-decker pulpit stands at a corner of the transept in the midst of the congregation. The original pews, high-backed to ward off drafts, are of natural-finish pine, while virtually all of the other wood, including paneling, is walnut, its dark color playing against the white of walls and ceiling.

Funds for the church, which occupies the site of an earlier fane (c. 1669), were provided by the famous Robert "King" Carter, and Carter graves can be seen in the chancel and outside. Because of its semiremote location, and the fact that it was owned by the Carter family until 1961, the church was fortunately spared injury following disestablishment and the War Between the States. Only minor restoration has been necessary. A slate roof was added in the 1890s, and a general overhaul, including the brick girdling wall mentioned, was undertaken in 1965–66 under the direction of Professor Frederick D. Nichols. Strangely, the architect is unknown. One of the greatest, or as Alan Gowans writes, "It may still claim to be the finest single piece of pure 18th-century classical architectural design in America" (*King Carter's Church,* University of Victoria, Maltwood Museum, 1969).

Open daily 9–5, except Dec. 25

20 King William Court House (c. 1725)
off VA 30
King William, Virginia

This little-known but evocative nugget has been in continuous use as a courthouse for over 255 years, making it one of the oldest in the nation still employed for its original purpose. But age aside, the courthouse and adjacent buildings, plus their setting, are picturesque and rewarding. Both county and village were named for William III and the courthouse became an important local seat. A low brick wall with stile-like steps—to keep out the animals—surrounds the group with the usual poignant monument to the Confederate dead amid a sturdy cluster of trees. The Court House establishes the scene with a five-arched arcade across its facade, close cornice, and well-pitched hipped roof—harmoniously changed from shingles to fireproof slate. (The courthouse at Hanover, some 30 miles/48 kilometers to the west and built ten years later, is almost identical.) The plan is T-shaped with altered and not impressive courtroom projecting behind, flanked at front

by chambers for the judge and by the jury room. The County Clerk's office stands at left and the jail to right. Though both were built in 1885 they respectfully bow architecturally to the Court House. (The arcade across the front of the jail was added in the 1940s.)

Open Mon.–Fri. 9–4, Sat. 9–12, except holidays

---

21   Oatlands (1804–27)
6.2 miles/10 kilometers S of town on US 15
Leesburg, Virginia

The exterior of Oatlands exhibits several puzzling features: one, it seems too towering, almost too urban, for its country site, and, two, the end bays, which were put on later, were not smoothly appended. The Corinthian front porch was added—fortunately from the design point of view as well as convenience—over twenty years after the house proper had been completed. Interestingly, a cupola was either taken off or never finished, for its drum exists in the attic. But though the overall form may not seem properly orchestrated, the interior with its Adam-inspired detail is excellent. All major rooms have been metic-

ulously attended to, the hall and octagonal drawing room in particular. Note the friezes and carvings throughout. The furnishings represent a cross section of years but there are only a few from the early nineteenth century. The boxwood gardens, which were restored and expanded (1903–10) should not be missed.

The house, according to most sources, was designed by its owner, George Carter, who used William Chambers' book *A Treatise on Civil Architecture in Which the Principles of That Art are Laid Down* (London, 1768): this is especially true of the design of the portico. All brick was made on the estate and the timber cut from its trees. In 1965 the property was graciously given to the National Trust for Historic Preservation by Mrs. David E. Finley and Mrs. Eustis Emmet. Since 1979 it has been operated by Oatlands of The National Trust Inc.

Open Apr.–mid-Nov., Mon.–Sat. 10–5, Sun. 1–5: admission

22 Belle Grove (1794–97)
W off US 11, 1.8 miles/2.8 kilometers S of Middletown, Virginia

An upper-bracket farmhouse of finely dressed local limestone which surveys from its knap the beginning of the famous Shenandoah Valley. The house from the outside is marked by high basement and the four tall inset chimneys. Despite a distractive element in the later addition of the western extension (c. 1820) at left, the scale remains pleasantly domestic. The prominent Tuscan porticos, a feature much favored by Jefferson—who also gave considerable advice concerning the final plan and design of this house—were added later to both north and south sides. (The precise date of these additions is still unknown.) As this was basically a farm residence, the drawing room and dining room are not of the imposing dimensions seen along the James, but their carved woodwork is of a respectable level, the detailing, especially in the parlor, showing a hint of the new Federal Style.

The house was ill-served during and after the Civil War (even in this century it was used as an inn), but in 1929 it was purchased by the late Francis Welles Hunnewell and fully restored by Horace Peaslee. Mr. Hunnewell then generously willed the house with 100 acres/40 hectares of rolling land to the National Trust for Historic Preservation which acquired it in 1964.

Open Apr.–Oct., Mon.–Sat. 10–4, Sun. 1–5: admission

---

23   Mount Vernon (mid-1730s/1757–58/1777–84/1787)
**Mount Vernon Memorial Highway/VA 235, c. 14 miles/23
    kilometers S of Washington, D.C.**
Mount Vernon, Fairfax County, Virginia

Ann Pamela Cunningham has not as yet appeared on a United States postage stamp. She should. For this energetic South Carolina lady not only alerted the female forces which saved Mount Vernon from disintegration in 1853, she and her cohorts saw to it that funds were raised to purchase (1858) and restore the house and grounds. During the Civil War they personally kept off troops of both sides! Not only was this great mansion preserved, America was made dramatically conscious of its major architectural heritage and the need to preserve it. (Washington's Headquarters in Newburgh, New York, built in 1750, had been rescued from demolition in 1850, but this is a small structure.) Unbelievably, the U. S. Government and the Commonwealth of Virginia had each refused to buy the house and property, when,

through the decline of its farming potential, the estate was offered for sale.

In a way it can be said that Jefferson's Monticello (q.v.) and Washington's Mount Vernon, violently dissimilar though they appear, share several key determinants: they are both Palladian in plan, with semidetached dependencies in the case of Mount Vernon, and they both took a great many years to build and rebuild, each starting life with a small initial core that was expanded enormously. Moreover each freely employed "textbook" details in doors and windows.

The additions to Mr. Washington's dwelling were so substantial and often so poorly coordinated in architectural terms that a price had to be paid: that price can be seen on the entrance side (only), where we are left with a less than satisfactory facade. An afterthought pediment (1778), seemingly tacked on, tries valiantly to pull this flat front together, while the irregular window spacing, instead of lending liveliness, merely looks amateurish. Moreover the second-story windows at the northeast end are fake (to disguise the high-ceilinged banquet room which fills this end of the house). However, all is not lost, for the rest of the exterior compensates. At the northeast, a broken-pediment Palladian window—taken direct from Batty Langley's *Treasury of Designs* of 1740—embellishes the end, while along the masterful southeast front we find the country's first two-story, full-width, squared column portico, a feature which is as functional as it is beautiful.

This "piazza" pioneered a unique architectural contribution we now imprecisely call "Southern Colonial" (even though it was completed after the Revolution). Domestic porticos were not previously unknown. Scores of houses—from Palladio's Villa Capra (possibly the first), to Colin Campbell's Mereworth Castle and Lord Burlington's Chiswick in England, then on to Ireland—had Palladian-inspired porticos adorning their fronts (and often sides and backs), but these were abutments, so to speak, a focal point on a facade (as were the earlier two-story columns on the Jumel Mansion of 1765 in New York). Washington made his airy, princely porch the facade itself, its ample depth (14 feet/4.3 meters) shielding this side from summer sun by day, while enabling the upper rooms to keep their bedroom windows open day and night even in heavy rain. And as a place to sit in the late afternoon, with its glorious panorama of the Potomac, this porch was Washington's open-air living room and entertainment center for much of the year. Like an urban arcade it serves as a spatial intermedium between architecture and setting, tying both together in mutual harmony. It was probably Washington's "ignorance" of "correct" architecture—abetted by his natural desire for an outdoor "room"—that prompted its creation.

The first Mount Vernon—ironically named for a British admiral under whom Washington's half-brother Lawrence had served—was a story-and-a-half, smallish dwelling (erected mid-1730s). In 1754 George acquired the title to the house, and in 1757–58, in anticipation of his marriage to Martha Dandridge Custis (1759), the house was enlarged by the addition of a full second floor, and expanded laterally by dependencies (which were later replaced). The original farmhouse and its new height and renovation form the central part of Mount Vernon today, the hall with two rooms on either side (of slightly unequal size) and chimneys at the ends being incorporated into the final building. The exterior of the house was sheathed with wood beveled in imitation of stone and painted with a sand-finished paint—a Kentish and New England technique not previously used in the South (cf. the Wentworth-Gardner House of 1760 in Portsmouth, New Hampshire). The popularity of the Washingtons—they were rarely without guests—and the attendant need for larger entertainment space prompted George to make the final expansions of the house which were carried out from 1777–84, largely during the General's absence. Two additions were made to the central core, that at northeast (23 feet/7 meters) forming the banquet room mentioned earlier, the one at southwest (22 feet/6.7 meters) providing for a library, another flight of stairs, and a pantry on the ground floor, with General Washington's room above. The present dependencies and their connecting colonnades were also constructed at this time as was the famous piazza. The cupola dates from 1787.

The interiors of Mount Vernon, while not as elaborate as some of the James River plantations, are suitably rich, the delicate Adamesque plaster work in the ceilings of the banquet room and dining room being noteworthy. But the main impact of Mount Vernon does not derive just from the house itself, or even its wonderful portico, but from the house, its situation, its outbuildings, and its extensive gardens (which should by all means be seen). All have been woven together to create a complex that provides one of the highlights of late-eighteenth-century American architecture.

The Mount Vernon Ladies' Association gives Washington complete credit for the design of what we see today. As a surveyor he was, of course, familiar with drafting instruments (a set of which is preserved in the house) and he had the usual English architectural books. Mount Vernon's house and grounds form one of our masterpieces—and not just because it sheltered our first President. The nation will be forever grateful to Ann Cunningham.

Open Mar.–Sept., daily 9–5, Oct.–Feb., daily 9–4: admission

24   Woodlawn Plantation (1800–5)
  **NW off US 1 at VA 235, c. 14 miles/23 kilometers S of
     Washington, D.C.**
  Mount Vernon, Virginia

WILLIAM THORNTON, ARCHITECT

Located a few miles from Mount Vernon, Woodlawn asserts a style
of architectural cohesion and elegance lacking in its earlier neighbor.
Dr. William Thornton was the architect. (In 1793 he had won the
competition for the nation's Capitol and had also designed the Octagon
House (q.v.) in Washington.) Thornton incorporated a key feature of
the James River plantations in his new work but gave it an unusual
direction for that time. Instead of a block for the house with flanking
but unattached dependencies on either side, he connected the central
block with hyphens to the kitchen dependency at right and the plantation office to left, with both units presenting a gabled end to the

approach. He then extended this frontage by semiattaching via a high wall the dairy beyond the kitchen and the smokehouse (left of the office), thus creating an imposingly long facade. It should be added that the hyphens and wings were unfortunately enlarged early in the twentieth century, with dormers put on the hyphens, making these once inconspicuous elements competitive with the main facade.

The interiors of Woodlawn are excellent: the central hall—used for the living area in hot weather, as was often the practice—is not distinguished, but the music room, the parlor, and the downstairs bedroom are well turned out and decorated, and furnished with many original pieces of furniture. Since 1951 the house and the nearby Pope-Leighey House by Frank Lloyd Wright (1940–41—q.v.) have been administered by the National Trust.

Open 9:30–4:30 daily, except Dec. 25: admission

---

25   Pope-Leighey House (1940–41)
Woodlawn Plantation
NW off US 1, c. 14 miles/23 kilometers S of Washington, D.C.
Mount Vernon, Virginia

FRANK LLOYD WRIGHT, ARCHITECT

Mr. Wright first created the Usonian series of houses—small houses for limited incomes—in 1937. These began with the Herbert Jacobs house in Wisconsin, then expanded into a whole series in the 1940s to form a key part in the development of domestic architecture in the U.S.A. When pneumatic "Colonial" and other so-called "styles" were peppering every suburb at that time, these modestly priced dwellings introduced the carport, low or flat roof, natural wood finish, and basement-free living, while the interiors of most of them were characterized by Wright's famous flow of internal spaces plus his well-known furniture. The Pope-Leighey, saved from destruction by being moved to this site in 1965, is not the most successful of these, primarily because the brick utility core housing the kitchen and heater is, from the outside, not well integrated with the rest of the house. Moreover, within, its living room is strangely closetlike, its sitting (i.e. far) end forming a solid U-shape with ranges of French doors "attaching" this to the house. (Cf. Wright's finer play of space and light in the Usonian Rosenbaum House of 1939 in Florence, Alabama.) Pope-Leighey is, however, a revealing, inexpensive house, and in it one can glimpse some of the Master's delight with three dimensions. Moreover it is the only small house of Wright's which is open to the public. It should be remembered that FLW was one of the few architects in this country to concern himself with developing a house for moderate-income clients.

Open Mar.–Oct., Sat.–Sun. 9:30–4:30: admission

---

26   Adam Thoroughgood House (c. 1636–40)
NE on Princess Anne Road to Northampton Boulevard (both VA
   166), S 1 block on Pleasure House Road, then Thoroughgood
   Drive and Parish Road, c. 8 miles/13 kilometers E of
Norfolk, Virginia

On a creek of Lynnhaven Bay, and only a short distance from the Chesapeake, stands what may be the oldest surviving brick house in the U.S.A. It is possibly the oldest of any material. (Cf. the much-added-to wood-frame Fairbanks House, c. 1637, at Dedham, Massachusetts. St. Augustine's "oldest house" obviously dates from post-1702 when the British sacked and burned the town.) The Thoroughgood House is a minuscule, medieval affair, one and a half stories high, girdled by two T-shaped chimneys. The one at right (south) is set on the outside of the wall, and marked by four belt

courses, the second of which wraps around the house at eave to define the upper floor level. The chimney at left lies within the wall to warm the house better (this is the north end). (Compare the great central chimneys of New England.) Brick set in English bond (rows of headers alternating with rows of stretchers) enclose the two sides and the wall facing the river, but the front wall is of the more exacting Flemish bond. The texture is rich, the sharp slope of the gabled roof, now covered with fireproof tiles but of oak shingles originally, medieval, and the whole picturesque. Note too the low door and the high-set windows. This dwelling represents a distinct advance over the earlier ones built in the Colonies.

There are only two rooms on each floor, with a "hall" (e.g. living room-kitchen) and parlor downstairs, passage and stair being added in 1745 at the time the bedrooms were converted from the original loft area. In 1957 the house was purchased by the City of Norfolk and completely restored, the facade being returned to two windows from three, the late dormers removed, and the window sash changed from double-hung to casement. (The largest casements found in the seventeenth century measure only 1 x 2 feet/.3 x .6 meter.)

The Thoroughgood House has been thoughtfully furnished in the late-seventeenth/early-eighteenth-century fashion, while its garden, with excellent box hedging, has been put back in fine if theoretic condition. There is little stylistic importance to the Thoroughgood House

—it is not high fashion—but it is very useful in showing the survival, with only small adaptation, of English medieval traditions in the earliest American colony.

Open Apr.–Nov., Tues.–Sat. 10–5, Sun. 12–5; Dec.–Mar., daily 12–5, except holidays: admission

---

27 **Moses Myers House** (1791–92/1797),
   325 Freemason Street at Bank
Freemason Street Baptist Church (1848–50),
   Freemason Street at Bank, T. U. Walter, architect
Old Norfolk Academy Building (1840),
   420 Bank Street, T. U. Walter, architect
Willoughby-Baylor House (1794),
   Freemason at Cumberland
Norfolk, Virginia

For some years downtown Norfolk has been undergoing an ambitious urban renewal program that has cleared (sometimes recklessly) many blocks and rebuilt others. One of the prime areas for redevelopment contains the four historic buildings mentioned here, all within a few hundred yards of each other. The city's planners have wisely preserved these cultural counterpoints.

The most important is the **Moses Myers House** (Open Apr.–Nov., Tues.–Sat. 10–5, Sun. 12–5; Dec.–Mar., Tues.–Sun. 12–5, except Jan. 1 and Dec. 25), which provides a business-district oasis with its still well-preserved garden. The exterior of the house is on the modest side but note the two entry doors, one per side, to aid cross ventilation in summer. The interior is marked by several elegant Adam-inspired chambers, particularly the dining room, which was added in 1797. Note its cornice and twin sideboards around which the room was built. Many of the furnishings are outstanding. The house was kept by descendants of the original builder until 1931, hence many pieces of furniture are original and intact. At that date it was purchased by a group of interested citizens and completely restored. The house and contents were given to the City of Norfolk in 1951 under the administration of the Museum of Arts and Sciences, now known as the Chrysler Museum at Norfolk.

The **Baptist Church** stands on the diagonal across the street from the Myers House. Though generally open only on Sunday mornings, its exterior alone merits a look for its vigorous Gothic Revival by Thomas U. Walter, who did so much work on the U. S. Capitol. The interior does not impress.

Farther down the street, at 420 Bank, stands, somewhat lonely, the **Old Norfolk Academy Building** (open during office hours), also by Walter. But here, because of its earlier date, is a stocky, muscular, double-ended Doric example of the Greek Revival. It was thoroughly renovated in 1972 and now usefully houses the Chamber of Commerce.

The nearby **Willoughby-Baylor House** (open Apr.–Nov., Tues.–Sat. 10–5, Sun. 12–5; Dec.–Mar., Tues.–Sat. 12–5, except Jan. 1 and Dec. 25: admission) is a good late-Georgian town house which has been fully restored and open to the public, having come under the aegis of the Norfolk Historic Foundation in 1963. The porch, of Federal inclination, was added in 1824. The garden should also be seen. Like the Myers House, it is managed by the Chrysler Museum at Norfolk.

Together these four neighbors add a stimulating touch to the edge of downtown. If better related by landscaping, they—and their private neighbors—would form an even more impressive historic core.

Open as indicated: admission to the two houses

---

28 Virginia National Bank (1968)
Main Street at Bank
Norfolk, Virginia

SKIDMORE, OWINGS & MERRILL, ARCHITECTS; WILLIAMS & TAZEWELL PARTNERSHIP, ASSOCIATES

Strategically situated downtown not far from the Civic Center, and enjoying a view overlooking the Elizabeth River, the Bank has been a key element in upgrading Norfolk's central business and waterfront

districts with its new building and its 3.5-acre/1.4-hectare landscaped park. The exoskeleton of the skyscraper creates good sun control in a generally hot climate, and, of course, gives a powerfully sculpted personality to the building (cf. SOM's John Hancock in New Orleans, etc.). The lower two floors are cast-in-place concrete, the upper nineteen are constructed of T-shape prefabricated members which weigh 20 tons/18.2 metric tons apiece. Note that the sunshade sections of these "Ts" do not quite touch—thus expressing their non-structural quality as well as giving visual bounce. The entry level seems overly compressed but the double-height banking floor is airy and cheerful. Over a hundred works of art by Virginia artists appear on the bank's walls. A 4-foot/1.2-meter-high podium with landscaped pool gives the building a distinctive base. Roy Allen was the design partner.

Open during business hours

---

29 SCOPE—Cultural and Convention Center (1971 and 1972)
Charlotte Street, Monticello Avenue, Brambletown Avenue, St.
   Paul's Boulevard
Norfolk, Virginia

WILLIAMS & TAZEWELL PARTNERSHIP, ARCHITECTS; PIER LUIGI NERVI, DOME ENGINEER

The two buildings of Norfolk's SCOPE, the larger a striking circular multipurpose hall, the second a rectangular theater, provide the city with outstanding cultural, assembly, and sports facilities. Occupying 14

acres/5.7 hectares on the eastern edge of downtown, SCOPE provides for the full range of public events and entertainments. The complex is raised slightly above street level because of the water table and also to offer under-cover parking for 640 automobiles (with additional parking nearby). An exhibit hall of 65,000 square feet/6,039 square meters with entrance off St. Paul's Boulevard is also located under the podium.

The magnificent structure of the Convention and Sports Hall immediately asserts itself as one approaches the group, with the incomparable late Nervi's aristocratically sculpted buttresses supporting the smooth reinforced concrete cap of the roof. The array of these twenty-four V-shaped buttresses gives ebullient verve to the plaza. They are structurally reminiscent of the Gothic cathedrals of the twelfth to fourteenth centuries and more directly of Nervi's Palazzetto dello Sport for Rome's 1960 Olympics. Note the manner in which the flying buttresses form broadly flattened rectangles at top, the better to receive the weight of the roof, and then are rotated 90° to transmit this thrust into the bases. Exquisite engineering and extremely competent workmanship.

The interior is dominated by the underside of the dome with its mathematical diagram of the stresses and strains which its 336-foot/102-meter span (inner diameter) sustains. Its nervation is composed of 2,500 beautifully precast concrete triangles—contained by a peripheral tension ring—with a thin roof of poured concrete on top. From the dome is hung a slender circular light-bridge 100 feet/30 meters in diameter and also of precast concrete. Unlike many lighting/audio mechanics, this is not intrusive. Arrayed below are 8,300 permanent seats with 3,700 portable ones readily available. For concerts and conventions the hall can accommodate 11,800–12,000; for sports, 9,500 for ice hockey, and up to 12,000 for boxing. There are also meeting rooms and banquet facilities for 5,000.

The exterior of Chrysler Hall (dedicated in 1972) is reminiscent of New York's Avery Fisher Hall in Lincoln Center, but the interior is fresh and the acoustics reputedly excellent. There are 2,500 seats, arranged in Continental fashion, in the theater/concert hall proper, with a 350-seat little theater adjacent. The orchestra lift can accommodate 90 musicians. Altogether a complex of which Norfolk can be very proud. Fraioli-Blum-Yesselman Associates were the structural engineers.

Open during events: grounds always open

30   Pohick Church (1769–74)
immediately E of US 1, and W of Fort Belvoir
Pohick Church, Lorton, Fairfax County, Virginia

The Pohick Church forms a compact hip-roofed rectangle, unlike many
towered and gabled churches of the New World Georgian era which favored a Greek cross or transept plan. And though it is almost domestic
in outward appearance, there is nothing domestic about the church
within. It possesses probably the most sophisticated interior of its time
in the Colonies. The outer walls, laid in the usual Flemish bond, are
quietly stated, being relieved by prominent white stone quoins, well-
pedimented doors (the main one in the long wall, two others at the
west end), fifteen roundheaded windows, and firmly denticulated cornice. The round-topped, keystone-less windows deliver a syncopation
to the facades. The sandstone enframements of the doors are capable
interpretations from standard English architectural books. On entering
one encounters an elegant single chamber, totally comprehensible,
whose only break is a gallery (restored) at west. Directly facing the
main entrance from the opposite wall rises the pulpit, with wineglass

base and cantilevered canopy sounding board above. A broken pedimented plaque at the chancel end, with small altar below, contains the usual scriptural references, while a "grid" of waist-high box pews with two long aisles fills most of the rest of the church. All elements have been fused by the clarity of the space and by being painted the same putty color. The results are admirable. George Washington, who was a member of the vestry at Pohick, had a strong hand in its design; in 1859 Benson J. Lossing published a plan and elevations which he claimed were drawn by Washington. William Buckland, who did most of Gunston Hall (q.v.) for George Mason (who, in his turn, was also on the vestry at Pohick), was responsible for the completion of the church according to parish records. He was probably involved in the interior carving, and possibly its completion, while James Wren, some feel, was the "architect" and builder who worked with Washington. The church was damaged in the Civil War and much of the interior gutted—hence most of what we see today dates from the restorations of 1874 and 1906, the latter putting the church as near its original condition as possible for the state's Tricentennial in 1907. Good outside, glorious within.

Open 8–4 daily

---

31 Reston New Town and Lake Anne Village (1965–   )
from Washington, D.C. NW on VA 7, then W on VA 606
Reston, Virginia

CONKLIN & ROSSANT, ARCHITECTS-PLANNERS; VARIOUS OTHER
ARCHITECTS OF HOUSING

The domestic tragedy of the United States is that it has produced almost no proper major answers to twentieth-century habitation. Compared to Europe, especially Sweden, Finland, and England, our record is disgraceful: we have nothing in a class with Vällingby (Stockholm), Tapiola (Helsinki), or Roehampton (London). Washington, where the power and decisions lie, and the large insurance companies and corporations, where the money to finance the so-called "New Towns" lies, are equally to blame, but in a democracy one reaps what one votes.

Reston, some 18 miles/29 kilometers WNW of Washington, was the first large-scale (7,419 acres/3,002 hectares), fully rounded living, ed-

ucation, recreation, and partial employment New Town of merit in this
country. It is, in part, an admirable effort, a brilliant tribute to its original developer, Robert E. Simon, Jr., and its planners, Conklin & Rossant. As such it glows with substantial lessons, while warning us by its
shortcomings, which are evident away from central areas.

Reston's main virtues are epitomized by Lake Anne Village and its
pedestrian plaza of shops, town houses, and a high-rise apartment
knowingly grouped around a 28-acre/11-hectare man-made lake. The
first of six proposed village clusters, this section, designed by Conklin
& Rossant, represents one of the distinctive achievements of American
planning, for it carries a sense of "belonging," of being a part of a
cohesive whole, which will not be found elsewhere. Moreover it is full
of surprise, efficiency, and imagination. And like Portofino and the
Piazza San Marco in Venice, it deploys its elements—its buildings—
with spatial élan, using water to unify and highlight.

Reston's shopping plaza, reached by a tempting passage with un-
derdefined entry, extends a relaxed welcome, one aided by first-rate
sign control. Near its cafe spouts frolicsome water sculpture, while the
piazza steps down to welcome the lake (cf. Portofino), which for many
months of the year is alive with the young gaming, swimming,
splashing, canoeing, sailing, flirting. Toward the middle of these waters
spurts a grandiose jet (40–50 feet/12–15 meters high). For a short
distance on both sides of the lake, extending from the plaza, stretch
town houses, the side at right climaxing in the tall apartment building.

This fifteen-story structure is not only strategically located to punctuate the view down the Mall, it is handsomely designed (by Conklin & Rossant). Note the play sculpture nearby. Across the lake are grouped both attached town houses and a few individual dwellings, the former designed by Chloethiel Woodard Smith. This housing, like most sections of Reston, can be reached by underpasses so that no one, child or adult, has to cross a major street to shop, go to school, or visit a friend —a simple and obvious ground rule, yet one little seen in this automad nation.

Thus, the central parts of Reston are admirable, but the farther one moves out from its cores, the more the licensed speculative builders move in, and the less the quality. On the fringes will be found houses indistinguishable from those in any Suburbia, U.S.A., except that the land planning and usage is far better. Moreover a self-conscious seeking of variety militates against a restful atmosphere.

Reston has had its well-publicized troubles, and its original developer did not have the financial staying power to maintain control of management. Chief among its difficulties is the strange lack of communication with downtown Washington, to which approximately one half of the working population commutes, either by rapid transit (now better with express buses) or by automobile (labyrinthine). Reputedly there were forces, both official (including a highway department and a governmental agency) and private, which conspired against a logical rapid transit system to serve both Dulles Airport (nearby) and Reston. If this had been done, most of the communication problems would have been solved—for both. It is worth noting that when Stockholm's town section of Vällingby was in the planning stage, the first item on the agenda, and the first to be built, was the excellent rapid rail system to the heart of the city. The introduction (1968) of express buses at Reston has, as mentioned, helped, as it has at Dulles, but an interconnected high-speed rail line should still be put in.

Reston will eventually (late 1980s) be a city of 68,000 (in June 1980 it had approximately 35,000 generally well-educated citizens in some 12,000 units). As the finest effort we have made toward "new city" living and working, it has many lessons to offer, as has Columbia, Maryland (q.v.). Its land planning and usage is on as high a plane as Columbia's—both exemplary—while the architecture and planning of Reston's central area is considerably better. Both have seemingly settled on distressingly routine house types, some more than distressing— in both cases done by speculative builders but on preplanned and prepared (with utilities) land. Hence this major sector is disappointing. But we have much to learn from each, and each should be intently studied for what it has, and what it has not, to offer. When this is constructively done, we can, in fact, we must, start building new towns that conceivably will match those in Europe. Happily, Reston has in recent years attracted a broad employment base (over 7,000 jobs), both governmental and corporate.

---

32   The Virginia State Capitol (1785–92)
Capitol Square between 9th and Governor Streets
Richmond, Virginia

THOMAS JEFFERSON, ARCHITECT

Mr. Jefferson's Virginia Capitol introduced the Classic World of Architecture to the budding nation. The country never recovered. This extraordinary statesman/architect, who honed his architectural wits while in Europe as our Minister to France (1784–89), despised the Georgian—its British derivation obviously influencing his post-Revolution taste—and considered the Wren-designed building at William and Mary an uncouth "brick kiln" and the facades of Independence Hall "puny." He turned more and more to the Classic of Rome and its

Palladian interpretations for his inspiration. Though Mr. Jefferson never got to Rome or to Greece one wonders what would have happened to the architecture of this country if he had studied the great Classic examples at first hand, instead of via books. (The Maison Carrée in Nîmes in the south of France was the only major Classical example he ever saw—though he got as far as Genoa to study rice cultivation.) Nîmes (A.D. 14) is certainly a well-preserved Roman temple (actually the best preserved of all the rectangular ones), but it carries little of the majesterial force of those in the Roman Forum.

In any event, Jefferson was the first architect anywhere to fit a major workaday building into a Classic-derived temple form—though not without difficulties. It was also the first building to include both houses of the legislature in a single structure. In this he had, while in France, the help of C.-L. Clérisseau, the architect who, interestingly enough, also worked with Scotland's famous Adam brothers.

Nîmes might have been the inspiration for the Richmond Capitol, but it was not altogether the model, the latter being far larger, with Ionic capitals instead of the more elaborate Corinthian, and unfluted columns instead of fluted. Neither does Richmond have any of the pseudo-peripteral, or "attached," columns which embrace the side of Nîmes, nor (originally) the steps up the front which introduce the French example. To quote the Virginia Historic Landmarks Commission, "It might also be noted that Jefferson *intended* that the building have front steps, they are shown in his drawing and model. Jefferson did not supervise the construction, and apparently the contractor took the liberty of leaving off the steps because the portico door led directly into the Supreme Court chamber. Only when that space was partitioned off to make a central corridor were the front steps finally erected."

The Capitol was, however, an extremely important and influential building, a pioneer in the evolution of architecture in this country, even if esthetically it is not comparable to Jefferson's brilliant University of Virginia or his piquant Monticello (q.v.). It should also be borne in mind that only the central part of the building we see today belongs to Mr. Jefferson and M. Clérisseau, for the two wings housing the Senate (west) and the House of Delegates (east) were added at the early part of this century (1904–6), and the south portico transformed to the main entrance, its steps installed and the intrusive pediment windows removed. (See the plaster model of the original.) Minor remodeling occurred in 1962–63. The interiors, because of the changes, are handsome but not completely harmonious. Note Houdon's famous statue of Washington in the Rotunda (the room is square but with a dome). The stately siting of the Capitol, its landscaping and even its fence (1819) are all excellent.

Open Mon.–Fri. 8:15–5, Sat. 9–5, Sun. 1–5, closed Dec. 25

Though the **Governor's Mansion,** just northeast of the Capitol, is closed to the public except during Garden Week, take a look at its capable, if partially altered, exterior (1810–13) when leaving. Alexander Parris was its original architect, although his design, some feel, was changed during construction.

---

33 Wickham-Valentine House (1812)
1015 East Clay Street
Richmond, Virginia

ROBERT MILLS, PROBABLE ARCHITECT

A fine example of Federal Style architecture which has been attributed to Robert Mills (1781–1855), the South Carolinian who was one of the country's first native-born professional architects. (Mills spent the

first year of his career at Monticello where Jefferson taught him to draw. He also had the run of the latter's great architectural library.) Although there is no documented proof that Mills designed the Wickham-Valentine House, it does feature architectural details which Mills and other architects were known to use at the time, such as the Classical entrance porch, triple-hung windows, oval-shaped parlor, and veranda on the garden side of the house. In addition, Mills was the known designer of the Monumental Church, 1814, Richmond's City Hall, 1816, and perhaps some private residences. Of these other buildings only the Monumental Church remains standing.

The quiet, pared restraint of the Federal period is typified on the exterior of the Wickham-Valentine House by its low-pitched roof, smooth stuccoed facade, and recesssd arches framing the windows. On the interior the palette-shaped stairway, curved walls with niches, and inventive trimwork give unusual distinction and an air of delicacy to the house. In the 1850s the interior was redone in the then-fashionable Victorian Style. From that period a Victorian parlor and bedroom still remain. Especially notable are its frescoed ceilings and walls in *trompe l'oeil,* marble mantel, and molded plaster cornice. Though the exterior is basically Federal the interior shows room settings typical of much of the nineteenth century.

The Valentine Museum—of which the house is a part—was opened in 1898 through the generosity of Mann S. Valentine II, who left his personal collections and an endowment to create a museum on the life and history of Richmond.

Open Tues.–Sat. 10–5, Sun. 1:30–5, except holidays: admission

---

34 Egyptian Building (1845), **College and Marshall Streets, Thomas S. Stewart, architect**
Monumental Church (1812–14), **1224 East Broad Street, Robert Mills, architect**
Old First Baptist Church (1839–41), **East Broad Street and 12th Street, Thomas U. Walter, architect**
Richmond, Virginia

From the batter of its walls to its cavetto cornice, and from its scarabaeus to its lotus-capped columns, the **Egyptian Building** (grounds and lobby open to public) rates as one of the great examples of the

Egyptian Revival in the U.S.A. (Another is Strickland's Downtown Presbyterian Church in Nashville—q.v.)

Built originally as the first unit of the Medical College of Virginia, it has been in continuous use since it opened. In 1939 the building was completely restored, outside and in, through the generosity of the late Bernard Baruch whose father had been an alumnus. A colorful lobby leads to an auditorium (of little interest) on the ground floor, with research laboratories and offices above. Note the details of the cast-iron fencing: the posts are in the form of mummies.

Just around the corner on Broad Street stand two other historic Medical College buildings which the college was careful to preserve and convert to contemporary use. The **Monumental Church,** by Robert Mills (open daily), is almost droll in its lightly coordinated accumulation of geometric forms. Note in the prominent porch that the columns are fluted only at top and bottom, the fluting thus serving as capital and base. The building's unusual name stems from the fact that it was built as a monument to those who lost their lives in a fire (1811) in a theater which previously stood on this site. Formerly an Episcopal church, it was remodeled into a Conference Center (1977) by Glavé, Newman, Anderson & Associates.

Almost adjacent, at East Broad and 12th streets, stands the **Old**

First Baptist Church, by Thomas U. Walter (both Mills and Walter had worked on the U. S. Capitol). This sharp-edged Greek Revival example is architecturally superior to Walter's 1840 "temple" at Norfolk (q.v.) and forms one of Richmond's important monuments. Considerably altered within, it now serves as a restaurant. (Open weekdays.) The college has threatened to demolish the ex-church to make way for a new health education facility. Fortunately it is listed in the National Register of Historic Places—as are the other two buildings mentioned.

Open as indicated

---

35   Cast-Iron Buildings (late 1860s)
East Main Street
Richmond, Virginia

Several years after the burning of Richmond in the Civil War, a half-dozen blocks of East Main were rebuilt with cast-iron structures. Of these only a few remain, but they are rewarding to those interested in this unique, early American prefabricated form of speedy construction. The three buildings at 1207-9-11 East Main are among the lonely survivors (but alas for the desecration of the central one by the State Liq-

uor Authority). Their fenestration is based directly on the Palazzo Rucellai (A.D. 1451) and the Palazzo Strozzi (1489) in Florence.

The group at 1009, 1011, and 1013, built as a unit, and the adjacent beautifully maintained Branch Building at 1015 East Main (note porch) form the finest collection. Both date from 1866–67 with the single iron front for the brick-sided 1009–1013 building made by the Hayward, Bartlett Foundry in Baltimore. This structure, officially The Ironfronts, was beautifully restored (1975–76) by Glavé, Newman, Anderson & Associates into highly successful office space. Cast aluminum instead of iron was used for some of the columns, capitals, and arches as being cheaper and rust-proof. They were manufactured in Salt Lake City.

The First and Merchants National Bank had to remove some cast-iron buildings when it constructed its new headquarters (1973), but their fronts were carefully saved and given to the Valentine Museum (Wickham-Valentine House—q.v.), where, it is hoped, they will eventually be re-erected.

The cast-iron buff might also like to see **James Monroe's Tomb** (1858) in the picturesque Hollywood Cemetery (1847), entered at 412 South Cherry Street, the tomb lying on the high ground of the southwest corner. Albert Lybrock was the architect.

Can be seen from street

36   Old City Hall (1887–94)
Broad and 10th Streets
Richmond, Virginia

ELIJAH E. MYERS, ARCHITECT

The exterior of the Old City Hall—the commission for which was won
by competition—stands hard and chiseled in the late Victorian Gothic
manner. Having been cleaned, its immutability stands boldly forth. Of
itself, the exterior is not unusual. The four-story interior stairhall and
"court," however, provide us with tiers of neo-Gothic levels, some
gilded, some crocketed, all potent. Now that the new City Hall is
completed, let us hope that this older bastion will not be destroyed—

as its previous City Hall by Robert Mills was wiped out (1874) to make room for this. Fortunately the building is listed in the National Register of Historic Places.

At present not open to the public: future in doubt

---

37   Jefferson Hotel (1893–95/1905)
116 West Main Street
Richmond, Virginia

**CARRÈRE & HASTINGS, ARCHITECTS; J. KEVAN PEEBLES,
ARCHITECT OF REMODELING**

Ancient Rome's most prodigal caravanserai in the United States can be found in the sumptuous lobby of the Jefferson Hotel. It speaks with nothing less than Neronean splendor, and if the fates are ever so unkind as to phase out the 342-room *Betthaus,* let us hope that the two-story lobby will always be kept: no hotel could have a finer introduction. Actually, the lobby seen today was "radically altered in style" by J. Kevan Peebles, who remodeled it (1905) following a serious fire. Massive columns of marbleized masonry replaced slender ones of iron, the new columns' metal capitols rich with gilt and flowered swags, the mezzanine walls refulgent with red and gold. Behind this sturdy classicism are grouped unobtrusive but efficient hotel facilities.

Open daily

---

38   Science Museum of Virginia—ex-Broad Street Station
(1917–19/1979–81)
West Broad Street between Davis and Robinson
Richmond, Virginia

JOHN RUSSELL POPE, ARCHITECT

Of all the neo-Classical railroad stations in this country, the former
Broad Street depot stood near the top, along with Burnham's Union
Station (q.v.) in Washington, D.C. It was not only well designed for
its eclectic times; far more important, it worked superbly (which many
of its peers do/did not). From the setback front entrance to one's train
there was but a short walk in Roman splendor, with immediately
graspable access to the proper track. Departing or arriving, there was
unequaled clarity of circulation—and exultant three-dimensionality.
Because of the drastic fall-off in rail passenger traffic, the station was
declared redundant, but in 1976 it was purchased by the Commonwealth and converted to the Science Museum of Virginia the following
year. The recycling—still under way—is being carried out by Oliver
Smith Cooke & Lindner with Samuel Crothers Associates. A brilliant
adaptive use.

Open Sat.–Thurs. 1–4, except Jan. 1 and Dec. 25: admission

---

39   Reynolds Metals Building (1955–58/annex 1968)
 **6601 West Broad Street (US 250) at Dickens Road, c. 5 miles/8
     kilometers NW of downtown**
 Richmond, Virginia

SKIDMORE, OWINGS & MERRILL, ARCHITECTS

The elegant Reynolds Building and the same architects' Connecticut General Life Insurance Building (Bloomfield, Connecticut, 1954–57—q.v.) gave an impetus to establishing corporate headquarters in the suburbs which has had a profound effect on American business and its architecture. Other headquarters have been built since —some of the best by SOM—but Reynolds and Connecticut General were significant innovators. Reynolds' site is rolling tree-rich countryside, with ample room for expansion and parking yet only a short ride from downtown. The three-story building, square in plan around a hollow court, rests on a low podium. A 250-foot/76-meter-long reflecting pool stretches in front, willow oak allées on either side. Two sides of the entry level are partly open and two closed by the L-shaped wing for reception and executive offices. A "freestanding" auditorium for 140 stands at the left of the entry. The two upper floors of offices describe a full square, while a basement accommodates services and a cafeteria, which, because of slope in grade, enjoys a sunny terrace to the south.

On approaching the inner, open courtyard, one is pulled to the entry, and tempted beyond to the fountain court itself. The courtyard is divided into sections of brick, grass, and water by bands of white concrete which mark the column spacings, producing thus a well-scaled "mosaic." A tall magnolia and a five-jet fountain lend their accents, with the east side left open as a loggia and spatial keyhole to provide views of distant Richmond. The reception lobby is a glazed "extension" of this court, even to the red Virginia brick flooring. The two office floors, which are columnless, are protected on east and west from the low sun by 880 vertical aluminum louvers, anodized gray on their south faces and painted blue on their north. The louvers (14 feet/4.3 meters high and 1.9 feet/.56 meter wide) are automatically operated and programmed by a master clock and photocells, and, being set out from the face of the building, they offer not only sun protection—with a consequent economy in air conditioning—but also provide platforms for window washing. The south front is shielded from the high sun by the horizontal projection of these platforms. Details throughout the building received meticulous attention, down to the hardware, the fabrics, and the numerous works of art of museum caliber. Aluminum was, of course, used whenever feasible.

The original headquarters was joined (1968) by a six-story annex which one sees to the right on approaching, and which is connected by underground tunnel to the main building. Designed by the same architects, it forms a trim building. Gordon Bunshaft was partner in charge of design; Marcellus Wright and Baskervill & Son, associates; Ebasco Services, Inc., were consultants.

Reception hall and grounds open to the public on weekdays

40 Philip Morris Factory (1972–74)
3601–4201 Commerce Road
Richmond, Virginia

SKIDMORE, OWINGS & MERRILL, ARCHITECTS

Relatively few architects pay sufficient heed to what might be termed velocity-impact when designing an industrial plant near a superhighway: a structure which could be effective at 20 mph/32 kph in town can be slurred into incomprehension at 55 mph/88 kph. The architects evidently had speed-grasping in mind when they came up with this enormous building (it measures 1,200 feet/366 meters long) directly on the Richmond-Petersburg Turnpike (IS 95). (It is, however, only accessible via the parallel Commerce Road.) There is sufficient rhythm in its cadence massing to be eye-catching at any highway speed, with, perhaps, a touch of dryness for the closeup pedestrian. A fountain in front adds welcome. Note that the fountain's (recirculated) water splashes back into its own retainer so that the mirror of the large ovoid reflecting pool will not be disturbed. The only element which breaks the formality of the approach and entry is that of visitors' automobiles.

The basic layout of Philip Morris is almost programmatic in its simplicity with a long, narrow, two-story administration wing across the entire front, an equal length cigarette production facility parallel to it and directly behind, and shop and related activities in a third wing (similar in size to that of administration) at rear. Two full-length garden courts separate the three buildings which are attached by five bay-point connectors. (The landscaping is visible from the production shops.) Other processing and warehouse units are grouped separately behind and to south. Ten cubic "towers" (cubic as seen in elevation), five on each side of the production building, contain specialized offices and rest rooms on lower level, with elaborate air-conditioning machinery above providing the exact temperature and humidity demanded for cigarette manufacture and employee comfort. These boldly projecting masses (94 feet/29 meters high) add greatly to the vibrancy of the building's profile. Two 25-foot/7.6-meter-wide circulation corridors parallel the production unit, their full 1,200-foot/366-meter length (glass-lined on one side) domesticated by the garden courts, their greenery echoed within by a leafy colored carpet. The mammoth manufacturing facility is spanned by trusses 210 feet/64 meters wide by 10 feet/3 meters deep, allowing maximum flexibility in placement of machinery. Its length is divided into five bays, each painted a different color.

Philip Morris Inc. wanted to produce a plant and office where all workers would find the environment congenial—thus the emphasis on working conditions, gardens ($1.5 million for landscaping), and works of art (mostly by Virginia artists). It was a wise investment, and even if this were not the largest and most automated cigarette-producing factory in the world (which it is with potential of 4,000 cigarettes a unit/minute or 500 million a day), it would be equally striking. It can be said that the complex is so precise and symmetrical as to be almost classical—it has been likened to Spain's Escorial (a mere 675 feet/206 meters long). Gordon Bunshaft was partner in charge of design. Zion & Breen were the landscape architects; Ivan Chermayeff of Chermayeff & Geismar was responsible for the tapestries, graphics, the small exhibition, and the fifteen-story "pop obelisk" in front. The Research Center just south of the factory group was designed by Ulrich Franzen (1968).

Tours Mon.–Fri. 9–4, except holiday weeks; telephone for confirmation: (804) 271-2000

41 **Skyline Drive** (1931–39)
North entrance—Front Royal at US 340
South entrance—Rockfish Gap at US 250
Shenandoah National Park, Virginia

**U. S. BUREAU OF PUBLIC ROADS, WILLIAM M. AUSTIN, RESIDENT
ENGINEER; T. C. VINT, CHARLES E. PETERSON, STANLEY ABBOTT,
LANDSCAPE ARCHITECTS**

In addition to affording one of the loveliest series of vistas in the
U.S.A., the 105.4-mile/169-kilometer-long Skyline Drive is, for a
welcome change, road engineering in complete partnership with nature.
Leisurely in its pace (35 miles per hour/56 kilometers per hour maximum speed, often less), the Drive is designed for the motorist who
wishes to encounter an unspoiled nature with soul-satisfying views of
hills and valleys to be had from its seventy-five parking overlooks. The
highway engineers and landscape architects understood the opportu-

nities well, and this road—plus its extension southward on the **Blue Ridge Parkway**—creates many pleasures for the non-pressed. (The motorist in a hurry will take IS 81, which parallels the Drive some 20 miles/32 kilometers to the west.)

Near the north entrance (Dickey Ridge) and near the midpoint at Big Meadows are visitor centers with exhibits, literature, and interpretive programs. At Big Meadows Lodge there are hotel accommodations (open all year), at 3,610 feet/1,100 meters altitude, plus a campground with two hundred fifty-five sites. Cabins are also available at Skyland Lodge (41.7 miles/66 kilometers from entrance) and Lewis Mountain (57.6 miles/93 kilometers from entrance) from late spring to fall. Other tent and campgrounds will also be found. To enjoy the drive's pleasures at their fullest, park and lock your car and hike for a few hours in the unspoiled Shenandoah Park. There are over 400 miles/644 kilometers of trails.

The almost equally lovely **Blue Ridge Parkway** is a southward continuation of the Skyline Drive which reaches its climax in Mount Mitchell State Park, near Asheville, North Carolina, at the highest peak east of the Rockies (6,684 feet/2,032 meters). Would that all of our highways and Interstates were as respectful of nature. This is not impossible, even at 55 miles per hour/88 kilometers per hour.

---

42   Shirley Plantation (c. 1720/1740/1831)
W off VA 5, turnoff 19 miles/31 kilometers SE of Richmond
Shirley Plantation, Charles City County, Virginia

Shirley stands on property established as a plantation just six years after the founding of Jamestown. Tall, precisely square, and boxlike, and with extraordinary outbuildings, it has a unique personality among the Virginia river houses; "it alone is of the old monumental style" (Thomas Tileston Waterman in his *The Mansions of Virginia,* University of North Carolina Press, 1945). While the house, as Waterman and Hugh Morrison (*Early American Architecture,* Oxford University Press, 1952) both show, stems straight from Palladio with its two-tiered porticos, the relation of house to dependencies is unique. These outbuildings are grouped to frame a courtyard on the land side of the dwelling, a relation almost suggestive of a French chateau—an impression strengthened by the original Mansard roof. Mr. C. Hill Carter, Jr., a ninth-generation Carter—the family has owned the plantation since

1660—feels that this possible French influence might have come from Louis XIV's abrogation of the Edict of Nantes (1685) which forced many Huguenots to flee to England, thence to the colony. As Mr. Carter wrote, "the considerable French Huguenot settlement at Manquin near Richmond may have provided the workmen who did much of the work and probably the master builder." In any case we find a carefully composed grouping, with a brace of two-story gabled houses, the one at right (north) originally for kitchen, that at left (south) for overseer, facing each other across the lawn on the land side of the mansion. Beyond lie two, story-and-a-half farm buildings whose L-shapes close the composition of the five buildings. These dependencies probably date from around 1720.

The main house (c. 1740) is of two full stories with a steeply Mansarded roof and overly prominent dormers sheltering a third floor. The porticos of Shirley, which are highly similar to those on several South Carolina houses of the period (cf. Drayton Hall near Charleston), were added in 1831 (as recent archeological research has brought out). The plan of the house is unusual in that there is no central hall, but a "hall room" in the northeast corner with a remarkable "flying" stair of walnut, three stories high. Note the details of the underside of the steps and the balustrade. The extensive interior paneling and the carving of fireplaces, overmantels, transoms, and cornice are very fine examples of Georgian work. Because the plantation has been continuously inhabited—even during the Civil War when nearby Richmond was in flames—the house is remarkably well preserved. Shirley is still a fully working plantation.

Open 9–5 daily, except Dec. 25: admission

43   Stratford Hall Plantation (c. 1725–c. 30)
**42 miles/68 kilometers E of Fredericksburg on VA 3 to Lerty,
    then 2 miles/3.2 kilometers NE on VA 214
Stratford, Westmoreland County, Virginia**

The visual pleasures of Stratford lie both in its low-springing mansion, probing the four points of the compass, and in its collection of dependencies and outbuildings. Stratford, like Shirley, resembles no other Virginia plantation house. Its H-shape plan derives from Italian books (Serlio) and English publications, a possible influence from the H-shaped Capitol at Williamsburg, and, it would seem from the plan (but not the appearance), of Tuckahoe (1712–30), a mansion west of Richmond. In addition to an unusual plan, Stratford also differs in that its main approach was generally by road, as it still is, not by the distant Potomac.

In any case the house presents a remarkable statement of interacting geometry with two symmetrical wings with squared ends jutting on either side of a recessed central block—and giving two exposures to each room. The *piano nobile* is elevated a half story by its raised basement with an unusual flight of stairs angled to the front doors. Above, topping the intersections of the uniform hipped ridges, erupt two enormous clusters of Vanbrughian chimneys comprised of four interlocked but independent flues. A balustered lookout couches in each. Flanking the house near the corners stand four dependencies, arranged with Palladian symmetry, the two on the approach side (kitchen at east, office on west) placed at right angles to the school and lumber and tool room which stand on the river side.

The mansion is elevated, as mentioned, by a raised basement: note that brick size of the lower part differs from that above the water table

—both are laid in Flemish bond—but that this lower brickwork with its glazed headers is picked up again in the chimneys.

The heavily balustraded flights of stairs, one on either side of the central or hall block, "vanish," that is narrow sharply from c. 13 to 5 feet/4 to 1.5 meters, as each ascends to its simple, brick-pedimented door. Their perspective thus creates a visual dominant in spite of the fact that the stairs are sandwiched between the challenging projections of the wings. It must be added that current research reveals that the late Fiske Kimball, who was in charge of a major stage of the restoration, made arbitrary decisions for the splayed stairs (south flight 1935, north 1940) for which there was no archeological evidence. There is, indeed, no documentation that the north stairs existed. These stairs, a few of whose balusters are original, lead onto the Great Hall with the major rooms disposed in identical rectangular wings on either side, thus producing the H-plan. The hall (28.5 x 28.7 feet/8.69 x 8.74 meters), with its inverted tray ceiling, handsome painted paneling, and sparkling chandelier, forms one of the country's great entrances. It is, moreover, the finest room in the house and one of the finest in the Colonies. With the Potomac shining on one side and the fertile land stretched on the other, the prospect pleases. The other rooms while noteworthy are less impressive, the so-called Mother's room in the southeast corner and the parlor being the finest, though it should be mentioned that they were later refinished with Federal Style woodwork. The minor bedrooms for children and the service quarters for housekeeper, offices, etc. were placed on the lower floor, and served only by a small interior stair. There were also outside stairs on either side.

Fortunes waned with time, changes were made (all outside stairs removed or pushed around, and most interiors, except hall, altered), but no permanent alteration—such as the insertions of hyphens at Westover or Carter's Grove—took place. In 1929 the Robert E. Lee Memorial Association purchased the house and grounds and undertook its masterful restoration, a process which began in 1933 (initially, as mentioned, under the direction of Fiske Kimball) and which still continues. The rehabilitating and refurnishing of the house cover the ninety-two-year occupancy of the Lee family, 1730–1822. No architect has been discovered. Unique.

Open 9–4:30 daily, except Dec. 25, lunch available Apr.–Oct., 11:30–3: admission

---

44   The Filene Center and Wolf Trap Farm Park (1968–71)
from D.C. take Washington Memorial Parkway to Beltway then
**   Dulles Access Road or VA 7 to Trap Road (the Dulles Access**
**   Road is only open for performances)**
Vienna, Virginia

MacFADYEN & KNOWLES, ARCHITECTS; ALFREDO DE VIDO, ASSOCIATE ARCHITECT

Wolf Trap, approximately 14 miles/23 kilometers west of Washington, provides an imaginative, inexpensive, covered but open-sided theater and concert hall. Designed as a summer shelter for the performing arts, it accommodates its activities in rustic splendor. The festivities include classic and folk music, recitals, jazz, ballet, musicals, and theater. Taking advantage of the largely natural grade, the architects let the covered auditorium, which seats 3,500, expand up the hillside on the greensward with open-air space for 3,000 more. The undercover balcony seats are entered near the top grade level via two dramatic gangplanks. The angled sides of the theater are open but the spaces between the "vanes" can be closed by top-seated awnings in case of wind or rain. Construction is of huge laminated wood beams and red cedar panels, which also enclose the fly loft and the ten-story-high stage

house. The stage itself measures 100 feet/30 meters wide x 64 feet/20 meters deep, with backstage facilities, dressing rooms, and services underneath. The orchestra pit holds 116 musicians.

The 130-acre/53-hectare park was given by Mrs. Catherine Filene Shouse in 1966 to be administered by the National Park System as "the country's first park for the performing arts." Mrs. Shouse then generously gave funds ($2.4 million) for the theater-concert hall to be called The Filene Center in memory of her parents. By day the center's architecture is intriguingly angled, while at night it comes spatially and dramatically alive. Lev Zetlin & Associates were the structural engineers; Paul Veneklasen, acoustic consultant; Clarke & Rapuano, landscape architects.

Open early June–mid-Sept. for performances; box office open 10–10: admission

---

45   **Westover** (c. 1730–c. 34)
S off VA 5, turnoff (same as for Berkeley) c. 22 miles/35
    kilometers SE of Richmond
Westover, Charles City County, Virginia

Westover is one of the preeminent houses in this country; however the visitor must keep in mind that what is seen today is only partially as originally built. For the house (like Carter's Grove) has been transformed from a central dwelling with separate flanking dependencies into one stretched-out mansion by connecting the three previously detached units with hyphens. The house stands close to the James River, with gigantic tulip poplars in front, planted almost two hundred years

ago, to shade the building from the sun yet not obstruct the view. Called "the most famous Georgian house in America" (Morrison), its central block is, indeed, superb. Its distinguished south door with an elaborate scroll pediment is one of the most copied in the country (as it, in turn, was largely copied from *Palladio Londinensis* of 1734: the Portland stone enframement itself came from London). William Byrd II, who commissioned Westover, and undoubtedly had a hand in its design, possessed a superb architectural library.

Note that the entablature of the door aligns with the pink-painted brick stringcourse to bind the entry to the whole facade. On either side are three segmental brick window frames with arched window heads to match their slight curve; generally such wood framing and glass are rectangular. Moreover these windows are repeated on the second floor and as they rise they diminish slightly in pane size, lending a highly unusual refinement to the facade. Here stands perfection of proportion with a nicety of detail unmatched in the Early Georgian architecture of the Colonies. Moreover the north (i.e. land) facade is almost equally rewarding, for though the doorway—from the same *Palladio Londinensis*—is not as exuberant, it displays equal workmanship. In front of this side of the house are wrought-iron gates which were made in England and, it is thought, installed around 1711, before the main house itself was commenced. These gates well merit detailed inspection. The gardens themselves possibly date from the late seventeenth or early eighteenth century. (The west dependency was also probably built at this time or earlier.)

It would be agreeable if this paean could continue in describing the remainder of the house, but it cannot because of the insensitivity of the hyphens which were put in (1901–05) to connect the house with the two dependencies. Not only are they weak in design themselves, the hyphens carry out the same ridge as the dependencies, thus slurring their junctures. In addition, the east dependency, which had been destroyed in the Civil War, was rebuilt with a gambrel roof so that we have gable, hip, and gambrel along one roof-line. (Cf. the much more accomplished result in joining together three units at Carter's Grove.) But concentrate on the exterior of the mansion proper and enjoy probably the greatest achievement of American domestic architecture. If possible, arrive during Garden Week, usually toward the end of April, when the interior is also open to the public. The design of the stair and the stunning marble mantel in the drawing room (from James Gibbs's *Book of Architecture,* London, 1728) are particularly recommended.

Grounds and garden open 9–6 daily; house not open except during April Garden Week

---

46   Colonial Williamsburg Restoration (1699–1780/1927–   ) Williamsburg, Virginia

PERRY, SHAW & HEPBURN, INITIAL ARCHITECTS OF RESTORATION (1927–34); THE COLONIAL WILLIAMSBURG FOUNDATION (1935–   )

For three quarters of the eighteenth century, Williamsburg epitomized Colonial building in America. Today it is the world's greatest open-air museum of architecture.

No other English settlement, either in the South or North, even approached the urbane sophistication, the civic unity, and the comeliness achieved here on the high land between the James and the York rivers. (The capital of Virginia was moved here in 1699 to get away from the malarial coast at Jamestown; it was transferred to Richmond in 1780 during the Revolution, where, of course, it remained.) It is beyond the scope of this guidebook to comment more than briefly on the individual buildings and gardens—excellent guides may be had on the

site—but let it be clearly stated that any architect, urbanist, or land-scape architect can profit enormously from a visit, while the non-professional will be immensely rewarded.

The plan of Williamsburg is no casual string of public buildings and houses, but an organized, dynamic play of axis and cross-axis that has immense vitality. The town's essential lesson is not so much one of a carefully restored, beautifully landscaped collection of picturesque, his-toric buildings as it is of spaces. There are pulsating axial and lateral spaces, building spaces respecting each other, building spaces working with garden spaces, the two together delimiting the street spaces. This finds a climax on Duke of Gloucester Street, where trees, bricks, and weatherboard are intertwined in an extended urban partnership. *photo above*

The town, as mentioned, did not simply accrete at random; it was the first major "composed" plan—not a repetitive unfocused grid—of the Colonies. This was based on a Baroque-derived urban layout with the two ends of its spinal avenue, Duke of Gloucester Street (99 feet/30 meters wide), nailed down by the existing college (Wren Building) and the new Capitol, .75 mile/1.2 kilometers away. A cross-axis of major importance, composed of a broad green, 210 x 825 feet/64 x 251 meters, with the Governor's Palace facing it, tapped onto this main thoroughfare. Having the key foci established, the lesser streets developed from this brilliantly off-center T-shape. The core in many respects anticipated L'Enfant's T-plan for Washington by ninety-three years.

Though there were ground rules for the placement of houses on their half-acre lots—rules which included mandatory fences against grazing animals—regimentation did not result. Sir Francis Nicholson (1655–1728), a too little-known but apparently extraordinary governor, or lieutenant governor, of *six* American colonies from Nova Scotia to South Carolina, was responsible for the urban plan of the new capital—as he was also for the plan of Annapolis a few years earlier. (The latter was a far less successful effort which dimly reflects both the never-built Wren Plan for London, and the Palace layout at Versailles, each of which Nicholson was familiar with.) For the town of Williamsburg, with a planned population of 2,000, he could scarce have done better. Alexander Spotswood, governor from 1710–22, made subsequent modifications.

The concept for restoring this notable town began in 1927 (the "dream" was nurtured twenty years earlier). It was then that the Reverend William Archer Rutherfoord Goodwin, rector of Bruton Parish Church, persuaded John D. Rockefeller, Jr., that if he would restore the town's splendid but run-down buildings, and reconstruct those whose foundations lay only a few inches beneath their feet, a cultural richness of the greatest magnitude would evolve. Mr. Rockefeller, who had visited Williamsburg the previous year to attend the dedication of Phi Beta Kappa Hall (the society having been founded at William and Mary in 1776), magnanimously agreed and preliminary work began shortly thereafter. Seven years later the major buildings were opened. Today, after an expenditure of prodigious sums of money and fifty years of work, important restoration and reconstruction still remain to be studied and executed, and the work continues.

The famous Wren Building of William and Mary College, the Colonies' second oldest college and their oldest surviving academic building, was still standing in the 1920s, as was Bruton Parish Church. Actually the only major structures which required total rebuilding were the Capitol (opened in 1934), the Palace (1934), and Raleigh Tavern (1932). Altogether 83 buildings have been completely restored, while 413 minor, many simple outbuildings, have been built afresh, generally on their early foundations, guided by drawings, inventories, wills, and, of course, excavations. To accomplish this, 454 buildings of the last hundred or so years were removed from the 130-acre/53-hectare historic core.

Some quarrel that the resulting Williamsburg "style" has blighted

American architecture by encouraging so many copies of its houses, much as the 1893 Chicago Fair congealed building of its time in a neo-Classical mold. But considering the state of architecture in the 1930s and '40s, such an accusation, in retrospect, does not seem as stultifying now as it did earlier. Moreover the restoration sparked a keen interest in architectural preservation all across the country. However one assesses Williamsburg, and there are those who say it is "sanitized," there are urban lessons for tomorrow that can readily be gleaned from this restoration of the past. Its architecture gives us an illuminating insight into eighteenth-century English influence on the buildings of the Mother Colony—its earliest, largest and (for a time) most populous possession in the New World. It is, thus, not to be missed.

Let us comment briefly on the major buildings. The Wren Building, which initially housed the young institution in toto, provided, as mentioned, the existing anchor by which the new town was secured. (The site, where a scattering of buildings stood in 1699, had been established in 1633 as Middle Plantation with a palisade at the west against the Indians.) First built from 1695–98, the college suffered several fires (1705, 1859, and 1862) which consumed the interior, but the external walls are almost all original, although the building was several times altered. As Professor Marcus Whiffen brings out in his encyclopedic *The Public Buildings of Williamsburg* (Colonial Williamsburg, 1958), the attribution of Christopher Wren as the architect is based solely, thus somewhat strangely, on a book written in 1724 by the Reverend Hugh Jones, a mathematics professor at William and Mary, a man who should certainly know. Jones wrote in *The Present State of Virginia* (London) that "The Building is beautiful and commodious, being first modelled by Sir *Christopher Wren* [Jones' italics]," immediately adding that it was "adapted to the Nature of the Country by the Gentlemen there," and after the fire of 1705, "altered and adorned by the ingenious Direction of Governor Spotswood." As it stands, the facade lacks the mastery of proportion we would expect from Wren, particularly in the central pedimented bay (too narrow for the building's length, with arched entry too wide for its bay). For this we can probably thank Alexander Spotswood. (A wide, triple-arched pedimented bay graced the buildings from the 1865 "rebuilding" to the present restoration.) The Hall, projecting at north rear, was part of the original L-shaped building and survived the fire mentioned. The Chapel, at south rear, was not added until 1729–32: the college initially was intended to form a complete rectangle. Incidentally the Main Building was not called the Wren Building until 1928. In front of the academic grouping at south stands The Brafferton, built, as the plaque proclaims, "as an Indian School in 1723." The near-identical President's House (1732–33) stands opposite on the north side of the College Yard. Accidentally burned in 1781, it was restored in 1786 with funds from the French Government. *Wren building opposite.*

The Bruton Parish Church seen today is the third for the community; the first, whose precise site and date are unknown, was probably built shortly after 1633, when, as mentioned, the area was settled. It was superseded by the second, which dates from 1681–83, and lasted until the college was established and the capital moved here (1699). Then in 1711, hard by the second church, the present larger edifice, designed by Alexander Spotswood, was started, reaching completion in 1715; a 22-foot/6.7-meter expansion, to make the chancel length equal that of the nave, was effected in 1752. In plan the church is symmetrical about both nave and transept axes, with square tower and bell steeple (of little elegance) added in 1769. The interior, several times altered, does not match for brio several of the other Virginia churches, being low of ceiling, but the exterior forms a highly useful nodal point, an urban fulcrum, at the intersection of Duke of Gloucester Street and the Palace Green. George B. Tatum points out in *The Arts in America—Colonial Period* (Scribner's, 1966) that the church "must be counted one of the earliest American examples of the use of the Georgian style by the Church of England."

The Governor's Palace is no arbitrary reconstruction. It is built on

the precise excavated foundations of the old, with a measured plan by Thomas Jefferson—who lived in it for six months while governor of Virginia—to fill in the details. The rebuilding of the exterior massing and window treatment was enormously facilitated by a sharp one-point perspective engraving found in the Bodleian Library at Oxford. (This engraving, invaluable to the reconstruction, contains views of four other major buildings at Williamsburg.) Extensive inventories and descriptions helped with the interior and its furnishings. The Palace was begun in 1706 and finished in 1720. It is a five-bay Georgian mansion in style (note that the bays vary symmetrically in width), almost square in plan, with two dependencies at right angles in front, the whole wrapped in a double-curved brick wall entered by a well-scaled gate. The dormered roof rises steeply to a balustraded deck flanked by paneled chimneys and topped by a high cupola. Some historians think that Dutch Palladianism was a source of inspiration. A ballroom was added at the north side in 1751, and other subsequent repairs carried out (1767–70), possibly to enable the building to meet the challenge of Tryon's Palace in New Bern, North Carolina (q.v.). Be certain to see the richly pedimented exterior of the ballroom, which shows by its floridness the later development of the Georgian. The gardens, too, should not be missed. The Palace was burned in 1781, when being used as a hospital for the wounded from nearby Yorktown.

The Capitol, which forms the climax of Duke of Gloucester Street, was begun in 1701 and finished four years later (but occupied before completion). Two and a half stories high, it is H-shape in plan (cf. Stratford), with two identical wings, round-ended on the south, coupled by a same-height nexus with open ground floor piazza framed by three archways. Like the Governor's Palace, it is built on the foundations of the first capitol, with its exterior restoration greatly helped by the aforementioned Bodleian plate. To avoid the danger of fire there was originally no heating, hence no chimneys—and no candles or smoking—until 1723. Ironically, twenty-four years later, the building burned almost to the ground. The second capitol, on the foundations of the first but differing somewhat in appearance, was commenced in 1747 and completed in 1753. (This, too, burned, in 1832.) It is the restoration of the first capitol which we see today, well proportioned outside, comely within. Incidentally, it is thought likely that the double-hung windows in the Capitol represented their first use in the Colonies. (The Venetian blinds are also authentically of the period.)

The houses of the Williamsburg Restoration, the vast majority of which are of wood weatherboards, merit careful attention, as do their gardens. Like the major buildings, some have been simply restored, others totally reconstructed, but all done meticulously. Two of the finest face each other across the Green near the Palace: the Brush-

Everard House (1717–19) of wood and with later additions, and the imposing Wythe House (1752–54) of brick. Both are owned by Colonial Williamsburg and open to the public. (For detailed handy guidance consult the *Official Guidebook and Map,* and William B. O'Neal's excellent *Architecture in Virginia,* published by the Virginia State Museum [1968]. For more serious research see Marcus Whiffen's *The Public Buildings of Williamsburg* [1958] and his *The Eighteenth-Century Houses of Williamsburg* [1960], both published by Colonial Williamsburg and both very knowledgeable.) All of the Williamsburg structures are, as would be expected, basically Colonial Georgian derived with a hint of the slightly earlier Queen Anne, plus an inevitable sea change. Elegance in architecture in the Colonies can be said to have begun here: moreover such stylish small houses were not found in England at that time. Peripherally, none of the buildings even anticipate the domestic "white pillars" of Greek Revival-Southern Colonial which first appeared across the entire front of Mount Vernon (q.v.) at the very end of the eighteenth century.

Perry, Shaw & Hepburn and their distinguished consultants were admirably successful in their formidable task of restoring and rebuilding —for the first time in the United States—a whole historic city. Following the completion of the original program for the restoration of the major buildings in 1934, Colonial Williamsburg set up its own architectural office to carry out the remaining work. The nation will be eternally grateful to Mr. Rockefeller. It is probably correct to say that the work he made possible here has been the single greatest factor, conscious or not, in our present and future concern for saving the great buildings of our past.

---

47   Main Street and the Nelson House (c. 1711)
Main Street
Yorktown, Virginia

Yorktown is more than a picturesque village: for the American, French, or British military history buff it is an essential one. Its Main Street well merits inspection. The finest house open to the public is the Nelson House, Main and Nelson Streets, acquired by the Colonial National Historic Park of the National Park Service and completely restored and opened in the spring of 1976. Its sturdy exterior—note the well-capped chimneys—is set off by prominent quoins of Aquia stone, while the segmental windows are accented by unusually bold key-

stones. Observe, also, the rich cornice and the pedimented gable, this last an unusual feature (which is also seen at Berkeley). The asymmetrically planned interior possesses several fine paneled rooms, the dining room being outstanding. An interesting detail is its unusual Corinthian "pilasters" with Prince of Wales "feathers" in the capitals. Though within sight of the Yorktown Battlefield and injured then and during the Civil War, the house escaped serious damage. The Edmund Smith House (1750) and the Ballard House (c. 1744) lie just behind and like it are under the protection of the National Park Service.

House open Memorial Day–Labor Day, Tues.–Sun. 9–5, but subject to change

West Virginia

•Wheeling 9

•Cresap 1

•Morgantown 5

Harpers Ferry 2 •

•Philippi 6

Charleston

• Hawks Nest 3

Lewisburg 4 •
• Sweetsprings 7

Union 8 •

WEST VIRGINIA

The buildings in boldface type are of general interest. The others are for the specialist.

Cresap

1 **Mitchell Power Station** (1970–71)— American Electric Power Service Corp.; The Marley Co.

Harpers Ferry

2 **National Historical Park** (1775–1859)

Hawks Nest

3 **Hawks Nest Lodge** (1967)—The Architects Collaborative

Lewisburg

4 Old Stone Presbyterian Church (1796)

Morgantown

5 **West Virginia University Coliseum** (1970)— C. E. Silling & Associates; The Osborn Engineering Co.

Philippi

6 Covered Bridge (1852)—Lemuel Chenoweth

Sweetsprings

7 **A. W. Rowan Home for the Aged** (1833)

Union

8 Rehoboth Church (1785–86/1927)

Wheeling

9 The Wheeling Suspension Bridge (1849/ 1856/1872)—Charles Ellet, Jr.

1 Mitchell Power Station (1970–71)
**on W VA 2, 10 miles/16 kilometers S of Moundsville, 16 miles/26
kilometers N of New Martinsville**
Cresap, West Virginia

AMERICAN ELECTRIC POWER SERVICE CORP., ENGINEERS;
COOLING TOWERS DESIGNED BY THE MARLEY CO.

The natural-draft hyperbolic cooling tower, long known to European
power plants, where water is scarcer than in the United States, is
becoming more and more a part of the American scene. The use of
these towers was pioneered in this country (1963) by the American
Electric Power System. By cooling the water needed in power-plant
operation, it can be recycled or returned to the river without harm.
The towers' hyperbolic shapes are superb mathematical diagrams and
when, as here, they are contrasted with the needle-profiled stack alongside, one encounters three-dimensional mathematics at its grandest
scale. This AEP stack, which serves both generating units, is, at 1,206
feet/367 meters in height, the second tallest in the country (and virtually as tall as the Empire State Building), with space between its concrete exterior and its liner to accommodate a maintenance lift. The two

cooling towers are 370 feet/113 meters in height, 395 feet/120 meters in diameter at base and 178 feet/54 meters at top, with a capacity of 250,000 gallons/1,136,520 liters of water per minute each. The geographic setup for this coal-fired power plant is ideal. Coal comes out of the adjacent hill on conveyor belts on one side of and above the highway (its boilers consume 7,000 tons/6,300 metric tons a day), while the essential waters of the Ohio River flow a relatively few yards away on the other side. Sandwiched between stand the power plant, its cooling towers, and its stack. Total electrical output 1.6 million kilowatts. Potent.

Plant not open to the public but can be seen from road

---

2   National Historical Park (1775–1859)
Shenandoah Street, W entry to town from US 340
Harpers Ferry, West Virginia

The meeting spot of two rivers, the Potomac and the Shenandoah, and three states, West Virginia, Virginia, and Maryland, produced impor-

tant engagements in U.S. military history. The buildings which gave them testament experienced rough going both during the Civil War— the area changed hands nine times—and thereafter, when the town's native and industrial importance withered with the closing of its U. S. Armory. Two heavy floods later in the century did their unwholesome bit. In 1944 Congress acquired over a thousand acres (405 hectares) of the historic center in and around Harpers Ferry, and dedicated it as a National Monument. The restoration of its important buildings has been going on since, beginning with the exteriors of all government-owned structures. The **Stagecoach Inn** (built in 1826 by J. G. Wilson, additions in 1834), which is the first building on the left when entering the town, has been carefully transformed into a Visitors' Center, where instructive slide shows and take-home information are available. It is a good example of regional architecture. The two houses adjacent date from 1845. The **Old** (1812, addition 1827) and **New** (1858) **Master Armorer's Houses,** farther along the other side of Shenandoah Street, now form a museum, with John Brown's famous "fort" down the street. On the hillside stands the **Harper House,** the oldest surviving structure in town, having been built in 1782, and altered in 1832 when it was joined to the houses next to it. (Open only during summer months.) None of the buildings show architectural expertise, nor were they designed to do so, but they do provide a valuable panorama of the time and the region.

Open mid-June–Labor Day, daily 8–8, Labor Day–Oct., daily 8–6, rest of year 8–5, except Jan. 1, Dec. 25

---

3   Hawks Nest Lodge (1967)
Hawks Nest State Park
on US 60, just W of Ansted (c. 45 miles/72 kilometers SE of Charleston)
Hawks Nest (Gauley Bridge), West Virginia

THE ARCHITECTS COLLABORATIVE, ARCHITECTS

The development of Hawks Nest Park by the State of West Virginia— one of four new state parks authorized by the Area Redevelopment Authority—is being carried out along refreshingly forward-looking lines. Hawks Nest comprises 480 acres/194 hectares of dramatically beautiful land in the center of the state, and the buildings have been

designed to fit into this natural splendor with the minimum of intrusion. The principal architectural achievement of what to do and how to do it is found in this lodge, which presents an understated two-story front off the highway, but a four-story cliff-hanger on the far side. Perched 585 feet/178 meters above New River Canyon, the lodge steps down its steep site with an exciting series of controlled views and spaces. Indeed this manipulation of spaces, the far and the near, the horizontal, the stepped, the open and closed, is the outstanding feature of the building. The lodge contains not only the usual bedrooms (thirty-one)—most of them with a balcony offering a panoramic view—but conference rooms, and facilities for the many day visitors. Construction is of rough-form concrete frame, reddish brick, and natural wood. These materials have been handled to develop maximum spatial enjoyment as one moves in and out, up and down. An aerial lift takes one down to the river for water sports. Very sympathetically conceived.

Open daily

4 Old Stone Presbyterian Church (1796)
200 Church Street
Lewisburg, West Virginia

While this substantially built church may recall Quaker meeting
houses, it was built by and for Presbyterians. (Some Pennsylvania German Presbyterians and many Virginia Scotch-Irish migrated to West
Virginia in the eighteenth century.) Additions and changes have been
made, with 25 feet/7.6 meters added to the east end (1830) and some
windows blocked up, but the hip-roofed, limestone church sets a surprisingly competent note for its date in the rumpled hills of the state.
The interior almost matches the assurance of the outside, although it is
more simple. A thorough restoration took place in 1962. The first
church for the parish, built in 1783, was of logs but on a nearby site.

Open daily 9–4

5 West Virginia University Coliseum (1970)
US 19 (Monongahela Boulevard) at Patterson Drive, 2 miles/3.2
**   kilometers W of**
Morgantown, West Virginia

C. E. SILLING & ASSOCIATES, ARCHITECTS; THE OSBORN
ENGINEERING CO., ENGINEERS

Echoing its hillside setting in the Mountain State, its circular roof
rippling with concrete ridges and valleys, this multipurpose coliseum
creates a powerful climax to the west end of the campus. The scale development is excellent as one approaches the building, entering under
an "intimate" marquee, then bursting into the cavernous, column-free
interior. The dome, of course, dominates both exterior and interior,
and its final profile was reached only after extensive computer calcula-
tions. 360 feet/110 meters in diameter, it is supported by forty peripheral columns on which rest forty precast concrete ribs. Haunched

triangulated gores, forming the roof-ceiling, rest on these ribs, which are contained on the periphery by a concrete tension ring. Note that the gores flair upward at their outer edges to emphasize their rhythmic quality. The playing floor is 27 feet/8.2 meters below grade to minimize the height of the building and to shorten the exterior columns. The dome, cleverly, was constructed before the excavation took place, thus minimizing scaffolding for its construction and providing cover in inclement weather for remaining work.

The coliseum serves functions from basketball, tennis, and other spectator sports, to assembly hall for the university. It has 13,500 fixed seats around a squared arena, with pull-out additional seats on two sides. There is chromatic coding for each entrance quadrant but all seats are a uniform blue. Even the suspended light frame—always a problem for such buildings—has been inconspicuously attended to. Squash and handball courts and physical education facilities project around the periphery at entry level. Note their striated concrete finish against the smooth-formed structural members. A fine job throughout.

Open for events

---

6   Covered Bridge (1852)
US 250 immediately N of town
Philippi, West Virginia

LEMUEL CHENOWETH, ENGINEER

The citizens of Philippi should be congratulated for saving this bridge which by the 1930s had become unequal to the heavy truck traffic then developing. Instead of erecting a new steel span to replace the picturesque and historic bridge—which had served critically in the Civil War —they jacked the old one up (1934–38) and reinforced it with steel beams which they rested on reinforced concrete piers. However, they also added a covered sidewalk and squared off the entries to clear high truck bodies. Thus, although Mr. Chenoweth's twin 138-foot/42-meter Burr-truss spans of yellow poplar are not as "pure" as they used to be, at least they are still there. But, please, O Philippians, remove the signs from the bridge.

---

7 A. W. Rowan Home for the Aged (1833)
W VA 3 (VA 311)
Sweetsprings, West Virginia

The Old Sweetsprings Resort began as a "watering place" in 1792 and its main building (the second on the site) was obviously influenced by the work of Thomas Jefferson. (Some claim, without documentation,

that it was based on a design by Jefferson.) Situated in an angle of the state abutting the road between Roanoke and White Sulphur Springs, the impressively long facade consists of a white arcaded base on which rest the two upper floors of red brick. Three double-height Doric porticos grace this considerable expanse, adding a welcome relief to the brick walls behind. Half-round windows in their three pediments pick up the geometry of the arcade, tying the facade together. Used for many years as a spa, then closed (1930) for a long time, it now serves as an old people's home. The interiors today are not of interest. The building is listed in the National Register of Historic Places.

Grounds only open to public

---

8   Rehoboth Church (1785–86/1927)
N off W VA 3, 2 miles/3.2 kilometers E of
Union, West Virginia

A log cabin church, built by Methodists, which reputedly is the oldest in the Alleghenies, and the farthest west church of its time still standing. It will not make the pages of any history of architecture, but it does offer an insight into the primitive building and worship conditions of this area almost two hundred years ago. (The pulpit is hand-hewn

and the "pews" split logs.) Upon its restoration (1927), the church was wisely covered by a protective, freestanding (but tight) shed. It is listed in the National Register of Historic Places.

For entry see note regarding key on front door

---

9   **The Wheeling Suspension Bridge** (1849/1856/1872)
10th Street
Wheeling, West Virginia

CHARLES ELLET, JR., ENGINEER

A venerable mixture of metal and stone which was the longest bridge in the world—and the first over the Ohio River—when built in 1849: 1,010 feet/308 meters. Designed by Charles Ellet, Jr., its decking was destroyed in 1854 by wind oscillation. The squat, almost medieval towers at Wheeling, with the seemingly delicate double cables stretched across the top of their turrets, epitomize stone's compressive and wrought-iron wire's tensile strengths.

It is pertinent to point out, according to research by Dr. Emory Kemp, Professor of History of Science and Technology, University of West Virginia, that Ellet himself supervised the rebuilding of the span in 1855–56, not John Augustus Roebling as has often been assumed. Roebling came to Wheeling in May and July of 1847 seeking the contract for the original bridge but his plans were rejected in favor of Ellet's. However, in 1871–72, Washington Roebling (John Augustus' son) undertook a major reconstruction—Ellet having died in 1862—utilizing all of his own and his father's expertise to strengthen and stiffen the span. The bridge was completely overhauled in 1956. A too little-known example of mid-nineteenth-century engineering: it is an asset both to state and nation. Fortunately it is listed in the National Register of Historic Places.

Wisconsin

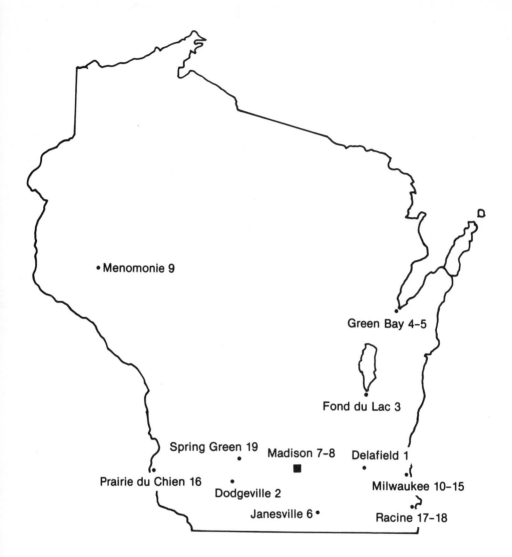

• Menomonie 9

Green Bay 4–5

Fond du Lac 3

Spring Green 19   Madison 7–8   Delafield 1

Prairie du Chien 16   Dodgeville 2   Milwaukee 10–15

Janesville 6 •   Racine 17–18

WISCONSIN

The buildings in boldface type are of general interest. The others are for the specialist.

Delafield   1 **St. John Chrysostum Church** (1851–53)—
                           Richard Upjohn

Dodgeville   2 Iowa County Court House (1859)—
                           Ernest Wiesen

Fond du Lac   3 Galloway House (c. 1847) and Village

Green Bay   4 **Roi-Porlier-Tank House** (1776–1850)
                         5 **The Baird Law Office** (1835) **and
                           The Cotton House** (1840)

Janesville   6 **Tallman House** (1855–57)

Madison   7 U. S. Forest Products Laboratory (1932)—
                           Holabird & Root
                         8 **First Unitarian Meeting House** (1949–
                           51)—Frank Lloyd Wright

Menomonie   9 Mabel Tainter Memorial Building
                           (1889–90)—Harvey Ellis

Milwaukee   10 **Mitchell Building** (1876–78) **and Mackie
                           Building** (1879–80)—Edward Townsend
                           Mix
                        11 Federal Building (1892–99)—Willoughby
                           J. Edbrooke
                        12 **Annunciation Greek Orthodox Church**
                           (1959–61)—Frank Lloyd Wright
                        13 Inland-Ryerson Building Systems Plant
                           (1966)—William Wenzler & Associates;
                           The Engineers Collaborative
                        14 **Center for the Performing Arts** (1968–
                           69)—Harry Weese & Associates
                        15 **First Wisconsin Center** (1973–74)—
                           Skidmore, Owings & Merrill

Prairie du Chien   16 Villa Louis (1843/1872)

Racine   17 **The S. C. Johnson Offices** (1936–39) **and
                              Laboratory** (1947–50)—Frank Lloyd
                              Wright
                           18 "Wingspread" Conference Center (1937)—
                              Frank Lloyd Wright

Spring Green   19 **"Hillside"** (1902–3/1952) **of the Taliesin
                              Fellowship**—Frank Lloyd Wright
                              The Spring Green (1953–69)—Frank
                              Lloyd Wright
                              Unity Chapel (1886)—John L. Silsbee

St. John Chrysostum Church (1851–53)
Church Street, W off Genesee (just N of IS 94)
Delafield, Wisconsin

RICHARD UPJOHN, ARCHITECT

Nineteenth-century "Village Gothick" in wood is still found in numerous states. Among the better examples is this Episcopal church—
named for the famous fourth-century Antiochean—some 25 miles/40
kilometers west of Milwaukee (and adjacent to St. John's Military
Academy). Set in an old cemetery, punctuated by a detached wood
belfry that owes a debt to Swedish bell towers, and painted a pinkish
red (a faded Swedish falun color), the church, its belfry, and its graveyard provide a cohesive ensemble. The nave—note the trusswork built
by English shipwrights—is on the dark side, but, fortunately, neither
the interior nor the exterior has been seriously altered through the
years. A complete restoration inside and out took place in 1973–76.
(The elaborately carved barge boards are well worth noticing.) Recent
research almost definitely confirms that Upjohn was the architect, even
though this is not mentioned in *Richard Upjohn, Architect and
Churchman* by Everard M. Upjohn (Da Capo Press, 1968). *Upjohn's*

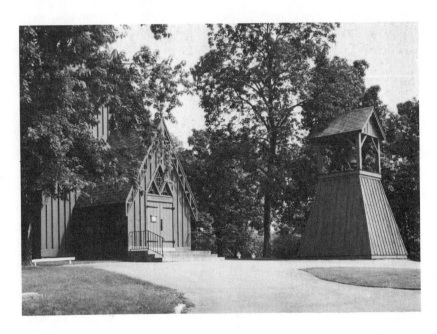

Rural Architecture—which helped so many small communities build their Gothic Revival churches "and Other Rural Structures"—was published in 1852, a year after St. John was commenced, and the church bears a very strong resemblance to examples in this volume. It might well be that this Wisconsin chapel was thus Upjohn "designed" —i.e. its drawings sent by him to the parish. Whatever the attribution, let us be grateful for the result.

Open for Sun. service and by appointment; telephone (414) 646-2727

---

2 Iowa County Court House (1859)
Iowa Street at Chapel
Dodgeville, Wisconsin

ERNEST WIESEN, ARCHITECT

The Greek Revival did not gain much foothold for public buildings in Wisconsin: the mainstream of the cultural climate was farther south. Moreover Wisconsin's early "official" buildings (statehood was only granted in 1848) tended to more basic expressions than purified entablatures from ancient Athens. In this courthouse, though, we have a

creditable example (except for the aluminum front door) which the specialist might enjoy. Detailing is primitive (no entasis in columns, cupola on heavy side), but for the state's oldest courthouse the results are good. There were additions in 1894 and 1927, with a full restoration in 1937. It is listed in the National Register of Historic Places.

Open during office hours

---

3   Galloway House (c. 1847) **and Village**
336 Old Pioneer Road, S edge of
Fond du Lac, Wisconsin

A restored thirty-room Victorian mansion, most of which was built about 1847. The house is surrounded by a group of end-of-century buildings furnished as if in use. The house itself shows Tuscan touches in its bracketed eaves, while on the inside it displays carved woodwork,

stenciled ceiling, and many original furnishings. The twenty other buildings on the 8-acre/3.2-hectare site range from a century-old log cabin to an operating gristmill, to a collection of old structures put together to represent a village street of the time. In 1954 the house and property were given to the Fond du Lac County Historical Society by Edwin P. Galloway, grandson of the original owner. Complete restoration was then undertaken.

Open Memorial Day–Sept., Tues.–Sun. 1–4: admission

4   Roi-Porlier-Tank House (1776–1850)
Heritage Hill State Park
2640 South Webster Avenue
Green Bay, Wisconsin

Though no more than a cottage, and devoid of stylistic significance, the house is of architectural interest in that part of it is the oldest still standing in the state, hence we have a token of frontier building means. As might be expected, these means were primitive and

consisted in their earliest and most rudimentary manifestations of *poteaux-et-pièces-en-coullisant,* a monolithic vertical log construction similar to French building techniques used in Canada. The central part of this house, built by a fur trader named Joseph (some references say "Francis") Roi, is the earliest (1776). The building was later clapboarded for greater weather protection, probably by Jacques Porlier, who purchased the house in 1805. The cottage was enlarged by adding wings on either side in the middle of the last century (1850) by a Norwegian family named Tank, and most of the furnishings shown are from their occupancy. The expansion was made using a "post and fill" construction, the clay fill mistakenly thought by some to be wattle-and-daub. The Tanks also undoubtedly covered the expanded house with new clapboards. The dwelling first stood on the west bank of the Fox River, but was moved to Tank Park (ex-Union Park) and finally to Heritage Hill State Park on the east bank of the Fox.

Open June–Aug., Mon.–Sat. 9–5, Sun. 1–5: admission

---

5   The Baird Law Office (1835) **and The Cotton House** (1840)
Heritage Hill State Park
2640 South Webster Avenue
Green Bay, Wisconsin

A small Greek Revival law office, built in downtown Green Bay and moved here in 1976. It makes an unexpectedly handsome pair with the nearby Cotton House built five years later and also moved to this site on the south edge of town along the east side of the Fox River. The Law Office, reputedly the first in the territory, with its portico upheld by two Ionic columns and two squared columns on the corners, is perhaps the more "correct" of the two, but the river (northwest) side of the house with its inset porch and two two-story Doric columns and flanking wings recalls Jeffersonian principles. This use of the Greek Revival undoubtedly reflected the eastern travels of its builders. Both house and office were well restored when moved and are now the property of the State of Wisconsin Department of Natural Resources. The National Register gives the date of 1831 for The Baird Law Office.

It should be noted that Green Bay, though on the northeast edge of the state, is the oldest settlement in Wisconsin, dating from 1669. It was settled in 1634, only twenty-seven years after Jamestown. It soon became an important French mission and fur-trading center, originally being called La Baye for the sparkling arm of water that leads from town to bay to Lake Michigan.

Open June–Aug., Mon.–Sat. 9–5, Sun. 1–5: admission

---

6   **Tallman House** (1855–57)
440 North Jackson Street (City Route 14)
Janesville, Wisconsin

The overall scale of the Tallman House, its opulent portico (note the columns and frieze), well-detailed windows, and deeply bracketed eaves combine to produce an outstanding example of an Italianate mansion. Moreover on the interior this well-preserved house contributes a variety of advanced conveniences which adds further interest. There is, for instance, running water for each basin in the major bedchambers, two indoor privies, a central-heating plant, while sliding slat shutters are built into the walls. When constructed (of Milwaukee cream brick on limestone base) it was the most advanced house in the state. Its owner and apparently its designer was W. M. Tallman, a New York State-born attorney, and ardent abolitionist, who made a fortune in land speculating. The design of the house is based on a "pattern book" by Samuel Sloan published in 1852.

Although relatively little of the furniture is original to the dwelling, which had been vacant for thirty-five years before being given to the city (1950) by the builder's grandson, most of its twenty-six major rooms have been refurnished in the prodigal fashion of its period. There are reputedly "several thousand" artifacts of quality. Its restoration was under the care of the Rock County Historical Society, which now operates it. Because of the excellent preservation and the scope and quality of the furnishings, the Tallman House is one of the most important of its period in the Midwest: historian Kenneth L. Ames puts it among "the top ten of mid-century structures" in the United States. It is listed in the National Register of Historic Places.

Note the **Carriage House** behind, now a gift shop and museum, and the 1842 Greek Revival **Stone House** (which was moved to this site in 1964).

Open June–Aug., Tues.–Sun. 11–4; also Sat.–Sun. 11–4 in May–Oct.: admission

7   **U. S. Forest Products Laboratory** (1932)
    501 Walnut Street
    Madison, Wisconsin

HOLABIRD & ROOT, ARCHITECTS

As an example of Early Depression Moderne and Art Deco, this laboratory is one of the country's significant pioneers. Its symmetrical composition atop the hill, its corner windows countering the verticality of its profusion of "fins" are all dated now. But this was one of the first large "contemporary" structures in the country when it was built, an exciting statement of its time. The original setting has been marred by unsympathetic additions, the exterior color scheme has been changed, and a nearby expressway does not help matters, but the laboratory still maintains much of its original vanguard conviction.

Tours 2 P.M. during business days

8   **First Unitarian Meeting House** (1949–51)
     900 University Bay Drive, 1 block N of University Avenue at W
       edge of University of Wisconsin campus
     Madison, Wisconsin

FRANK LLOYD WRIGHT, ARCHITECT

This famous Unitarian church settles on its low ridge, cozily simpatica
with nature like all of Wright's buildings. Symbolically its green copper
prow-roof suggests—as Mr. Wright was wont to point out with his eloquent fingers—hands folded in prayer, indeed "the whole edifice is in
the attitude of prayer" (FLW). However suggestive the exterior might
be, the interior is, in some respects, disappointing—at least to this observer. This is because of the source and treatment of natural light.
Mr. Wright wanted to develop Unitarian "open-endedness" and "to
make the outdoors a part of the room," but as the large windows
behind the pulpit supply almost the sole source of daylight some glare

results. It should be immediately added that, according to the minister, this is a distinctly minority point of view. (Because of the church's triangular "prow" there is no chancel in the regular sense of the term, only a pulpit.) The triangular plan of the interior develops a brilliant intimacy between minister and congregation and among the congregation itself. The very flexible auditorium, which seats 250, can be turned into a parish hall, with its seats reversed, when it then "faces" the hearth room which opens off the rear. An educational wing, a large assembly room, and offices complete the church.

Open Tues.–Fri. 9–4, Sat. 9–12, except holidays

9   Mabel Tainter Memorial Building (1889–90)
205 Main Street
Menomonie, Wisconsin

HARVEY ELLIS, ARCHITECT

Richardson was the godfather of this accomplished structure and the great carved sandstone arched narthex—which opens onto an Italian marble and mahogany lobby—would not be to his discredit. Nor, indeed, would the massing of the turreted facade. The building, much of which is occupied by a library, was built as a community center by a

local timber baron and his wife in memory of their daughter, who died at the age of nineteen. A fully restored, compact theater forms an integral part of the building and should also be seen. It is in active use by the Menomonie Theater Guild. This assertive example of rural Romanesque Revival is on the list of the National Register of Historic Places.

Open Mon.–Fri. 9–5, except holidays

---

10   Mitchell Building (1876–78) **and Mackie Building** (1879–80)
207 and 225 East Michigan Street
Milwaukee, Wisconsin

EDWARD TOWNSEND MIX, ARCHITECT

Two of the most ebullient office buildings of the 1870s—designed by the same architect and built within a few years of each other—stand adjacent and lightly connected in downtown Milwaukee. Their unabashed architectural hedonism, the frenetic modulation of their facades, their presumptuous ambitions, bring harmonic cheer to the central business district. Between the two—a veritable Damon and Pythias of office buildings—they conjure up a panoply of architectural gar-

nishing. The window treatment alone furnishes a handbook for the stop-at-nothing school, but achieved, nonetheless, with knowing talent. Note in each that the fenestration progresses from one large pane of glass at street (elevated basement) level, to coupled windows on main floor, then two separate windows, and finally three at top, all crowned with both broken segmental and triangular pediments. The entrances, too, are glories of their kind, that on the Mackie (also Chamber of Commerce Building) suggesting the influence of Frank Furness (see Index). The more restrained, semi-Baroque front door of the Mitchell Building is flanked by gryphons at the ready. Well preserved inside and out (except for two inexcusable signs), they are among the finest which, their improbable era produced. W. A. Holbrook was associated with Mix in the design of both.

Open during business hours

---

11   Federal Building (1892–99)
515 East Wisconsin between Jefferson and Jackson Streets
Milwaukee, Wisconsin

WILLOUGHBY J. EDBROOKE, PROBABLE ARCHITECT

A *fin de siècle* granite glory so indestructible that it will probably be around at the turn of the next century. Combining a bit of Richardson with a suggestion of Loire chateaux—all topped by an enormous tower (empty)—it well represents an age of municipal opulence not repeated until Washington's Rayburn Office Building (1956). Its architect is not precisely known but the design was prepared for the Treasury Department in Washington by its Supervising Architect—to which post Willoughby Edbrooke was appointed in 1892. An eight-story addition was grafted on in 1931. It is listed in the National Register of Historic Places.

Open during office hours

---

12   Annunciation Greek Orthodox Church (1959–61)
**North 92nd and West Congress Streets (W from downtown on
    WIS 190, N on 92nd)**
Milwaukee (Wauwatosa), Wisconsin

FRANK LLOYD WRIGHT, ARCHITECT

The problem of establishing for today a valid exterior and a proper interior setting for the Greek Orthodox Church presents the architect with a difficult task. Most observers will respond favorably to the

Byzantine-influenced exterior, inner iconography, and golden setting which Mr. Wright and his associates have achieved in this Milwaukee suburb. Other observers might be more reticent with their praise; in any case, scale, color, relationships of parts to the whole, lighting, and decoration demand firsthand experience. The exterior suggests, of course, reference to that Greek Mother Church, Santa Sophia (A.D. 537)—the most audacious building in the history of architecture—which the Emperor Justinian commissioned, and of which he reputedly said on entering for the first time, "I have surpassed even thee, O Solomon!" Frank Lloyd Wright had long admired the Byzantine: "I was thrilled by Mayan, Inca and Egyptian remains, loved the Byzantine" (*A Testament*, Horizon Press, 1957) and, as in most Greek Orthodox churches in the United States, some obeisance to the dome atop Istanbul's great example seems inevitable. The blue-tiled dome of the Wauwatosa church, incidentally, is at 104 feet/32 meters in diameter just 3 feet/.9 meter smaller (but much shallower) than that topping Santa Sophia. Its exterior employs not only a dome on top but an inverted counter-dome or bowl on bottom, the two cupped together. Their roof is surrounded by a scaled series of lunettes which progress from small on the eave edge, to medium in the band of windows, to bay-size at entry.

On the interior this interlocked circular and semicircular geometry almost erupts. This begins with the plan itself which expands from a small inner circle containing nave and chancel to a large, upper "nave" for the majority of the congregation. This elevated ring of five banks of walnut seats with blue cushions overlooks the sanctuary, almost like a cockpit. The inner curve of the upper section is broken by the counter-curves of the stairwells down to the small, main nave. A reredos and chancel screen of uninhibited color and complexity provide the focus.

Open Mon.–Sat. 10–3, except holidays: admission

---

13   Inland-Ryerson Building Systems Plant (1966)
West Calumet Road at North 73rd Street
Milwaukee, Wisconsin

WILLIAM WENZLER & ASSOCIATES, ARCHITECTS; THE ENGINEERS COLLABORATIVE, ENGINEERS

A simple, but cagily designed industrial plant which rises to excellence in the relation of side paneling to frame and in the handling of lateral fenestration. Materials are concrete in the low base with steel framing

and ribbed steel panel walls above. Two ventilating and illumination strips line the long sides: a 2-foot/.6-meter-high, all-glass lower one, permitting eye-level views out plus ventilation, and a 4-foot/1.2-meter-high, partially slotted band near the ceiling, primarily for ventilation. The glass portions of this upper band are hooded to keep out direct sun, and to cast shadows. Entrances are at both east and west ends to allow railroad cars and trucks to pass through. The interior forms one vast industrial space and is of little interest (and is not open to the public). A small executive building stands nearby. The design, completed under pressure conditions, utilizes many of the plant's own building components.

Executive building only open to the public during office hours

14 Center for the Performing Arts (1968–69)
North Water Street between East Kilbourn Avenue and East State Street
Milwaukee, Wisconsin

HARRY WEESE & ASSOCIATES, ARCHITECTS

The Performing Arts Center acts as a strong drawing card for Milwaukee's downtown resurgence. Well sited along the river, well landscaped, and within view of City Hall, it would be an asset to any com-

munity. Its travertine facade is one of symmetrical formalism, but the terrace down to the river and the landscaping soften the solemnity. The building houses not only a concert hall-opera house, but also a repertory theater, small recital hall, and banquet pavilion.

The main auditorium, Uihlein Hall (entry from Water Street via a tight lobby), forms an impressive room seating 2,331, with an unusual treatment of "framing" on walls of both auditorium and stage, visually making them one family when used as a concert hall. The metal stage "shell" is quickly retractable for opera and/or theater. At the back of the stage there is a pit for the organ. The architect sought to reveal, not mask, the elements which produce proper acoustics and proper visual ambience in this combination chamber. An ingenious canopy of Plexiglas "clouds" hovers over the concert stage. Fully mechanized, its sound-reflective angles can be changed to suit full orchestra or single voice. A suspended circular chandelier enlivens the ceiling. Acoustics are very good.

The Todd Wehr Hall, at the southwest corner, houses the Milwaukee Repertory Theater Company. Its 504 seats embrace a thrust stage on three sides, and as the theater was designed for a resident company with intimate productions, elaborate backstage facilities were not necessary. A steel light grid over the thrust of the stage fills much of the ceiling, while the seats which bank high on three sides, including the balcony, almost hide the brick walls. The shape and straightforward result induce a close sense of audience participation.

The Charles P. Vogel Hall, which occupies the northwest corner, is basically a recital hall seating 500. Its walls and especially its coffered ceiling are broken into prominent divisions; acoustics are reportedly fine. Bradley Pavilion, used for festivities, feasts, and meetings, occupies the well-windowed space above Wehr and Vogel, with the center's offices in the projecting "cornice" above. George C. Izenour Associates played a substantial role in the theater program; Bolt, Beranek & Newman and Dr. Lothar Cremer were acoustic consultants; Dan Kiley was landscape architect.

Open during performances

---

15   First Wisconsin Center (1973–74)
East Wisconsin Avenue between North Cass, North Van Buren,
    and East Michigan
Milwaukee, Wisconsin

SKIDMORE, OWINGS & MERRILL, ARCHITECTS

Imaginatively conceived in structure, expressively detailed, First Wisconsin forms a highlight on Milwaukee's lakefront. Much of the drama of the forty-two-story building derives from its base of three boldly expressed structural floors, a "subsystem" of trusses which act as stiffening belts for the framed tube of the tower. This trussing also spans Michigan Street to the separate 850-car garage. The sleekness of the tower, which rises from a two-story podium, comes from the contrast of its triangulated freestanding "bones" versus the smooth skin of white aluminum and dark glass. The double-height banking floor for the First Wisconsin National Bank projects across the entire site—the tower rising above it in the middle—and offers, particularly on the Wisconsin Avenue side, a dramatic interior with skylighting, large trees (moved in before final glazing), and outsize paintings. One might

regret the lack of sun control (note the use of awnings on the 1911 building across the street), but overall First Wisconsin numbers among the high-rise elite. It was designed by the Chicago office of SOM in association with Fitzhugh Scott Inc. and Cosentini Associates.

Open during office hours

---

16 Villa Louis (1843/1872)
521 Villa Louis Road at Bolvin Street
Prairie du Chien, Wisconsin

Although the Villa Louis/Dousman House which we see today represents a drastic remodeling of the 1843 mansion built by Hercules Louis Dousman, its forms a valuable niche as a domesitc index of its

time and place. (Mr. Dousman was an extremely able and successful fur factor for John Jacob Astor.) To judge from old photographs, the first dwelling was a stretched-out building with prominent enclosed veranda, the whole having little sense of style. After Mr. Dousman's death in 1868, his widow set about to remodel, in effect to rebuild the house—with the aid of architect E. Townsend Mix in the then popular Tuscan Style. The length was shortened, a trimly bracketed low third floor added, and the whole wrapped with yellow brick instead of the routine red of the original. The results were (and are) sumptuous, particularly the interior and its furnishings.

Variously occupied until 1934, the house and 84 acres/34 hectares of grounds were given the following year to the town of Prairie du Chien (the name, we understand, derives from seventeenth-century French traders to honor Indian Chief Alim of Big Dog). Complete restoration of the property has taken place since then under the aegis of the remaining Dousman family, who have given it time, money, and many of the original furnishings. Being one of the representative landmarks of its region, the house was acquired (1951) by the State Historical Society of Wisconsin. A Fur Trade Museum, built as a warehouse for the American Fur Company in 1829, was opened on the grounds in 1977.

Open May–Oct., daily 9–5: admission

17   The S. C. Johnson Offices (1936–39) **and Laboratory** (1947–50)
Franklin Street between 15th and 16th
Racine, Wisconsin

FRANK LLOYD WRIGHT, ARCHITECT

Pietro Belluschi wrote of the Johnson complex. "These buildings shine
in uncompromising purity and deliver all that the spirit may wish"
(*Architectural Record,* July 1956). Of its impacts it is the interior of
the main administrative unit that gleams the most. This magnificently
fashioned room was modern architecture's first substantial administrative beachhead on the then reactionary shores of U.S. corporate wis-
dom (Wright's demolished Larkin Building excepted). It was, and is
forty years after its completion, one of the Great Spaces—and there
are precious few. The fifty-four (thirty-two freestanding) dendriform
columns (24 feet/7.3 meters high) uphold the 128 x 228 feet/39 x 69
meters ceiling—structurally they hold up mostly themselves. In shape
they vaguely recall those which supported King Minos' Palace in Crete
of about 2000 B.C.; and they were so beyond the building code concept
of base size to load that they were immediately challenged by the state.
Thereon, Mr. Wright—who studied engineering before beginning architecture—had a prototype column constructed and piled with sandbags until it exceeded by twelve times the load it was normally calculated to carry. The city engineer was among the first in hailing FLW's
triumph. (The columns are hollow and were poured integrally with
steel mesh.) Whether this forest of columns with conical necks and
lily-pad tops (18 feet/5.5 meters in diameter) supports as much as is
suggested, the fact remains that these exquisitely tapered shapes with
their glass tube interstices provide us with a noble, suffusively illuminated hall. It is also one which creates a "family" ambience for work
in a non-stimulating industrial environment.

The desks and cabinets of the typing and accounting activities at the
column bases are all in a cheerful Cherokee red—and were designed
by the architect. One of the essential features of the space quality of
the two-story-with-balcony room can be seen in the juncture of three
of its sides with the ceiling plane. This is effected by a continuous glass
tube clerestory which lends spatial freedom to the enclosed volume
plus delivering a glowing emanation outside at night. (The extensive
exterior use of 2-inch/50-millimeter Pyrex glass tubing, in 5- and
10-foot/1.5- and 3-meter lengths, occasioned initial leakage problems
but these have been solved by a silicone rubber sealant.) Note that, as

has been already mentioned in connection with many of Wright's buildings, the entrance rarely announces itself; here at Racine it is mischievously tantalizing. There is no ambiguity about the great forested work space, however: it is masterful. As Mr. Samuel C. Johnson, a fourth-generation Johnson, and chairman and chief executive officer of the company, adds: "We became a different company the day the building opened. We achieved international attention because that building represented and symbolized the quality of everything we did in terms of products, people, the working environment within the building, the community relations and—most important—our ability to recruit creative people" (*AIA Journal,* January 1979).

Behind the administrative building rises the fourteen-story Research Tower (not open to the public), swathed in slightly streamlined bands of glass tubing and red brick, its vertical accent welcome amid the low units about it.

Tours several times daily, Mon.–Fri.: telephone (414) 554-2000 for hours

18   "Wingspread" Conference Center (1937)
The Johnson Foundation
4 Mile Road, E off WIS 32 (or Main Street), NE edge of Racine, Wisconsin

FRANK LLOYD WRIGHT, ARCHITECT

Wingspread, the former Herbert F. Johnson residence, "the last of the Prairie Houses," was named by Wright himself for its four "wings" which spring toward the cardinal points from an octagonal core. One wing was for the master bedrooms, children occupied the second, guests and carport filled the third, while kitchen and services took up the fourth. (Compare the "windmill" plan of Wright's Isabel Roberts House of 1907 and Mies van der Rohe's 1923 plan for "a brick country house.") It provides a fascinating spatial experience. One enters via a somewhat "cautious" front door into a purposefully low prehall, then steps into the towering, climactic Great Hall, literally crowned with rings of light at the top, while garden vistas lure one at eye level.

Banked around the periphery of an immense chimney-bulwark are living, reading, dining, and music areas set off by changes in levels and by low screens or built-in furniture. A flood of light which slants in through a triple clerestory gives dramatic emphasis to the visual role of the fireplace so that whatever the hour the sun is out it puts a spotlight on this great brick core, "a massive kernel," as Giedion summed up Wright's centricity. Repose from this exciting and inevitably somewhat restless communal space can be sought in the quiet study rooms in the wings.

Fortunately, the house and sensitively landscaped grounds were given to the Johnson Foundation as a high-level international Conference Center. With the exception of a few minor changes to adapt it to group sessions, the dwelling and grounds are as Mr. Wright designed them.

Open to visitors by appointment only: telephone (414) 639-3211 for information

19 **"Hillside"** (1902–3/1952) **of the Taliesin Fellowship
on WIS 23, S of river and of
Spring Green, Wisconsin**

FRANK LLOYD WRIGHT, ARCHITECT

Frank Lloyd Wright's architecture does not reveal itself fully to the impatient eye. His interiors, especially the domestic ones, are not immediately graspable in the Renaissance and Miesian sense, but unfold their subtleties only with study and quiet movement. At their best they possess spatial sorcery. It is startling to find that the conjoined buildings which form Hillside were originally constructed at the beginning of this century, so far ahead of their eclectic contemporaries were they. (Since 1933 they have been used as the office and drafting room of Taliesin.)

Hillside was built as a school with six smallish classrooms and several large chambers for assembly, gym, lab, etc. They were easily converted to their present drafting room and office divisions (and also underwent earlier modifications following fires). Though lacking the homogeneity of Mr. Wright's later houses, this is a primordial grouping, its random ashlar local stone walls stretching out to grasp the land. The school was rebuilt in 1952 after a fire. Open to the public in summer on guided tours, the experience of exploring and encountering unexpected spaces can be had by all. Fortunately upkeep has been excellent—parts of the building have been renovated each year since 1960—so that the trip to Spring Green (some 35 miles/56 kilometers west of Madison) is very worthwhile.

The Taliesin residence, which lies nearer the village, is not open to the public, but an excellent restaurant, **The Spring Green,** is. Designed by Wright (1953) and finished (1969) by Mrs. Wright and students, it stands picturesquely on the bank of the Wisconsin River and is open all year round. Incidentally, Mr. Wright was buried nearby off County Road T, next to the 1886 wood-shingled **Unity Chapel** designed for Wright's uncle by John L. Silsbee, in whose office Wright first (1887) began work in Chicago. A golf course and ski facilities originally planned by Taliesin Associated Architects occupy the neighborhood.

*Daily tours July–Labor Day, Mon.–Sat. 10–4, Sun. 12–4;
telephone (608) 588-2511 for information: admission*

Glossary

abacus	The topmost, blocklike element of a capital, that on which the architrave (i.e. beam) rests
acropolis	Literally a city on a hill, the most famous example being in Athens
acroterion	A small pedestal at ends and/or on top of a pediment to hold a statue (Greek or Roman temples); the word often includes the figure(s); also commonly an eave ornament
Adam/Adamesque	Influenced by the Scot Robert Adam (1728–92) and his brother James (1732–94), the most important British architects of their time
adobe	Sun-dried brick generally mixed with straw binder
aggregate	Gravel or crushed stone mixed with cement and water to form concrete
agora	An open square or marketplace in ancient Greece generally surrounded by a peristyle
allée	An avenue of trees
anthemion	Foliated leaf pattern in clusters in Greek and Roman friezes
architrave	The bottom part of an entablature—that which rests on the columns
archivolt	The outside molding of an arch; also the ornamental molding on the face of an arch
Art Deco	The "jazzed," zigzag design approach popular in the late 1920s and the 1930s. Its name stems from L'Exposition Internationale des Arts Décoratifs et Industriels Modernes of 1925 in Paris, also known as Moderne
ashlar masonry	Stone cut in rectangles: it can be smooth or rough faced, aligned or random
atrium	An open inner courtyard in a Roman house generally surrounded by a colonnade
baldachino	The canopy supported over an altar. Also called a ciborium
balloon frame	Framing of precut light wood studs, generally 2 x 4's, often two stories long and spaced less than 2 feet/.6 meter apart
baluster	The upright supports of a railing
balustrade	The railing around the head of stairs or atop some buildings
band course	See stringcourse

barge board	A decorative, often scroll-cut board at gable ends
batten	A narrow board nailed to cover the joint of two vertical boards
bay	A vertical wall module (as between structural columns in a skyscraper)
belt course	See stringcourse
bema	A raised platform from which religious services are conducted, generally applied to synagogues
berm	A man-made low earth "boundary"
betonglass	Thick faceted glass (1 inch/2.5 centimeters generally)
blind arcade	An "arcade" indicated by pilasters applied to a wall surface
blind arch	A relieving arch built into a wall to distribute overhead weight
bolection mold	The prominent roll mold which covers the juncture of door panel and frame
box girder	A rectangular, hollow girder usually of steel
brackets	Angled supports, often elaborate, to uphold overhang
brise-soleil	Exterior louvers, fixed or movable, to control sun load on a building
cartouche	A shield or coat of arms used as a decorative panel on a wall
cavetto cornice	An outward-curved, usually quarter-round, cornice used in Egyptian Revival
CBD	The Central Business District of a city
cella	The inner room(s) of a Classical temple, primarily the sanctuary
chamfer	A beveled edge at the meeting of two planes
chancel	The (east) end of the church, the part reserved for the clergy
Chicago window	A large fixed central pane of plate glass flanked by sash windows
ciborium	See baldachino
clapboard	A covering board thin on inner (upper) edge, thicker at butt; the boards are overlapped horizontally for weather protection. Sometimes called weatherboards
clerestory	The topmost windows of a church nave, those

	above the aisle roof, thus any high band of windows
console	An elaborate bracket, often scroll-shaped
coquina	A soft limestone of marine origin found in Florida; it hardens on exposure to air
corbel	A (series of) cantilevered short projection(s) supporting an overhang
Corinthian Order	The richest of the Greek and Roman orders, the capital representing stylized acanthus leaves; at ten diameters its column is the most slender of all
cornice	Technically the top and most projected element of an entablature; in contemporary buildings it refers to the entire projecting eave
cortile	A small courtyard
crockets	Ornamental decorations, usually vegetation-derived, on Gothic members
cupola	A domed accent on a roof with either round or polygonal base
curtain wall	An enclosing wall or wall panel independently attached to the frame of a building
dendrochronology	Dating of a wooden building by counting annual tree rings in a beam cross section or core. The method was developed by Professor A. E. Douglass of the University of Arizona
dentils	A continuous line of small blocks in a Classical molding just under the fascia
dependencies	Smaller buildings symmetrically placed on either side of a major one: flankers
distyle in antis	Two Classical columns set between end walls
dogtrot	A breezeway separating two sections of a (log) house, early popular in Southern vernacular
Doric Order	The oldest and simplest of the Classical orders. The Greek Doric column is fluted and has no base
drum	The (circular) base and support of a dome
Eastlake Style	The Eastlake Style, named for the English architect C. L. Eastlake, was popular toward the end of the nineteenth century. It helped popularize the Stick Style
ell	An addition to a house making an L-shape
English bond	A brick pattern with alternating rows of headers (brick ends) and stretchers (brick sides)

entablature	The horizontal element which tops Classical columns. The lowest part—that resting on the columns—is the architrave, the middle (and often decorated) the frieze, and the top the cornice
entasis	The slight swelling profile curve of a Greek or Roman column as it diminishes upward (an optical correction)
exedra	A semicircular (or rectangular) niche, often half-vaulted and with seats
extrados	The outside face or edge of an arch
facade	The face of a building, usually the main elevation
fanlight	A window over an entry, either semicircular or semielliptical
fascia	The flat band(s) of an entablature; also the flat top edge of a building
Federal Style	The planar, tightly restrained yet elegant style which budded in the U.S.A. following the Revolution. Found largely in the Northeast, it lasted until the 1830s
fenestration	The disposition of the windows of a building
flankers	Flanking wings or dependencies usually symmetrically disposed about the main building
Flemish bond	Alternate brick headers and stretchers in the same row
Four Corners area	The juncture of Utah, Colorado, New Mexico, and Arizona
frieze	The mid-member of the three-part entablature (architrave, frieze, cornice), often with decorative panels
furring	Inner blocking of an exterior wall to create air space with inside wall
gable	The (triangular) upper wall established by the roof planes
galleria	Typically a glass-roofed urban passageway
gambrel roof	A roof with two slopes on each side, the lower sharply pitched. It stems from the French Mansard roof
Georgian architecture	In the U.S.A. the period of increasing architectural richness beginning under the reign of George I (1714–27) to the Revolution. Symmetry and classically derived details are characteristic

ghorfas	A series of long, mud-brick paraboloid "warehouses" (like horizontally piled cigarettes) found in south Tunisia
girder	A major horizontal supporting beam
girt	A heavy beam at the ends (and often flanking the chimney) of a Colonial house to receive upper floor joists and sometimes the summer beam
Greek cross	A (church) plan with all four arms of equal length
Greek Revival	A style based on Greek architectural prototypes or details, popular in the first half of the nineteenth century
hall	The name given to the living room of a seventeenth-century New England house
hammer beam	A short cantilevered beam or bracket supporting a timber roof arch
hatchment	An escutcheon with armorial insignia
headers	Bricks laid with their ends facing out
hexastyle	Having six columns at one end
hip roof	A roof with four sloping planes, at times meeting in a flat roof-deck
hogans	The traditional semirounded, earth-covered log dwellings of the Navajo
Howe truss	A (bridge) truss made up of a series of X-frames; similar to Long truss but with vertical wrought-iron or steel tie rods
hyphen	A connecting link between the main house in Georgian architecture and the flanking dependencies
impost	The springing point or block of an arch
in antis	The end of a (Classical) building with columns between the side walls
International Style	The first organized architectural movement against Academism: it dates largely from the 1920s and '30s
intrados	The under surface or soffit of an arch
Ionic Order	One of the major Classical orders; its capitals are immediately identified by their volutes or scrolls
IS	Abbreviation of Interstate Highway

jalousies	Slatted exterior blinds, often adjustable to control light and air
jerkin-head	The small triangular nipping off of the gable end of a roof
joist	The parallel secondary beams upholding a floor
lantern	A small geometric structure atop a roof, most frequently glazed and usually for appearance only
lights	The panes of glass of a window
lintel	A beam over an opening, or over two or more vertical members (post-and-lintel)
Long truss	A bridge truss composed of continuous boxed X-panels
lunette	Small round or half-round window generally in a gable
Mansard roof	Like the gambrel roof (q.v.), a roof with two sloping planes per side, the lower much more sharply pitched. Named for François Mansart (1598–1666)
mastaba	A flat-roofed, slope-sided tomb from Egypt's Old Kingdom
metope	The panel between the triglyphs of a Doric frieze, either plain or sculptured
Moderne	See Art Deco
modillions	Small scroll brackets, larger and wider than dentils
mortise	A cut-out hole in a beam or member which receives a tenon
mullion	The vertical division between windows (and windows and doors)
muntin	The pane divider within a window frame
oculus	A circular opening in the crown of a dome
oriel window	A bay window projecting on brackets or corbels
P/A	The abbreviation of *Progressive Architecture* magazine
Palladian	Architecture influenced by the Italian architect Andrea Palladio (1508–80). Characterized by majestic symmetry often with flanking dependencies. Palladian windows have a broad arched central section with lower flat-headed side portions

passerelle	A footbridge
pavilion	A projecting center section—for prominence—of a (usually) symmetrical building
pediment	The triangular space of the gable end of a building; also at small scale used over doors and windows—triangular, segmental (curved), and "broken" pediments
pendentive	A triangular spheroid section used to effect the transition from a square or polygonal base to a dome above
pent roof	A small "attached" roof used over first-floor windows
peripteral	Having columns completely surrounding a temple (or building)
peristyle	A colonnade surrounding a building on the outside or a court inside
piano nobile	The main floor of a mansion, generally elevated a full floor above grade
pilaster	In effect a column reduced to a thin rectangle to establish wall divisions; an engaged pier
pilotis	Columns which uphold the upper floor(s) of a building leaving ground level largely open
plate	The top horizontal member of a wood-framed wall: the rafters spring from the plate
platted	Surveyed and laid out, as of a town
plinth	The square block under a column; also the base for a statue
portal(es)	The covered porch or veranda fronting a Spanish building
portico	A columned shelter at entry; a porch
post-and-lintel	Construction by vertical uprights supporting horizontal beams
prestressed concrete	Reinforced concrete whose end-threaded steel bars or cables are prestretched to develop extra strength
purlin	Secondary horizontal beams supporting roof rafters
quadriga	A representation of a four-horse Roman chariot used as decorative feature
Queen Anne Style	A late-nineteenth-century, almost frantic mélange of styles, often with prominent triangular gable

quoins	Prominently beveled stones (or wood in imitation of stone) used to give emphasis to corners: from French *coins* or corners
rafters	The (generally) angled framing members which directly support the roof
raised basement	A "basement" partly or totally above grade
random ashlar	Miscellaneously sized, non-aligning, rectangular stones
reredos	An ornamental screen placed on the wall behind an altar
retable (retablo)	The niches and shelves behind a Spanish altar (in Gothic architecture often an encased shrine)
return	The carrying of a molding partly around a corner, often on gabled ends
reveal	The depth of inset from the wall face of a window or door
ridgepole	The topmost horizontal roof member receiving upper ends of rafters
rinceau	A low-relief vine-like running ornament
riser	The vertical measure between stair treads
roundel	A small circular opening or window
rustication	Exaggeration of joints and/or surface of stone or wood imitating stone
saltbox	The name for a New England cottage with rear addition and asymmetrically extended roof
segmental arch	A partial arch over a window
shaft	The part of a column between base and capital
shakes	Hand-split shingles, generally large and thick
sheathing	Boards or panels enclosing a structural frame
shed roof	A one-slope roof
Shingle Style	A late-nineteenth-century domestic style using (unpainted) shingles on walls as well as for roof; a term made popular by Professor Vincent Scully
sill	A wood (or metal) member atop and fastened to foundation walls to which the upright framing is attached
single-loaded	Rooms on one side only of a corridor
soffit	The underside of an arch or overhead beam

spandrel	In high-rise construction the enclosing panels between window head below and windowsill above; the solid bands between rows of windows
spire	The tapered section of a steeple
steeple	A church tower and its spire
stepped gable	A gable whose slope or rake is stepped rather than straight (or curved). Also called crow-foot and Dutch gable
stereotomy	The art of stone cutting and placing
Stick Style	A middle-late-nineteenth-century style of complex projections, roof, and wood outrigging
stile	The vertical framing member of a door or window
stretchers	The long sides of bricks laid facing out
stringcourse	A generally flat band of minute projection horizontally stretching across a brick facade. Also called a belt course or band course
studs	The (secondary) upright members of a wood-framed wall, often 2 x 4's
stylobate	The base, usually stepped, for a columned building or colonnade
summer beam	A heavy intermediate beam, mainly used in seventeenth-century New England, which carries floor joists and is itself supported by chimney and end girts
tache	Literally a spot, used here as a wall accent
temenos	A sacred confine
tenon	A projection on a wooden beam designed to fit the mortise in another beam to effect juncture. The two are fastened with a dowel
tholos	A round building, especially Greek
tie beam	A horizontal beam connecting the ends of rafters to make a truss
Town truss	A lattice panel truss with alternate closely spaced diagonals
trabeated	Post-and-lintel construction
tread	The step of a stair
triglyphs	The rectangular blocks in a Doric frieze with two vertical channels and half channels on edges
truss	A combination, generally triangulated, of wood,

	concrete, or metal members to span a space and provide structure for supporting the roof
Tuscan Order	A Roman adaptation of the Greek Doric without fluting but with base; the frieze is plain
tympanum	The framed (triangular) inner area of a pediment; also framed semicircular panel above door
vermiculated	Grooved stone imitations of worm tracks
vigas	The projecting roof beams in Indian pueblo and Spanish Colonial architecture
volutes	Spiral ornament as on an Ionic capital
voussoirs	The wedge-shaped stones or bricks which make up an arch
wainscot	The paneled protective wall lining of a domestic interior, usually not to ceiling
weatherboard	Lapped horizontal wood siding using boards often of parallel faces—as opposed to radial-cut clapboards which they resemble

Index

State abbreviations are the U. S. Post Office Department designations—i.e. Alabama is AL, Indiana is IN, etc.

KIDDER SMITH is an architect and Fellow of the American Institute of Architects who has devoted most of his professional life trying to make architecture a more significant part of our culture. Supported by a number of major foundation grants, he has produced a series of distinguished articles, books, and exhibitions on the architecture of twenty-four countries. He has also lectured on four continents, often under the auspices of the Department of State. Mr. Smith received the ENIT Gold Medal from the Italian Government for his *Italy Builds,* and he and the late Philip L. Goodwin were decorated by the Brazilian Government for their *Brazil Builds* book and exhibition for the Museum of Modern Art. His *New Architecture of Europe* and *New Churches of Europe* were published in the U.S.A., England, Italy, and Germany; his *Pictorial History of Architecture in America* was one of the major books at the Moscow International Book Fair of 1979. He has also contributed to the Encyclopaedia Britannica. The twelve-year undertaking which produced these volumes on *The Architecture of the United States* represents his most ambitious effort.

Mr. Smith was born in Birmingham, Alabama (1913), and received his A.B. and M.F.A. from Princeton University. He and his wife, Dorothea, live in New York City, with one son teaching in California and the other in Switzerland.